THE FATHERS
OF THE CHURCH

A NEW TRANSLATION
VOLUME 12

THE FATHERS OF THE CHURCH

A NEW TRANSLATION

EDITORIAL BOARD

Hermigild Dressler, O.F.M.
Quincy College
Editorial Director

Robert P. Russell, O.S.A.
Villanova University

Thomas P. Halton
The Catholic University of America

Robert Sider
Dickinson College

Sister M. Josephine Brennan, I.H.M.
Marywood College

Richard Talaska
Editorial Assistant

FORMER EDITORIAL DIRECTORS

Ludwig Schopp, Roy J. Deferrari, Bernard M. Peebles

SAINT AUGUSTINE

LETTERS

VOLUME I (1-82)

Translated by
SISTER WILFRID PARSONS, S.N.D.

THE CATHOLIC UNIVERSITY OF AMERICA PRESS
Washington, D.C.

NIHIL OBSTAT:

> JOHN M. A. FEARNS, S.T.D.
> Censor Librorum

IMPRIMATUR:

> ✠ FRANCIS CARDINAL SPELLMAN
> Archbishop of New York

May 15, 1951

The Nihil obstat and Imprimatur are official declarations that a book or pamphlet is free of doctrinal or moral error. No implication is contained therein that those who have granted the Nihil obstat and Imprimatur agree with the contents, opinions or statements expressed.

Library of Congress Catalog Card No.: 64-19948
ISBN-13: 978-0-8132-1556-3 (pbk)

Copyright © 1951 by
THE CATHOLIC UNIVERSITY OF AMERICA PRESS, INC.
All rights reserved
Second Printing 1964
Third Printing 1981
First paperback reprint 2008

CONTENTS

Letter *Page*

1. To Hermogenianus 3
2. To Zenobius 5
3. To Nebridius 6
4. To Nebridius 11
5. Nebridius to Augustine 12
6. Nebridius to Augustine 13
7. To Nebridius 14
8. Nebridius to Augustine 20
9. To Nebridius 21
10. To Nebridius 23
11. To Nebridius 25
12. To Nebridius 30
13. To Nebridius 31
14. To Nebridius 33
15. To Romanianus 36
16. Maximus to Augustine 37
17. To Maximus 39
18. To Caelestinus 43
19. To Gaius 44
20. To Antoninus 45
21. To Bishop Valerius 47
22. To Bishop Valerius 51
23. To Maximinus 58
24. Paulinus and Therasia to Bishop Alypius 66

25. Paulinus and Therasia to Augustine 70
26. To Licentius 75
27. To Paulinus 87
28. To St. Jerome 93
29. To Bishop Alypius 99
30. Paulinus and Therasia to Augustine 109
31. To Paulinus and Therasia 111
32. Paulinus and Therasia to Romanianus 117
33. To Proculeianus 126
34. To Eusebius 131
35. To Eusebius 135
36. To Casulanus 138
37. To Simplicianus 168
38. To Profuturus 169
39. St. Jerome to Augustine 171
40. To St. Jerome 179
41. Alypius and Augustine to Bishop Aurelius. . . . 179
42. To Paulinus and Therasia 181
43. To Glorius, Eleusius, the Felixes, Grammaticus, and Others 182
44. To Eleusiu, Glorius, and the Felixes 207
45. Alypius and Augustine to Paulinus and Therasia . . 219
46. Publicola to Augustine 220
47. To Publicola 225
48. To Eudoxius 231
49. To Honoratus 234
50. To the Leaders of the Sufes 237
51. To Crispinus 238
52. To Severinus 243
53. Fortunatus, Alypius, and Augustine to Generosus . . 245
54. To Januarius 252
55. To Januarius 260
56. To Celer 293
57. To Celer. 295

58. To Pammachius	296
59. To Victorinus	298
60. To Bishop Aurelius	300
61. To Theodore	302
62. Alypius, Augustine, and Samsucius to Bishop Severus	304
63. To Bishop Severus	306
64. To Quintianus	309
65. To Xanthippus	312
66. Against the Schismatic Crispinus	314
67. To St. Jerome	316
68. St. Jerome to Augustine	317
69. Alypius and Augustine to Bishop Castorius	320
70. Alypius and Augustine to Naucellio	323
71. To St. Jerome	324
72. St. Jerome to Augustine	328
73. To St. Jerome	332
74. To Praesidius	341
75. St. Jerome to Augustine	342
76. To the Donatists	368
77. To Felix and Hilarinus	373
78. To the Church of Hippo	375
79. To a Certain Manichaean Priest	385
80. To Paulinus and Therasia	386
81. St. Jerome to Augustine	389
82. To St. Jerome	390

WRITINGS
OF
SAINT AUGUSTINE

VOLUME 9

INTRODUCTION

THE-LETTERS of St. Augustine are not as well known as they deserve to be. It may be that they have suffered by comparison with the *Confessions* or the *City of God,* and the reader who takes them up expecting to be entertained by the revelation of a rich personality or thrilled by the recital of an eventful life is due for a disappointment. Augustine made his personal revelation of his early life in the *Confessions,* and it stops with them. If he wrote any purely social or familiar letters, they have not been preserved. We have not a single one from or to a member of his family. The Letters we have are of quite another nature: they are one of the weapons of his armory in his warfare against ignorance, error, paganism, schism, and heresy. They are sharp and hard-hitting weapons, because a letter, unlike a treatise, can be directed to a single person or group of persons, and can be aimed at some special erroneous opinion. Some of them, indeed, have the form of a treatise, and repeat material which was used in the treatises.

This is not, however, to deny the interest of the Letters, which are a human document of great value, giving us the picture of one of the most powerful minds of all time. They show us an Augustine recognized and respected even in his own time, for his ability to treat with penetrating insight of widely diverse subjects, while remaining humbly aware of his own possible fallibility. They gave us on idea of the position he occupied among his contemporaries, of the deference paid to him by all kinds of folk, both high and humble. With equal ease and authority, he settles the scruples of an almost illiterate layman who was worried about his dealings with pagans, and dissects with merciless logic the pretentious arguments of a Donatist bishop. Each letter had its own purpose—to instruct, to counsel, to exhort, to encourage or to attack. The tastes and inclinations of the writer are rarely evident, except his overmastering love of truth, and here and there his regret that he cannot have more personal contact with his dear friends, like Paulinus of Nola. The range of subjects is wide, including most of the theological controversies of the day, interpretation of passages of Scripture, explanations of Church doctrine and discipline, solution of cases of conscience. There are many interesting sidelights on Church life and customs in Africa, and of abuses which required for their suppression a rare combination of tact and firmness. The amount of sheer information the Letters offer is astonishing.

Chronologically, the Letters are divided into four classes: (1) Those written between the year of Augustine's conversion, 386, and his consecration as bishop, 395 (Nos. 1 to 30); (2) Those written between the year of his consecration, 395, and the council of Carthage, 411 (Nos. 31-123); (3) Those written between 411 and 429 (Nos. 124-231); (4) Those of the third period not positively assignable to any fixed date (Nos. 232-277). Of the total number, fifty letters were written by Augustine's correspondents, and are included because he answered them or they answered him.

For convenience of handling, the present translation of the Letters will be in four volumes, the division being more or less mathematical, with an index in the last volume. In the first group the most interesting are probably the letters to and from Nebridius. These are more nearly personal than almost any others, and in them something of the writer's tender affection for his young friend, who died so soon after his own and Augustine's conversion, is apparent, even through the formal philosophical explanations he has to make. Augustine's labors in defense of the doctrine and discipline of the Church began before his consecration as bishop; consequently, in these early letters, we find him entering the lists against paganism, against Donatism—this was to be a long campaign —and against certain reprehensible practices of his fellow Catholics. He also opened that long and spirited discussion with St. Jerome about the translation of the Scriptures. The first twenty letters were written before he became a priest. The letters of the second group included in this volume range over such topics as Church discipline on fasting, the excellence of monastic life, rules of stability for clerics, and St. Jerome's proposed translation of the Scriptures.

According to subject matter, the Letters may be classified as: (1) theological; (2) polemical; (3) exegetical; (4) ecclesiastical; (5) moral or of spiritual direction; (6) philosophical; (7) historical; (8) familiar. Some of the Letters spread over more than one of these groups. In the first such group we find explanations of the doctrine of the Incarnation, of the Trinity, of the presence of God, of the various mysteries of our Lord's life, of free will, of grace, of baptism, of the Holy Eucharist. In the second group are found the controversies with the Arians, the pagans, the Manichaeans, the Donatists, the Novatianists, the Priscillianists and the Pelagians. In these, Augustine shows himself a powerful and formidable opponent of error, heresy, and schism. In the exegetical group are letters dealing with the explanation of various parts of Scripture: Daniel, Jonas, many of the Psalms, some of the parables in the Gospels, disputed passages in the Epistles. It was in this field that he found himself carrying on a long debate with St. Jerome. The ecclesiastical questions treated include the universality of the Church, the celebration of Easter and other feasts, fasting, the duties of priests and bishops, questions of ecclesiastical jurisdiction, monastic life, church property, punishment of delinquent clerics and the singing of psalms and hymns. Those on moral questions cover topics such as exhortations to a higher life, rules of conduct for soldiers, judges, monks, nuns, married people; discourses on prayer, charity, penance, on various virtues and various sins. The philosophical letters treat of such topics as memory, imagination, dreams, the nature of ideas, the condition of the soul separated from the body. Those classified as historical give information on acts of the emperors against heresy and schism; accounts of various councils of the Church and action taken at them against the Donatists and Pelagians; an exhaustive history of Donatism, the election of Pope Celestine, the siege of Rome by Alaric. The familiar letters are few, and include those to Nebridius, to Romanianus and Licentius and to St. Paulinus of Nola.

The persons to whom Augustine wrote his letters, or who wrote to him, form a good cross section of the society of his time. People of all ranks and classes appear in these pages: clerics of every grade, laymen of every calling, from emperors who did not think it beneath them to send him copies of official pronouncements, to a humble stenographer who needed to be set right on certain practices of the good life. Fellow bishops submitted their perplexities in matters of jurisdiction and of clerical discipline, and received uncompromising answers. A pagan rhetorician writes cynically about the substitution of the ridiculous Punic names of Christian martyrs for the noble gods of the pagan pantheon, and gets a pungent reply, complete with quotations from Vergil (43,44). Licentius, a young pupil of Augustine in his teaching days, sends him a long poem of pretentious and artificial style, full of imitations of Vergil, Ovid, and Lucan, and receives, instead of the literary criticism he craves, a serious exhortation to consider the needs of his soul (26). Dioscorus presents a long list of difficulties arising out of his readings in Cicero's philosophical works, and asks to have them solved so that he need not appear stupid when asked about them. He is favored with a sharp request (118) that he stop loading busy and preoccupied bishops with extra work on trivial pretexts, followed by a short sermon on vainglory and a long analysis of the tenets of certain schools of Greek philosophy. A priest named Deogratias wanted the answer to six miscellaneous questions which were often raised by pagans, beginning with the Resurrection of Christ and ending with the account of Jonas and the whale. They had been submitted by a friend of his, whose conversion he thought might ensue if the questions were satisfactorily answered. They were all discussed (102) luminously and convincingly, with the rather wry comment that persons who believed in the magical tricks of Apollonius of Tyana and Apuleius of Madaura were hardly consistent in ridiculing the biblical narrative. However unnecessary or trivial the questions might seem—and all sorts of people asked him all sorts of questions—he answered all real difficulties with painstaking thoroughness and often with an impressive array of Scripture references. Count Boniface, commander of the Roman forces in Africa, where the last stand was made against the Vandals, was one of Augustine's most distinguished correspondents, and received secular as well as spiritual advice from the great bishop. In the correspondence with St. Paulinus of Nola and his wife, Therasia, Augustine shows the capacity of his heart for friendship. Apparently, the two saints never met, but they had the greatest admiration for each other, and their letters are full of the most religious mutual compliments. They are also a mosaic of Scripture quotations, for Paulinus could hardly make the simplest statement without backing it up with a passage from the Bible, and Augustine falls into the same practice when he writes to Paulinus.

Special mention should be made of a little group of letters to women, interesting beeause they show so clearly the high level of education and of theological knowledge among women of the fifth century. The nature of the subjects treated and the manner in which they are developed are no less profound for the women correspondents than they are for the men. There is no more spiritual nourishment in the whole range of the Letters than the treatise on Prayer addressed to Proba (130) or that on the Vision of God which he wrote for Paulina (147). In a letter (211) addressed to a community of nuns, he settles a point in dispute, and then proceeds, in admirably terse Latin, to outline a rule of life for the religious, many points of which are as practical today as they were fifteen centuries ago. With the same clarity he gave advice on more worldly and everyday affairs. He rebukes Ecdicia for giving alms without her husband's knowledge and permission, and for dressing herself like a widow (262). He writes to Sapida, a virgin, to thank her for a tunic which she had sent him, and to say that he is willing to comfort her by wearing it in memory of her dead brother, for whom she had originally woven it (263). He encourages Florentina, a 'studious girl,' to continue her studies, and to call on him any time for help in understanding the Scriptures (266).

The correspondence with St. Jerome has a character of

its own, and shows an apologetic tone not found elsewhere. Augustine opened it in 394 or 395 after the return of his friend Alypius from a visit to the Holy Land where Jerome was living. He had just heard that Jerome was contemplating a translation of the Bible from the Hebrew, and he thought it would be far better for him to correct the faulty Latin versions by bringing them into accord with the Septuagint. One of the reasons he gave was that many people knew Greek and could compare the Latin with the Septuagint version, but hardly anybody knew Hebrew. Besides, the Septuagint had been used by the Church from the beginning, and it was known and loved by all. In this connection he told the story of the congregation that almost rioted because the new translation of Jonas had been read to them, in which the vine that shaded the prophet was called an ivy, whereas it had always been a gourd vine. Jerome's reply to this was hardly logical, but it was unanswerable. Another point brought up in this first letter to Jerome was to start a prolonged duel on the proper interpretation of St. Paul's rebuke to St. Peter as reported in Galatians 2.11-14. This introduced the question of the so-called officious or polite lie, to which Augustine was unalterably opposed. Apparently, he knew little of the rather testy temper of his correspondent, and he made his attack with some sharpness. He had a strong feeling of objectivity about his own opinions, when they were not matters of faith, and he was always open to conviction by an argument stronger than his own. Naturally, he thought a learned man like Jerome would feel the same way. But Jerome did not feel the same way. He was quite sensitive about his opinions, which to him were always true, and he resented adverse criticism. He had had a good deal of this, especially in the matter of his translation of the Bible, and he may be forgiven for defending himself with heat and asperity. He took Augustine's criticism as a personal affront, and the situation was complicated by the fact that Augustine's second letter was neither delivered to him nor returned to the writer, but by some mischance was circulated through Italy. In his reply to another letter he showed himself deeply hurt both by Augustine's criticism of his work, and by what he thought was a 'book' against him, supposedly sent by Augustine to Rome, for the purpose of injuring his reputation. It took all of Augustine's tact and humility to smooth him down, and to prove to him that it was a letter, not a book, and that he had not known of the untrustworthiness of the messenger to whom he had entrusted it for delivery. In spite of apology and explanation, Jerome continued to be fairly gruff about it, and to repeat over and over: 'Please see that letters addressed to me reach me first.' Augustine had greatly desired a real debate between himself and Jerome, in the course of which, by the clash of ideas, they might both arrive at the truth. He was distressed at the idea that charity could be wounded by an honest difference of opinion, and was sadly prepared to give up the attractive prospect of a thoroughly good argument between two well-balanced opponents. But, after considerable diplomatic coaxing, he succeeded in getting Jerome to answer his objections and to accept his viewpoint about a really impersonal exchange of ideas. It is noticeable in his own arguments after this experience that he drops the hammer-and-tongs technique which he used with devastating effect against other opponents, and that he advances his arguments with a sort of deprecating firmness. Thanks to his humility and detachment, the holy friendship between the two saintly scholars was never breached.

The style of the Letters is far from uniform, and they naturally vary in tone according to the subject matter and correspondent. Some are concise to the point of curtness; some, simple enough to be understood by persons of no great intelligence; others, highly rhetorical, even florid. When the thought becomes obscure, the language is apt to be involved and the sentence structure ponderous. Some of the sentences, with their endless parentheses, could never have been used in sermons, because the orator would have been out of breath long before he reached the end. Sometimes, the pure exuberance of his thought carries the writer on for a page or so of subordinate clauses without a stop, and once in a while he even loses sight of his subject. The more studied letters, those in which he is answering questions or explaining points of doctrine, by request, show the highest degree of literary finish; when he is refuting heresy or inveighing against schism, his style becomes so oratorical that he is evidently in imagination haranguing a hostile audience.

Augustine's literary style was the product of his time, and it shows the characteristics of that time: deliberate archaism, use of colloquial words, influx of foreign words, and freedom of inventing new words. He also makes frequent use of the rhetorical adornments common to the sophists. Three other factors, however, enter into the making of his style. First of all, he was an African, and his Latinity has a distinctively African coloring: it is lush, vivid, highly figured, often artificially phrased. But he was also a classical scholar of no mean attainment, a man who admired Cicero and Vergil so intensely that he found Scriptural Latin uncouth and repulsive when he first made acquaintance with it. This classical taste helps to keep within bounds any extremes of innovation in his use of new words, or in outright abandonment of the customary rhythms of the periodic structure. It does not keep him from adorning his phrases with a rich embroidery of figures of all kinds. We have to admit that he overdoes some of them at times, especially antithesis and some of the figures of sound. These latter not infrequently betray him into puns —not always good ones. In addition to being an African and a classical scholar, Augustine was an ecclesiastic, and this also influenced his style. In his choice of metaphors he prefers those of Scriptural origin, favoring such as refer to the parables of the Gospel, and he likes to drive home an idea by a succession of images. He also necessarily makes wide use of ecclesiastical terms, many of which were of Greek origin.

We may say in general of the style of the Letters that Augustine had evidently made his own the dictum of St. Paul, of being all things to all men, and that in his correspondence he was quite literally all things to all those to whom he wrote, both men and women, clerics and seculars.

The form of the Letters is that usual in Christian epistolography, with rather elaborate introductory addresses and free use of honorary titles. The purely conventional 'If you are well, it is well, I am well.' of Cicero had yielded to a more ceremonious introduction, lavish with complimentary phrases. Obviously, many of these had lost their original meaning, but they usually give a clue to the respective rank of writer and recipient. At times, the terms of the address are repeated or summarized at the end of the letter. In the body of the letter, unless it is purely a treatise with an attached introduction, many honorary titles are apt to be found, some of which sound strange to us. The title 'your Holiness,' used today only to the Pope, was addressed freely to bishops and occasionally to lay persons. Even the word *papa,* pope, was used by his friends to Augustine. Some of the most common titles of excellence are: your Charity, your Benignity, your Blessedness, your Benevolence, your Dignity, your Piety, your Paternity, your Reverence (not confined to clergy), your Serenity, your Worthiness, and the one used today, your Excellency. A curious usage, akin to this, is that of titles of depreciation, used by a writer of himself. Such are: my Insignificance, my Mediocrity, my Humbleness, as we say 'my humble self,' or 'your humble servant.' These are often balanced against extravagant titles of excellence applied to the addressees.

The Letters bear neither date nor place of writing, details so indispensable to modern letter writing. Sometimes a clue is given in the letter itself; otherwise, it has been the laborious task of scholarship to establish the date and sequence of the Letters. There was no regular postal service in the ancient world, except for couriers carrying official despatches. Private correspondents had to depend on the kindness of friends who might be traveling in the direction in which the letter was being sent. This accounts for the frequent references in the Letters to the necessity of using every such occasion, and sometimes of writing in great haste, because the messenger has been warned by the captain that the ship will sail on the tide. This also accounts for the fact that letters went astray sometimes, with disagreeable consequences for the writer, and explains why an interval of as much as three or four years might elaspe between a letter and its answer.

Scriptural quotations are offered in the Douay-Challoner version. In his citations, Augustine ranges over the whole Bible and it has seemed advisable to use a single English translation. The question of what Latin version he used will not be discussed here; the Vulgate was not in general use, as the Letters themselves indicate. Where his quotations differ from the Vulgate, the corresponding reference to the Vulgate is marked by Cf.

The text used is that of Goldbacher in the Vienna *Corpus Scriptorum Ecclesiasticorum Latinorum*. For the dates of the Letters, reliance has been made on Migne, *Patrologia Latina* 33.

SELECT BIBLIOGRAPHY

Texts:

J. P. Migne: *Patrologia Latina* (Paris 1886) 33.
A. Goldbacher: *Sancti Aurelii Augustini Hipponensis Episcopi Epistulae*, in *Corpus Scriptorum Ecclesiasticorum Latinorum* (Vienna 1895-1911) 34.1-2; 44; 57.

Other works:

E. Amann: *The Church of the Early Centuries* (Catholic Library of Religious Knowledge 15, London 1930).
G. Bardy: *Christian Latin Literature of the First Six Centuries* (Catholic Library of Religious Knowledge 12, London 1930).
J. H. Baxter: *Introduction to St. Augustine: Select Letters* (Loeb Classical Library, London and New York 1930).
P. De Labriolle: 'La Correspondance,' *Histoire de la Litterature latine chréstienne* (2nd ed., Paris 1924).
Monument to St. Augustine: Essays on Some Aspects of His Thought Written in Commemoration of His 15th Centenary (London 1930).
Sister Mary Bridget O'Brien: *Titles of Address in Christian Latin Epistolography to 543* A.D. (The Catholic University of America Patristic Series 21, Washington 1930).
Sister Wilfrid Parsons, *A Study of the Vocabulary and Rhetoric of the Letters of St. Augustine* (The Catholic University of America Patristic Series 3, Washington 1923).
H. Pope, O. P.: *Saint Augustine of Hippo* (Westminister, Md. 1949).
Possidius: *Vita Sancti Aurelii Augustini Hipponensis Episcopi*, in Migne, *PL* 32.33-66.
J. Tixeront: *Handbook of Patrology* (London 1920).
F. E. Tourscher: 'The Correspondence of St. Augustine and St. Jerome,' *American Ecclesiastical Review* 57 (1917) 476-492; 58 (1918) 45-46.
———: 'Some Letters of St. Augustine—A Study,' *American Ecclesiastical Review* 60 (1919) 609-625.
W. Watts: *St. Augustine's Confessions* (Loeb Classical Library, London and New York 1931).

LETTERS

1-82

Translated
by
SISTER WILFRID PARSONS, S.N.D.
Emmanuel College
Boston, Mass.

1. Augustine to Hermogenianus[1] (386)

I SHOULD not venture, even in jest, to criticize the Academicians,[2] whose influence has always weighed strongly with me, if I did not think they have been in far other repute than is commonly believed. Therefore, as far as possible, I have imitated them rather than attacked them—which latter I am quite unable to do. If any untainted stream flows from the Platonic spring, it seems to me that in these times it is better for it to be guided through shady and thorny thickets, for the possession of the few, rather than allowed to wander through open spaces where cattle break through, and where it is impossible for it to be kept clear and pure. For, what is more acceptable to the common herd than the idea that body and soul are identical? Contrary to men of this type, I think that that method or art of concealing the truth is a useful invention. But, in this age, since we find no true philosophers—and I consider that those who go around dressed in philosophers' cloaks are quite unworthy of that honorable title—men need to be led back to the hope of

---

1 Not otherwise known, except that his knowledge of the Academicians was great enough to cause Augustine to ask his opinion on a new book.
2 Academicians, school of philosophy founded by Plato (428-350 B.C.) In the *Confessions* (5.10), Augustine says: 'For there arose in me a conceit that those philosophers, which they call the Academics, should be wiser than the rest, for that they held men ought to make a doubt upon everything, and decreed that no truth can be comprehended by man.'

discovering truth, especially those who have been deterred from understanding things by the subtlety of Academic phrases. Otherwise, what was devised in its time for the uprooting of deep-seated error might now begin to be a hindrance to the cultivation of knowledge.

In their time, the eagerness of the various schools was so ardent that the only thing to fear was acceptance of error. Thus, whenever by those arguments a man was dislodged from an opinion which he had considered firm and unshaken, he sought another, and he did this with a persistence and care proportioned to the energy of his character, and the profound and involved truth which was felt to be hidden in the universe of phenomena and of ideas. But, nowadays, there is such shrinking from effort and such poor esteem of study that it is enough for shrewd thinkers to declare that nothing can be understood, and men forthwith give up the quest and doom themselves to eternal darkness. Even the more persistent do not venture to commit themselves to these studies, having no hope of discovering what Carneades[3] could not discover, in spite of his deep and prolonged study, his genius, his great and manifold learning, and his very long life. And if anyone who tries to throw off sluggishness, even a little, should read those treatises in which it is proved that understanding is impossible for the human mind, he falls into so deep a sleep that even the last trumpet would not awaken him.

Therefore, since I so willingly trust your opinion of my books, and since I rely on you so completely, that for me there can be no defect in your prudence nor deceit in your friendship, I beg you to think over very carefully and write back to me whether you approve my conclusion at the end

---

3 Philosopher of Cyrene (*c.* 155 B. C.), pupil of the Stoic, Diogenes, founder of the New Academy in Athens. He held that the senses, the understanding, and the imagination frequently deceive us, and therefore cannot be infallible judges of truth.

of Book Three,[4] a conclusion which I regard with more misgiving than assurance, but which I think is in accord with facts and worthy of credence. Finally, whatever the value of my writings, my chief delight is not your having said—with more affection than truth—that I have outdone the Academics, but the fact that I have broken a most hateful bond by which I was held back from tasting the sweetness of philosophy by despair of attaining to truth. And truth is the food of the soul.

2. Augustine to Zenobius[1] (386)

We had agreed, I think, that none of the things which a bodily sense reveals to us can remain unchanged for even an instant, and that everything shifts, flows away, and has no hold on the present, which is to say, in Latin, that it has no being. The true and divine philosophy warns us to check and tame the love of such things, so dangerous and so full of penalties for us; and, while the body is engaged in its own activity, the mind should be carried away and entirely enamored of what alone remains unchanged, of what is not a passing attraction for us wayfarers. In spite of which, and although my mind regards you as a sincere and candid person, such a one as can be loved without misgiving, I nevertheless confess that I miss the physical sight and presence of you when you are in far places, and I long for you as brothers may do. If I know you well, you undoubtedly like this defect in me, and, although you wish all good things for your nearest and dearest, you would shrink from curing them of this weak-

---
[4] *Contra Academicos* 3.37-42.

[1] Bishop of Florence, to whom Augustine dedicated his *De Ordine*.

ness. But, if you are so strong-minded as to recognize this snare and to laugh at those caught in it, then you certainly are a great and unique soul! For my part, when I miss an absent friend, I want to be missed by him. I am on my guard, as far as possible, and I strive to love nothing which can be taken from me against my will. While I am struggling with this difficulty, I warn you meantime, such as you are, that the discussion begun with you must be concluded, if we have any regard for each other. I would not allow it to be concluded with Alypius,[2] even if he wished, which he did not; for he is too much of a gentleman not to lend me his aid in keeping you with us by as many letters as possible, when you leave us for some reason or other.

3. Augustine to Nebridius[1] *(387)*

I am not sure whether this is to be put down to your flattery, so to speak, or whether it is really so. For the thought suddenly occurred to me, without deliberation, how far people

---

[2] Augustine's very dear friend, the 'brother of his soul,' of whom he says *(Conf.* 6.7): 'Alypius was born in the same town with me, whose parents were of the chief rank there, and himself younger than I. For he had also studied under me first, when I set up school in our own town and at Carthage afterwards. He loved me very much, because I seemed of a good disposition to him: and I loved him again, for his great towardness to virtue, which was eminent enough for one of no great years.' He followed Augustine in his conversion, and afterwards became Bishop of Tagaste.

[1] His 'sweet friend,' a youth of a wealthy family, who followed Augustine, to Milan. He was converted and baptized not long after Augustine, as is related in the *Confessions* (9.3): 'Whom not long after our conversion and regeneration by thy baptism, being also baptized in the Catholic faith, serving Thee in perfect chastity and continence amongst his own friends in Africa, having first converted his whole family to Christianity, didst Thou take out of the flesh; and now he lives in the bosom of Abraham.'

can be trusted. You wonder what this means. What do you think? You almost convinced me, not, indeed, that I am happy, for that is the reward of the wise man alone, but that I am comparatively happy, as we say that a man is comparatively a man when measured against that man whom Plato knew, or that a thing is comparatively round or square, as we look at it, although it is far from those qualities, as the mind of the expert perceives them. I read your letter by lamplight after dinner; it was almost time for bed, but not quite time for sleep: so I reflected for a long time, sitting on my bed, and Augustine held this conversation with Augustine. Is it not true that I am happy, as Nebridius claims? Not entirely; for even he does not dare to deny that there are still fools, and how could happiness be the portion of fools? That is a hard problem: as if happiness were an insignificant thing or as if there were any other misery than folly. How, then, did he reach this conclusion? Was it by reading those treatises that he came to call me wise? But eager joy is not that bold, especially in a man whose reasoning power I know how to estimate. This, then, must be it: he wrote what he thought would give me most pleasure, because what I had set down in those works had given him pleasure, and he wrote eagerly, without thought of what should be allowed to an eager pen. But, if he had read the *Soliloquies*,[2] what then? He would have been much more enthusiastic, and yet he would not have found anything else to call me but happy. So he poured this supreme title out on me, and reserved to himself no other term to use in case he should be feeling even more enthusiastic. See what joy does!

But, where is happiness to be found? Where? Oh where? Oh, if it were to consist in rejecting the indivisible particles

---
[2] Augustine had finished this work shortly before he wrote this letter.

of Epicurus![3] Oh, if it were to know that there is nothing here below but the material world! Oh, if it were to know that the outer edge of a sphere revolves more slowly than its center, and other such things which I likewise know! But, now: how or in what fashion I am happy, I do not know. But, why should the world be of such a size, when the nature of its dimensions does not prevent if from being as much bigger as anyone should wish? But, should it now be said to me, would I not rather be forced to admit that matter can be divided infinitely, so that from a certain foundation a certain number of particles would develop into a certain quantity? Therefore, as no material body can be conceived as the smallest possible, how can we admit that anything should be the largest possible, without possibility of increase? Unless something I once confided secretly to Alypius should have validity: namely, that an ideal number can be infinitely increased but cannot be infinitely diminished, because it cannot be reduced below the number one; whereas a real number —and what else is a real number but a quantity of particles or objects?—can be infinitely diminished but cannot be infinitely increased. And that is why philosophers wisely place wealth in the realm of ideas, and poverty in the world of sensible objects. For what is more distressing than for something to become continually less and less? And what more enriching than to increase as much as you wish, to go where you wish, to return when and where you wish, and to love greatly that which cannot be diminished? Whoever understands the science of numbers[4] puts his satisfaction in the number one, and no wonder, because from it he can form

---

[3] Greek philosopher, 341-270 B.C., materialist and atheist, best known through the work of Lucretius, *De rerum natura*.
[4] Among his other aberrations, Augustine had been a numerologist, and seems never to have lost his fascination for arguments based on numbers.

others for his delectation. Nevertheless, why is the world of such a size? It could have been larger or smaller. I do not know—such it is. And why is it in this place rather than that? In that matter there ought to be no question, for, wherever it would be, the question would still arise. But that one point impresses me deeply: that matter can be infinitely divided; and the answer to it lies, perhaps, in the contrary nature of ideal numbers.

But wait: let us examine this thought that comes to mind. Surely, the real world is said to be an image of a certain ideal one. It is a matter of wonder that in the case of images we see what mirrors reflect: for, however large the mirrors, they do not reflect larger images, even of the most minute objects. But, in small mirrors, such as the pupils of the eye, even if a large object is presented, a very small image is formed in proportion to the reflecting surface. Therefore, it is possible for the images of objects to be diminished if the mirror is diminished; but they cannot be enlarged if the mirror is enlarged. Doubtless, there is some mystery here. But, now it is time for sleep. For I do not appear happy to Nebridius by searching for something, but by finding it. But, what is this something? Is it that power of reasoning which I cherish as my best beloved, and in which I find my greatest joy?

Of what do we consist? Of soul and body. Which of these is the better? Doubtless, the soul. What is praised in the body? Nothing else than beauty. What is beauty of the body? A harmony of its parts with a certain pleasing color. Is this form better when it is true or when it is false? Who could doubt that it is better when it is true? But, where is it true? In the soul, of course. Therefore, the soul is to be loved more than the body. But, in what part of the soul is that truth? In the mind and in the understanding. What is opposed to these? The senses. Therefore, it is clear that the senses are to be resisted with the whole force of the mind. But, what if sensible things give us too much pleasure? They must be prevented from giving pleasure. How? By the practise of renouncing them, and aiming at higher things. What if the soul dies? Then, truth dies, or truth is not in the understanding, or the understanding is not in the soul, or something can die in which there is immortality. My *Soliloquies*[5] set forth and prove conclusively that none of these things can be so; in spite of which I am frightened and I stumble because of my acquaintance with evil. Finally, even if the soul dies, which I admit is completely impossible, I have demonstrated for this time that happiness does not consist in sensible pleasures. In these things, perhaps, and in others like them, I seem to my Nebridius, if not happy, at least comparatively happy. May I seem so to myself! For, what do I lose thereby, or why should I forfeit his good opinion? This was the conversation I held with myself; then I prayed, according to my custom, and fell asleep.

It has given me pleasure to write this to you, for I am glad that you thank me for telling you everything that comes into my head. I like to give you pleasure. And with whom would I more willingly play the fool than with one whom I cannot displease? If it is destined that a man should love a man, see how blessed I am in having these additional joys—and I hope the crop of them will be richly increased. Truly, wise men are the gift of fortune, the only ones who can rightly be called happy, who do not wish to be feared or desired. (Is that verb *cupi* or *cupiri?* find that out for me.)[6] It is a

---
5 *Solil.* 2.33.
6 At this time, Nebridius was lecturing under Verecundus, a grammarian of Milan, and could be supposed to be an expert on questions of inflection.

good thing that has come out, for I should like you to set me right about that inflection. Whenever I use verbs like that, I begin to doubt; for *cupio* is like *fugio, sapio, iacio, capio,* but I am never sure whether the infinitive should be *fugiri* or *fugi, sapiri* or *sapi.* I could add *iaci* and *capi,* but I am afraid that someone, in jest, would *catch* me and *throw* me, by wishing to prove that *iactum* and *captum* are one thing; *fugitum, cupitum, sapitum* something else. Likewise, regarding these last three, I do not know whether they are to be pronounced with a long and accented penult, or with a short, unaccented one. I should like to challenge you to a longer letter, and I beg of you to let me have a long one, for I cannot tell you how much I love to read your letters.

4. Augustine to Nebridius (387)

When I was looking to see how many letters of yours still remained to be answered, for a wonder, and quite unexpectedly, I found only one which still keeps me your debtor; the one in which you hope and desire that I may have plenty of time for you, so that I can tell you what progress I have made in the distinction between the real[1] and the ideal. I think you know that anyone is more easily involved in false opinions, the more he is exposed to them, and the same happens to the mind in the case of truth. Thus, we progress little by little as we go through life. Certainly, there is a great difference between the boy and the grown man, but no one who was questioned daily from boyhood would ever say at any given time that he is a grown man.

I do not wish you to conclude from this that I have reached

---

1 Or, perhaps, sensible versus intellectual. This report is made from the country place at Cassiciacum lent by Verecundus, the grammarian friend of Nebridius.

a certain maturity of mind, by reason of a stronger intelligence. We are children—good ones perhaps, as the saying goes—at least not bad ones. When people are frightened and overwhelmed by the apprehension of temporal troubles, you know well how this course of reasoning brings relief: namely, that the mind and the understanding are superior to the eyes and the common sense of sight. This would not be so unless the things we understand are superior to those we perceive by the senses. I ask you to consider with me whether there is anything opposed to this reasoning. After I had refreshed myself with it for some time, and after I had called on God for help, I began to be lifted up to Him and to those things which are most completely true. I was so penetrated with a knowledge of eternal things, that I wondered how I had ever needed to reason about them, since they are as intimately present as a man is to himself.

But do you also count up, for you are more skilled at that sort of thing than I am, and see whether, unwittingly, I owe you any letters. For this sudden relief from many burdens, which I had once counted up, does not reassure me, although I would not doubt that you may have received letters from me of which I have no copies.

5. *Nebridius to Augustine (388)*

My dear Augustine, it is true?—that you show such courage and patience in serving your fellow citizens, and that the much-desired leisure is not granted you? I ask you, why do they impose on you when you are so good? I suppose it must be because they do not know what you love and what you desire. But, is there none of your friends who could declare your preferences to them? Why not Romanianus?[1] or Lucinianus?[2] Surely, they would listen to me. I will shout, I will testify that God is your love, that you long to serve Him and cling to Him. I wish I could call you off to my country house and there rest with you. I will not fear being called your tempter by your fellow citizens, whom you love too much and by whom you are too much loved.

6. *Nebridius to Augustine (389)*

Your letters are as precious to me as my eyes. For they are great, not in length, but in the subjects they treat and the proofs of weighty truths which they contain. They speak to me of Christ, of Plato, of Plotinus.[1] To me they will always be sweet to hear because of their eloquence, easy to read because of their brevity, and safe to understand because of their wisdom. You must take care to teach me whatever seems good and holy to you. You shall answer this letter when you have reached a more accurate conclusion about imagination and memory. It seems this way to me: that not every image is connected with memory, but that memory cannot occur without an image. But, you will say: what about our remembering that we have understood or thought something? To this I answer by saying that this happens because, when we have understood or thought anything corporeal or temporal,

---

[1] A wealthy citizen of Tagaste, who more than once helped Augustine financially, making it possible for him to continue his studies. His son, Licentius, became one of Augustine's pupils.
[2] Also spelled Lucianus and Lucilianus; probably another wealthy and influential friend.

---

[1] Philosopher of the Neo-Platonic school at Lycopolis, Egypt, A.D. 205-270.

we produce what is needed for an image; we either add words to our understanding and our thoughts, and these words have a time element and are connected with a sense perception or a concept, or our understanding and intellect have been subject to an impression, which could leave a memory trace in the imagination. I have expressed myself ineffectually and confusedly according to my wont; you will sift out the true from the false and set me right in your letters.

Here is another point: why, I ask you, could not the imagination have all its images from itself rather than from the senses? It could be that just as our reasoning faculty is directed by the senses to the perception of things intelligible to it, and does not receive a passive impression, so the imagination could be directed by the senses to the contemplation of its own images without deriving them from outside itself. And this is how it happens that the imagination perceives things which the senses cannot perceive, which is a sign that it has all its images in and from itself. About this, too, tell me what you think.

7. *Augustine to Nebridius (389)*

I shall dispense with an introduction and begin at once on what you wish me to discuss, but I shall not leave off quickly. You claim that memory[1] cannot exist without images or those mental pictures which you wish to call fantasies. I think otherwise. Now, in the first place we must note that we do not always remember things past, but often things still in existence. And, although memory retains a firm hold on things past, it is evident that it is partly of things that have left us behind and partly of those we have left behind. When I remember my father, I likewise remember that he left me

---

1 Cf. *Conf.* 10.8-21.

and is no longer alive; when I remember Carthage, I recall that it still exists and that I left it. The memory retains the past in both these instances. I remember both the man and the city from what I saw and not from what I see.

Here you perhaps ask: where is this leading us?—especially when you notice that neither of these things can come into the memory without that mental picture. It is enough for me at present to have shown that the word memory can be used of things that have not passed out of existence. Note carefully how this helps my argument. There are some who attack in a sophistical manner that well-known Socratic theory in which it is asserted that the things which we learn are not presented to us as something new, but are recalled to mind by recollection. These critics say that memory is only of past events, but that the things we learn by our understanding, on the authority of Plato himself, remain always, cannot be destroyed, and therefore cannot become past. They do not admit that that kind of knowledge can be past, because at any time we can advert to it mentally. As for those mental experiences which we leave behind us, when we begin to take note of other things and in a different manner, then we recall those previous experiences only by means of the memory. Therefore, to pass over other examples, if eternity itself always remains, and needs no mental image by means of which it may come into the mind, as it were on a vehicle, and yet if it were unable to enter our mind unless we recalled it, then there can be memory of certain things without imagination.

Now, as to your idea that the soul which is deprived of the bodily senses can imagine corporeal objects, it is proved false in the following manner. If the soul, before it has the use of the senses for perceiving corporeal things, can imagine those things, and can form better images of them before it becomes entangled in the deceitful senses—which no sane person contends—then the minds of sleepers have more correct images than the minds of persons awake, and insane people are better off than those in mental health; for they would have the images antecedent to those produced by the unreliable senses: and either the sun they see in their minds will be more like the original than the one seen by persons who are sane and awake, or false things are preferable to true ones. If this is absurd, as it is, then that imagination you speak of, my dear Nebridius, is nothing but a wound inflicted by the senses, and what is effected thereby is not, as you write, a kind of recollection forming such images in the mind, but the introduction, or to speak more exactly, the imprint, of error. Certainly, whatever impresses you impresses you deeply, and so it happens that we represent mentally faces and forms which we have never seen. For that reason I shall extend this letter beyond the customary length, although it will not be too long for you, for whom no page is more acceptable than the one which brings me to you in my more wordy mood.

All these mental images, which you, like many others, call fantasies, I think can be most conveniently and most correctly divided into three classes: the first comprises true sense impressions; the second, images of things supposed; the third, of things thought. An example of the first class occurs when I form a mental image of your face, or of Carthage, or of our former comrade, Verecundus,[2] or of any other thing now existing or having existed in the past, which I have actually seen or experienced. To the second class belong those images of things we imagine to have been so or to be so, as when, for the sake of an argument, we build up a certain case not repugnant to truth, or when we picture a situation

---

2 The grammarian who lent Augustine his summer house.

to ourselves while a narrative is being read, or while we hear or compose or conjecture some fabulous tale. When it pleases me or when it comes to my mind, I can picture to myself the appearance of Aeneas, or of Medea with winged serpents yoked to her chariot, or of Chremes or of some Parmeno.[3] In this class, also, are those images which the learned make use of as figures to illustrate truth, and those which the ignorant, founders of various superstitions, allege as true: for example, the infernal Phlegethon,[4] and the five caverns of the inhabitants of the dark regions,[5] and the northern stake supporting the sky, and a thousand other portents of poets and heretics. Thus we say, in the course of an argument: imagine three worlds like this one, piled one upon another; imagine the earth confined in a square figure, and such things. For we imagine and suppose all these things according to the tenor of our thought. As to the third class of images, they pertain chiefly to numbers and dimensions: partly, as they are found in nature, as when the shape of the universe is conceived, and an image follows this concept in the mind of the thinker; partly, in mathematics, when we deal with geometrical figures or musical rhythms or the infinite variety of numbers. Although these may be truly understood, as I assert, they beget false images such as reason itself can scarcely withstand; and it is not easy for the very act of arguing to escape this defect, since in our divisions and classifications we picture to ourselves counters.

In this whole forest of images, you do not, I suppose, claim that the first class refers to the mind before it has the use of the senses; so we shall not argue this point further. Of the other two classes, the question might properly be raised

---

[3] Stock names in Roman comedy, especially in Terence.
[4] One of the rivers of the lower world.
[5] One of the beliefs of the Manichaeans; cf. *Conf.* 3.6.

if it were not evident that the mind, which is not yet subject to the vanity of the senses and sense impressions, is less exposed to error. But, who will doubt that those imaginings are much more false than the images of things experienced? It is equally true that the things which we suppose and believe or imagine are utterly and completely false and those which we see or experience are far more true. Now, in the third class, I may imagine to myself any sort of physical space, and to the trustworthy reasonings of logic my thought may seem to have created it, but by the same reasonings I prove this to be false. Consequently, I do not believe that the soul, before it has the use of a body, before it is beaten upon by the vain senses in a mortal and perishable substance, lies in such degradation of error.

Whence, then, does it happen that we think of things which we do not perceive? How else, do you think, but by a power innate in the mind of increasing and diminishing, which it must necessarily bring with it from wherever it comes? This power can be noticed especially in regard to numbers. So, for example, the image of a crow may be, as it were, set before the eyes, recognizable in all its features; but by subtracting or adding certain details it may be changed into something never seen anywhere. Thus it happens that, when people are accustomed to deal in such fictions, images of this sort break in on their thoughts almost spontaneously. Therefore, it is possible for the imagination to alter the data brought in by the senses, and by subtraction, as we said, or by addition, to produce things which in their totality have been experienced by none of the senses, although parts of them have been experienced in one or another instance. Thus, we who were born and brought up among Mediterranean peoples were able, even as children, to imagine the sea, from seeing water in a small cup; whereas, until we had tasted them in Italy, the flavor of strawberries and cherries could in no wise come into our minds. That is why those who are born blind are unable to answer when they are questioned about light and color: they cannot imagine color because they have never perceived any.

Do not wonder that those things which are pictured according to nature cannot first be imagined by the self-activity of the conscious mind, when it has never perceived them exteriorly. When, by anger or joy or other emotions of the sort, we produce in our body many facial expressions and colors, it is not our thought, as far as we can act, that causes such effects. Those consequences follow upon your thought in marvelous and unifying manner, when hidden numbers are dealt with mentally without any falsifying of bodily images. From this I should like you to understand—since you realize that there are so many activities of the mind free from these images about which you are inquiring—that the soul acquires a body by some other activity than by the thought of sensible forms, which I think it can in no wise experience before it has the use of a body and senses. Therefore, my dearest and most cherished, by our friendship and by your faith in the divine law, I exhort you most earnestly to form no friendship with those diabolical shadows and to lose no time in breaking off the friendship you have formed.[6] It is impossible to resist the bodily senses, according to our most sacred practice, if we feel pleasure in the blows and wounds they inflict on us.

---
6 The aberrations of the Manichaeans.

8. *Nebridius to Augustine (389)*

In my haste to get to the point, I shall dispense with preface and introduction. How does it happen, my dear Augustine, or what method is used by the spiritual powers—I mean the heavenly ones—when they wish to set before us in our sleep certain dreams? I repeat: what method? That is, how do they do it, by what art, what devices, what instrumentalities, what spells? Do they project their own thoughts into our mind, so that we represent those things to ourselves in our thought? Or do they in their own body[1] or in their own imagination present and show to us these happenings? But, if they do these things in their own body, it follows, also, that in our sleep we have other bodily eyes within ourselves with which we see those scenes formed by them in their body. If, however, they are not aided to that end by their body, but arrange details in their imagination and so touch our imagination, and there ensues a vision, which is a dream, why, I ask you, does not my imagination force yours to produce the same dreams which I have formed in mine? Certainly, I have an imagination, and it is able to fancy whatever I wish, but I cannot produce a single dream in you; all I perceive is myself producing my own dreams. For, when the body is ill, through its close connection with the soul, it forces us to form images of this suffering in wonderful ways. Often in sleep, when we are thirsty we dream that we are drinking, and when hungry we seem as if eating, and many other such experiences are transferred from the body to the soul by a certain industry of the imagination. Do not wonder if these problems, by reason of their own obscurity and my lack of skill, are presented without elegance and without subtlety. It shall be your part to offset this as far as you are able.

---

1 He does not seem to mean a material body.

9. Augustine to Nebridius (389)

Although you know my mind, still, perhaps, you do not know how much I should enjoy your company at present. However, God will grant us this great favor some time. I have read your latest letter, in which you complain of loneliness and of a certain desertion by your friends, in whose company life is sweet. But, what other thing can I tell you to do, except what I do not doubt you do yourself? Retire into your own mind and lift it up to God as best you can. There you will surely find us, not by means of corporeal images such as our memory is obliged to use, but by that power of thought by which you understand that we are not together in one place.

When I was reviewing your letters, in which you express confidence of receiving satisfactory answers to your questions, that one frightened me greatly in which you ask how it happens that certain thoughts and dreams are produced in us by supernatural powers or demons.[1] That is an important matter and your keen mind will recognize that it should not be answered in a letter, but in a personal conversation or in some treatise. I shall try, nevertheless, to shed over your clever mind some light on this question, so that you can either work out the rest of it yourself or, at least, will not despair of reaching a probable solution of so serious a matter.

I am of the opinion that every act of our mind produces some effect in the body, and that, however heavy and slow our senses may be, they feel this effect, in proportion to the intensity of the mental act, as when we are angry or sad or joyful. From this it may be concluded that, when we think something which has no apparent effect on our body, it can nevertheless be apparent to the supernatural and heavenly

---
1 Cf. *Conf.* 10.30.

spirits, whose perception is so very keen that ours does not deserve the name of perception in comparison with it. Therefore, those traces of its activity which the mind imprints, so to speak, on the body can both remain and take on a certain appearance; and when they are subconsciously aroused and activated, they easily produce in us thoughts and dreams, according to the intention of the arouser and activator. For, if our earth-bound and utterly unresponsive bodies can be so' unbelievably affected by the playing of organ music, or by rope-dancers and numberless other such spectacles, as it is clear that they can, then it is certainly not unreasonable to suppose that spiritual and heavenly beings, acting with faculties which have a penetrating natural effect, possess a far greater ability to arouse in us whatever they wish, without our being aware of it even while we are the subjects of it. We are likewise unaware of how the overflow of bile drives us to frequent anger—yet it does so drive us—while, as I have said before, this very overflow is caused by our being angry.

But, if you do not wish to receive this comparison I make in passing, examine this thought as thoroughly as you can. For, if there continually arises for the mind some difficulty in doing or fulfilling what it desires, it is continually angered. According to my way of thinking, anger is the turbulent urge to overcome those obstacles which hinder our freedom of action. Therefore, we are often angry not only at men, but at a pen in writing, so that we slash it and break it—as dice-players do with their dice, or painters with their brushes, or anyone with any kind of implement from which he thinks he suffers frustration. Even doctors admit that the bile increases with this continual state of being angry; and with the increase we fall into anger again and easily and almost without external cause. Therefore, the effect which the mind has produced in the body will react to affect it again.

These points can be treated much more at length, and, by adding many proofs drawn from experience, they will lead to a firmer and fuller conviction. Add to this letter that other one which I sent you recently, on the subject of memory and mental images, and study it more carefully, for it is clear from your answer that you did not fully understand it. Therefore, when you match with this one which you are now reading that section of the other letter which treats of a certain natural power of the mind to add to and subtract from an idea, perhaps you will no longer be troubled by the fact that shapes of bodies which we have never seen are presented to us in our thoughts and in our dreams.

10. *Augustine to Nebridius (c. 389)*

Never has any of your inquiries kept me in such a tempest of thought as that one which I read in your latest letters, where you claim that I am negligent in making arrangements for us to live in the same place. That is a serious charge, and, if it were not false, it would carry a grave penalty. But, since a very persuasive argument seems to prove that we can live here more satisfactorily than at Carthage or even in the country, I am somewhat uncertain what to do with you, my dear Nebridius. Should a vehicle be all fitted up and sent to you? Our friend Lucinianus suggests that you could be safely carried in a litter; but I think of your mother who can hardly bear to have you away when you are in good health, much less when you are ill.[1] Should I myself, then, come to

---

[1] It was evidently his illness that made Nebridius peevish and unreasonable. He was at this time at Carthage, and died not long after. Cf. *Conf.* 9.3.

you? But, there are friends here who could not come with me, and whom I should think it shameful to desert. You can live agreeably in your own mind, but it is doubtful that these can do the same. Should I, then, go backward and forward frequently, so as to be now with you and now with them? But, this is no way of living, either together or satisfactorily. Besides, you know that my health, too, is poor, and I am not able to do what I wish, unless I cease to wish what I am not able to do.

Therefore, to spend one's whole life planning quiet and easy journeys, such as you cannot have, is not the proper conduct of a man who thinks of that one last journey, called death, on which alone, as you understand, one's thought should rightly be expended. God has indeed given to a certain few, whom He willed to be rulers of the churches, not only to look forward to death with fortitude, but even to desire it with eagerness, and to undertake the labors of their administration without anxiety. But I think that it is not to those who are drawn to this sort of administration by love of worldly honor, nor again to those who long for the busy life when they have been deprived of it, that this great boon is granted, of acquiring, in the midst of the bustling confusion of goings and comings, this familiarity with death which we seek. To both groups, however, it is possible to be sanctified in peaceful quiet. If this is not true, then I am certainly the most cowardly, not to say the most stupid, of men, since I cannot taste and relish that true good unless a certain measure of carefree leisure falls to my lot. Believe me, a man does not achieve freedom from fear through his own insensibility, or boldness, or greed of empty glory, or superstitious credulity, but only by a considerable detachment from perishable things. From this comes that firmly established joy, which cannot be compared in any respect whatsoever to other delights.

But, if such a life does not fall to the lot of human nature, why does that freedom from fear sometimes befall us? Why does it occur more frequently in proportion as one adores God in the innermost recesses of his soul? Why does that interior peace permeate even our human activity, when we return to that activity from our inner shrine? Why is it that, when we are speaking, we sometimes feel no fear of death, but, when we have ceased speaking, we even desire it? I say to you—and I would not say this to anyone else—but I say to you, whose upward strivings I know well: will you, since you have experienced how sweet life can be when the soul is dead to corporeal love, will you deny that the whole life of man can be freed of fear, so that he can rightly be called wise? Or will you dare to assert that this state of mind, which reason strives after, has ever been yours except when you were inwardly recollected? Granting these arguments, you see that there is only one thing left to do: that is, to consider on your part how we may reside together. What is to be done about your mother, whom your brother Victor will certainly not leave alone, you know much better than I. I will write no more, lest I draw you off from that thought.

11. Augustine to Nebridius (c. 389)

Although I had been greatly disturbed by a recent problem of yours, set forth with a certain friendly reproach—namely, how we might be able to reside together; and although I had determined to write to you about this alone, and not to turn my pen to any other subject of mutual interest to us until this one had been settled, your latest letter, with its brief and very reasonable proposal, has quickly set me at ease. We shall, therefore, not have to think about this again, since it is agreed that either we shall go to you when we can, or you, when you can, shall inevitably come to us. Therefore, as I had been set at rest on that point, as I said, I reviewed all your letters, to discover to which ones I owed answers. I found so many questions in them that, even if they could easily be solved, their very number would outweigh anyone's ability and time. And they are such difficult questions that, if even one of them were put before me for solution, I should have to admit that it laid on me a very heavy burden. The purpose of this introduction is to induce you to stop asking me any more questions for awhile, until we are free of the entire debt, and to write to me only of your own conclusions. Yet, I know what a loss it will be for me to put off awhile sharing in your divine thoughts.

Here, then, is what I think about the mystery of the Incarnation,[1] which the religion in which we are both steeped proposes to us as an object of knowledge and belief; that it was accomplished for our salvation. I have selected this question, not as the easiest of all, or the one I was best able to answer, but as the one that seemed to me more worthy than others of thought and attention. For, those questions which arise on matters of this world seem to me to have no bearing on the achievement of happiness; even if it gives us pleasure to search into them, it is to be feared that time is spent on them which ought to be devoted to better things.

Therefore, in regard to this present question, of God becoming man: in the first place, I am surprised at your finding it hard to understand why the Son is said to have become man, and not the Father or even the Holy Spirit. For, according to the Catholic faith, the Trinity[2] is proposed to our

---

1 The term used by Nebridius and Augustine is *susceptio hominis.* It has been translated by Incarnation because the latter term is more familiar to present-day readers.
2 Cf. *Conf.* 13.11.

belief and believed—and even understood by a few saints and holy persons—as so inseparable that whatever action is performed by It must be thought to be performed at the same time by the Father and by the Son and by the Holy Spirit. Consequently, the Father does not do anything which the Son and the Holy Spirit do not also do; the Son does not do anything which the Father and the Holy Spirit do not also do; nor does the Holy Spirit do anything which the Father and the Son do not also do. From this it seems to follow that the whole Trinity became man, for, if the Son took on human nature and the Father and the Holy Spirit did not, They no longer act jointly. Why, then, in our mysteries and our sacred rites is the Incarnation celebrated as if attributed to the Son? This is a very deep question, and so difficult and of such great import that it cannot be solved in a sentence, nor can its proof be wholly satisfying. Nevertheless, when I write anything to you, I venture rather to outline than to develop what is in my mind, leaving you to work it out for yourself, according to your own gifts of mind, as well as what you know of me through our long friendship.

There is no nature, my dear Nebridius, and certainly no substance, which does not possess and show forth these three characteristics: first, that it should be; second, that it should be this or that; third, that it should continue to be what it is, as far as it is able. The first shows us the very cause of nature from which all things come; the second shows us the appearance (species) in which all things are fashioned and in a certain manner formed; the third shows a certain continuance, so to speak, in which all things are maintained. But, if it could happen that something should be, and should not be this or that, and that it should be, and should be what it is as long as it remains in its own genus, or that it should be this or that, but should not be nor remain in its own genus as far as it able, or that it should remain in its own genus according to the powers of its genus, but nevertheless should not be, or should not be this or that, then, indeed, it could happen that in that Trinity one of the Persons would do something without the other Persons. But, if you perceive that it inevitably follows that whatever is must forthwith be this or that, and must remain in its own genus, as far as it is able, then the Three perform no act except jointly. I see that I have thus far treated the part of this question of which the solution is difficult, but I wanted to make known to you briefly—if I have done what I wanted—what subtlety of understanding is needed in dealing with the inseparability of the Trinity according to Catholic truth.

Now learn how it is possible for that which moves not to move the mind. That distingushing characteristic which is properly attributed to the Son refers to a system of life and to a sort of art, if we can rightly use this word in such matters, and also to the understanding by which the mind is formed in its thought about things. Therefore, since it has been brought about by the Incarnation that a certain method of living and example of precept has been conveyed to us under the majesty and clarity of His teachings, it is not without reason that this whole operation is attributed to the Son. For, in many things, which I leave to your prudent consideration, although many truths are implied, there is something which stands out and which rightly demands for itself special notice. Just as, in those three sorts of questions, if one were to ask whether a thing exists, there is implied also the question of what it is, for it certainly cannot exist unless it is something; and, likewise, there is implied whether it is to be approved or disapproved, for, whatever it is, it is worthy of some esteem; so, too, when one asks what it is, there is necessarily implied both that it exists and that it deserves some consideration; the same consequence follows if one asks what sort of thing it is, for it is certainly something. Thus, all these arguments are inseparably joined together, but the question does not take its name from all of them, but according to the intention of the questioner. Therefore, a way of life was necessary for men that they might be thoroughly versed in it and formed according to it. Now, as to what is accomplished in men by that rule of life, are we to say that it does not exist or is not to be desired? First we propose to know on what we may construct an argument, and on what ground we may stand. That is why a certain rule and standard of reasoning had first to be proved. This has been accomplished by that dispensation of the Incarnation, which is properly to be attributed to the Son, so that there proceeds from the Father Himself, as from the single principle from whom are all things, both understanding through the Son, and a certain interior and ineffable sweetness and delight in that understanding (outlasting and looking down upon all mortal things), which is rightly ascribed to the Holy Spirit as gift and attribute. Therefore, although all these operations occur with the most complete union and inseparability, they nevertheless had to be proved separately, by reason of our weakness through which we have fallen from unity into multiplicity. For, no one raises another to the place where he is, without stooping somewhat to the place where the other is. You now have a letter which may not solve your difficulty on this point, but will, perhaps, set your own thoughts on a firm foundation, so that you may complete the argument with that genius which is so well known to me, and continue with that tender devotion to which we must cling, above all.

12. Augustine to Nebridius (c. 389)

You write that you have sent more letters than I have received—a matter in which I can neither disbelieve you nor you me. I may not be able to keep up with you in answering, but I keep your letters with no less care than you use in multiplying them. We agree on this, that you have received only two of my longer letters; I did not write a third. I notice by the copies I have kept that I have answered almost five of your questions, except that one of them was treated rather cursorily. This was a compliment to your own ability, even if it did not satisfy your insatiable desire. You will have to curb this a little and put up with summary arguments sometimes, but on this condition, that, if I cheat your intelligence of anything by being sparing of words, you do not spare me, but demand the whole of what is owed. That will be a binding obligation to me, and even an agreeable one. You will therefore count this letter among my short ones, which do not diminish the pile either for you or for me. But you are not the sort of person to send short ones—the kind which do not increase the pile.

Now, as to that question of yours about the Son of God, why He rather than the Father is said to have become man, whereas He and the Father are one. If you will recall my discussions, in which I have treated as well as I have been able—for it is an ineffable subject—who the Son of God is, in whom we are united, you will easily understand this. To sum it up briefly, I will say that the plan and form of God by which all created things are made is called the Son. All that was done by Him in becoming man was done for our enlightenment and instruction.[1]

---

[1] According to the Vatican MS., there is a lacuna of sixty-seven lines at the end of this letter.

13. Augustine to Nebridius (c. 389)

I do not like to write you on trite subjects, and I am not able to deal with new ones; I see that the former do not suit you, and for the latter I have no time. Since I left you, I have not had a chance nor any leisure for thinking over and working out those subjects which we usually discuss together. It is true, the winter nights are very long, and I do not sleep through the whole of them; but, when I have some time, more importunate matters demand my attention, and they necessarily use up all my leisure. So, what am I to do? Shall there be complete silence between us? Neither you nor I want that, so you will have to do with this which I worked out at the end of the night—for as long as it lasted—when this letter was written.

You must remember that we have often tossed the ball of argument back and forth, following it, panting and breathless, as we argued over that certain sort of indestructible body or semblance of body which belongs to the soul; and you recall that by some it is called the vehicle of the soul. Certainly, this is evidently not an intelligible thing, if it possesses motion; and what is not intelligible cannot be understood. But, what is outside the range of the understanding, if at least it falls under the senses, allows some probable estimate to be made of it, whereas what can neither be understood nor perceived begets only a baseless and valueless opinion. And this matter, of which we are treating, is such, if, indeed, it is anything. Why, then, I ask you, don't we declare a holiday on this little question, and, after we have prayed to God, why do we not raise ourselves to the utter peace of the highest living being?

Here you may perhaps say that, although there are some corporeal things which cannot be perceived, there still are many facts about the body which it is possible for us to understand; as for example, that we know there is a body. Would anyone deny this, or claim that it is more probable than true? Thus, although this body itself is a probable thing, it is true that some such thing exists in nature. Therefore, it is a sensible body, but it is judged to be intelligible, also, for it could not otherwise be perceived. Thus, that indefinite sort of body about which we are inquiring is believed to be one to which the soul is attached, so that it may move from place to place; and, although it is not perceptible to our senses, it might be so to more powerful ones; in any case, it can be reasonably known whether it exists.

If you agree to this, recall that what we mean by understanding is accomplished in us in two ways: either by the mind itself and the reason acting within us, as when we understand that the understanding exists; or through information furnished us by the senses; as we have said before, when we understand that the body exists. Of these two kinds of knowledge, we understand the first, that is, the one which is concerned with what is within us, by considering God; and the second, which concerns knowledge brought to us by the bodily senses, we likewise understand by considering God. If this is accepted as proved, then no one can know anything about that sort of body, or even whether it exists, unless his senses bring him some information about it. If there is any such in the number of living beings, as we have no experience of any, then I think that point is carried, which I had begun to indicate above; namely, that this question has nothing to do with us. I should like you to think this over carefully, and let me know what conclusions you reach.

14. Augustine to Nebridius[1]

I have decided to answer your latest letters, not because I have no regard for your earlier inquiries, or that they gave me less pleasure, but because in answering I am undertaking a greater task than you think. You did, it is true, give me orders to send you a letter longer than the longest, but I have not as much time as you think, or as you know that I have always longed and still do long to have. Do not ask me why that is: I could more easily tell you what my handicaps are than why I am handicapped.

You write of a matter of which I am to try to find the cause: why you and I, although we are separate persons, do many of the same things, whereas the sun does not do the same things as the other stars. But, if we do the same things, then he also does the same things as they do; and if he does not, then we do not either. I walk and you walk; he moves and they move; I wake and you wake, he shines and they shine; I argue and you argue, he revolves and they revolve. However, a mental act is in no wise to be compared with what we see. But, if you compare mind with mind, as is proper, if there is any mind in the stars, they, much more than men, must be considered to think or contemplate the same objects, or to perform any other mental action which may be appropriately mentioned. On the other hand, if you consider attentively, as is your wont, the motion of bodies, no two can possibly perform the same action. When we two are walking up and down together, do you suppose that we are doing exactly the same thing? You have more sense than that. The one of us who walks on the northern side must either precede the other, if they walk with equal steps, or he must proceed

---

[1] Written some time before 391, this is the last of the letters to Nebridius, who died before Augustine became a priest. Cf. *Conf.* 9.6.

more slowly.² Neither of these facts is perceptible; but, you, if I mistake not, are thinking of what we understand, not what we perceive. If we turn toward the south, arm-in-arm and close together, and if we press as hard as we can, upon a smooth marble or ivory floor, the movement of both of us can no more be the same than can the beat of our pulse, or our physical form or our faces. Remove us, place Glaucia's twins³ there, and you will get no other result; for, although they are exactly alike, they are just as much bound to move individually as they were to be born separately.

You will probably say that this is a matter of reasoning only, but the fact of the sun's differing from the stars is clear and obvious to the senses. If you force me to consider the matter of size, you know how many opinions there are about distances, and how unreliable our guesses are apt to be. But, if I grant that this matter is as it appears to be—and I suppose it is—whose sense of size, pray, was deceived by the height of Naevius,⁴ taller by a foot than the one who was tallest at six feet? You must have been looking for somebody that tall, and, when you did not find one, you wanted our letter to be stretched out to match. Considering that such a prodigy exists on earth, I think nothing in heaven ought to be wondered at. If you are stirred by the fact that no other star but the sun gives light to our day, who, I ask you, appeared so great to men, as the Man whom God received far otherwise than He does the rest of saints and wise men? If you compare Him with other men, they are separated by a greater distance than are the other stars in comparison with the sun. Consider this analogy carefully, and you may find in

---
2 This is clear only if we imagine them to be walking in a circle.
3 Perhaps a neighbor's children.
4 Obviously not the poet Naevius, but probably some contemporary giant, whose height Nebridius was supposed to guess.

the depths of that superior mind of yours that I have answered indirectly a certain question posed by you about Christ becoming man.

You likewise ask whether that supreme truth and wisdom, the form of things, through whom all things were made, whom our sacred rites hail as the Son of God, contains within Himself the form of man in general, or of each one of us in particular. That is a great question. It seems to me that, if we consider the creation of man as such, there is in Him the form of man only, not yours or mine; but, if we consider the sequence of time, there exists in that absolute perfection the various forms of men. I admit that this is far from clear, and I think of no illustration to simplify it, except by having recourse to those branches of knowledge which are familiar to our minds. Thus, in the science of geometry there is one form for the angle and one for the square. If I wish to demonstrate the angle, no other form comes to my mind but that of the angle; whereas, I should try in vain to draw a square if I did not have in mind the form of four angles together. Thus, any man is created according to one form by which he is understood as a man; but, in the case of a whole people, it is one and the same form, yet not the form of a man but of men. If, then, Nebridius is part of this universal whole, as he is, and if the whole is composed of parts, then God the Creator of the whole could not fail to have in mind the form of the parts. Consequently, the fact of the form of many men being therein does not refer to the particular man, although again in wondrous wise the whole is conformed to the one. But, you will think this out more suitably. I ask you to be satisfied with this for the present, although I have outdone Naevius in size!

15. Augustine to Romanianus (c. 390)

This letter points to a scarcity of paper, but does it not at least show that there is plenty of parchment? I sent my ivory tablets to your uncle, with a message, but you will more readily pardon this bit of parchment, because what I wrote to him could not be delayed, and I thought it would be foolish not to write to you, too. But I wish you would send back any tablets of mine that are with you, to meet such emergencies as this. I have written something on the Catholic religion, within the limits of what the Lord has granted me to do, and I want to send it to you before my arrival, if paper does not fall short. You, however, are one who will welcome any sort of writing from the workshop of Maiorinus. Of finished books, except one on the orator, I haven't one with me, but, as I gave you full permission before to take what pleases you, I still feel the same way about it. In my absence, I can't think of anything else to do.

It gave me great pleasure that you shared your domestic joy with me in your last letter. But, *Dost thou bid me shut my eyes to the sea's calm face and peaceful waves?*[1] You would not bid me do this, nor would you shut your own eyes. So, then, if a period of quiet is given you for deeper thought, seize this divine opportunity, but do not take credit to yourself when such good fortune falls to your lot. We owe our thanks rather to those whose just and efficient management of temporal affairs, both peaceful and tranquilizing, makes possible the receiving of heavenly gifts, a management which does not entangle when it is increased, so long as it does not possess its holder, nor overwhelm when it is at peace.[2]

---

1 Vergil, *Aen.* 5.848,849.
2 Goldbacher indicates a lacuna here, but the reading *pacatur* for *putatur* makes that supposition unnecessary.

By the mouth of Truth itself it has been said: 'If you have not been faithful in that which is another's, who will give you that which is your own?'[3] Therefore, letting go our care of fleeting things, let us seek the secure and certain goods; let us rise above our earthly possessions. The bee has wings for a good purpose, when there is abundance of honey, but it kills the stay-at-home.[4]

16. Maximus the Grammarian[1] to Augustine (c. 390)

Because I often long for the pleasure of your words and the prick of your speech, with which you goad me most delightfully and in all kindness, I cannot refrain from answering you, lest you think that my silence means a change of mind. So, I ask you to treat me with the indulgence of kindly ears, even if you think these are the wiles of an old man. There is a Greek myth of uncertain authenticity to the effect that Mount Olympus is the dwelling-place of the gods. We, on the other hand, see and prove that the forum of our city is held by a throng of saving deities. Yet, could anyone be so mad, so touched in the head, as to deny that there is one supreme God, without beginning, without natural offspring, like a great and powerful Father? His powers, scattered throughout the material world,[2] we call upon under various

---
3 Luke 16.12.
4 *Necat enim haerentem* seems to be a sort of proverb, and may refer to the bee trying to kill anyone laying hold on its honey or to the slaughter of drones in the hive.

---
1 Maximus, a grammarian, probably a sophist of Madaura, a town not far from Tagaste. This town was the scene of some of Augustine's earlier excesses. Cf. *Conf.* 2.3.
2 Cf. *City of God* 7.6.

names, since, undoubtedly, none of us knows His true name. For, 'god' is a word common to all religions. Thus, when we honor His separate parts by different forms of prayer, we seem to worship Him wholly.

I cannot pretend that I am not intolerant of such an error. For, who could allow Miggin to be preferred to Jupiter, brandishing his thunderbolt, or Sanamen to Juno, Minerva, Venus, and Vesta, or, horrible to say, the arch-martyr Namphano to all the other immortal gods? Among them, Lucitas is honored with no less worship, and others in unending number, names hateful to gods and men, who, stained with the consciousness of unspeakable deeds, heaping crimes upon crimes, and with the pretense of a glorious death, find an end worthy of their character and their acts. Yet, fools throng to their tombs as if worthy of remembrance, and, leaving the temples empty and forsaking their own household gods and those of their ancestors, they fulfill the prophecy of that despairing poet: *'And in the temples of the gods, Rome will swear by phantoms.'*[3] It almost seems to me at present as if the battle of Actium were being re-enacted, when perishable Egyptian monsters dare to brandish their weapons against the gods of the Romans.

But, I ask you one thing, wisest of men: that you set aside and leave untried the force of that eloquence in which you excel others, and those Chrysippean[4] arguments which you use as weapons, and even, for a little while, that method of reasoning which in the contest of wits strives to leave no ground of certitude for an adversary, and that you show me by facts alone who that god is whom you Christians claim as your own, and whom you feign that you see present in

---

3 Lucan, *Pharsalia* 7.459.
4 Chrysippus was a Stoic philosopher of Cilicia, 291-208 B.C., who would often argue on opposite sides of the same question, enjoying subtleties and distinctions for their own sake.

hidden places. For our part, we adore our gods openly, by daylight, before the eyes and ears of all men, and by reverent prayers and acceptable victims we win their favor, and we try to have these acts of ours known and approved by all.

From now on, as I am an old man and a sick one, I withdraw myself from this sort of contest, and I gladly go along with the sentiment of the Mantuan writer: *'Let each one follow his own bent.'*[5] After this I do not doubt, excellent sir, as you have left my religion, that this letter will be stolen by someone, or will perish in the fire or some other way. If this happens, it will be a loss of a page, but not of my words of which a copy will remain with all religious men. May the gods preserve you, whom we and all men, one at heart despite multitudinous differences, adore and worship as the common father of all mankind.

17. Augustine to Maximus (c. 390.)

Are we dealing seriously together, or do you want to joke? From the tone of your letter, I am not sure whether it is because of the weakness of your case, or the charm of your manners, that you prefer to be witty rather than exact. In the first place, there is a comparison of Mount Olympus and your forum—although I do not know what that has to do with it, except to inform me that Jupiter pitched his camp there when he was making war on his father, as that history which your people call sacred narrates—and in that forum I could recall that of two statues of Mars, one is unarmed, the other armed, while a statue of a man placed opposite, with three fingers outstretched, is supposed to control this evil spirit, unlucky to citizens. Am I to suppose that, by

---
5 Vergil, *Ec.* 2.65.

mentioning that forum, you wished to renew my memory of such divinities, or that you preferred to jest rather than to argue seriously? As to the statement of yours that such gods are, as it were, members of one great god, I warn you strongly, as you deserve, to refrain from such sacrilegious witticisms. If you claim that that god is one, on which, according to the ancients, learned and unlearned agree, do you say that these are members of that god whose monstrous cruelty or, if you prefer, power is kept in check by an image of a dead man? I could say more on this point, but your own clear mind shows you how that postition lays you open to attack, and I refrain, lest you should think I was speaking rhetorically rather than truthfully.

Coming now to those Punic names of our dead, which you have collected, and which you seem to think furnish amusing insults to be used against our religion, I am not sure whether to refute them or to pass them over in silence. If they seem as light to your serious mind as they are, then I have no time for jesting, but, if they seem serious to you, I wonder that this absurdity of names did not remind you that you have Eucaddirs among your priesthoods, and Abaddirs among your divinities.[1] I suppose you did not think of those when you were writing, but, in your mood of affability and charm, you wanted to give us a little relaxation of mind by showing how ridiculous such things are in your creed. Yet, I do not think you could have forgotten that an African writing to Africans, since we are both settled in Africa, would scarcely think that Punic names were objectionable. For, if we translate those words, what else does Namphano mean but a man of good feet, or one whose coming brings some happiness? We usually say that someone comes in on a favorable foot when some good luck follows his entrance.

---

1 The names are Punic.

If this tongue is objectionable to you, refuse to admit that many things have been learnedly handed down to memory in Punic books, as is the tradition of the most learned men, but at least be ashamed that you were born where the origins of this tongue are cherished. But, if our language does not reasonably displease us, and you concede that I have interpreted that word correctly, then you have reason to be angry with your Vergil, who invites your Hercules to the sacrifices which were being offered in his honor by Evander, in this wise: *'Graciously with favoring foot visit us and thy rites!'*[2] He asks him to come with favoring foot; therefore, he wants a Hercules Namphano, about whom you condescend to deride us so much. However, if you really want to laugh, you have plenty of material of your own: a god Dunghill, a goddess Sewer, a bald Venus, a god Fear, a god Paleness, a goddess Fever, and any number of others of the sort, to which the ancient Romans set up temples with worshipers of their statues, deeming them fit for worship. If you refuse to accept these, you refuse to accept the gods of Rome, and you are classed as someone not initiated into Roman rites; yet, devoted to the altars of these too numerous Romans, you scorn and despise our Punic names.

It seems to me that you make even less of those sacred rites than we do, while you draw some pleasure from them to beguile the passing of this life, seeing that you do not think twice about appealing to Vergil, as you write, and defending yourself with that verse of his: *'Let each one follow his own bent.'*[3] If Vergil's authority pleases you, as you show that it does, doubtless this other quotation will please you, too: *'First from heavenly Olympus came Saturn, fleeing from*

---

2 Vergil, *Aen.* 7.302.
3 Vergil, *Ec.* 2.65.

the weapons of Jove, and exiled from his lost realm.[4] and other passages in which he gives us to understand that he and the other gods of that sort were men. He had read many a tale, supported by the authority of the ancients, which Cicero had read, too, and which he develops in his dialogues[5] even more than we could venture to expect, and even tries to draw men's attention to them as far as the times allowed.

When you say that your religious rites are to be preferred to ours, because you adore your gods publicly, whereas we have small and secret meeting-places, I ask you, first of all, whether you have forgotten about Bacchus, whose cult you people have thought proper to entrust to the participation of a few initiates. In the second place, you imagine that the only thing you are trying to do by reminding us of the public celebration of your cults is to have us place before our eyes, as a sort of show, the public officials and leading citizens of your city dancing and raging in bacchanalian orgy through the streets. If you are truly possessed by the god in that sort of worship, you surely see what sort of god he is, who steals away your mind. If you only pretend it, what secrets of yours are displayed in public? Or what is the purpose of this disgraceful deceit? Finally, why do you not predict the future, if you are prophets? Or why do you plunder the bystanders, if you are in your right mind?

Therefore, when you write of these and other things which I think unworthy of notice, such as our making fun of your gods, wouldn't anyone who knows your type of mind, and who reads your letters, understand that your gods are much more subtly mocked by yourself? So, if you wish any discussion between us, such as befits your age and wisdom, and such as can be asked by those dearest to us, according to

---

4 Vergil, *Aen.* 8.319,320.
5 Cicero, *De natura deorum* 1.42.119.

established custom, seek something worthy of our consideration, and be sure to speak of your gods so that we may think you a sincere defender of them, because you give us more arguments against them than for them. Finally, let this be very clear to you, and let it keep you from falling into blasphemous insults, that we Christian Catholics, whose church is established in your town, adore no one of the dead, and worship nothing as a divinity which is made and fashioned by God, but we adore the one only God who made and fashioned all things. With the help of this one true God, I shall discuss these matters more at length when I see that you are serious in your desire to treat of them.

18. Augustine to Caelestinus[1] (c. 390)

How I wish I could speak with you at length! That, indeed, is something—to be stripped of vain cares and clothed with useful ones. But, I doubt whether any security is to be hoped for in this world. I have written to you and had no answer. I sent you my books against the Manichaeans[2]—the ones I had finished and corrected—but I have not had any indication of your impression of them or your criticism of them. So, now, I must ask them back and you must send them back. I ask you to do so at once, with your comments, for I especially want to know what you make of my writings, and what you think is needed as a weapon for overthrowing that fallacious belief.

---
1 Probably a lay friend, as he is addressed without title.
2 The heretical sect in which Augustine became involved during his student days. This sect believed in a dual principle of divinity: one the creator of good, the other of evil things. They had been powerful in Africa, but Augustine helped to give them their death blow. The work referred to may have been *Contra Faustum*.

Since I know you so well, here is something both great and short. There is a nature, which is subject to the changes of both time and space, as the body; and there is a nature which is not subject to space but only to time, as the soul; and there is a nature which is subject to neither space nor time, and that is God. What I have portrayed as changeable is called creature; what is unchangeable, the Creator. Since, therefore, we postulate of all being continuity and unity, doubtless every form of beauty is a form of unity, and you see at once in that classification of natures what is highest; what is lowest, yet existent; what intermediate, being greater than the lowest and less than the highest. The highest is Beatitude itself; the lowest can be neither happy nor wretched; but the intermediate lives wretchedly by inclination, blessedly by conversion. He who believes in Christ does not love the lowest, is not proud in the intermediate nature, and thereby becomes fit to cling to the highest. And this is the whole of what we are commanded, urged, and aroused to do.

19. *Augustine to Gaius*[1] (*c. 390*)

After I had left you, the memory of you filled me with indescribable sweetness—and still does. I recall that, in spite of the ardor of your questions, which was extraordinary, there was no lack of restraint in your arguments. I could not easily find another who questions so eagerly and listens so quietly. I wish I could talk much with you, although it would not be much, however much it was, if only I could talk with you. But, because it is difficult, what need is there to seek reasons? Certainly, it is difficult. Perhaps it will be easier

---
1 One of Augustine's converts.

sometime—may God grant it!—but now it is far otherwise. Therefore, I have charged our brother to show all my writings to your most prudent charity; I know that he will not impose anything of mine upon you against your will, but I also know your kind dispositions toward me. If, then, you approve what you have read, and esteem it to be true, do not attribute to me anything but the giving, whereby there is an opportunity of your conversion, and whence it is given you, too, to approve. For, no one who reads believes that truth is in the printed book or in the writer, but in himself, especially if his mind is illumined by the light of truth, that light which is far removed from any material torch or anything which is commonly called bright. But, if you discover in my writings anything false or blameworthy, you may know that it is bedewed by a human cloud, and you may attribute that to me as truly my own. I would encourage you to the search, if I did not seem to see the mouth of your heart wide open; I would even encourage you to hold strongly to what you know to be true, if the strength of your mind and intention was not so perfectly evident. This was completely revealed to me in a short time, almost as if I had seen through your fleshly covering. Surely, the most merciful providence of our Lord will not permit that so good and so true-hearted a man as you should remain aloof from the Catholic fold of Christ.

20. Augustine to Antoninus (c. 390)

Although letters were owed to you by both of us, the better part of the debt is being discharged with interest, because you are seeing one of us in person, and from him you can hear news of me. This could have relieved me of the necessity of writing, because his journey seemed to make it superfluous, but at his bidding I have done so. Perhaps, after all, I shall have a more profitable talk with you than I should have in a personal conference, since you both read my letter and listen to him in whose heart I live by affection, as you know. I have read and interpreted with great joy the letters of your Holiness[1] because they show me a mind both truly Christian, without any contamination of this wicked age, and most friendly to me.

I congratulate you and I give thanks to God our Lord for your hope and faith and charity, and I thank you in Him that you think so well of us that you deem us to be faithful servants of God and that you love us with sincere affection. Yet, on this score, there is more ground for congratulation than for thanks to your goodness of heart, because it is to your own advantage to love goodness. Whoever loves someone whom he believes good loves goodness, whether that person is what he is esteemed to be or something quite different. There is just one mistake to avoid, and that is false judgment—not about man but about man's good. But you, most beloved brother, are not wrong in believing and in knowing that the great good is to serve God, freely and chastely. Whenever you love a man as a sharer in this good, you have your reward, even if he is not actually so. This is my reason for congratulating you rather than the one loved, unless he is such as the lover esteems him to be. He whose judgment is unerring, not only of man's good but of man himself, will recognize what we are, and what progress we make toward Him. Believing us to be such as it befits servants of God to be, you will win the prize of

---

[1] This method of address was chiefly used to ecclesiastical equals or superiors, often of bishops to bishops. This letter was presumably written before Augustine's elevation to the priesthood. The rank of his correspondent is unknown.

blessedness, as far as it can be won in this way, by embracing us with the wide charity of your heart. We give you bountiful thanks, because, when you praise us as if we were such as we should be, you encourage us exceedingly to desire so to be, and we should thank you even more heartily if you would remember us in your prayers, or, rather, if you would pray for us unceasingly. And prayer for a brother is more pleasing to God when the sacrifice of love is offered.

I send kindest greetings to your little son, and I hope he will grow up in the practice of the saving precepts of the Lord. I pray earnestly for the members of your household that they may progress in the one faith and true devotion, which is found only in the Catholic religion. If you feel the need of my or any other help in this matter, in the name of the Lord and our mutual affection, do not hesitate to ask it. I should like to suggest to your most religious Prudence that you instill a reasonable fear of God into your weaker vessel,[2] by offering the nourishment of spiritual reading and serious conversation. Certainly, no one who is properly concerned over the state of his own soul, and humbly desirous of seeking the will of the Lord, will fail to distinguish the one Catholic faith from any kind of schism, especially if he has the help of a good teacher.

21. Augustine, priest, gives greetings in the Lord to the most blessed and venerable father Valerius,[1] bishop, most dearly beloved in the Lord (391)

First of all, I beg your religious Prudence to consider that there is nothing in this life, and especially at this time, easier

---
2 His wife; cf. 1 Peter 3.7.

---
1 Bishop of Hippo, a Greek who was scarcely able to preach in Latin.

or more agreeable or more acceptable to men than the office of bishop or priest or deacon, if it is performed carelessly or in a manner to draw flattery; but in God's sight there is nothing more wretched, more melancholy, or more worthy of punishment. On the other hand, there is nothing in this life more difficult, more laborious, or more dangerous than the office of bishop or priest or deacon, but nothing more blessed in the sight of God, if he carries on the campaign in the way prescribed by our Commander. Neither in childhood nor in youth did I learn what that way was, but, just as I was beginning to learn, I was constrained[2] as a punishment for my sins—I can think of no other reason—to accept the post next to the helmsman before I had even learned to handle an oar.

I think my Lord wanted to correct me, because, without adequate virtue and experience, I had dared to reprimand what was there being done before I had experienced the misdeeds of many sailors.[3] But, after I had been plunged into the midst of things, I began to realize the rashness of my reprimands—although even then I had considered it a most dangerous duty. That was the cause of those tears which some of the brethren noticed me shedding when I was newly ordained; and knowing the cause of my grief, they tried to comfort me, with good intentions, no doubt, but with words which left my inner wound untouched. I have since learned much, very much, more than I expected, not because I have seen any new waves or storms which I had not previously seen or heard or read or thought of, but because I had not known the extent of my skill and strength in avoiding or overcoming them, thinking I was of some use. Then the

---

[2] According to the custom of the time, he was presented to the bishop by the people who demanded that he be made priest, a custom later abolished.

[3] Sailors, in this rather elaborate metaphor, seems to mean other clerics.

Lord laughed at me and willed to show me myself in action.

If He did this, not as a punishment, but out of mercy—which I earnestly hope, now that I know my weakness—then I ought to study all His remedies in the Scriptures, and by praying and reading, so to act that strength sufficient for such perilous duties may be granted to my soul. I did not do this before, because I did not have time, but, as soon as I was ordained, I planned to use all my leisure time in studying the Sacred Scriptures, and I tried to arrange to have leisure for this duty. Truly, I did not know what I needed for such a task, but now I am tormented and weighed down by it. If I have learned by experience what is needful for a man who administers the sacrament and the word of God to the people—and I do not lay claim to what I do not possess—do you, Father Valerius, give me a command which is my destruction? Where is your charity? Do you truly love me? Do you truly love the Church itself, to which you wish me to minister? I am sure you love both me and the Church, but you consider me fit, whereas I know myself better. And I should not have known myself if I had not learned by experience.

Perhaps your Holiness[4] may say: I should like to know what is lacking to your training? So much is lacking that I could more easily tell what I have than what I lack. I venture to say that I know and hold with firm faith all that is necessary for my own salvation. But, how am I to make use of this for the salvation of others? 'Not seeking that which is profitable to myself, but to many, that they may be saved.'[5] Perhaps there are—I should say there undoubtedly are—some instructions written in the Sacred Books, which a man of God may learn and hold so as to act with authority in

---
4 The contemporary title of a bishop.
5 1 Cor. 10.33.

ecclesiastical matters, or, if not that, at least to live with safer conscience in the midst of sinners or to die without losing that life to which alone meek and humble Christian hearts aspire. How can this be done, except as the Lord Himself says, by asking, seeking, knocking: that is, by praying, reading, weeping? For this purpose, I wanted the brethren to secure for me from your most sincere and venerable Charity, a little time, at least until Easter, and this I myself now ask.

What answer am I to make to the Lord Judge?—that I was not able to seek because I was prevented by the cares of a church? If, then, He should say to me: 'Thou wicked servant,[6] if the state of the church should fall into the hands of an unjust steward, who should gather the fruits with great industry, but neglect the land, which I have watered with My Blood, and if you should appear in his defense before an earthly judge and the verdict went against you, would you not, with the consent and even with the command and compulsion of all, go away and remove yourself far across the sea? In that case, no complaint would recall you from your annual or even longer absence, lest another take possession of the land necessary, not for the soul, but for the body of the poor, since My living trees, if they were carefully tended, would much more easily and agreeably satisfy their hunger. Why, then, do you allege your lack of leisure for learning My [divine] agriculture?' Tell me, I beg you, what am I to answer? Do you want me, perhaps, to say: 'Valerius, who is old, believed that I was well instructed in all this, and, because he loved me so much, he would not allow me to study?'

Give heed to all this, venerable Valerius, I beseech you, by the goodness and the severity of Christ, by His mercy and

---

6 Matt. 18.32.

His judgment, by Him who has breathed into you so great a love for me that I dare not offend you, even for the saving of my soul. As you make the Lord Christ a witness of your innocence, and of the charity and sincere affection you feel for me, I am almost unable to take oath in my own defense. Therefore, I beg you, by that charity and affection, to take pity on me and grant me as much time as I have asked, for the reason I have asked. Help me also with your prayers, that my desire may not be vain nor my absence unprofitable to the Church of Christ and the service of my brethren and fellow servants. I know that the Lord does not despise the charity of prayers in such cause, but perhaps He will accept them as a sacrifice of sweetness, and will restore me in a shorter time than I have asked, armed with saving knowledge from the Scriptures.

22. Augustine, priest, to Valerius, bishop (c. 392)

With what thankfulness I was ready to answer the letters of your Holiness—which I looked for in vain for a long time—and to what a high pitch the reading of your letter stirred me as I rose from sleep, so that the affection of my heart exceeded all bounds! I thereupon commended myself to God, begging Him to work upon my powers so that I might write to you in turn what should accord with our mutual zeal for the Lord, and our care of the Church, as befits your high estate and my position as helper. First of all, that word of yours, that you feel yourself helped by my prayers, is something I do not deny, but welcome with eagerness, for, if our Lord will not hear my prayers, He surely will hear yours. There are no words to express my thanks to you for so kindly allowing Brother Alypius to remain in our company as an example to the brethren, who wish to shun the cares of this world. May God repay you! The whole community of brothers which is beginning to gather around them is devoted to you with such loyalty that, though we be scattered into the most distant places, your direction guides us as if you were present in spirit. Therefore, to the limit of our strength, we apply ourselves to prayer that the Lord may deign to support the flock entrusted to you, and may never abandon you, but be ever present as a helper, in due time[1] showing mercy[2] to His Church through you His priest, that He may make you such as spiritual men, with tears and groanings, beg of Him.

You must know, also, most blessed Lord, revered for your abundant charity, that we do not despair—nay, we ardently hope—that the Lord our God, through the authority of the character you bear, which we trust is impressed not on your flesh but on your spirit, can heal by the authority of councils[3] and by your influence the many carnal taints and weaknesses which the Church in Africa suffers in many and bewails in few. Whereas the Apostle has set down briefly in one place three sorts of vices to be detested and avoided, because from them springs an unlimited crop of sins, the Church attacks one of them severely—the one which he puts in second place; but the other two—his first and third—seem to be treated with toleration. So, it could happen by degrees that they would no longer be considered vices, as the Vessel of Election[4] says: 'Not in rioting and drunkenness, not in chambering and impurities, not in contention and envy; but put ye

---

1 Ps. 9.10.
2 Ps. 17.51.
3 A lacuna is suggested here in the Vienna text; I have used the Migne edition, which gives a complete sentence at this point.
4 St. Paul.

on the Lord Jesus Christ, and make not provision for the flesh in its concupiscences.'[5]

Therefore, of these three, chambering and impurities are considered so great a crime that no one who is stained with that sin would be deemed worthy of participation in the sacraments, much less of the clerical office. And with very good reason. But, why only this one? Rioting and drunkenness are considered so lawful and permissible that they are part of the observance in honor of the holy martyrs, not only on feast-days, but even daily. And who that looks upon this with unworldly eyes can behold it without weeping? If it were merely sinful and not actually sacrilegious, we might think it should be borne with some measure of toleration. But, what of that other saying of the same Apostle, who, after enumerating several vices, includes drunkenness, and concludes: 'With such a one not so much as to eat'?[6] If we must overlook these things in the shameful luxury of those banquets which are held in private houses, if we must receive the body of Christ in company with those with whom we are forbidden to eat bread, at least let this scandal be kept away from the tombs of the saints, from the place of the sacraments, from the houses of prayer. For, who dares to forbid in private a practice which is called honoring the martyrs when it is done in holy places?

If Africa should take the lead in stamping out these abuses, she ought to be worthy of imitation; but, as far as the greater part of Italy is concerned, and in all or most of the overseas churches, these practices either were never introduced, or, if they sprang up and took root, they were suppressed and destroyed by the vigilant care and censure of holy

---

5 Rom. 13.13.14.
6 1 Cor. 5.11.

bishops, who had a true view of the life to come.[7] Why, then, do we shrink from correcting such debased customs, with this well-known example before us? Moreover, we have for bishop a man from those places,[8] for whom we give great thanks to God. Although he is a man of such moderation and mildness, of such prudence, also, and vigilance in the Lord, that, even if he were an African, he would be readily convinced from Scripture of the necessary of remedying a wound which licentious custom and false freedom have inflicted, yet it is so widespread an evil that I doubt if it can be cured by anything short of the authority of a council. On the other hand, if the correction is instituted by a single church, it might be considered as bold to change what the Church in Carthage holds as it would be shameless to wish to keep what the Church in Carthage has corrected. What bishop could be so desirable for such a task as the one who condemned these practices while he was a mere deacon?

What you then grieved over, you must now eradicate, not harshly, but, as it is written, in the spirit of meekness[9] and mildness. Your letters, indicative of your innate charity, embolden me to speak to you as I would to myself. According to my way of thinking, those abuses are not done away with by harsh or severe or autocratic measures, but by teaching rather than by commanding, by persuasion rather than by threats. This is the way to deal with the people in general, reserving severity for the sins of the few. And, if we make threats, let it be done sorrowfully, in the words of Scripture, and in terms of punishment in the world to come. In this way, it is not we who are feared because of our power, but God because of our words. In this way, too, the

---

7 Another lacuna is noted here in the Vienna text; Migne again has been followed.
8 He was not an African, but from 'overseas.'
9 Gal. 6.1.

spiritual-minded, and those who are influenced by them, will be aroused; by their influence the majority of the people will be won over by very gentle but very insistent warning.

Finally, since these drinking bouts and extravagant banquets in cemeteries are believed by material-minded and ignorant people to be not only an honor to the martyrs but even a solace to the dead, it seems to me it would be fairly easy to turn them from that foulness and disgrace, if the prohibition is put in Scriptural terms, and if offerings for the spirits of the dead—which are rightly believed to be efficacious—should be furnished readily, but not sold, to all seekers, without ostentation. And if anyone wishes to make a money offering for a religious purpose, let him expend it on the poor in person. Thus they will not seem to give up remembering their dead—something which could cause no slight grief—and at the same time the commemoration which is made in a religious and honorable manner will be carried out in the church. This will be enough about banquets and drunkenness for the present.

Now, what is there proper for me to say about contention and envy, since these vices are more serious in our ranks than among the people? Pride is the mother of these maladies, and so is hunger for human praise, which too often begets hypocrisy. There is no way of resisting this temptation except by instilling the fear and love of God, through frequent pondering of the Sacred Books. But, he who does this must show himself a model of patience and humility by attributing to himself less honor than is offered, neither swallowing all nor refusing all from those who honor him. What praise and honor he accepts he must receive not for himself—for he should refer all to God and despise human things—but for the sake of those whom he could not help if he were to lose dignity by too great self-depreciation. Applicable to this is the saying: 'Let no man despise thy youth,'[10] recalling that he who said that said in another place: 'If I yet pleased men, I should not be the servant of Christ.'[11]

It is a great thing not to rejoice in the honors and praises of men, but to cut off all empty show, and, if any should be necessary, to refer it wholly to the profit and salvation of those who confer the honor. For, this is no idle saying: 'God hath scattered the bones of them that please men.'[12] For, what is so weak, what so lacking in stability and strength— as signified by bone—as a man whom the tongue of detractors casts down, even when he knows that what is said is false? The pain of such suffering would certainly not tear the fibers of the soul, if the love of praise had not broken his bones. I rely on the strength of your mind, and I share with you the things I say to myself, for you are willing, I believe, to consider with me how serious and difficult these matters are. Only he who has declared war on this enemy knows its strength, because, however easy it may be to do without praise when it is withheld, it is hard not to take pleasure in it when it is offered. Nevertheless, our minds ought to be so fixed on God that, if we are praised undeservedly, we correct, if we can, those who praise us, either because they believe us to be what we are not, or credit us with a good that comes from God, or extol qualities which we possess or even abound in, but which are not praiseworthy, such as the benefits we have in common with animals or even with wicked men. However, if we are praised because of God, we thank those who recognize the true good, but we take no credit to ourselves for pleasing men. The condition for this, however, is that we be such before God as they believe us to be, and that the

---

10 1 Tim. 4.12.
11 Gal. 1.10.
12 Ps. 52.6.

praise be referred to God, since all that is praiseworthy is His gift. This is my daily refrain to myself, or rather to Him whose saving precepts these are, whether they are met in spiritual readings or are communicated to the inward mind. In spite of all this, I am often wounded in my struggles with the enemy, because I cannot always put away my pleasure in praise when it is offered.

It may be that your Holiness has no need of these thoughts, either because your own reflections are better and more practical, or because you do not need this remedy; but I have written thus that my defects may be known to you, and that you may have good reason to deign to pray to God for my weakness. That you may do this most earnestly I make my plea by the humanity of Him who gave us the precept of bearing one another's burdens. There are many things in my life and my intercourse with men which I weep over, but which I would not have reach you by letter. Between your heart and mine let there be no intermediary except my mouth and your ears. However, I saw, when I was with you, that the venerable Saturninus[13] was loved and esteemed by you as a brother, as he is regarded with sincere affection by all of us. If he should deign to come to us when he finds it convenient, I shall confide in his holy and spiritual affection, and it will be almost the same as if I were dealing with your worthy self. I cannot express in words how deeply I wish that you would ask and obtain this favor from him. As for my absence, the people of Hippo are in a state of extreme anxiety, and they are not nearly as ready to trust me as I am to trust you.

Before your letter came, we learned through our holy brother and fellow servant Parthenius,[14] about the land which

---
13 Probably the one praised in *De civitate Dei* as Bishop of Uzala or Upsala.
14 Probably a priest of the same diocese with Augustine.

was given to the brethren by your far-seeing generosity. We also heard many other things which we had been longing to know, and the Lord will satisfy our desire for still further news.

23. Augustine, priest of the Catholic Church, sends greeting in the Lord to his most beloved lord and honorable brother, Maximinus[1] (392)

Before I come to the point of what I wanted to write to your Benevolence, I shall give you a brief explanation of the inscription of this letter, which might disturb you or someone else. I have written 'lord,' because it is written: 'For you, brethren, have been called unto liberty: only make not liberty an occasion of the flesh, but by the charity of the Spirit serve one another.'[2] Since, therefore, I serve you by the charity of this ministry of letters, it is not unreasonable for me to call you lord, because of our one and true Lord who gave us this precept. And I have written 'most beloved' because God knows that I love you as myself, and I am conscious of wishing you the same good that I wish for myself. I also added 'honorable,' but not out of respect to your position as bishop, because you are not my bishop. You must not take this amiss, because it comes from the heart, as our words should be: 'Yea, yea, no, no.'[3] You know, and so does everyone who knows us, that you are not my bishop, and I am not your priest. I willingly call you honorable, on the principle that I know you are a man, and a man made to the image and likeness of God, and placed in honor by that

---

[1] Donatist bishop of a neighboring church, who later embraced the Catholic faith. Cf. *De civ. Dei* 22.8.
[2] Gal 5.13.
[3] Matt. 5.37.

origin and that natural right. Let my act of recognition of this essential fact conduce to your honor. For it is written: 'Man when he was in honor, did not understand: he is compared to senseless beasts, and is become like to them.'[4] Why, then, should I not call you honorable, inasmuch as you are a man, and I may not despair of your salvation and correction as long as you are in this life? You are aware that I have a divine precept for calling you brother, and that even to those who refuse to be our brothers we say: you are our brethren. And this is a good addition to my reason for wishing to write to your fraternity. Now that I have given you my reason for erecting such a gate to my letter, give a kindly ear to what follows.

When I was in that part of the world, I noticed a horrible and lamentable custom, whereby men who boasted of the name of Christian did not shrink from rebaptizing Christians, and with what words I could I showed my detestation. Some of your admirers told me that you did not do it. At first, I admit, I did not believe it. Then, reflecting that it is possible for the fear of God to take hold of a soul that thinks of the life to come, and to restrain it from such manifest wrong-doing, I believed it and I credited you with not wanting to be so far removed from the Catholic Church in such a practice. I was even seeking an occasion for a talk with you, so as to smooth out, if possible, the small remaining difference of opinion between us, when lo and behold, a few days ago, the news reached me that you had rebaptized our deacon Mutugenna. I felt very deeply both his wretched lapse and, my brother, your unexpected backsliding. I know, indeed, what the Catholic Church is. The nations are the inheritance of Christ, and the ends of the earth are His pos-

---
4 Ps. 48.13.

session.[5] You know this, or if you do not know it, take heed of it: it can easily be learned by those who wish to learn. To rebaptize a heretic, who has received this sign of salvation, according to the Christian custom, is certainly a sin, but to rebaptize a Catholic is a monstrous crime. As I still did not believe it, because I had such a good opinion of you, I tried to reach Mutugenna himself, but was unable to see the poor man. Then I heard the truth from his parents that he had already become your deacon. In spite of this, I thought so well of you that I could not believe that he had been rebaptized.

Therefore, I beseech you, most beloved brother, by the divinity and the humanity of our Lord Jesus Christ, to be so kind as to write me what was done, and to write such a statement as you know I will be willing to read to the brethren in church. My intention in writing thus has been to avoid wounding charity when I do afterwards what you hope I will not do, and also to prevent you from having any just complaint of me among our friends. So I do not see what can stand in the way of your answering me. If you do rebaptize, you have no reason to fear your colleagues, if you answer that you do what they command in spite of your own unwillingness. But, when you defend this practice with what arguments you can, not only will they be aroused, but they will preach it abroad. If you do not baptize, then, brother Maximinus, lay hold on Christian liberty, lay hold on it, I beg you, and do not fear the reproach of any man, as you contemplate Christ, nor shrink from any one's power. The glory of this world passes, ambition passes. In the future judgment of Christ, neither the steps of the choir, nor the tapestries of the chair, nor the bands of singing nuns coming to meet you will avail to your defense, when conscience

---

5 Ps. 2.8.

begins to accuse and the arbiter of conscience to judge. What things here do you honor, there are a burden; what here lifts you up, there weighs you down. Those things which are undertaken temporarily for the benefit of the Church will redound to our honor and may be defended with a truly good conscience, but there is no defense for wrong-doing.

What you do with so good and religious an intention, if you do it—that you do not repeat the baptism of the Catholic Church, but you approve the baptism of the one most true Mother, who opens her arms to all nations to save them, and offers her breasts to the saved as the unique possession of Christ, reaching to the ends of the earth—if you truly do this, why do you not break out into a free and rejoicing cry? Why do you hide this valuable splendor of your light under a bushel?[6] Why do you not tear off those wretched animal skins, the sign of cowardly slavery, and put on Christian confidence and come out and say: 'I know one baptism, consecrated and signed with the Name of the Father and of the Son and of the Holy Spirit. When I find it in this form, I must perforce accept it. I do not destroy, when I recognize the banner of the Lord my King, I do not blow it away.' Those who divided the garments of Christ[7] did not dishonor Him, because they saw Him dying and did not believe that He would rise again. If the garment of the One hanging on the cross was not torn by His persecutors, why is the sacrament of the One reigning in heaven destroyed by Christians? If I had been a Jew in the times of the ancient people, when there was nothing better to be, I would surely have accepted circumcision. That 'seal of the justice of the faith'[8] had so much power at that time, before it was rendered void by

---
6 Matt. 5.15; Luke 11.33; 8.16; Mark 4.21.
7 John 19.24.
8 Rom. 4.11.

the coming of the Lord, that the angel would have strangled the infant son of Moses[9] if his mother had not taken up a stone and circumcised the child, and thus by this sacrament warded off his imminent destruction. This sacrament even tamed the River Jordan and reduced it to a brook. The Lord Himself received this sacrament after birth,[10] although on the cross He made it void. These observances were not condemned, but gave place to later and more timely ones; for, as the first coming of the Lord abolished circumcision, so His second coming will do away with baptism. Just as now, when liberty of faith has come and the yoke of slavery has been removed, no Christian is circumcised in the flesh, so then, when the just are reigning with their Lord and the wicked have been condemned, no one will be baptized, but that which they prefigure—the circumcision of the heart and the cleansing of conscience—will remain forever. If, then, at that time I had been a Jew, and a Samaritan had come to me and wished to give up his wrong belief, which even the Lord condemned, saying: 'You adore that which you know not; we adore that which we know, for salvation is of the Jews'[11]—if, as I said, he wished to become a Jew, and the Samaritans had circumcised him, there would be no bold demand for a repetition of what had been done in heresy, but according to the precept of God, and we should be obliged not to repeat it, but to approve it. But, if in the flesh of a circumcised man I could find no place to repeat circumcision, because there is only one such member, much less could a place be found in one heart, where the baptism of Christ could be repeated. You, therefore, who wish to baptize again, certainly need two hearts.

---

9 Exod. 4.24.
10 Luke 2.21.
11 John 4.22.

Cry out, therefore, that you do right if you do not rebaptize, and write me this, not only without fear, but even with joy. Let no councils of your people trouble you, my brother; for, if this displeases them, they are not worthy to have you; but, if it pleases them, we believe, by the mercy of the Lord, who never abandons those who fear to displease Him and who strive to please Him, that there will soon be peace between you and us. Otherwise there would be risk that in saving our personal dignity, of which reason is a dangerous piece of baggage, the poor people who believe in Christ would have their food in common in their homes, but they could not have the Table of Christ in common. Do we not groan because a man and wife, joining themselves in faithful wedlock, swear to each other by Christ, and then tear asunder the body of the same Christ by communion in different sects? If by your moderation, and prudence, and the love which we owe to Him who shed His blood for us, this great scandal, this great triumph of the Devil, this great destruction of souls were removed from our midst in these regions, who could describe in words the palm prepared for you by the Lord, because you originated a remedy worthy of imitation for the healing of all the members which lie wretchedly wasted with disease throughout all Africa? How I fear, since you cannot see my heart, that I may seem to speak to you with arrogance rather than love! But I cannot think of anything else to do except to offer my words to your eyes and my soul to God.

Let us dispense with mutual useless charges such as ignorant partisans hurl at one another: so that you do not bring against me the times of Macarius,[12] nor I against you the

---

[12] Emissary of Emperor Constans, sent to Africa to carry out the imperial edicts against Donatism. When bribery did not succeed, he used force, which caused resistance, and bloodshed. The Donatists called their fallen sectaries 'martyrs' and referred to the incident as the Macarian persecution.

cruelty of the Circumcellions.[13] If the latter has nothing to do with you, so the former has nothing to do with me. The threshing floor of the Lord has not yet been winnowed;[14] it must still contain some chaff. Let us pray and act to the best of our ability, so that we may be good grain. I cannot pass over in silence the rebaptizing of our deacon; I know how dangerous silence can be to me. I am not thinking of spending idle time on ecclesiastical dignities; I am considering how I shall give an account to the Prince of all shepherds of the sheep entrusted to me. If you do not like my writing this to you, my brother, then you will have to excuse my fear; for I greatly fear that if I pass it over in silence and pay no attention to it, others also will be rebaptized by your group. I have determined, therefore, that, as far as the Lord will grant me strength and ability, I will so plead this cause that all who are in communion with us may know by our peaceful conferences how far removed the Catholic Church is from heresies and schisms, and how constantly we should be on guard against pestilence and cockle and the branches which have been cut off from the vine of the Lord. If you will willingly undertake a joint statement with me, which can be read to our people in the form of letters from both of us in agreement, I shall rejoice with unspeakable joy. But, if you do not agree to this, what else can I do, my brother, except read our letters—whether you like it or not—to the Catholic people for their instruction? And, if you do not even condescend to answer me, I have decided to read my letters only, so that they may be shamed by your lack of faith into giving up rebaptism.

I shall not take any action while the army is present,

---

13 A violent, direct-action group of Donatists, guilty of cruel excesses against the Catholics.
14 Luke 3.17.

lest anyone of yours should think that I wanted to use force rather than a peaceful method. After the departure of the army I shall see to it that all who hear us may know that it was no part of my plan that men should be forced into any communion against their will, but that truth should be manifest to those seeking it in quietness. On our side, there shall be no more fear of the temporal power; on yours, let there be an end to the terror of the bands of Circumcellions. Let us really take action, according to reason and the authority of the Divine Scriptures, and, in peace and quiet, let us do our utmost to ask, seek and knock,[15] so that we may receive and find, and the door may be opened to us. And may it thus be possible, with the Lord's help, that our united efforts and our prayers may begin the destruction in our lands of the disgrace and impiety of many parts of Africa. If you do not believe that I am willing to wait before acting until after the departure of the army, then do you await that departure before you answer my letter. For, if I should want to read my letters to the people in the presence of the soldiery, the publication of my letter will prove me a breaker of my word. And may the mercy of the Lord, who allows me to bear His yoke, preserve me and my establishment from that!

My bishop would probably have preferred himself to write to your Benevolence, if he had been here, or I should have written by his order or permission. In his absence, since this rebaptism of the deacon is or is said to be something new, I could not let the matter grow cold by delay, and I was moreover deeply moved by bitter grief over the true death of a brother. Pehaps by the mercy and providence of the Lord of peace there will be some comfort to outweigh my sorrow. May the Lord our God deign to inspire peace to your heart, my lord and most beloved brother.

---

15 Matt. 7.7; Luke 11.9.

24. Paulinus[1] and Therasia,[2] sinners, to the right honorable lord and most blessed father, Alypius[3] (394)

This is the true charity, this is the perfect love for you, which you have shown to be innate in our lowliness, truly holy lord, rightly blessed and desirable. When our man Julian returned from Carthage, he brought us letters so filled with the light of your sanctity that we seemed not so much to learn as to recognize your charity for us, since doubtless that charity flows from Him who chose us in Him before the foundation of the world,[4] in whom we were made before we were born, because He made us and not we ourselves,[5] who made also what is to be. Formed, therefore, by His foreknowledge and power to a likeness of wills and a unity of faith or a faith of unity, we are joined by a love which has preceded acquaintance, so that, before actually meeting, we have known each other by the revealing force of the Spirit. We give thanks, therefore, and we rejoice in the Lord, because, being one and the same, He produces His love in His own, everywhere on the earth, by the operation of the Holy Spirit, whom He pours out on all flesh[6] by the stream of the river, making joyful His city,[7] among whose citizens He has set you on the apostolic seat, as a leader, with the princes of

---

1 Pontius Meropius Anicius Paulinus (353-431) was born at Bordeaux of an illustrious Roman family. He held several public offices but was converted in 389, baptized by Delphinus, Bishop of Bordeaux, and thereupon sold most of his property, and went with his wife Therasia to Spain to lead an ascetic life. Ordained priest by the Bishop of Barcelona, about 394, he retired to Nola in Campania, to live as a monk near the tomb of St. Felix of Nola. He was unwillingly elected Bishop of Nola during the period of the barbarian invasions.
2 Wife of Paulinus; eulogized by Augustine in Letter 27.
3 Now Bishop of Tagaste.
4 Eph. 1.4.
5 Ps. 99.3.
6 Joel 2.28.
7 Ps. 45.5.

His people,[8] and has lifted us up also who were cast down,[9] and has raised the needy from the earth,[10] and deigned to enroll them in your band. We are even more thankful for that bounty of the Lord, whereby He has made us to dwell in your heart, and has deigned to establish us in its innermost parts. Emboldened by these privileges, we claim as our personal possession the pledge of your love, and, in our turn, we cannot but love you trustfully and sincerely.

We have received, as a special sign of your love and regard, the work, complete in five books,[11] of that holy man perfected in the Lord Christ, our brother Augustine, and we so admire and look up to it that we believe it was divinely inspired. Relying, therefore, on your wholehearted support, we have ventured to write to him, taking for granted that you will make excuses to him for our inexperience and recommend us to his charity, as also to all the saints.[12] As you have deigned to refresh us with their good deeds, even in their absence, without doubt you will care for us with equal affection, and thus through your Holiness all shall be mutually greeted by our salutations, both the companions of your holiness among the clergy, and those who imitate your faith and virtue in the monasteries. For, although you exercise power among peoples and over the people, ruling the sheep of the pasture of the Lord[13] as a watchful shepherd keeping unsleeping guard, yet by your renunciation of the world and repudiation of flesh and blood you have made to yourself

---

8 Ps. 112.8.
9 Ps. 145.8.
10 Ps. 112.7.
11 These could have been any of the following: *De moribus ecclesiae, Catholicae et de moribus Manichaeorum, De Genesi contra Manichaeos, De duabus animabus contra Manichaeos, Contra Fortunatum disputatio*—all of which were completed before 394.
12 The usual name given to Christians.
13 Ps. 99.3.

a desert, where you are separated from the many, but called among the few.

I have sent you a sort of return gift, though one unworthy of you in every respect, but according to your request: the universal history of Eusebius,[14] the venerable Bishop of Constantinople. My delay in complying with your request was caused by the fact that I did not have the volume with me, so, at your suggestion, I looked for it at Rome and found it with our relative, Domnio, that holy man, who doubtless obliged me the more readily because I said it was for you. As you had told me where you would be, I wrote, as you advised, to that venerable member of your circle, our father Aurelius,[15] and asked him, if you should be staying at Hippo Regius, to be so kind as to send our letters to you there, and also the manuscript copied at Carthage. We asked those holy men, Exodius[16] and Comes, whom we recognized by their own kindness and your description, to do the copying personally, so that our relative Domnio would not have to be without his volume too long, and you could keep the one sent you, without the necessity of returning it.

I ask one particular thing of you, since you have filled me with such great love of you, unworthy as I am and not daring to hope for so great honor, that, in return for this general history, you would give me the details of your own history, such as: *'Of what race are you? from what home?'*[17] and called by so great a lord, set apart by what impulses from your mother's womb, did you go over to the mother of the sons of God, rejoicing in her offspring, by renouncing

---

14 Eusebius of Caesarea (260-340), the 'Father of Church History,' assisted in editing the Septuagint and was the author of a monumental *Chronicle,* and of a *Church History,* in ten books.
15 Archbishop of Carthage.
16 A monk of Augustine's group at Tagaste, afterward Bishop of Upsala.
17 Vergil, *Aen.* 8.113.

flesh and blood, and how were you admitted to the royal and sacerdotal race?[18] I admit that I am somewhat curious to learn what you hinted at finding out about the name of our lowliness at Milan when you first went there, for, indeed, I should like to know you wholly, and I should think it is a matter of personal joy if you were received into the faith by our worthy father Ambrose, or even consecrated to the priesthood by him, for then we should seem to have the same father in God. It is true I was baptized by Delphinus at Bordeaux, and ordained priest, suddenly, by the pressure of the popular demand, at Barcelona by Lampius; but I have been nourished in the faith by my constant love of Ambrose and now I am supported by him in the priesthood. He has been so kind as to number me among his clergy, and, although I live in various places, I am counted as his priest.

That you may know everything about me, you must know that I am a long-standing sinner, not so long ago brought out from darkness and the shadow of death,[19] that I have breathed the spirit of his life-giving air, that I have not so long ago put my hand to the plow[20] and taken up the cross of the Lord, and I hope to be helped by your prayers to persevere to the end. This reward will be added to your merits, if you relieve our burdens by your intercession. For, the saint who helps the toiler—we do not dare to say brother —shall be exalted like a strong city.[21] You, indeed, are a city seated upon a mountain;[22] you shine with seven-fold brightness as a candle lighted upon a candlestick, but we lie hid under the bushel of the sinners. Visit us by your letters, and lead us forth into the light in which you live,

---

18 1 Peter 2.9.
19 Ps. 106.14.
20 Luke 9.62.
21 Prov. 18.9.
22 Matt. 5.14.

seen by all on the golden candlestick; your words will be a light to our paths;[23] our head shall be anointed with the oil of your light;[24] and faith shall be enkindled when we receive from the breath of your mouth food for our mind and light for our soul. Peace and the grace of God and the crown of justice remain with you on the last day, my lord, most dearly loved father, venerable and most desired. We ask also, with deep affection and due respect, that the companions and imitators of your Holiness be blessed, our brothers in the Lord, if we may call them so, in the churches as well as the monasteries at Carthage, Tagaste, Hippo Regius and in all your parishes; in fact, in all the places known to you throughout Africa, where they serve the Lord as Catholics. If you have received the parchment of the holy Domnio, please send it back to us after it has been copied. And I ask you to write me which hymn of mine you know. We have sent a loaf of bread[25] to your Holiness in token of unity, in which the substance of the Trinity is contained. By graciously receiving this bread, you will make it a blessing.

25. Paulinus and Therasia, sinners, to the venerable Augustine, their lord and beloved brother (394)

The charity of Christ, which presseth us[1] and binds us together even in absence by the unity of faith, lends us confidence to set aside our awe of you and to write to you. It binds you also to me in my innermost fibers, especially through

---

23 Ps. 118.105.
24 Ps. 22.5.
25 Little loaves, blessed and sent by bishops and priests in sign of fraternal affection, or of Christian unity.

---

1 2 Cor. 4.18.

those works of yours which I now have in five books, overflowing with scholarly authority and sweet with heavenly honeycomb—medicine and nourishment for my soul. We have received them through the gift of our blessed and venerable Bishop Alypius, not only for our own instruction, but for the profit of the Church in many cities. These, then, are the books I now have to read, in these I find my pleasure, from them I take food, not that which perisheth,[2] but that which produces the substance of everlasting life, by means of our faith, by which we are made one in Christ Jesus our Lord, which looks not at things which are seen, but at the things which are not seen,[3] and by charity, which believes all things through the truth of the omnipotent God, and is strengthened by the writings and examples of the faithful. O true salt of the earth,[4] whereby our hearts are preserved against the wickedness of the world! O light worthily placed upon the candlestick of the Church,[5] fed with the oil of gladness from the seven-fold lamp, giving forth light to Catholic cities far and near, how you dispel the dense darkness of heretics and by the force of your brilliant language free the light of truth from the clouds of darkness!

You see, beloved brother, esteemed and looked up to in Christ our Lord, how intimately I know you, with what respect I admire you, with what great love I embrace you, as I daily rejoice in the converse of your books and feed on the breath of your mouth. Rightly may I call your mouth a pipe of living water, and the source of an unending fount, because Christ has become in you a fountain of water springing up into life everlasting.[6] With this desire my soul hath

---

2 John 6.27.
3 2 Cor. 4.18.
4 Matt. 5.13; Mark 4.21; Luke 8.16; 11.13.
5 Matt. 5.15.
6 John 4.14.

thirsted for thee,[7] and my soul has desired to be inebriated with the plenty of thy stream.[8] Therefore, with this Pentateuch of yours you have armed me well against the Manichaeans, and if you have prepared any other weapons against other enemies of the Catholic faith, I beg you to supply me with them from your armory, and not to refuse me the armament of justice, for our enemy, who has a thousand harmful arts,[9] must be attacked with as many kinds of weapons as he uses snares against us. For I am even now a sinner weighed down with a grievous burden; I am a veteran in the ranks of sinners, but a raw recruit in the celestial army of the eternal king. Wretch that I am, I have until now admired the wisdom of the world, and, through a false prudence, have been mute and voiceless before God, though engaging in useless writings. But after I grew old among my enemies[10] and became vain in my thoughts,[11] I lifted up my eyes to the mountains,[12] looking upon the precepts of the law and the gifts of grace, whence help comes to me from the Lord,[13] who, not rewarding us according to our iniquities,[14] has given sight to the blind, unfettered the prisoner and laid low the proud, so as to raise up the truly humble. Therefore, I follow with halting gait the heroic footsteps of the just, if, perchance, by means of your prayers I may be able to apprehend, as I am apprehended[15] by the mercies of God. Guide this little one creeping along uncertainly, then, and teach him to walk in your footsteps, for I wish to regard not my physi-

---

7 Ps. 62.2.
8 Ps. 35.9.
9 Vergil, *Aen.* 7.338.
10 Ps. 6.8.
11 Rom. 1.21.
12 Ps. 120.1.
13 Ps. 120.1,2.
14 Ps. 102.10.
15 Phil. 3.2.

cal but my spiritual age. It is true my age according to the flesh is the same as his who was healed with a word of power by the Apostles at the Beautiful Gate,[16] but in terms of birthdays of the soul I am still in that infancy which was immolated by blows aimed at Christ,[17] and which by the meritorious blood of the Lamb preceded the Victim and prepared the way of the Lord's Passion. Therefore, as I am still an infant to the Word of God, and of a spiritual age requiring milk, do you nourish me with your words, feeding my eagerness with the breasts of your faith, wisdom, and love. If you consider the office we both hold, you are my brother, but in maturity of mind and experience, you are my father, although in years you are younger than I, because hoary-haired prudence has advanced you in your youth to the maturity of one who has served in the ranks of the elders. Warm me, then, and strengthen me in sacred letters and spiritual studies, new-born as I am, as I have said, and inexperienced, by reason of long dangers and frequent shipwrecks; you who have long since taken up your stand on solid earth, receive me with open arms, that we may, if you will allow, sail together into the harbor of salvation. Meantime, as I strive to escape from the perils of this life and the abyss of sin, support me by your prayers as with a plank, so that I may be rescued from this world, as a naked man from shipwreck.

To this end, I have tried to lighten myself of baggage and burdensome garments, that by the command and help of Christ, free of fleshly entanglements and anxiety for the morrow, I may swim out of this stormy sea of the present life, where our sins, like howling monsters, try to cut us off from God. Not that I boast of having achieved this, although, if

---
16 Acts 3.2,10; 4.22. The lame man was 'above forty years old.'
17 Matt. 2.16; a reference to the massacre of the Holy Innocents.

I could glory, I should glory in the Lord[18] who must accomplish what is present to us to will;[19] but my soul still covets to long for the judgments of the Lord.[20] See how far I am from accomplishing the will of God, I who still desire to desire! But, as far as it lies in me, I have loved the beauty of the holy house,[21] and, as far as I could, I have chosen to be an abject in the house of the Lord.[22] But, He who was pleased to separate me from my mother's womb[23] from the friendship of flesh and blood, and to draw me to His grace, has also been pleased to raise me up needy [of all merit] from the earth[24] and to bring me out of the pit of misery and the mire of dregs,[25] that He might place me with the princes of His people[26] and might place my lot in your care so I might become like you, by sharing the same authority, though you surpass me in merit.

It is not an act of presumption on my part, then, but by the decree and ordinance of the Lord, that I enter upon a partnership with your Fraternity, and, though unworthy, raise myself to such a great honor, because I am certain that as far as your Holiness is concerned—for you are truly wise— you do not mind high things, but consent to the humble.[27] Therefore, I hope you will receive the charity of our lowliness, which, indeed, I trust you have already received through our father, that most blessed priest, Alypius—he deserves the title. He certainly has given you a personal example of loving

---

18 2 Cor. 10.17.
19 Rom. 7.18.
20 Ps. 118.20.
21 Ps. 25.8.
22 Ps. 83.11.
23 Gal. 1.15.
24 Ps. 112.7.
25 Ps. 39.3.
26 Ps. 112.8.
27 Rom. 12.16.

us before he knew us, beyond our deserving, because he was able to see us by loving, and to reach out to us by conversing, even when we were unknown to him, and separated by the remoteness of our country or the intervening sea,[28] and this he did by the spirit of true affection which spreads and is poured abroad everywhere. He gave us the first proofs of his affection, and the pledges of your love by the above-mentioned gift of books. He made a great effort to have us love your Holiness in no ordinary way, not only because of his words, but through our own fuller knowledge of your eloquence and faith, and we believe that he has been equally intent on having you love us in return, in imitation of him. We pray that the grace of God may remain with you forever, as it now is, beloved brother in Christ the Lord, venerable and most desired. With the affection of cordial brotherhood we salute your whole household, and all the companions and imitators in the Lord of your Holiness. We have sent you a loaf of bread as a token of our unity with your charity, and we pray you to receive and bless it.

26. Augustine to Licentius[1] (395)

I have had a hard time finding an occasion to write to you. Who would believe it? But Licentius must believe me and I do not want you to go spying out causes and reasons, because, even if they could be found, they do not belong to the trust which you have in me. I could not send you back

---

28 Probably when they were in Spain.

1 Son of Romanianus, Augustine's pupil at Cassiciacum; a spoiled child capricious, vain, changeable, given to sudden enthusiasms: for poetry, Greek tragedy, Church music. He remained a pagan in spite of the admonitions and entreaties of Augustine.

an answer by those who brought me your letters. What you asked me to request I have taken care of by letter, as far as it seemed possible to promote it; you will see what success I have had. If I have not yet succeeded, I will act again more urgently when I find out, or when you yourself insist. Thus far I have discussed with you the clashing fetters of this life, now you must hear briefly the anxieties of my heart about your eternal hope, and how you may find your way to God.

My dear Licentius, you have been drawing back and shrinking from the fetters of wisdom, and I fear that you are too strongly and too dangerously attached to mortal things. For, wisdom first fetters her votaries and then tames them with training exercises; afterwards she sets them free and gives herself to be enjoyed by them. Those whom she has made expert by temporary obligations she will afterwards hold in an eternal embrace—and there is nothing more delightful than this or more enduring. I admit that these beginnings are somewhat hard, but I would not call achievement hard because it is so sweet, nor would I call it soft because it is so lasting. What more, except what cannot be said, but can be believed and hoped for and loved? The fetters of this world have a true harshness, a false joy; a certain suffering, an uncertain pleasure; a hard labor, an uneasy rest; wealth full of wretchedness, hope empty of happiness. Is it in this sort of thing that you ensnare yourself, neck and hands and feet, when you aim at subjecting yourself to such honors; when you think your life otherwise unprofitable, and when you go around intruding yourself in places where you ought not to go, even if you were invited or compelled?

Here, perhaps, you will answer me like the slave in Terence: *'So you're pouring out your maxims here, old Wisdom?'*[2]

---

[2] Terence, *Adelphoe* 769.

Better catch them, then, because I am pouring out, not outpouring. If I sing and you dance to another tune, it will not bother me, for my song has its own charm, even if it does not stir feet to the dance, because it is sung in the full key of charity. Some expressions in your letter troubled me, but I thought it silly to pause over them when I am concerned so deeply with the conduct of your whole life.

The Poem of Licentius to His Master Augustine

Scanning the mystery-haunted way of Varro,[3] the profound,
My mind falters and, frightened of the light, essays to flee.
No strange thing that; for all my zeal for study falls away,
And fears to stand alone without thy helping hand.
No sooner does my love persuade me to unroll the tortured
*   page*
Of garnered wisdom of so great a man; and plunge into his
*   holy lore,*
To which he gave the sounds of rhythm, and the world he
*   taught*
To sing and dance in graceful bands to hail the Thunderer;
Than straight the rust of things o'erwhelms my heart
With many-colored mist, and clouds my mind;
Frenzied, I seek for forms of figures bodiless,
Only to bruise myself on other heavy forms of darkness.
In fine, the causes of the stars and their bright wanderings,
[I seek] whose unknown ways he traces through the clouds.
Thus I lay stunned as one beholding total ruin,
Since none was there to bid me not to gaze
Upon the hiding-places of the sky,
Nor any guide whose function it would be to lead

---

[3] The youthful poet probably wishes to show that he was acquainted with the *Origines* of Varro (B. C. 116-27).

Across its vast expanse to caverns dark.
The ancient Greeks their tale of Proteus told,[4]
Who to the anxious would not prophesy,
But raged as boar, flowed as stream, roared as lion,
Hissed as snake; or, caught betimes,
Became a little bird and flew away.
So to me, with too great cares weighed down,
Is Varro's message hid, though sweets I seek
Of mind, or less sweet food implore.
With suppliant song what guardian do I call,
What nymph, what rivers am I to invoke?
Am I to summon thee, whom over unsung springs
Shining Olympus' lord has set, and bid thee send
The hidden, bursting flood afar to feed the mind
With richness? O master, send me aid at once,
Delay not to support my failing strength,
Begin with me to till the sacred glebe,
For time, if mortal things betray me not,
Runs on and drags us into hoary age.
But our Apollo fills thy heart, and wins his sire[5]
And father of the gods to thee, and his good law
And blood-stained peace reveals—all veils withdrawn—
And opens all his mysteries to thee.
Perchance a score of far-off orbs of sun
Thou hadst traversed, when all the lovely plan
Of universe, richer than realms of power, sweeter far
Than any nectar, seized thee and stopped thy steps,
And in the midst placed thee, from whence thy glance
Could sweep afar, beholding all that is.
O excellent one! set forth on time's long road,
Behold how wisdom grows with love of its own self,

---

4 Vergil, *Georg.* 4.387-529; Ovid, *Met.* 8.732-737.
5 Cf. Vergil, *Aen.* 3.434; 1.65.

New heights on heights forever finding there!
Seek out the path, whereon the famous son
Of Thunderer shall lead thee, making rough ways plain![6]
And when the evening star, with rising light,
Has stirred thy heart, and thou hast blessed the holy fire,[7]
Be mindful then of me. And you who lend an eager ear[8]
To conquering laws, strike breasts with hands,[9]
Bow down your bodies to the ground,
Due sufferings accept, and turn from evil ways.
God has for all one mandate; in His name[10]
His vicar speaks; His threats of future woe
Strike fear to all.[11]
Oh, would to me some early-shining dawn,[12]
In chariot of joy, might summon back
Those long-past, sun-filled days
I spent with thee in carefree hours,
The while we conned the guiltless laws of right,
And traveled mid-Italian plain or mountains high.[13]
Not freezing winter with its hoary rime,
Nor cruel blasts of Zephyr, nor Boreal roars
Would hinder me from pressing after thee
With anxious step. What task thou biddest me,
Though blood bedew my steps, I will fulfill.
To tropic Neuri will I fare, or fog-bound Ister;[14]

---

6 Luke 3.5.
7 In the early Church the sacred fire was blessed each evening, a ceremony now retained only in the liturgy of Holy Saturday.
8 Persius, *Sat.* 4.50.
9 The Confiteor, with striking of the breast as a sign of penitence, is part of the Office of Compline, recited in the evening.
10 Vergil, *Aen.* 5.197; Ovid. *Met.* 10.322.
11 *Ibid.* 1.230.
12 *Ibid.* 8.560.
13 *Ibid.* 7.563.
14 The Neuri were a people in European Scythia who were regarded as magicians; the Ister was the lower part of the Danube.

*The unknown African shall loose for me his tribal bonds;
And, fleeing from Exampean lake, Sarmatian stream*[15]
*Shall foam and crash in fruitless rage its Scythian waves,
Where people of Callippides*[16] *now dwell.
We'll fare to Belgic Gaul, whose easternmost of towns
Liège is named; and then the lonely peaks of Casius's mount,*[17]
*Whose rocks would emulate the ridge of Antioch;
From whence, while still the night is dark, I'd view
The tranquil dawn and sun's descending chariot,
And end of day. At thy demand all these I'll seek,
Nor toil nor any fear shall stay my step,
When God to prayers of pure in heart gives ear.
And now the palaces of sons of Romulus,*[18]
And empty heights[19] *where Remus took his stand, I will
To leave, and home where revels hold full sway, and vain
Tumultuous crowds; and I would come at last, alone,
To stay with thee, but that my mind withholds my steps,
Reminding me of wedlock's bond. O learned one!
Believe my troubles and my grief oppress me sore,
Because, without thy help, my sails no harbor find,
And I am borne afar on stormy waves of life,
As those who sail, beset by blinding fog,
Whom austral rage and hissing blasts of east have struck,
Whom whirlwind has of pilot's skill deprived;*[20]

---

15 A spring of bitter waters in Scythia (southern Russia), between the Dnieper and Hypanis (Bug) Rivers.
16 A Scythian people around the Hypanis River.
17 According to Pliny (*Nat. hist.* 5.22.18), this Syrian mountain, near Antioch, was so high that from its summit the sunrise could be seen during the fourth watch of the night (3 to 6 A.M.); while it was day on the east side, it was still night on the west.
18 The Palatine, in Rome.
19 The Aventine; cf. Livy (1.6).
20 Vergil, *Aen.* 5.867.

*Too soon the wretched ones by mountainous waves are tossed,
No gangway and no prow, no sails against the wind
Avail to stand; all hope of steering given up:*[21]
*So am I, a prey to winds and storms of fierce
Desire, on deadly ocean tossed. Yet, land is not
Too far to be attained, and, thinking on thy words
Of shining truth, O master loved, I deem it well
To trust the more to thee in this: 'A crafty thing it is,
Deceiving us and building up a snare to catch
Our souls.' Forgetful of the past, and all its years,
I take upon myself all present duties dear
To thee, no longer from thy heart estranged.
Alas! where shall I turn, from whence shall I reveal
My mind and heart to thee? The dove its gentle nest
Beneath Aegean wave shall build; the halcyon bird
Shall make its home in tallest tree; and hungry calf*[22]
*Pursuing after lioness, herself a-hungered,
Shall by her be fed; and starving wolf shall give
To tender lambs their food; and changing parts of earth
To them assigned, the Libyan*[23] *shall plough the mount
Of Taurus;*[24] *or tribe of Caspian's shore on Afric's strand
Shall till the earth; the orb of day in fright shall turn
At sight of Thyestean feast,*[25] *to try again
To be the dawn; the clouds shall make a Nile;
The deer shall gambol on the sea; the mountains sing*

---

21 Ovid, *Trist.* 1.2.32.
22 The kingfisher, which does not rest in trees.
23 African.
24 A mountain range in southeastern Asia Minor.
25 Thyestes, brother of Atreus, was induced to accept reconciliation of a long-standing feud by partaking of a banquet offered by the latter. Atreus had killed his brother's two sons, and then served their flesh to their father. The sun is said to have checked his chariot in mid-course, in horror at the deed.

*And rivers raise their hymns of praise—all this shall be
Before my heart forgets thy benefits, O master mine!
Love is my jailer, love the bond of reverence
Between us; here ah! here is friendship's throne, all foes
Cast out. 'Tis not the gleam of crystal wealth
Nor hard-won gold that makes the meeting of our minds,
Nor fickle favor of the crowd that daunts all effort;
No! but coming o'er thy inmost thoughts on learned page
Set forth, and poring o'er the meanings of thy mind,
Thy lofty teaching and thy bold replies—by these
Am I borne on. And my sweet Muse, Calliope,
Although she dreads thy lofty presence now and hides
Her face while futile themes she treats, yet this strong bond,
These faithful fetters of the heart, not he will break
Who tamed the rocky Alpine peaks, and pressed the siege
Of strong Italian towns,*[26] *nor shall he from my breast
This true love tear.
Flow on, ye springs of tortuous windings sprung, and haste
To separate with swelling flood the Scythian hills
From Scythian tribes, or Caspian towns or homes Cimmerian,
And let Maiotic waves*[27] *which Hellespont o'erwhelms
The barriers be twixt Asia and Europa's lands.
Did not Dodona,*[28] *wearying on either side
Her herd of cattle, separate Molossi*[29] *from
The fields of Talari*[30] *and Arab kin?
No friendly pact of peace the kings of Greece have kept
With Tyrians or with sacrilegious Troy, although
For long the bond of hospitality had been.
What, then, have I to do with brothers' strife and wars?*

---

26 Hannibal, in the Second Punic War.
27 The present Sea of Azov.
28 A celebrated oracle and city in Epirus.
29 People of Epirus.
30 A Molossian people around Pindus.

*Or shall I sing the honored curse of sires, or wrath
Of mothers and unfilial sons? The dissonance
Of earth some heavenly harmony may mean,
And many a custom turns to law by public voice.
But one love binds us two. And though the northern blast
A hundred voices gave with breath from hundred mouths,[31]
And though he howl with freezing tongue, I could not say
What bonds of ancient places once we had, which now
Are severed, and their glory wears away
With time's hard file. But as for us, one city gave
Us birth; one hearth was ours; one strain of gentile blood
Flows in our veins; and one we are in Christian faith;
So what to us the far-dividing space,[32] the waves
Of sea that part us—love derides them both—and though
We joy not in each other's presence now, nor see
The light of eyes, yet each in heart his friend enjoys,
Since love is of the heart, and there it finds its food,
Within the very marrow.
Meantime, whatever writings of thy pen shall come
Filled with all good, and with life-giving words, and those
Of former days, more sweet than honey-comb, wherein
Thy deepest thoughts, like nectar are distilled, all these
Shall make thee present—yea thy very self to me,
If thou wilt favor me, and send those books, in which
Thy gentle music rests; for them my spirit yearns.
Grant this: that truth may be by reason manifest,
May it more freely flow than Eridanus,[33] may
The world's attraction flit in vain around the fields
Tilled by our toil.*

---

[31] Vergil, *Georg.* 2.43.
[32] *Ibid.* 4.480.
[33] Mythical and poetic name of the River Po.

If your verse were defective by reason of unregulated rhythm, if it did not abide by its own laws, if it offended the ear of the listener by uneven quantities, you would certainly be ashamed, and you would neither delay nor leave off your study and practice of the metrical art, counting no effort or toil too much so long as you could regulate, correct, straighten out and smooth off your lines. But, when you yourself are disordered and undisciplined, when you do not abide by the laws of your God, when you are not in accord with the honorable wishes of your friends, or even with your own reputation as a scholar, do you think all that is to be disregarded and forgotten? Your self-esteem is lowered by the sound of your own language, but you think it is a smaller thing to offend the ears of God by your disorderly behavior than to arouse the criticism of the grammarians by your disordered lines. You write:

> *O would to me some early-shining dawn,*
> *In chariot of joy, might summon back*
> *Those long-past, sun-filled days*
> *I spent with thee in carefree hours,*
> *The while we conned the guiltless laws of right,*
> *And traveled mid-Italian plain or mountains high.*
> *Not freezing winter with its hoary rime,*
> *Nor cruel blasts of Zephyr, nor Boreal roars*
> *Would hinder me from pressing after thee*
> *With anxious step. What task thou biddest me,*
> *I will fulfill.*

Unfortunate that I am, if I do not bid, if I do not compel and force you, if I do not plead and beseech. If your ears are shut to my voice, let them be open to your own speech; let them heed your own poem; hearken to yourself, utterly hard, cruel and deaf that you are! Where shall I find a tongue of gold and a heart of steel? Not verses, but lamentations, are what I need to mourn over your poetry, in which I see a soul, a genius, which I cannot seize and immolate to our God! You are waiting for me to command you, that you may be good, tranquil and happy; but, if any day could dawn more happily for me than that on which I might enjoy your genius, may you never truly know how I hunger and thirst for you, or at least not admit it in your poem. Recall your mood when you wrote that; now tell me: 'My only need is that you command me.' Here is my command: Give yourself to me, if this is your only need; give yourself to my Lord, who is the Lord of us all, who gave you that genius. What am I but your servant through Him, and your fellow servant under Him?

Does He not give His own command? Listen to the Gospel. It says: 'Jesus stood and cried: Come to Me all you that labor and are burdened, and I will refresh you. Take up my yoke upon you, and learn of Me, because I am meek and humble of heart, and you shall find rest for your souls; for My yoke is sweet and My burden light.'[34] If these words are not heard or not heeded, do you, my Licentius, expect Augustine to give orders to his fellow servant, instead of mourning rather that His Lord commands in vain? Nay, He does not command, He invites and begs, so to speak, that those who labor should be refreshed by Him. Of course, the yoke of the world is more agreeable than the yoke of Christ to the strong and self-confident neck. If He were to force us to labor, consider who would force, and at what price. Go into Campania, learn how Paulinus,[35] a noble and holy servant of God, has unhestitatingly shaken off the yoke of

---
34 John 7.37; Matt. 2.28.
35 Cf. Letter 24 n. 1.

great worldly pomp, with a generosity only equaled by his humility, in order to subject his neck to the yoke of Christ, as he has done; and now, with Him for guide, he goes his way with quiet and modest joy. Go, learn with what wealth of genius he offers the sacrifice of praise, returning to Him whatever good he has received, lest he lose all if he did not return all to its source.

Why do you waver? Why do you hesitate? Why do you attend to the vain urging of poisonous pleasures, and turn away from us? They lie, they die, and they lead to death. They lie, Licentius! 'That truth may be by reason manifest,' as you desire, 'may it more freely flow than Eridanus.' Truth alone speaks truth: 'Christ is the truth.'[36] Let us come to Him that we may not labor. Let us take His yoke upon us that He may refresh us, and let us learn from Him because He is meek and humble of heart, and we shall find rest to our souls, for His yoke is sweet and His burden light.[37] The Devil is using you for his adornment. If you found a golden chalice on the ground, you would give it to the Church of God. You have received from God a mind that is spiritually golden, and you use it to minister to lust; you offer yourself as a drink to Satan! Do not do it, I beg of you. May you sometime understand with what sad and pitying heart I have written this. Then, if you sink low in your own eyes, have pity on me.

---

36 1 John 5.6.
37 Matt. 2.28.30.

LETTERS

27. *Augustine gives greeting in the Lord to his brother, Paulinus, truly holy and venerable lord, worthy of high praise in Christ (395)*

O good sir and good brother, you have been hiding from my heart. And I tell it to endure your still hiding from my sight, but it scarcely obeys me; in fact, it does not obey me at all. Does it truly endure this? Then, why does the longing for you torment the innermost part of my being? If it were pains of body that I were bearing without losing the serenity of my soul, I should be considered to be bearing them properly, but, when I am disturbed at not seeing you, it is unbearable to call that bearing something. But, with the kind of person you are, to be away from you should perhaps be borne as something too unbearable. It is a good thing that I cannot take this cheerfully, for, if I could take it cheerfully, I should be no cheerful companion myself. It is strange what has happened to me, but it is true; I suffer because I do not see you, and my very suffering consoles me. Even the virtue of fortitude, which consists in bearing patiently the absence of good—such as you are—is displeasing to me. It is true, we long for the heavenly Jerusalem, and the more impatiently we long for it, the more patiently we bear all things on account of it. Could anyone, then, be sad at seeing you, so that he could be glad as long as he did not see you? I am not able to do either of these things, for, if I could, it would be monstrous; so, I am glad of my inability, and this being glad is some comfort to me. In this state of mind, my grief comforts me, not by being assuaged, but by being embraced. Do not reprove me, I beg of you, from the height of that holier gravity in which you excel, by saying that I cannot properly grieve because I do not yet know you, when you have laid open to my gaze your soul, your very innermost self. If I found out that you, my brother and lover and hero in the Lord, were anywhere in your earthly city, do you think I should feel no grief at not being able to see your house? Why, then, should I not grieve at not knowing your face, which is the house of your soul, as well as I know my own?

I have read your letters overflowing with milk and honey, displaying the simplicity of heart with which you seek the Lord, breathing forth His goodness and rendering Him glory and honor. The brethren have read them, also, and they rejoice unceasingly and exceedingly over the rich and excellent gifts of God which are yours. As often as they read them they carry them away, because they are carried away when they read. The sweet odor of Christ which they distil, their fragrance, is something beyond telling. When those letters present you to us so that you are almost seen, how they rouse us to seek you! For they make you clearly visible and desirable, and the more they show your presence among us, in some sort, the more they make it impossible for us to bear your absence. In them all love you and wish to be loved by you, while God is praised and blessed because by His grace you are such as you are. Then Christ is awakened so that He may deign to calm the winds and the seas for you as you make your way to His solid earth.[1] Your wife is also made visible to your readers, not as one leading her husband into luxury, but rather as leading him back to strength in his innermost being. We salute her, also, with the greetings owed to your Holiness alone, because she is joined in close union with you, and is attached to you by spiritual bonds which are as strong as they are chaste. There, the cedars of Libanus are laid on the ground, there they are joined by the thongs of charity to be the material of the Ark, and are incorruptibly

---

1 Matt. 8.26.

floated on the waters of this world;[2] there, glory is despised that it may be acquired, and the world given up that it may be held; there, the little ones or even the growing children of Babylon are dashed against a stone;[3] that is, the vices of disorder and worldly pride.

These and other ideas most sweet and sacred do your letters present to their readers, those letters, letters of unfeigned faith, letters of high hope, letters of pure charity. How they pant for us with your thirst and with the longing and fainting of your soul for the courts of the Lord![4] What purely holy love they breathe forth! With what wealth of truth and purity they overflow! What thanks they render to God! What favors they win from Him! They are kindly, yet spirited; enlightening, and fruitful. It is amazing that they should soothe us as much as they rouse us, that they should bring us, so to speak, both abundant showers and fair weather. I ask you how this can be, or how I can repay you for those letters, except by being wholly yours in Him to whom you wholly belong? If this is not enough, I certainly have nothing more to give; but you have made me out to be something in my own eyes, by so kindly loading me with praises in your letter. Consequently, I must not think too little of myself when I pay myself back to you, for fear of being proved to disbelieve you. Indeed, I am ashamed to think so much good of myself, but I should feel worse not to believe you. There is something I can do; I will not believe myself to be such as you think, because I do not know, but I will believe myself to be loved by you, and that I fully understand and experience. In that way I shall not be bold in my own regard, nor ungrateful to you. And when I offer myself to you wholly,

---

2 3 Kings 5.6,9.
3 Ps. 136.9.
4 Ps. 83.3

it is not a small thing, for I offer what you deeply love, and, if what I offer is not what you think, at least it is the one for whom you pray, that he may deserve to be such as you think he is. I am more insistent in asking you to pray for me, for, if you do not, I may lose that additional grace, because of your thinking that I have become what I am not.

The one who brings this letter to your Excellency and your excelling Charity is one who is exceedingly dear to me, and one of my most intimate friends from early youth. His name[5] is in the book *On Religion,* which your Holiness has read with pleasure, as you have said in your letters. He is doubtless welcome to you because of the recommendation of the one who has sent him to you, even such a one as I. However, I should like you not to believe this intimate friend of mine, if he happens to say anything in praise of me. I have noticed that he is often mistaken in his judgment, not from any propensity toward lying, but through the bias of his affection, and because he thinks I have received gifts, which I merely yearn to receive from the Lord with the open mouth of my heart. And if he does this to my face, you could imagine how much more likely he is, in his enthusiasm, to make statements in my absence that are more flattering than true. He will make a store of my books available to your estimable zeal, for he has everything I have written, either to those outside the Church of God or to the brethren. But, when you read, my holy Paulinus, let not the words which truth speaks through my weakness so carry you away that you pay less attention to what I say of myself; for, while you eagerly drink in the good and true things which are granted me to say as agent, you may neglect to pray for the mistakes and sins which I commit. In those parts, then, of my writings, which rightly displease you, I am to be

---

5 Romanianus.

seen; but in those other parts, which rightly please you because they are the gift of the Spirit, which you have also received, He is to be loved, He is to be praised, with whom is the fountain of life, and in whose light we shall see light,[6] without obscurity, and face to face, but we see now in a dark manner.[7] In the things, then, which I have uttered of the old leaven[8] I judge myself with sorrow as I read and recognize them; but in those which I have spoken by the gift of God, of the unleavened bread of sincerity and truth,[9] I tremble with joy. What, then, have we that we have not received?[10] He is better who is rich in more and greater gifts of God than he who has lesser and fewer gifts. Everyone admits that. But again it is better to thank God for His smaller gift than to wish to be thanked oneself for a great one. Pray for me, brother, that I may always think thus and that my tongue may not be at variance with my heart; pray, I beseech you, that I may not wish to be praised, but that, praising, I may call upon the Lord and I shall be saved from my enemies.[11]

There is another reason why you should love this brother more deeply; he is a relative of the venerable and truly blessed Bishop Alypius, whom you love with your whole heart, and rightly. For, whoever has kind thoughts of that man has them of the mercy of God and of His wonderful gifts. So, when he had read your request, in which you showed that you wanted him to write the story of his life, he both wanted to do it because of your goodness and did not want to do it because of his own modesty. When I saw him thus

---

6 Ps. 35.10.
7 1 Cor. 13.12.
8 1 Cor. 5.7.
9 1 Cor. 5.9.
10 1 Cor. 4.7.
11 Ps. 17.4.

wavering between love and reserve, I took the burden from his shoulders to my own, for he gave me this commission in a letter. With the Lord's help, I will speedily put the whole Alypius in your heart, for my greatest fear was that he would shrink from disclosing all the favors which the Lord has bestowed on him. Knowing that his words would be read by others besides you, he feared that some unobservant reader might think he was extolling himself instead of admitting the divine origin of gifts given to men; at the same time, he did not want his regard for the weakness of others to cheat you (who would know how to read his words) of the tribute due to brotherly affection. I should long since have pushed this matter through and you would now be reading him, except that the unexpected journey of a brother offered a sudden opportunity. I commend him to your heart and tongue, and I hope you will give him as friendly a reception as if you had not only now come to know him, but had met him with me. If he is not too shy in revealing himself to your heart, he will be cured entirely or in great part by your words, for I want him to be accosted on all sides by the voices of those who do not love their friends as the world does.

His son, also, our son,[12] whose name you will find in several of my works, although he will not be physically present to your charity, I have decided to entrust to you by letter, so that he may be consoled, encouraged, and instructed by the example of your strength, if not by the sound of your voice. I desire very earnestly indeed that, while he is still green wood, he may change the cockle into good grain, and trust the experience of others, for he is now dangerously anxious to make his own experience. From his poem, and from the letter which I have sent him, your very kind and

---

12 Licentius, son of Romanianus; cf. Letter 26.

gentle prudence may understand my concern, my fear and my wish for him. I hope by the Lord's help and by your ministry to be delivered from this tempest of anxieties about him. As you are going to read many of my writings, your affection will be more precious to me if you will correct those points which displease you and as a just man reprove me in mercy, for I do not fear to have the oil of such a one as you fatten my head.[13] The brethren in general, not only those who live with us, but those who live where it pleases God to have them serve Him, and who know us well, send greetings. They esteem and long to experience your brotherly spirit, your happy state, your kindness. I dare not ask, but, if you have leisure from your ecclesiastical duties, look how Africa and I thirst for you.

28. Augustine to Jerome,[1] his brother and fellow priest, most beloved lord, most worthy of being received and embraced in the bonds of sincere affection (394 or 395)

Never has anyone been so well known to another by face, as the quiet joy and scholarly pursuit of your studies in the Lord are known to me. Although I greatly desire to know you wholly, I have a little bit of you, namely, your physical appearance. I owe this to brother Alypius, now a blessed bishop, but even then worthy of the episcopate; for, after he

---

13 Ps. 140.5.

---

1 St. Jerome (347-419) was one of the great Biblical scholars of his own and all time. He made the translation of the Scriptures known as the Vulgate, adopted by the Church as the official version. A man of positive opinions, and somewhat difficult character, he made many enemies, but had also many friends. Augustine shows him great deference, even when differing from him. He spent the last years of his life in seclusion in Bethlehem.

had seen you and I had seen him at his return, I confess that you were made almost present to me by his description; and even before he came back, while he was still seeing you, I saw you, too, through his eyes. Anyone who knows us will say that we are two in body but one in mind, at least so far as perfect agreement goes and faithful intimacy; not in merit, however, in which he excels. Therefore, since you love me in the first place because of the meeting of our minds—we have a common aim—and in the second place because of his recommendation, I think it is not too bold of me, as if I were a total stranger, to commend to your Fraternity our brother Profuturus. I hope that through my efforts and your help he will truly benefit;[2] he may even turn out to be someone through whom I shall gain in your friendship rather than he through me. Perhaps I ought to end my letter here, and so I should if I were satisfied with the conventional type of formal letter. But my mind bubbles over with thoughts which I want to share with you about the studies which we pursue in Christ Jesus our Lord, who deigns to bestow on me, through your Charity, a great abundance of useful ideas and provision for the road mapped out by Him.

Therefore, I ask, and the whole group of students of the African Churches joins me in asking, that you would spare neither trouble nor labor in translating the books of those who have treated so well of our Scriptures in Greek. You can bring it about that we, too, should have such men as those—and especially one—whom you display so freely in your letters.

---

[2] Benefit is a pun on the name Profuturus; literally, 'will benefit.' Profuturus was afterward consecrated Bishop of Cirta and did not make the proposed journey to Palestine; consequently, this letter did not reach Jerome at this time. It circulated in Africa, and came to Jerome's attention, with another letter of similar fate, in an indirect manner, causing him much annoyance. Augustine had to smooth things out in later letters.

In translating the sacred canonical scriptures into Latin, I should like you to do the same thing you did in translating Job, that is, to point out by appropriate signs the variations between your version and the Septuagint, which has such preponderant authority. I should be greatly surprised if anything should now be found in the Hebrew texts which had escaped the notice of so many learned interpreters of that language. I say nothing of the Seventy, whose unity of thought and intention is greater than that of a single writer would be, and I do not venture to express as certain an opinion on any part of their work, except that I think an overwhelming authority is to be attributed to them in this matter, without question. But those others disturb me more, who, in making later versions, bite too hard, as they say, on the rule and method of Hebrew words and expressions, and not only disagree among themselves, but leave many points to be explained and elucidated later. And these points are either obscure or they are clear. If they are obscure, you may get the blame for error; if they are clear, those authors get the credit for trustworthiness. Now that I have set forth my reasons, I should like you to be so kind as to let me know what you think of the matter.

I have read certain writings, said to be yours,[3] on the Epistles of the Apostle Paul, in which you were attempting to explain some difficulties in Galatians, and I came upon that passage where the Apostle Peter is rescued from a dangerous dissimulation. I confess that I regretted very keenly that lying should be defended either by such a man as you or by someone else, if someone else wrote it; and I shall go on feeling this way until it is refuted—if what disturbs me can be refuted. I think it is extremely dangerous to admit that anything in the Sacred Books should be a lie; that is,

---

[3] Hieron. in Pauli. ep. ad Gal. 2.11-14.

that the men who have composed and written the Scriptures for us should have lied in their books. It is quite another question whether a good man should ever lie, and still another whether a writer of the Holy Scriptures ought to lie—but no, that is not another question: it is no question at all. If we once admit in that supreme authority even one polite lie, there will be nothing left of those books, because, whenever anyone finds something difficult to practise or hard to believe, he will follow this most dangerous precedent and explain it as the idea or practice of a lying author.

For, if the Apostle Paul was lying when he rebuked Peter, saying: 'If thou, being a Jew, livest after the manner of the gentiles, and not as the Jews do, how dost thou compel the gentiles to live as do the Jews?'[4] and if Peter seemed to him to have acted rightly, although he both said and wrote that he had not acted rightly—which he did in order to appease the objectors—what, then, shall we answer when wicked men rise up forbidding marriage, as he foretold that they would do;[5] and when they say that the whole passage of the same Apostle on the inviolability of marriage is a piece of falsehood, inserted not because he thought so, but to forestall the objections of those who might make a disturbance because of their love of their wives? We do not need many examples. It could even seem that there were polite lies about the praises of God, to make His love glow more brightly in slothful men. And, so, nowhere in the Holy Books will there be the absolute authority of pure truth. Do we not note with what care for safeguarding truth the same Apostle says: 'And if Christ be not risen again, then is our preaching vain, and your faith is also vain. Yea, and we are found false witnesses of God, because we have given testimony against God, that He

---
4 Gal. 2.14.
5 1 Cor. 7.10,16.

hath raised up Christ, whom He hath not raised up'?[6] If anyone should say to him: 'Why do you shudder at this lie when you have said something, which, even if it is untrue, greatly redounds to the glory of God?' would he not detest this madness and, with whatever words and expressions he could, would he not lay open to the light the innermost parts of his heart, crying out that falsehood is blamed with no less guilt than truth—or even more—in the matter of praising God? We must see to it, then, that the man who desires to have knowledge of the Divine Scriptures should be such a one as to esteem highly the holiness and truth of the Holy Books, and to refuse to be pleased in any part of them with polite lies. Let him pass over what he does not understand rather than betray his own heart to that truth. Certainly, when he says this, he expects to be believed, but he acts so that we do not believe the authority of the Divine Scriptures.

With whatever strength the Lord gives me, I should like to show that all those proofs which are offered in support of the utility of lying ought to be understood as teaching the necessity of truth everywhere. For, just as witnesses should not be untruthful, so they should not support untruth. But I leave this to your understanding. With your greater application to reading, you will doubtless see this more readily than I do. Moreover, your spirit of devotion will force you to this conclusion, and make you recognize that the authority of the Divine Scriptures is undermined—leaving anyone to believe what he likes and to refuse to believe what he does not like—once the opinion has gained ground that the men through whose ministry the Scriptures have come down to us could be guilty of falsehood. Of course, you could lay down certain rules to let us know when it is proper to lie and when it is not, but, if you do, I beg you not to explain the process

---

6 1 Cor. 15.14.

by false and doubtful reasonings. I also ask by the most truthful humanity of our Lord that you do not set me down as officious or bold. For, it will be no fault on my part—or, at least, no great one—for error to support truth, if on your side truth can rightly tolerate falsehood.

There are many other points of Christian learning which I should like to mention and to discuss with you in your straightforward way, but no letter can satisfy this desire of mine. I can accomplish it more profitably through the brother whom I am glad to send to you, that he may take part in and be nourished by your sweet and beneficial conversations. With his permission, I would say that even he does not absorb as much of you as I should like. I do not mean to prefer myself to him, but I admit that I can take in more of you, whereas he is becoming fuller of you, and in that he certainly surpasses me. And when he comes back, which I hope will be soon, by the help of the Lord, and when I share in the stored-up riches of his mind, even then he will not fill up that part of me which is empty and hungry for your opinions. So it will still be that I shall be more needy and he more affluent. This same brother is carrying some of my writings with him. If you will be so kind as to read them, I ask you to treat them with a frank and brotherly severity, for this is how I understand what is written: 'The just man shall correct me in mercy, and shall reprove me, but let not the oil of the sinner fatten my head.'[7] The healing critic loves me more than the flatterer anointing my head. I find it hard to judge my own writings, for I am either too cautious or too ready to agree with myself. It is true that sometimes I see my faults, but I would rather hear them from someone better than I, because I am likely, after having taken myself to task, to justify myself by making out that my self-criticism has been exact in detail rather than correct as a whole.

---

7 Ps. 140.5.

29. Augustine, priest, to Alypius, Bishop of Tagaste (395)

Concerning that matter which I cannot help being concerned about, I could not give you any definite news while brother Macarius[1] was away, but I hear that he will soon be back, and, whatever can be carried through, with the help of God, will be carried through. Although our brethren and fellow citizens, who were present, could set you at ease about our anxiety for them, nevertheless a circumstance deserving of the sort of epistolary conversation with which we console each other has been granted by the Lord, and in furthering it I believe we are much helped by your own anxiety, which certainly cannot exist without your prayer for us.

Therefore, let us not fail to describe to your Charity what happened, that you may join with us in prayers of thanksgiving for a favor received, as you did in prayers of petition. After your departure, when news was brought to us that people were rioting and saying they could not bear to have that celebration forbidden—they try in vain to conceal the word drunkenness under that of festival, and, in fact, this news had started to come in while you were still here—it happened most fortunately, by a secret dispensation of almighty God, that the following text occurred in the Gospel of that Wednesday, for comment: 'Give not that which is holy to dogs, neither cast ye your pearls before swine.'[2] I therefore commented on dogs and swine to such effect that those who were snarling with continual barking against the precepts of God and those who were involved in the filth of carnal pleasures were forced to blush for shame, and I drew the conclusion so strongly that they saw how wicked

---
1 Apparently, one of Augustine's fellow clerics.
2 Matt. 7.6.

it is to do in church and under the name of religion what would cause them to be shut out from the holy place and from the pearls of the church if they continued to do it in their own homes.

Although my words were well received, I was not satisfied with the result, because so few had assembled. In addition to that, my sermon met with much contradiction when it had been noised about by those who were present, according to each one's ability and industry. But, when Ash Wednesday[3] came and a large crowd had assembled for the sermon, that passage in the Gospel was read where the Lord, after driving the sellers of animals from the Temple, and overturning the tables of the money-changers, declared that the house of His Father, which should be a house of prayer, had been turned into a den of thieves.[4] When I had my audience aroused by bringing up the question of wine-drinking, I read the same chapter of the Gospel, and I added an argument proving how much more indignantly and vigorously our Lord would have driven drunken banquets out of the Temple, since these are always shameful. What He had driven out had been legitimate trade, engaged in selling victims needed for the sacrifices of the Law, and I asked them which seemed more like a den of thieves: a place for selling necessities or one of excessive drinking. And, since I was expected to comment further on the Lessons of the day, I added that

---

3 There is some difficulty in fixing this day. The expression used is *dies Quadragesimae*—a day of Lent: but, which day? He had spoken of a Wednesday above. If the reading were *dies quadragesima*, it would mean the 'fortieth day,' that is, Ascension Day, which was one of those celebrated in the fashion described. The celebrations were apparently connected with the feast day of St. Leontius, the saint of their church. In the year mentioned, Ascension Day coincided with the feast of the Deposition of his relics. The Gospel spoken of is not at present read on either Ash Wednesday or Ascension Day.

4 Matt. 21.12.

the Temple was not a place where the Body and Blood of the Lord was offered; that the Jewish people, still material-minded, did not hold even moderate banquets in the Temple, let alone drinking parties; and that their history has no record of their drinking in public under the guise of a religious ceremony, except the time when they kept a feast in honor of the idol which they had made.[5] After I had said that, I took up the book and read the whole passage. I added to this with sorrow, as I very well could, since the Apostle, desiring to distinguish the Christian people from the hard-hearted Jews, says that his Epistle was written, 'not in tables of stone, but in the fleshy tables of the heart,'[6] and since Moses, a servant of God, broke the two tables of stone, because of those leaders, why can we not break the hearts of those, who, though men of the New Testament, wish to continue practices in honor of the saints, which the people of the Old Testament performed only once in honor of an idol?

Then I laid aside the text of Exodus, and, attacking the crime of drunkenness, as far as time permitted, I took up the Apostle Paul, and I showed what kinds of sins he classes with it, by reading that passage: 'If any man that is named a brother be a fornicator or covetous or a server of idols, or a railer, or a drunkard, or an extortioner, with such a one not so much as to eat.[7] I warned them with groans how great danger we run when we banquet with those who are drunkards even in their homes. I also read this other passage, which follows not long after: 'Do not err; neither fornicators, nor idolators, nor adulterers, nor the effeminate, nor liers with mankind, nor thieves, nor covetous, nor drunkards, nor

---
5 Exod. 32.6.
6 2 Cor.3.3.
7 1 Cor. 5.11.

railers, nor extortioners, shall possess the kingdom of God. And such some of you were, but you are washed, but you are justified in the name of our Lord Jesus Christ and the Spirit of our God.'[8] When I had finished reading, I told them to reflect how it was possible for the faithful to hear: 'But you are washed,' when they were ready to admit to their hearts, that is, to the interior temple of God, men who are stained with such guilt, against which the kingdom of heaven is shut. Then I came to that chapter: 'When you come therefore together in one place, it is not now to eat the Lord's supper. For everyone taketh before his own supper to eat. And one indeed is hungry: and another is drunk. What! have you not houses to eat and drink in? Or despise ye the Church of God?'[9] When I had quoted this, I recalled to them insistently that not even seemly and moderate banquets should be held in church, since the Apostle did not say: 'Have you not houses to become drunk in?' as if it were only unlawful to become drunk in church, but: 'to eat and drink in,' which can be done legitimately, but outside the church, by those who have houses where they can be refreshed by necessary food. However, we are so straitened by the corruption of the times and the laxity of morals that we do not yet expect moderate feasting but merely a domestic regime of drinking.

I likewise recalled the passage of the Gospel which I had discussed the previous day, where it is said of false prophets: 'By their fruits you shall know them.'[10] Then I reminded them that fruits in that text means works; I asked them among what fruits drunkenness was included, and I quoted the following from Galatians: 'Now the works of the flesh are manifest, which are fornication, uncleanness, luxury, idolatry, witch-

---
8 1 Cor. 6.9-11.
9 1 Cor. 11.20-22.
10 Matt. 7.16.

craft, enmities, contentions, emulations, wraths, dissensions, sects, envies, drunkenness, revellings and such like, of which I foretell you, as I have foretold to you, that they who do such things shall not obtain the kingdom of God.'[11] After these words, I asked how we Christians, whom the Lord bids to be known by their fruits, are to be known by the fruit of drunkenness. I recommended them to read the following: 'But the fruit of the Spirit is charity, joy, peace, longanimity, benignity, goodness, faith, mildness, continency,'[12] and I made them realize how shameful and how lamentable a thing it would be if they should not only aim at living privately by those fruits of the flesh, but should deprive the Church of honor, since they would even fill the whole space of a great basilica, if they were allowed, with their mobs of feasters and drinkers; while, on the other hand, of the spiritual fruits, to which they are invited by the authority of the Divine Scriptures and by our sorrowful words, they will not make offerings to God, and by this means most properly celebrate the feasts of saints.

After this, I returned the book, and, calling for prayer as forcibly as I could, under the urgency of a sense of danger and with the strength which the Lord deigned to grant me, I set before their eyes the common danger, both of themselves who are committed to us and of ourselves who have to give an account of them to the Prince of pastors, and I begged them by His humility, His terrible humiliations, the blows and spittle on the face and hands, the crown of thorns, the cross and bloodshed, that, if they had committed any offense against Him, they would have pity on us, and would recall the boundless charity of the venerable old man Val-

---

11 Gal. 5.19,21.
12 Gal. 5.22.

erius[13] toward me. For, he did not shrink for their sake from laying on me the dangerous duty of speaking the words of truth, and he often said that his prayers had been heard when we came. Certainly, he did not rejoice at our coming, if it meant our common death or even the sight of their death, but only their common labor for eternal life. Finally, I said that I had determined to put my trust in Him who cannot deceive, who promised by the mouth of His Prophet concerning our Lord Jesus Christ: 'If his children forsake my law, and walk not in my judgments; if they profane my justices, I will visit their iniquities with a rod, and their sins with stripes, but my mercy I will not take away from him.'[14] In Him, I said, I put my trust, because, if they despised these great truths which had been read and spoken to them, He would visit them with a rod and with a scourge, but He would not allow them to be damned with this world. Thus I acted in this rebuke, with all the courage and energy furnished me by our guide and ruler, according to the importance of the matter and the degree of danger. I did not rouse their tears by mine, but I admit that, after saying such things, I was overcome by their weeping and could not restrain my own. So, when we had wept together, I finished my sermon with the fullest hope of their amendment.

But, when the morrow dawned, a day on which they were wont to indulge their palates and stomachs, word was brought me that some of them, even those who had been present at my sermon, had not stopped grumbling, and that the force of evil habit was still so strong in them that they had only one comment to make: 'Why do they do this only now? Or were those who failed to forbid it before not Christians?' When I heard this, I was completely at a loss what greater

---
13 Bishop of Hippo.
14 Ps. 88.31,34.

devices I could use to impress them, but I made ready, in case they thought of keeping it up, to read them this passage from the Prophet Ezechiel: 'The watchman is held guiltless if he warn of danger, even if those who are warned will not heed,'[15] and after this to rend my garments and depart. Then, indeed, the Lord showed that He does not desert us, and that He urges us to put our trust in Him; for, just before I was to mount the pulpit, those very ones who had been reported as the grumblers against abolishing the old custom came in to me. I received them kindly, and in a few words I was able to bring them to the right frame of mind. Thus, when the period of discussion came, I omitted the reading which I had prepared, because it seemed no longer necessary, and I said only a few words about their question, to the effect that the shortest and truest answer to their 'Why now?' was 'Yes, now!'

However, not to appear to reflect discredit on those before us who had either allowed or had not dared to prevent such open abuses on the part of an unruly mob, I explained to them how the Church was constrained to permit such things in the beginning. With the advent of peace, after so many such violent persecutions, when throngs of pagans desiring to enter the Christian fold were held back by the fact that they were wont to spend the feast days in honor of their idols in excess of eating and drinking; as they could not easily renounce these evil but traditional pleasures, it naturally seemed good to our predecessors to indulge this weakness of theirs, and in place of the feast days which they were leaving behind them, to allow them others, in honor of the holy martyrs, to be celebrated, if not with the same sacrilegious rites, at least with equal lavishness. But, now, the binding force of Christ's name and the yoke of His

---
15 Cf. Ezech. 33.9.

authority should avail to make them receive the saving precepts of sobriety, which they can surely not refuse if they honor and reverence the Teacher. Therefore, now is the time, if they dare to profess themselves Christians, to begin to live according to the will of Christ, and, since they are Christians, to renounce what was granted to them that they might become Christians.

Then I exhorted them to become willing imitators of the overseas Churches, some of which never had admitted these customs, while others had corrected them with the cooperation of good pastors and obedient people.[16] And since examples were being cited of daily wine-drinking in the basilica of the blessed Apostle Peter, I said that in the first place we had heard that it was forbidden, but because the locality is too far for the bishop's personal attention, and because in such a large city there are many carnal-minded people, especially pilgrims and strangers who keep coming, and who cling to that custom with a violence equaled only by their ignorance, it had not yet been possible to control or abolish that abuse. But if we would truly honor the Apostle Peter, we ought to harken more eagerly to his teachings and to the epistle in which his will appears, rather than turn our eyes to the basilica in which it does not appear. Then I took up the book and forthwith read the passage where it says: 'Christ therefore having suffered in the flesh, be you also armed with the same thought; for he that hath suffered in the flesh hath ceased from sins; that now he may live the rest of his time in the flesh, not after the desires of men, but according to the will of God. For the time past is sufficient to have fulfilled the will of the gentiles, for them who have walked in riotousness, lusts, excess of wine, revellings, banquetings, and unlaw-

---

16 This had been done by St. Ambrose at Milan.

ful worshipping of idols.'[17] When this much had been accomplished, I saw that they were unanimously well disposed to the abolition of the evil custom, and I encouraged them to spend the noon hour in holy readings and psalm-singing; thus, they would be glad to have celebrated that day more virtuously and more purely, and from the crowd of those present it would be evident which of them were feeding their minds and which ones their stomachs. My sermon ended with the conclusion of the readings.

In the afternoon, there was an even greater crowd than there had been before noon, and there was an alternate reading and psalm-singing until we came out with the bishop; as we appeared, two psalms were read. I was very anxious to have done with this hazardous day, but the old man[18] obliged me under obedience, much against my will, to speak to them. I said a few words in which I gave thanks to God, and, as we had heard that in the basilica of the heretics the customary banquets had been held, and that they had passed the time in their cups, while we had been occupied as we had, I said that the beauty of day is enhanced by comparison with night, as the color white is more lovely by contrast with black. So, perhaps our meeting for a spiritual celebration might have been less pleasing if it had not been compared with the carnal guzzling of the other side, and I urged them, if they had tasted how sweet the Lord is, to desire such feasts with eagerness. Those others, however, who keep the first kind of feast have to fear that it will sometime be destroyed, since each one becomes part of the thing which he loves, and the Apostle reviles such people, saying: 'Whose God is their belly,'[19] and, likewise, in another place: 'Meat for the belly

---
17 1 Peter 4.1-3.
18 His bishop.
19 Phil. 3.19.

and the belly for the meats; but God shall destroy both it and them.' [20] Therefore, it befits us to follow what will not be destroyed, but that which, farthest from the affection of the flesh, is preserved by the sanctification of the spirit. And when I had finished saying these and things of like tenor, which the Lord deigned to inspire in me, according to the time, Vespers was celebrated as is the daily custom. As we were retiring with the bishop, the brethren continued to sing hymns in the same place, while no small crowd of both sexes remained and sang until dark.

I have outlined for you what I thought you particularly wanted to hear. Pray that God may deign to remove all stumbling-blocks and weariness from our efforts. We join with you in relying for the most part on the eagerness of fervor, because we have such frequent news of the good deeds of the spiritual church of Tagaste. The ship has not yet arrived with the brethren. At Asna, where brother Argentius is the priest, the Circumcellions[21] raided our basilica and shattered the altar. The case is now being tried, and we beg you earnestly to pray that it may be decided peacefully, and in a manner befitting the Catholic Church, in such wise as to restrain the unbridled tongue of heresy. We have sent a letter to the Asiarch.[22] Persevere blessedly in the Lord and remember us. Amen.

---

20 1 Cor. 6.13.
21 Cf. Letter 23 n. 13.
22 One of the civil officials of the Roman administration of Asia Minor, in charge of public worship and public games.

30. Paulinus and Therasia, sinners, to Augustine, their holy and beloved lord and brother (395)

Some time ago, my dearly beloved brother in Christ the Lord, although I realized that you were unacquainted with me, and that you were absent and engaged in your holy and pious labors, I made haste to approach you by letter, embracing you with my whole heart in a brotherly and intimate conversation. And I believe that, by the favor of the Lord, my words were delivered into your hands; but as the messenger whom I had sent before the winter set in to deliver greetings to you and others, equally dear to God, has not yet returned, I can no longer delay this duty or restrain my very ardent longing for a word from you. Therefore, I am now writing a second time, if my former letter deserved to reach you, or a first time, if it did not have the good fortune of being put into your hands. But you, spiritual brother, judging all things,[1] do not weigh our love for you by duty alone or by the time of the arrival of letters. The Lord is my witness, who, one and the same, worketh[2] His charity everywhere in His own, that from the first time I knew you in your works against the Manichaeans, through the kindness of the venerable bishops, Aurelius and Alypius, that love for you was so deeply rooted in me that I seemed not so much to take on a new friendship as to renew a long-standing affection. Now, at length, I write to you, unskilled in word, perhaps, but not in love, and recognize you mutually in spirit through the interior man. It is not strange, then, that we should be together, though apart, unacquainted yet well known to each other, since we are members of one body, we have one head, we are refreshed by one grace, we live by one bread, we walk by

---
1 1 Cor. 2.15.
2 1 Cor. 12.11.

one road, we live in the same house.³ Finally, in everything that we are, we strive for the future by the full hope and faith which sustains us in the present; we are equally one in the spirit and in the body of the Lord, and we should become nothing if we fell away from the One.

What insignificant thing does bodily absence deprive us of, except that satisfaction which feeds the eyes, always looking for temporal rewards? And yet, not even bodily presence ought to be mentioned as temporal among the spiritual gifts with which the resurrection will endow our immortal bodies, as we, though unworthy, shall presume to hope through the merit of Christ and the goodness of God the Father. Therefore, I would that the grace of God might allow us this benefit, so we might see your face even in the flesh. Not only would great joy be granted to our desires, but light would also increase in our minds, and our poverty would be enriched from your abundance. You can do this even for the absent, especially at this time, when our sons, beloved and most dear to us in the Lord, Romanus and Agilis,⁴ whom we commend to you as our other self, will return to us, in the name of the Lord, after fulfilling the work of charity. In this work, we ask particularly that they may feel the effect of your charity, for you know what exalted rewards the Most High promises to the brother helping his brother. If you wish to make use of them to enrich me with the gift of grace which is entrusted to you, you can do so safely. For I should like you to know that they are one heart and one soul in the Lord with us.⁵ May the grace of God remain with you as it now is, my dear brother in Christ, venerable, beloved and desirable. Greet all the saints

---

3 Rom. 12.45; 1 Cor. 12.12; 10.17.
4 These two seem to have been regular messengers between Paulinus and Augustine.
5 Acts 4.32.

in Christ for us, who are strongly united with you, and recommend us to the saints, that they may be so good as to join with you in prayer for us.

31. Augustine gives greeting in the Lord to the most beloved, sincere and truly blessed brethren, Paulinus and Therasia, most conspicuously endowed with the most abundant grace of God (396)

I had greatly desired that my letters, in which I answered your previous ones—if it is at all possible for me to answer yours—should come quickly into the hands of your Charity, so that I could be with you in some wise, even though separated from you. My delay has brought me the gain of your letter. The Lord is good, who often does not give us what we want so as to grant us what we would rather have. Your intention of writing after receiving my letter is one thing, but your having written without receiving mine is something else. Happy as I am to read yours, something would have been lacking to my joy, if my letter had reached your Holiness as quickly as I so greatly wished and prayed that it might. Now I have the double joy of possessing this letter and of hoping for an answer to that one of mine. Thus, I do not have to be blamed for my delay, and the more ample goodness of the Lord has done what He judged would be more in accord with my desire.

We received with great joy in the Lord the holy brothers Romanus and Agilis,[1] as if they were another letter of yours, but one hearing and repeating your words, and a most sweet part of your presence, such as to make us long more eagerly to see you. Whence or when or how would it be possible for

---
[1] Fellow clerics of Paulinus.

you to grant, or for us to demand, that you should teach us as much about yourself by writing as we have learned from their words? For, they had so much joy in the telling—something that could be found on no written page—that we read with indescribable joy, from their faces and eyes as they spoke, how deeply you were imprinted on their hearts. There was also this further advantage, that any given page, whatever good things may be written on it, does not gain thereby, although it may be unrolled for the benefit of others; but this letter of yours, namely, this fraternal soul, we read in their conversation, so that, the more fruitfully it was inscribed by you, the more blessed it appeared to us. Therefore, by carefully gathering up all the details about you, we have copied that letter into our hearts in imitation of their good fortune.

That is why we did not let them go so quickly from us without regret, even though they were returning to you. Look, I beg of you, at the affection with which I am stirred. Certainly, the more eagerly they wished to obey you, the more quickly should they have been let go, but the more they wished this, the more vividly they portrayed you to us; and in that they showed how dear you are to them. On the other hand, the more reasonably they asked to be let go, the less we wanted to let them go. O unbearable state of affairs, unless we do not really depart by that departure from us, unless 'we are members of one body, we have one head, we live by one bread, we walk by one road, we live in the same house.'[2] Why, then, should we not use the same words? I suppose you recognize that these words are from your letter. But, why should they be your words rather than mine, since they are certainly true, and they proceed from our union with the same head? If they have any special quality given by you,

---

2 Quoted from Letter 30, from Paulinus to St. Augustine.

I loved them the more for that, so that they blocked the way of my breast, and did not allow words to come forth from my heart to my tongue, until they came forth more pure, because they were more yours. Holy brothers, beloved by God, and members of each other, who could doubt that we are strengthened by one spirit, except he who does not perceive the love which binds us together?

However, I should like to know whether you endure this physical absence with more ready patience than we do. If that is so, I confess that I do not like that strength of character of yours, unless it is perhaps caused by the fact that we are less worthy of being desired than you are. Certainly, if I found in myself that ability to bear your absence, it would displease me; it would slow me down in my attempts to see you, and could anything be more ridiculous than slothfulness as a result of fortitude? But, it is well that your Charity take heed to the care of the Church with which I am weighed down, and you will know it from this that the most blessed father Valerius[3]—and you will hear from the brethren how earnestly he salutes you with us and how he longs for you—was not satisfied with having me for his priest, but he must lay on me the greater burden of a share in the episcopate.[4] Indeed, I greatly feared to refuse it, because I believed that the Lord's will was shown by his great charity and the great desire of the people, at the same time that several previous examples were offered which shut the door to all excuse on my part. Although the yoke of Christ is of itself sweet, and

---

3 His bishop.
4 In the year 395. He wished to refuse it because he thought it was contrary to the custom of the Church for him to be consecrated while his bishop was living. He yielded when he was convinced that it was not unusual, by examples of the practice in the overseas and African Churches. He later wrote that he should not have allowed it because it was forbidden by the Council of Nicea.

the burden light,⁵ still, if, by reason of my immaturity and weakness, this bond wears on me and this burden weighs me down, it would be somehow rendered unspeakably more tolerable and supportable by the comfort of your presence. I hear that you lead a life completely free and unburdened by cares of this sort,⁶ and therefore I do not feel shameless in begging and beseeching and demanding that you deign to come into our Africa which is suffering more from a drought of such men than from the better-known sort of dryness.

God knows how we long to have you corporally present in these lands, not only because of my own desire, nor even because of those who have learned of your manner of life either through us or through public rumor here and there, but even more because of the others who either have not heard of it or do not believe what they have heard, but who can be made to love what they have learned. Though your conduct is circumspect and merciful, I nevertheless beg that you let your works shine before the men of our lands, 'that they may see your good works, and glorify your Father who is in heaven.'⁷ When the Lord called the fishermen,⁸ and they left their ships and their nets, they took pleasure in remembering that they had left all and followed the Lord. And, truly, he despises all things who renounces not only what he is able to have but also whatever he wishes to have. God's eyes behold what is desired; man's, what is possessed. But, in some way or other, when worldly goods are loved to excess, we are more closely attached to what we have than to what we desire. When the young man inquired of the Lord how to attain to eternal life,⁹ and heard that he must sell all his goods and distribute them

---

5 Matt. 11.30.
6 He was then living in seclusion at Nola.
7 Matt. 5.16.
8 Matt. 19.27; Luke 18.28.
9 Matt. 19.21,22; Luke 18.22,23.

to the poor, and have his treasure in heaven, why else did he go away sad, except that he had, as the Gospel says, great riches? It is one thing not to wish to hoard up what one has not, and another to scatter what has been accumulated: the former is like refusing food; the latter, like cutting off a limb. With how great and how wonderful joy does Christian charity behold the happy fulfillment in our times of the Lord's Gospel, which that rich young man heard with sadness from the Lord Himself!

Although I can find no words in which to form and utter the thoughts of my heart, nevertheless, with your prudence and candor, you understand that the glory—of human esteem —is not yours, but the Lord's, and this you do because you are sufficiently on guard to perceive the enemy, and, like disciples of Christ, you devoutly strive to be meek and humble of heart.[10] So, I repeat, because you rightly understand that the glory is not yours, but the Lord's, you will see how inadequate and trifling are my utterances. I have spoken of the praises of Christ, to which even the tongues of angels are unequal. Therefore, we desire that this glory of Christ be set before the eyes of our countrymen, as an example offered in one marriage, of pride to be trampled underfoot by both sexes, and of perfection no one can despair of attaining. I know not if you do a greater kindness than you would if you were as unwilling to live in seclusion as you are willing to be such as you are.

I commend to your kindness and charity the boy Vetustinus, an object of pity even to the irreligious. You shall hear from him in person the cause of his misfortune and his wandering. A more extended time and a more robust age and the passing of fear will prove his intention, by which he promises to serve God. I have sent to your Holiness and Charity three

---
10 Matt. 11.29.

books[11]—and I would that they were adequately great expounders of a great question, for the question at issue is that of free will. Knowing the ardor of your desire, I am sure that you will not shrink from the labor of reading them. I know that brother Romanianus[12] does not have these, at least not all of them, but he is the one to whom I have given whatever I have been able to write for general circulation, and I have told him that they are to be read, not to be carried around by reason of your great affection for us. He had them all and was carrying them about with him, because I circulated all the first copies through him. I believe that your Holiness has already experienced, through that spiritual insight which the Lord has granted you, what good qualities of mind that man has, and in what part of his character he limps, so to speak, through weakness. Therefore, you have read, I hope, with what anxiety I have commended both him and his son[13] to your kindness and charity, and with what close attachment they are bound to me. May the Lord build them up through you. That is something which we must insistently ask of Him, for I know how much you wish it.

I have heard from the brethren that you have written against the pagans.[14] If I deserve anything of your heart, send it without distinction, that we may read it; for your heart is such an oracle of the Lord that I expect from it only pleasing answers, and extremely detailed ones against too wordy questions. I believe that your Sanctity has the books of the most blessed Bishop[15] Ambrose; I greatly long to have those which he wrote with such care and fluency against certain

---

11 This was the treatise *De libero arbitrio*.
12 Cf. Letter 5 n. 1.
13 Licentius. Cf. Letter 26 n. 1.
14 *Carmen 32*, a poetical epistle to Ausonius.
15 The word used is *papae*, which was not at that time restricted to the head of the Church, but was used generally of bishops.

very ignorant and proud persons, who claim that the Lord used for his own profit the books of Plato.[16]

Most blessed brother Severus[17] one of our fellow disciples, bishop of the church of Milevis, well known to the brethren in that city, sends to your Holiness due greetings together with us. All the brothers who serve the Lord with us also greet you as sincerely as they long for you, and they long for you as much as they love you, and they love you as much as you deserve love. The loaf of bread[18] which we have sent will become a more fruitful blessing through the love of your Benignity in receiving it. May the Lord preserve you from that generation forever, most beloved and upright lords, brothers truly good and excelling in the most abundant grace of the Lord.

32. Paulinus and Therasia to the worthy lord, estimable and honorable brother, Romanianus (396)

On the day before we sent this letter, our brothers,[1] returned from Africa—and you saw how eagerly we awaited them—bringing us the longed-for letters from Aurelius, Alypius, Augustine, Profuturus, Severus, all of them now bishops. Therefore, rejoicing in the latest messages of so many holy men, we have hastened to relate our happiness to you, so as to share with you, also, by these delightful announcements the joy which is looked forward to in the midst of this our care-laden pilgrimage. If you have heard the same tidings from

---

16 These books of St. Ambrose are not extant.
17 Severus, Bishop of Milevis, one of the members of the religious community at Tagaste.
18 Cf. Letter 24 n. 25.

---

1 Romanus and Agilis.

venerable and esteemed men, who have arrived on other ships, learn it again from us, and be glad with renewed joy. But, if this messenger from us is the first one to reach you, thank the great love felt for you in our country, which is effected by the gift of Christ, so that whatever Divine Providence does there, wonderful always, as it is written,[2] in His saints, we may be the first, or among the first, to know. We do not write this to express our joy only because Augustine has been made bishop, but because the Churches of Africa have deserved, as a mark of God's care, to hear heavenly words from the mouth of Augustine, who has been proposed and consecrated in the new fashion—to the greater credit of the Lord's gift —not to succeed the bishop on his throne, but to share it with him. For, Augustine has been consecrated coadjutor bishop of Hippo, while Valerius is still alive.[3] And that fortunate old man, on whose unsullied mind no dark envy casts a shadow, receives from the Most High fruits worthy of the peace of his heart, and the one whom he desired simply as his successor in the priesthood he now deserves to have as colleague. Could anyone have believed this before it happened? But, of this work of the Almighty, these words of the Gospel also can be used: 'With men this is impossible, but with God all things are possible.'[4] Let us therefore exult and rejoice in Him 'who alone doth wonderful things'[5] and who 'maketh men of one manner to dwell in a house,'[6] since 'He looked down upon our affliction'[7] and hath visited His people unto good, and 'hath raised up an horn of salvation unto us, in the house of

---

[2] Ps. 67.36.
[3] Cf. Letter 31 n. 4.
[4] Matt. 19.26; Mark 10.27; Luke 18.27.
[5] Ps. 71.18.
[6] Ps. 67.7.
[7] Deut. 26.7.

David, His servant,'⁸ and now He has raised up the horn of His Church among His elect, that He may 'break the horns of sinners'⁹—that is, of the Donatists and the Manichaeans—as He promised by His Prophet.

And may this trumpet of the Lord, on which He plays through Augustine, now strike the ears of our son Licentius, that he may hear with that ear by which Christ enters, from which the enemy does not take away the seed of God.'¹⁰ Then, truly, Augustine will seem to him the high priest of Christ, because he will then feel that he has been heard by the Most High, if the one whom he worthily brought forth to you in literature he may also now beget to himself as a worthy son in Christ. I want you to know that he has now written to us about him with the most acute anxiety. We trust in the omnipotent Christ that the spiritual aims of Augustine may prevail over the carnal aims of our young man. Believe me, he will be won over, even against his will; he will be won over by the faith of his most devout father; otherwise, he would win an evil victory, if he should choose to go his own way, to his own ruin, rather than yield to his own salvation.¹¹

Not to seem lacking in the duty of fraternal charity, we have sent to you and to our son, Licentius, jointly, five loaves of bread, soldier's biscuits¹² of the Christian campaign, in which military enterprise we daily wage war to supply our frugal wants, for we could not deprive ourselves of the blessing¹³ which we desire to draw into our inmost being. We

---

8 Luke 1.69.
9 Ps. 74.11.
10 Parable of the Sower: Matt. 13.4,19; Mark 4.4,15; Luke 8,5,12; Paulinus does not hesitate to mix metaphors.
11 This prophecy was not realized.
12 *Bucellatum,* a term used of bread baked in 'morsels'—to speed the process—for soldiers' use.
13 The formula was: 'By receiving this bread, may you make it a blessing.'

must, however, say a few words to himself,[14] lest he should say that what we have written about him was not written to him. What Micio hears is said to Aeschinus.[15] But, why speak of others' affairs when we can say everything about our own, since it is not a sign of a sane mind to speak of irrelevant things. We whose head is Christ are, thanks be to God, of sane and balanced mind. May we always find you safe in Christ all your life, and always happy with your whole household, honorable brother, most esteemed and most desired.

'My son, hear the law of thy father,' that is, the faith of Augustine, 'and resist not the counsels of thy mother,'[16] which name the love of Augustine can rightly and justly claim over you, because he held you on his lap when you were only so big, and from your babyhood fed you with your first milk of worldly wisdom. But now he longs to give you milk and strengthen you for the Lord from his spiritual breasts. Since he sees that, though you are physically grown up, you are still wailing in your spiritual cradle, still an infant in the word of God, still creeping or making your first steps in Christ with tottering gait, may the teaching of Augustine, like the hand of a mother or the arm of a nurse, guide your unsteady childhood. If you listen to him and follow him, I will again entice you with the speech of Solomon: 'My son, thou shalt receive a crown of graces for thy head.'[17] Then shall you truly be, not someone dreamed in a vision, but a consul and

---

14 Licentius; the last part of the letter and the poem are addressed to him.
15 Terence, *Adelphoe* 96,97: 'When I say this to him, Micio, I say it to you.' The rest of this line is: 'You are letting him be spoiled,' but it is not clear that Paulinus meant the whole line to be included in his reference.
16 Cf. Prov. 1.8.
17 Prov. 1.9. The Douay version reads: 'that grace may be added to thy head.'

priest formed by truth itself, when Christ shall replace the empty images of falsehood with the profound effects of His action. Licentius will be truly priest and truly consul, if you[18] will follow the prophetic footsteps and apostolic discipline of Augustine, as blessed Eliseus followed those of the sacred Elias,[19] and as the youthful Timothy was the inseparable companion of the illustrious Apostle on his divine journeys.[20] May you so learn to serve with the perfect heart of a priest, to seek the people's welfare with the mouth of a governor.

But, enough of advice and exhortation. With a little preaching and effort, I think that you, my dear Licentius, can be won to Christ; you who from your childhood have been fired with enthusiasm by the spirit and eloquence of Augustine, for the pursuit of truth and wisdom. But, Christ is both of these; of all good, He is the supreme Good. If he has so little influence on you, what can I do, so inferior to him and so poor in his resources? But, trusting in the power of his ability and the refinement of your own character, I hope that fuller and greater things have been accomplished in you than still remain to be accomplished, and I dare to aspire to this twofold grace, that I may be compared to that man [Augustine] in the debt of charity shown by our anxiety for you, and that I may be be counted as one of proved affection among those who seek your welfare. For, I know that the palm of winning you to perfection will fall most assuredly to Augustine. I fear, my son, to offend your ears by the harshness of my presumptuous speech, and through your hearing to arouse your disgust with me, and so wound your heart. But I thought of your letter, in which I learned of your proficiency in metrical rhythms, a pursuit to which I was not averse at your age.

---
18 The writer seems unaware that he has changed from third to second person.
19 4 Kings 2.1.

Thereupon, this recollection brought to my mind a way in which I could soothe your feelings, in case I had irritated you, namely, to summon you to the Lord, the Creator of every sort of harmony, by the music of poetry. I beg you to lend an ear, and not to despise the plea for your salvation, presented in my words, but willingly to accept my loving care and fatherly affection for you, even though set forth in commonplace words. In them the name of Christ is entwined, 'that name which is above every name,'[21] and to which is owed a veneration not to be refused by any believer.

Come, then, shake off delay[22] and the clinging fetters of
  time,[23] and fear not the sweet yoke of the gentle Lord.[24]
Indeed, the aspect of nature is fair and wonderful to un-
  anchored minds, but the wise soul is not astounded at this.
Now it is alluring Rome, strong enough to overthrow the
  strongest, that holds you enchanted by its varied charms.
But, my son, I pray that father Augustine may always bar
  your way against the myriad enticements of the city.
Looking on him, and holding him ever in your heart, you will
  be safe amid the great dangers of this uncertain life.
Repeating this over and over, I will utter my warnings,[25]
  that you may flee the pitfalls of this harsh warfare.
Honor is a sweet word, but a vile slavery, difficult to shake
  off, and he who but now desired it repents of his desire.

---

20 Acts 16.1-3.
21 Phil. 2.9.
22 Vergil, *Aen.* 4.412. Here begins a poem of 108 lines in elegiac couplets, each couplet, for the most part, a single sentence and a separate thought. The translation has been made to conform to this arrangement.
23 Vergil, *Georg.* 4.412.
24 Matt. 11.30.
25 Vergil, *Aen.* 3.436.

*Joyful it is to mount the heights, but fearsome from heights to
 descend; if you stumble, great is the fall from lofty
 strongholds.
False are the goods which now delight you; now you are tossed on every wind of ambition, and carried along in the
 frail clasp of empty fame.
But, when you shall be girded about with accursed heat, and
 your futile toil shall be broken off,
Too late and in vain shall you decry the baseless hopes, and
 strive to break the bonds which now you weave.
Then, without recourse, shall you recall to mind your father,
 Augustine, and grieve that you had scorned his truthful
 warnings.
Therefore, son, if you are wise and truly devoted to us, hear
 and heed the words of your fathers and the counsel of
 your elders.
Why does your untamed neck refuse the yoke? 'My yoke is
 sweet, and my burden light;'[26] so runs the loving word
 of Christ. Trust God,
Bow your head to the yoke, submit to his gentle halter,[27]
 bend your shoulders meekly to his light burden.
This you can do while still your life is free, while no bonds
 hold, no care of marriage couch, nor prideful honor.
This is true liberty, to serve Christ, and in Him to be
 above all things. No lords of men,
No vices does he serve, no haughty kings,
 who gives himself alone to Christ the Lord.
Let not nobility of rank seem free to you, though now you
 see it borne aloft through the admiring city,
But see how, with its seeming freedom, it disdains to bend the
 neck before its God.*

---
26 Matt. 11.30.
27 Vergil, *Georg.* 3.188.

Wretched is he who is a slave to many men,[28] *and even to slaves, and buys himself handmaids that they may lord it over him.*
They who have suffered life in lofty palaces know the eunuchs, and any unfortunate who endures Rome knows at what price of toil and loss of honor this one attains rank in the army, that one high office of state.
But, he who gains power, who buys his way to eminence over all others, does not attain to such height as to be subject to none.
Though he rightly boasts of being master over the whole city, he is a slave to demons, if he adores idols.
What sorrow, if for the sake of such as these you dwell in the city, Licentius, and to please them you despise the Lord!
Do you recall those lords, and salute them with bowed head, whom you see to be slaves of wood and stone?
They honor gold and silver as gods, and what the malady of their greed loves, that is their religion.
Let him love such, I pray, who does not love Augustine;
 let him not worship Christ to whom these gods are dear.
Hence, God Himself has said: 'No man can serve two masters,'[29] *since one must be the mind that pleases Him!*[30]
 One faith, one God!
And Christ, the Father's only Son,
 No double allegiance can there be for one single Lord.
As far as heaven is from earth, so far
 the things of Caesar and his rule from Christ's.
Rise from the ground, and now, 'while breath still sways these limbs,'[31] *pierce the heavens with your thought; let flesh no barrier be.*

---

28 Horace, *Carm.* 1.24; an imitation, not a quotation.
29 Matt. 6.24; Luke 16.13.
30 Cf. Eph. 4.5; not an exact quotation.
31 Vergil, *Aen.* 4.336.

*Though you are now involved in carnal deeds, ponder with
   mind unclouded the joys of the heavenly life.
Though prisoned in the flesh, you are spirit, if with faithful
   heart you win the victory by destroying carnal works.
Impelled by faithful love, dear son, I write these things; if
   you are won by them, you will be loved by God.
Believe that now through me you hear Augustine; heeding
   me, you will find two fathers with a single love.
If we are scorned, the loss of you will be the greater for us
   both, if we are heeded, you shall be a precious pledge to
   both.
Both your fathers labor over you with anxious care; how
   great a prize for you to make us both rejoice!
I do not rate myself as one of equal worth with Augustine,
   but in our love for you alone I make myself his peer.
Shall I, a mere rivulet, bedew you with sparse drops?
   You have a twofold stream in which to plunge,
Alypius is your brother, and Augustine your teacher;
   one your friend in the flesh, one the planter of the
   garden of your soul.
Strong in the support of such a brother and such a master,
   Licentius, how can you not seek out the stars on tireless
   wings?
Whatever you may do—and let the world not hope for you
   as friend—your soul is owed to Christ, not to the earth.
Though you may aim at love and lofty honors,
   think rather how to make yourself your Lord's possession.
Two just men, I think, avail to win one sinner,
   and the prayers of brothers will prevail over your desires.
Return, then; hear your father's voice, your brother's love,
   both priests of God, who bid you turn to Him.
Seek out again what is your own, for that which you now seek
   is alien; these things, rather, which still have dominion
   over you, are truly yours.*

Turn to these, pant after them; you waste your time on useless aims; if what is yours is unpleasing to you, who will give you what is another's?

You will no longer be your own, and wandering afar in wilderness of sense, alas! you shall be an exile from your own heart.

This must suffice for an anxious father to address to his son, and you shall know that I wish and fear for you what I do for myself.

This page, if you receive it, will bring you life soon; if you refuse it, it shall be a witness against you.

May Christ preserve you safe for me, dearest son, and may He make you His servant forever.

Live, I pray you, but live for God. To live for the world is death; real life is to live for God.

33. Augustine to the honorable and well-beloved Proculeianus[1]

Because of the vanity of the unlettered, I should no longer discuss with you the salutation of my letter. As we are trying each to draw the other out of error, although without an open discussion of the case, it may not be clear to some which of us is in error; still, by dealing together in good faith, we do each other the service of freeing ourselves from the misfortune of discord. In any case, whether or not this is evident to the majority of men, He, before whom all hearts lie open, sees that I am acting with sincerity of heart and with due observance of Christian humility. You easily understand what it is that I am ready to honor in you. Naturally, I do not consider the error of schism worthy of honor, since I long to cure all men of it, as far as I can. But, without any shadow

---

[1] Donatist bishop of Hippo.

of doubt, I think you are worthy of honor: first, because you are bound to us by the very bond of human society; secondly, because there are in you clear signs of a peaceful mind, which support the hope that you will readily embrace the truth when it has been demonstrated to you. Indeed, I owe you as much love as He commanded us to have who loved us unto the ignominy of the Cross.

If you wonder why I have so long failed to address your Benevolence, it was because I did not believe that you were of that state of mind which brother Evodius[2]—and I am bound to believe him—joyfully announced to me. For, when it had happened that you had come together into a certain house, and your conversation turned upon our hope, that is, the inheritance of Christ, he said that your Benignity had expressed a wish to confer with us in the presence of other good men. I am very happy that you deign to offer this opportunity to our humility, and I could not possibly fail to make use of this occasion offered by your kindness. Therefore, as far as the Lord will give me strength, I will search out and discuss with you the cause, the origin, and the nature of the sad and lamentable division which has arisen in the Church of Christ, to which He said: 'My peace I give unto you, my peace I leave with you.'[3]

I heard, however, that you had complained of the above-mentioned brother, that he had given you an insulting answer. I beg of you not to attribute that to haughtiness, because I am quite sure it was not the result of pride—I know my brother. If, however, in the heat of discussion, he spoke perhaps too strongly, because of his faith and his love of the Church, and his words were offensive to your dignity, that is to be set down not to obstinacy but to loyalty. He wanted to

---
2 Cf. Letter 24 n. 16.
3 Cf. John 14.27.

compare and to discuss, not to agree and to flatter. This is the oil of the sinner with which the Prophet does not want his head to be anointed, as he says: 'The just man shall correct me in mercy and shall reprove me: but let not the oil of the sinner fatten my head.'[4] Thus, he prefers to be corrected by the severe mercy of the just rather than to be praised by the soothing unction of flattery. Whence, the Prophet said: 'They that call you blessed, the same deceive you.'[5] Therefore, of a man whom false flattery has made arrogant, the popular saying puts it rightly: 'He has a swelled head'; that is, his head has been fattened by the oil of the sinner, and this is not the effect of the harsh truth of correction but of the soothing deceit of praise. However, I do not want you to draw the conclusion that you are to be understood to be corrected by brother Evodius as by the just. I am afraid you may think I am saying something insulting to you, and that is what I am avoiding as far as I can. But He is just who said: 'I am the truth.'[6] Therefore, when the truth from any man's mouth sounds too harsh to us, we are not being corrected by that man, who may be a sinner, but by Truth itself, that is, by Christ, who is just. And this is to prevent the unction of sweet but fatal flattery—that is, the oil of the sinner—from fattening our head. Besides, even if brother Evodius was somewhat carried away by his defense of his Church, and spoke too emphatically in the heat of his feeling, you ought to make allowance for his age and for the urgency of his case.

However, I ask you to remember what you agreed to promise: that those whom you yourself chose should be seated, and that we should inquire peaceably into a matter so important and so closely connected with the salvation of all;

---
4 Ps. 140.5.
5 Isa. 5.12.
6 John 14.6.

provided that our words should not be wasted on the air, but be taken down in writing, and that we carry on our discussion calmly and in due order; and if anything said by us slipped from memory, it should be recalled by reading from our notes. However, if you prefer to carry on the discussion by letters, without intermediary, or by private conference, or, if you like, by reading—and this might be better, because impulsive hearers might be more interested in looking for a quarrel between us than in thinking of their own salvation during our conference—then, when we have reached a conclusion, let the people hear of it from us afterward. Or, if we have agreed to communicate by letters, let them be read to our peoples, so that at some future time we may say not peoples, but people. Finally, I readily agree to whatever you wish, whatever you command, whatever pleases you. And on the part of my blessed and venerable father, Valerius[7], now absent, I promise, with all certainty, that he will hear of this with great joy, for I know how much he loves peace, and how far he is from being swayed by any empty vanity or personal dignity.

I ask you: What have we to do with those old quarrels, that the wounds, which the antagonism of proud men has inflicted on our members, should have lasted so long? By the putrefying of those wounds we have lost the feeling of pain, which ordinarily makes one call in a doctor. You see with what great and what wretched foulness the families of the Christian home are defiled. Husbands and wives agree about their bed and disagree about the altar of Christ. They swear by Him in order to have mutual peace, but they cannot have it in Him. Sons share one home with their parents, but they do not share the same house of God. They wish to receive the inheritance of those with whom they quarrel about

---

7 Bishop of Hippo.

the inheritance of Christ; slave and master tear asunder the common God who 'took the form of a servant'[8] that He might free us all from slavery. Yours honor us, ours honor you; yours swear to us by our crown, ours swear to you by yours. We take the word of everyone, we wish to offend none, but what injury has Christ done us that we tear His members apart? Men, wishing to advance their worldly aims through us —as far as we are useful to them—call us saints indeed and servants of God, so as to further the interest of their own land; let us, then, work at the business of their salvation and of our own. We are daily greeted by men with suppliant heads, begging us to settle their quarrels, but the disgraceful and dangerous division between us is not a question of gold or silver, or of lands and flocks; it is a dispute about our very Head. Those who salute us may bow their heads as low as they will, begging us to reconcile them on earth, but our Head has bowed down from Heaven to the Cross, and we are not reconciled in Him.

I beg and beseech you, if there is any of that human feeling in you which many extol, that your goodness—if it is not assumed for the sake of passing honors—may be manifest here and that your innermost being may be moved to compassion. May you wish this matter to be treated by persevering in prayer with us, and by discussing all of it peaceably, lest our wretched flocks, which pay homage to our position, may overwhelm us with that homage in the day of God's judgment. By our unfeigned charity may they be recalled from error and dissension to the way of truth and peace. I pray that you may be blessed in the sight of God, honored and beloved lord.

---

8 Phil. 2.7.

34. Augustine to his brother, Eusebius,[1] excellent lord and honorable brother, worthy of admiration

God, to whom the secrets of the human heart lie open, knows that, much as I desire Christian peace, I am deeply moved by the sacrilegious deeds of those who unworthily and impiously persist in separation from Him. And He knows that this disturbance of my mind is peaceful, and that I do not intend that anyone should be forced into the Catholic communion against his will. On the contrary, it is my aim that the truth may be revealed to all who are in error, and that, through our ministry, with the help of God, it may be made manifest so as to induce all to follow and embrace it of their own accord.

To pass over other things, what, I ask you, could be more detestable than what has now happened? An insane youth is corrected by his bishop for having frequently beaten his mother, and for having laid his impious hands on her, even on those days when the strictness of the laws forbears to punish even wicked criminals, thinking thus to recall to him that he was born of her. Thereupon, he threatens this same mother with his intention of going over to the Donatist sect, and says that he will kill her, whom he is accustomed to beat with such unbelievable fury. He threatens her; he goes over to the Donatist sect; in his wrath, he is rebaptized; raging against his mother's life, he is clothed in a white garment;[2] he is admitted within the sanctuary[3] as a prominent and noteworthy person; to the grief of all, although he is known as a

---

[1] A Donatist bishop, apparently one superior in the hierarchy to Proculeianus (of Letter 33).
[2] Worn by the newly baptized.
[3] In early churches, the sanctuary was separated from the nave by a lattice or grille.

man who intends to murder his mother, he is displayed as if he were newly cleansed by baptism.

Can you approve of this, eminent sir? I should be most unwilling to believe it of you, for I know your point of view. A mother in the flesh is beaten in that very body from which she bore and nourished her ungrateful son. The Church, our spiritual mother, forbids this, and she, also, is struck in the sacraments by which she bore and nourished this ungrateful son. Does he not seem to you to have said in his matricidal raving: 'What shall I do to the Church which forbids me to strike my mother? I have found something to do. Let her be struck by all the injuries I can inflict on her; let there be in me something to make her members suffer; let me go to those who know how to blow away the grace in which I was born in her, to destroy the form which I received in her womb; let me torture both my mothers with cruel torments. May the second one who bore me be the first to cast me out; may I die spiritually to cause her sorrow, so long as I live carnally to bring death to my first mother.' What else can we look for, honorable Eusebius, but his being armed securely as a Donatist, against a poor woman, worn down by age, bereft by widowhood, whom as a Catholic he is forbidden to strike? What other intention did he have in his raging heart when he said to his mother: 'I will go over to the Donatists and I will drink your blood?' Look how he has fulfilled the first part of his promise, bloody in conscience, spotless in his robes; the second part remains—to drink his mother's blood. If this is acceptable to you, let him be encouraged by the clerics, his sanctifiers, to pay the whole of the vow he had made, within his octave.[4]

Indeed, the right hand of the Lord is powerful enough to ward off that boy's fury from the poor, desolate widow, and

---

4 The newly baptized wore their white baptismal robes for eight days.

in His own ways to prevent him from committing such an accursed act. But I, pierced with such grief as I am, what can I do except speak? Or do they do such things and then say to me: 'Be silent?' May the Lord preserve me from such cowardice that I should hold my peace through fear of their wrath, when He commands me through His Apostle, saying that 'they ought to be reproved' by the bishop for 'teaching the things which they ought not.'[5] The reason I wanted this wicked sacrilege to be preserved in the public records is that I did not wish anyone to imagine that in deploring these excesses I was only playing a part—as they might do, especially in those towns where it would be advantageous, and this more likely since in Hippo itself it is now being said that Proculeianus had not sanctioned this, as he had given up his public office.

Could we, then, do anything more moderate than to take up so serious a case with you, a man endowed with most evident dignity, a peaceful man, of recognized fairmindedness? I ask, then, as I have asked through our brothers, good and honorable men, whom I have sent to your Excellency, that you would agree to inquire whether Victor, a priest of Proculeianus, did or did not receive this mandate from his bishop, as he claimed in the published report, or whether, perhaps, when Victor had said one thing, they set it down falsely in the records, since they are of the same communion with him. On the other hand, if he agrees to treat of the whole question of our dissension peaceably, so that the error which is now evident may become more evident, I willingly agree to that. For I heard the suggestion he made, that, without public disturbance, there should be with us ten men of influence and honor from each side, and that with them we should search out in the Scriptures what is true. As to that

---
5 Titus 1.11.

other report which some brought to me, that he had asked why I did not go to Constantina,[6] since they were in the majority there, or that he said that I ought to go to Milevis,[7] because they were about to hold a council there—so they say—it is nonsense to make such claims on me, because I have no other authority than that over the church at Hippo. The whole burden of this controversy is between me and Proculeianus. However, if he feels himself at a disadvantage, let him ask the help of any colleague he wishes. In other cities, we go as far, in Church matters, as our brothers and fellow priests, the bishops of those same cities, permit or induce us to go.

In any case, I do not quite understand why he, who claims to be a bishop for so many years, should be afraid of me, a raw recruit, or why he should shrink from an argument with me. Perhaps he fears my knowledge of literature, which he may not have studied himself, or at least not deeply; but what has that to do with this controversy, which has to be based on Sacred Scriptures, or on ecclesiastical or public records, in which he is better versed than I? Finally, I have a brother and colleague, named Samsucius, Bishop of Turris,[8] who has no such literary skill, as this one is said to fear; let him appear and treat with him; I will ask him, and I trust in the name of Christ that he will readily do me this favor of undertaking this discussion in my stead. The Lord will help him, I trust, in his contest for the truth, for, although he is crude of speech, he is well-grounded in the true faith. There is no reason, then, why he [Proculeianus] should push this question off on to other obscure individuals, when it should be taken up by us whose concern it is. Still, as I said, I do not even object to that sort of person, if he asks their help.

---

6 Also known as Cirta, a city in Numidia.
7 Another city in Numidia.
8 Turris Tamalleni, in southern Numidia.

35. Augustine to his excellent and beloved brother,[1] truly worthy of consideration.

Not in a spirit of unwanted encouragement or interference have I imposed on your reluctant will, as you say, a settlement to be agreed on between bishops. Indeed, even if I had wished to suggest that, I could have shown easily, perhaps, how well you yourself are able to judge between us in a case so clear and evident, and what sort of thing you do, in your avoidance of a settlement, when you do not shrink from rendering a one-sided verdict, without hearing both sides. I had asked nothing else of your honorable Benignity —and I should like you kindly to note this, especially in this letter—but that you ask Proculeianus whether he said to his priest, Victor, what the official account reported that he said, or whether, perchance, those who were sent to report forwarded what was wrongly set down in the records, not what they heard from Victor. Ask him, also, what he thinks about discussing this whole question between us two. However, I think a man does not become a judge by being asked to question someone, and by consenting to write down the answer he receives. If he had been willing to do that, I should certainly not be taking it up now with your Excellency. But, since he does not wish to do it, and since the responsibility of my position will not allow me to pass it over in silence, what more moderate action could I take than to have this questioning done by a man like you, and a friend of his besides? Your Gravity is displeased by the story of the mother being beaten by her son, but you say: 'If he [Proculeianus] knew it, he would expel such a wicked youth from his communion.' I answer briefly: 'He knows it now; let him expel him now.'

---

[1] The Donatist bishop, Eusebius, addressed in Letter 34.

I have another point. A subdeacon named Primus, formerly of the Spanish church, who had been forbidden communication with the nuns because of his undisciplined behavior, and who had disregarded this wise command and precept, was dismissed from the clergy. In his anger against the discipline of God he went over to them [the Donatists] and was rebaptized. Moreover, two of these nuns, fellow countrymen of his, who had lived on the estate of the Catholic Christians, were either taken over with him or followed him of their own accord, and they were also rebaptized. He is now boldly rushing around with bands of Circumcellions,[2] in the midst of vagabond crowds of women, who shamelessly refuse to have husbands so as not to be subject to them, and in his orgies of revolting drunkenness, he rejoiced at the unlimited license of immoral behavior now open to him, which was forbidden to him in the Catholic Church. Perhaps Proculeianus does not know of this letter. Let it be brought to his notice, therefore, by your gravity and modesty, and let him order the youth to be expelled from the communion which he chose for no other reason than that he had lost his clerical standing through his insubordination and immorality.

I myself, if it pleases the Lord, follow this course of action; when anyone of theirs, unfrocked for reasons of discipline, wishes to come into the Catholic Church, he is received as a lowly penitent, a state they would probably have forced him to assume if he had wished to remain with them. In view of these facts, I beg you to reflect what an accursed thing it is that immoral men whom we have disciplined with ecclesiastical punishment should be induced to go to another baptismal font, and, in order to receive baptism again, should answer that they are pagans. How many martyrs shed their blood

---

2 Cf. Letter 23 n. 13.

sooner than let such words come from a Christian mouth! Then these men, as if cleansed and sanctified, but in reality debased by the sacrilege of a new fury under the appearance of a new grace, mock at the discipline which they were not able to bear. However, if I am wrong in trying to have these abuses corrected by your Benevolence, no one can blame me if I have them brought to public notice in the public records —a privilege which cannot be refused to me, I think, in a city which enjoys Roman citizenship. For, when God commands that we speak and preach the word, and that we refute and condemn 'in season and out of season'³ those who 'teach the things which they ought not'⁴—as I can prove by the words of the Lord and the Apostles—let no man think that I can be enjoined to silence in these matters. Whatever bold acts of violence or brigandage they may think up, the Lord will not fail to protect His Church, since He has made all earthly kingdoms subject to His yoke, including all in His worldwide embrace.

There was the case of a certain farmer of our Church, whose daughter had been a catechumen of ours, but who was led astray by them,⁵ and, without her parents' consent, was baptized in their sect and even received the habit of a nun. Her father wanted to bring her back to the Catholic communion by severe measures, but I would not allow her to be received—a woman whose mind had been deceived—unless she willingly and freely chose the better course of her own accord. Thereupon, the farmer began to insist with blows that his daughter obey him, which I at once forbade absolutely. On the other hand, as we were passing through Spania,⁶ one of his priests, standing on the property of an estimable Catho-

---
3 2 Tim. 4.2.
4 Titus 1.11.
5 The Donatists; Augustine is quite unwilling to name them.
6 Probably a suburb of Hippo.

lic lady, called after us in a most insulting tone that we were traitors and persecutors, and he even hurled his insults at the lady—a member of our communion—on whose property he was standing. Hearing his words, I not only refrained from any personal retort, but I restrained the large group of persons who were with me. Yet, if I were to say: 'Let us see who are or were traitors or persecutors,' I would get this answer: 'We do not wish to enter into any controversy and we do wish to rebaptize; let us prey upon the sheep of your flock with the treacherous fangs of wolves, but you, if you are good shepherds, keep silence.' And what else did Proculeianus command, if he was really the one who did command? If you are a Christian, leave this to the judgment of God, and if we do not do it, you keep silent. But that same priest even dared to threaten the farmer, who was the steward of the estate of the church.

I ask you to let Proculeianus know all these things from you; let him restrain the mad excesses of his clerics, about which, honorable Eusebius, I have not left you uninformed. And you will be so kind as to write me in answer, not what you think of all this—for I would not have you suppose that I am imposing on you the burden of judging—but what answer they make. May the mercy of God keep you safe, excellent lord, truly estimable and beloved brother.

36. Augustine gives greeting in the Lord to Casulanus,[1] his brother and fellow priest, beloved and most desired (396 or early 397)

I do not know how it has happened that I have not answered your first letter; I know I did not do so through any

---
1 A priest of Augustine's diocese.

lack of consideration for you, for I take delight in your scholarly pursuits and even in your conversation, and I pray for you and urge you in this time of your youth to make progress in the word of God, and to bring forth abundant fruit for the edification of the Church. And now I have received your second letter, in which you beg me by the fraternal and most just bond of the charity in which we are one that I would finally write to you sometime. So I have decided that the longing desire of your love is not to be put off any longer, and, involved as I am in the most exacting duties, I have undertaken to acquit myself of my debt to you.

In the first place, you ask me whether it is allowable to fast on Saturday, and I answer that, if it were not allowable, then certainly neither Moses nor Elias nor the Lord Himself would have fasted for forty successive days. Of course, it can be concluded from that argument that it is not unlawful to fast even on Sunday. Yet, if anyone were to think that this day should be set aside for fasting, as some observe Saturday as a day of fasting, he would cause no small scandal to the Church, and not without reason. In these matters, about which the Divine Scriptures have made no definite pronouncement, the custom of the people of God and the traditions of our forefathers are to be held as law. If we should wish to start an argument about this, and to reprove others who act according to their own custom, there would arise an endless contest, which might indeed, with labored speech, show that no trustworthy documents of truth exist, but it would still be necessary to guard against allowing the clear sky of charity to be overcast by the storm of controversy. The man whose treatise you thought fit to send me, so that I could answer it, together with your previous letter, was not careful to avoid that danger.

I have not enough time at my disposal to spend on refuting every one of his opinions, because I need my time for developing some very important works. But do you yourself, with that keenness of mind which you display in your letters to me, and which I love in you as a gift of God, examine carefully the treatise of that certain Urbicus,[2] as you term him, and you will see that he has not feared to wound with most abusive words the Church of Christ, which is almost universal from the rising to the setting of the sun. I should not have said 'almost universal,' but simply 'universal.' For, it turns out that he has not spared even the Romans, whose custom he seems to defend, but he does not know, because he does not notice, how the flood of his reproaches pours out over them, also. When arguments fail him, with which to prove that one ought to fast on Saturday, he launches out into abusive attacks on the luxury of banquets, and drunken feasts, and detestable intoxication, as if not fasting were the same thing as being drunk. But, if this is why it is advantageous to the Romans to fast on Saturday, what about the days on which they do not fast; are they, according to his argument, to be judged drunkards and gluttons? Moreover, if it is one thing to weigh down one's conscience with tippling and drinking, which is always wrong, it is quite another thing to relax one's fast, with all due observance of moderation and temperance, something which no Christian will condemn, when it happens on the Lord's day. Let him, then, distinguish the modest meals of the saints from the greediness and wine-drinking of gluttons—otherwise, he makes the Romans out to be gluttons on the days when they do not fast—and let him inquire, not whether it is lawful to be drunk on Saturday, which is not permissible on Sunday

---

[2] A pseudonym, as the writer indicates later when he supposes that Casulanus had withheld the real name for motives of charity.

either, but whether it is proper to fast on Saturday, as it is not customary to do on Sunday.

I wish that he would so inquire, and so state as not so openly to slander the Church spread over the whole world—always excepting the Romans, and a few, as yet, westerners. Among all the eastern and even many western Christian peoples, no one should tolerate his saying of so many and such great servants of Christ, men and women, dining frugally and moderately on Saturday, that 'they are in the flesh and cannot please God';[3] and that it is written of them: 'Depart from me, you that work iniquity';[4] I do not wish to know their way; and that they are gluttons preferring Jewry to the Church; and as sons of the handmaid[5] they are devoted to their appetite by an unjust and voluptuous law, rebellious to discipline; and that they are flesh and they savor death; and other things of this sort. If he said such things about a single servant of God, no one, surely, should listen to him and everyone should avoid him. But when, indeed, with his insults and calumnies, he attacks the Church which is bearing fruit and increasing throughout the world, and which almost everywhere dines on Saturday, I warn him, whoever he is, to restrain himself. I suppose you have not wanted me to know his name, so that I might not judge harshly of him.

'The son of man,' he said, 'is lord of the sabbath,'[6] on which it is much more lawful to do good than to do evil. If, therefore,' we do evil when we dine, then we do not live well on any Sunday. When he admits that the Apostles ate on the sabbath and says that it was not then the time to fast, according to the

---
3 Rom. 8.8.
4 Gal. 4.23.
5 A reference to Ishmael, son of Agar the bondwoman of Abraham: 'Cast out the bondwoman and her son.' Cf. Gen. 21.10.
6 Matt. 12.8; 12.12.

Lord's words, 'The days will come when the bridegroom shall be taken away from them, and then the children of the bridegroom shall fast'[7] because there is a time of joy and a time of mourning,[8] he should first have noticed that the Lord is there speaking of fasting, not of fasting on the sabbath. In the second place, when he wishes it to be understood that mourning is to be considered as fasting, and joy as food, why does he not reflect that what God meant by what is written of Him—'On the seventh day He rested from all His works'[9]—was not mourning, but joy? Perhaps he would like to say that the repose of God and sanctifying the sabbath meant joy to the Jews, but mourning to the Christians. Yet, when God sanctified the seventh day, because on it He rested from all His works, He did not mention fasting or eating on that day of the sabbath; nor, when He afterwards enjoined its observance on the Hebrew people, did He say anything about taking or not taking food. Abstinence is only enjoined on man from his own or from servile works, a law which the former people receiving as 'a shadow of things to come,'[10] abstained from work as we now see the Jews do, but not, as it is thought, because the carnal Jews do not rightly understand what Christians understand. Certainly, we do not understand these things better than the Prophets did, who at that time, as was then fitting, observed the sabbath rest, which the Jews think is still to be observed. Hence that instance of God's commanding a man to be stoned for gathering wood on the sabbath;[11] but nowhere do we read of anyone being stoned or judged worthy of any punishment for either fasting or dining on the sabbath. Which of these two conduces to rest

---

7 Matt. 9.15.
8 Cf. Eccle. 3.4.
9 Gen. 2.2.
10 Col. 2.17.
11 Num. 15.35.

and which to labor, let him decide who attributes joy to those who eat and mourning to those who fast—or who thinks that the Lord so attributes, when, making a reply about fasting, He says: 'The children of the bridegroom cannot mourn as long as the bridegroom is with them.'[12]

As to what he says about the Apostles eating on the sabbath because it was not yet time to fast on the sabbath, because the tradition of the ancients obviously forbade, was there then ever a time when they were not to rest on the sabbath? Could it be that this tradition of the ancients both forbade and obliged them to rest? However, on that very sabbath day on which we read that the disciples ate,[13] they likewise plucked ears of wheat which was not lawful on the sabbath, because the tradition of the ancients forbade. Let him see, then, whether a more consistent answer to his objection might be that the Lord wishes both these things to be done by His disciples on that day—plucking wheat and taking food—so that the former might be an argument against those who demanded an absolute sabbath rest, the latter against those who require fasting on the sabbath. With a change of time, He indicated that the former practice had now become too scrupulous an exaction, but the latter He wished to be free at both times.[14] I shall not develop this argument, but I will show him how much more fittingly we can make a rebuttal than he made his objection.

'How,' he says, 'shall we not be condemned with the Pharisee for fasting twice in the week?'[15]—as if the Pharisee

---

12 Cf. Matt. 9.15.
13 Matt. 12.1.
14 Under the Old and the New Law.
15 Luke 18.11. It is to be noted that the word *sabbatum* is used in this Letter with three meanings: the Jewish sabbath or seventh day; the Christian sabbath or first day; and the week of seven days. The days of the week were not known, in the time of Augustine, by the names we now give them. Sunday was *Dies Dominica* or *Dominicus* (Augustine prefers the masculine); Monday, Tuesday, Wednesday,

was condemned because he fasted twice in the week, and not because he puffed himself up and preferred himself to the publican. He can even say that those who give tithes of all their goods to the poor are condemned with the Pharisee, because the latter detailed that, also, among his good works—something we wish we could find among many Christians, but find among very few. Or he might say that the unjust, the adulterer, the extortioner will not be condemned with the Pharisee, because he boasted of not being that sort—and anyone who thinks that is foolish. Moreover, if these unquestioned virtues which the Pharisee listed as his are not to be found with prideful boasting, such as he displayed, but are to be found associated with humble piety, such as he did not have, then to fast twice a week is without merit in a man like that Pharisee, but in a man of humble faith and faithful humility it is an act of devotion. In any case, the Gospel does not say that the Pharisee was condemned, but that the publican was justified rather than he.

But, if that one thinks we must understand the Lord's words, 'Unless your justice abound more than that of the scribes and pharisees, you shall not enter into the kingdom of heaven,'[16] to mean that, unless we fast twice in the week, we cannot fulfill His commandments, then it is a good thing that there are seven days, which, as they roll on, come back on their own traces. Therefore, if anyone subtracts two from these, so as not to fast on Saturday and Sunday, there remain five days out of which he can surpass the Pharisee who fasted twice a week. I suppose that if anyone fasts three times a week, he surpasses the Pharisee who fasted twice a week. But, if he fasts four or even five times a week, so as to leave

---

Thursday, and Friday were, respectively, *Feria secunda, tertia, quarta, quinta, sexta;* Saturday was *sabbatum.* In translating, the modern names have been used.
16 Matt. 15.20.

out no days except Saturday and Sunday, as many do all their lives, especially those in monastic communities, then not only is the Pharisee surpassed by them in the practice of fasting, since he fasted twice a week, but even by the ordinary Christian, who has been accustomed to fast on Wednesday and Friday, as well as on Saturday, as the people commonly do at Rome. Yet, if anyone fasts on five successive days, except Saturday and Sunday, and never wholly satisfies his appetite, that somebody of yours, that city arguer, as you call him, says that such a one is carnal, as if food and drink had no relation to the body on other days, and he judges him to be a glutton, as if Saturday's meal were the only one that went down his throat.

He is not satisfied with what suffices to surpass the Pharisee, namely, that one fast three times a week, but he demands fasting on six successive days, except Sunday, saying: 'Since the original stain[17] has been removed, two in one flesh[18] living under the discipline of Christ ought not to share luxurious sabbath banquets with those outside the law, and with the rulers of Sodom[19] and with the people of Gomorrha, but in company with those who dwell in monasteries, and with those vowed to God by a solemn ecclesiastical bond, they ought to fast with increasing regard for the law. Thus, the slight sins of six days may be washed away by the waters of fasting, prayer, and almsgiving, and so we shall be refreshed by a Sunday meal, and shall be worthy to sing with unburdened heart: "Thou, O Lord, hast filled the empty soul"[20] and hast given the thirsty soul to drink.' Saying things like this, and excepting only Sunday from the frequency of fasting, he rashly and

---
17 The stain of Original Sin.
18 He probably means the indwelling of the Holy Spirit in the baptized soul.
19 Isa. 1.10.
20 Cf. Ps. 106.9.

boldly accuses not only the Christian peoples of east and west, when he says that 'those living under the discipline of Christ ought not to share luxurious sabbath banquets with those outside the law, and with the rulers of Sodom and with the people of Gomorrha, but in company with those who dwell in monasteries, and with those vowed to God by a solemn and ecclesiastical bond, they ought to fast with increasing regard for the law,' and then, defining and developing what he means by regard for the law in fasting, he says: 'Thus, the slight sins of six days may be washed away by the waters of fasting, prayer, and almsgiving.' No doubt, he thinks that those who fast less than six days in the week do not practice fasting according to the law, or that they are not vowed to God, or that they do not wash away the stains of sin which are a consequence of our mortality. Let the Romans, then, see what they are doing, since they are treated so harshly by this one's argument, for how few are found among them, except a very few clerics and monks, who practice this daily fasting six days a week. Besides, they do not observe the custom of fasting on Friday.

In the next place, I ask this: if the slight sin of any one day is blotted out or washed away by the fast of that day—for so he says: 'the slight sins of six days are washed away by the waters of fasting'—what shall we do about the sin which slips in on Sunday, on which it is a scandal to fast? Or if on that day no sin creeps in on a Christian, look you how that man, that great faster, who accuses other men of being gluttons, does honor to the stomach, if men commit no sin on days when they dine. Or perhaps the fast of Saturday has such great merit that it alone—this Saturday fasting—can wipe out the sin, however slight, as he says, of the other six days, including Sunday; and that the only day on which one does not sin is the one on which he fasts completely?

What reason is there, then, for preferring the first day to the seventh in the Christian dispensation? Behold, according to him, the sabbath day is found to be much more holy, since one commits no sin on it if one fasts all through it, and by the same fast the sins of the other six days, and even of Sunday, are blotted out. I imagine this conclusion does not meet your approval.

But, now that he wishes to seem a spiritual man and accuses those who dine on Saturday of being carnal-minded, take note that he is not refreshed on Sunday by a modest meal, but he indulges in a banquet or *alogia*. For what else is an *alogia*, a word taken from the Greek, but a real banquet, not confined by the restraints of reason? Hence, animals, bereft of reason, are called *aloga*—irrational or dumb—and those who are slaves of the appetite are said to be like them. Therefore, an immoderate meal, in which the mind, supposed to ruled by reason, is, so to speak, deadened by excess of eating and drinking, is called an *alogia*. Moreover, it is not the food and drink of the mind, but of the gullet, which is said to be the reason for singing at the Sunday *alogia*: 'Thou, O Lord, hast filled the empty soul and hast given the thirsty soul to drink.' Oh spiritual man! Oh valiant faster! Oh reprehender of the carnal-minded, but no glutton yourself! Look who warns us not to break the law of the Lord by indulging our appetite, lest we sell the bread of heaven for earthly food! He even adds that, because of food, Adam lost paradise[21] and Esau his birthright![22] And look who says: 'The temptation of hunger is a common deceit of Satan; he tempts his victim to a little in order to make him take too much.' And he adds: 'The explanation of these principles has little effect on gluttons.'

---

21 Gen. 2.17; 3.1-6.
22 Gen. 25.29-35.

Does he not seem, by these words, to be urging us to fast on Sunday? Otherwise, the sabbath day, on which the Lord rested in the tomb, would be more sacred than the Sunday on which He rose from the dead. Certainly, according to him, Saturday is a holier day, if all sin is avoided by fasting, and if the sin contracted on the other days is thereby blotted out; whereas, on Sunday, the temptation of greediness is associated with eating, and paradise is lost and one's birthright sold. But, why does he then contradict himself by inviting us, not to refresh ourselves with a modest, simple meal on the Christian Sunday, but to yield to the pleasures of an *alogia*, praising ourselves and singing: 'Thou, O Lord, hast filled the empty soul and hast given the thirsty soul to drink'? If we do not sin on days when we fast, and if we even wash away the faults of six days when we fast on Saturday, then, obviously, no day is worse than Sunday and no day better than Saturday. Believe, dearest brother, that no one understands the law as he does, except one who does not understand it at all. It was not food that caused Adam's fall, but forbidden food; it was not food that ruined Esau, nephew of holy Abraham, but food coveted at the price of despising the mystery of his own primogeniture. Likewise, good and faithful souls may dine religiously and sacrilegious and unbelieving ones may fast wickedly. Sunday is preferred to Saturday, because of our belief in the Resurrection, not because we are accustomed to take food, or to let ourselves go in bibulous song.

'Moses,' says he, 'neither ate bread nor drank water for forty days.'[23] And he adds something to explain why he said this. 'See how Moses, friend of God, dweller in a cloud, communicator of the law and leader of the people, by continuing his fast for thrice two sabbaths gained merit, not blame.'

---
23 Exod. 24.18.

But, does he notice what objective can be made in consequence of his statement? Certainly, if, in proposing the example of the fast of Moses, he wishes to advocate fasting on Saturday, because in those forty days, as he says, there were thrice two sabbaths, then one can equally well argue for fasting on Sunday, because in those forty days Moses likewise fasted thrice two Sundays. He goes on to say: 'But up to that time, Sunday was being saved by God for the Church which was to come with Christ.' I do not know why he says that. If he means that there is greater reason for fasting after Sunday came in with Christ, and therefore we should fast on Sunday, far be it from us to do that! But, if he feared by his use of the forty-day fast to have a rebuttal made that fasting on Sunday is thereby approved, and if that is why he added that 'up to that time, Sunday was being saved for the Church which was to come with Christ,' so that Moses might be understood to have fasted on the day which follows the sabbath, because Christ had not yet come —and with Him came the Sunday on which it is not proper to fast—then why did Christ Himself likewise fast forty days? Why did He not on those thrice two days which followed the sabbath give up His fast, so as to commend dining on Sunday even before His Resurrection, just as He gave His Blood to drink before His passion? Surely, you see that this forty-day fast which that one brings up has nothing to do with the question of fasting on Saturday, just as it has nothing to do with fasting on Sunday.

Moreover, he does not realize what objection can be made to him about Sunday when he uses the same abusive terms against dining on Saturday as could be used against drunken banquets and every sort of greedy and bibulous extravagance, although Saturday meals can be both modest and restrained. Therefore, there is not much use in answering him point by point, since his criticisms do not distinguish between dining on Saturday and the vice of gluttony, and since he keeps saying the same thing over and over, using the same futile and irrelevant arguments. The question is whether one should not fast on Saturday, not whether one should not commit gluttony on Saturday, an action which those who fear God do not perform on Sunday either, although they certainly do not fast on that day. Who would say what he dares to say? 'How' he says, 'can those practices be sanctioned for us or through us, or how can they be worthy of God, which on a holy day lead us into sin?' He confesses that Saturday is a holy day and he says that men are led into sin because they dine. That means, according to him, that either Sunday is not a holy day, and that makes Saturday a better day, or, if Sunday is a holy day, we are led into sin because we dine.

And he tries to prove by divine authority that we should fast on Saturday, but he does not find any text to prove it. 'Jacob,' he says, 'ate and drank wine and was satisfied, and withdrew from God his salvation, and there fell in one day, twenty-three thousand'[24]—as if it were said: 'Jacob dined on the sabbath and withdrew from God his salvation.' When the Apostle related how many thousand fell, he did not say: 'Let us not dine on the sabbath as they dined,' but he said: 'Neither let us commit fornication, as some of them committed fornication, and there fell in one day three and twenty thousand.'[25] What does he mean when he says: 'The people sat down to eat and drink and rose up to play'?[26] Certainly the Apostle used this text to draw people from serving idols, not from eating on Saturday. This one does not prove that

---

24 A badly garbled misreading of 1 Cor. 10.8.
25 1 Cor. 10.8. Augustine confronts Urbicus with the correct text.
26 Exod. 32.6; 1 Cor. 10.7.

this was done on Saturday, but, following his fancy, he suspects it. Indeed, it can happen that a man fasts, and, when the fast is over, if he is a drinker, he may drink to excess, just as it can similarly happen that someone would not fast, and, if he is a temperate man, he may dine moderately. There is no point, either, in his trying to prove the validity of the Saturday fast by adducing the words of the Apostle: 'And be not drunk with wine, wherein is luxury,'[27] as if he were saying: 'Do not dine on the Sabbath, wherein is all luxury.' But, just as this command of the Apostle, not to be drunk with wine, in which is all luxury, is observed by God-fearing Christians when they dine on Sunday, so it is observed when they dine on Saturday.

'That I may more emphatically controvert those who are in error,' says he, 'no one will offend God by fasting, even if he does not gain merit thereby, since not to offend is to gain merit.' No one who thought what he was saying would make a statement of this kind. Then, when pagans fast, they do not thereby offend God the more; or, if he wishes what he said to be understood of Christians, who would not offend God if he insisted on fasting on Sunday to the scandal of the universal Church? He then adds some proofs from Scripture, of no use to the cause which he is defending. 'It was by fasting,' he says, 'that Elias was rewarded with paradise, and that he reigns while still in the flesh'[28]—as if those who do not fast on Saturday will not preach fasting, just as those who do not fast on Sunday do preach fasting; or else, that Elias fasted at that time when the people of God used to fast even on Saturday. What we answered regarding the forty days' fast of Moses, I think should be offered as rebuttal concerning the forty days' fast of Elias. 'It was by fasting,' he says,

---

27 Eph. 5.18.
28 3 Kings 19.8; 4 Kings 2.11.

'that Daniel escaped unscathed and dry-eyed from the rage of the lions'[29]—as if he read this passage to mean that he fasted on Saturday, or even that he was with the lions on Saturday; when we read, that, as a matter of fact, he did dine. 'It was by fasting,' he says, 'that the three faithful brothers overcame the flames of their fiery prison, and adored the Lord whom they welcomed to the hospitality of their pyre.'[30] These examples of the saints have no validity in proving the worth of fasting on any day at all, much less on Saturday. Not only do we not read that the three men were cast into the fiery furnace on Saturday, but we do not even read that they were there long enough so that we could say that they fasted. On the contrary, it took hardly an hour for them to sing their hymn of praise, and they did not walk among the harmless flames after they had finished their song. Perhaps that one thinks an hour is enough to call a fast. In that case, he has no quarrel with those who dine on Saturday, since there is a much longer space of foodlessness up to the time of dinner than that which elasped in the fiery furnace.

He adds this other testimony of the Apostle, where he says: 'For the kingdom of God is not meat and drink, but justice and peace and joy in the Holy Ghost'[31]—and by the kingdom of God he means the Church in which God reigns. Now, I ask you, when the Apostle said that, was he making any reference to Christians fasting on Saturday? He was not speaking of fasting on any day at all when he said it. It was said against those who followed the custom of the Jews in the Old Law by believing that there was cleanness in certain foods, and he was warning these brethren not to scandalize the weak by failing to make this distinction in their food and

---
29 Dan. 6.16-23.
30 Dan. 3.23-93.
31 Rom. 14.17.

drink. Therefore, when he said: 'Destroy him not with thy meat, for whom Christ died' and 'Let not then our good be evil spoken of,' he then added: 'The kingdom of God is not meat and drink,' and so forth. For, if he understands these words of the Apostle to mean that the kingdom of God, which is the Church, is not in eating and drinking but in fasting, then we ought not merely to fast on Saturday, but we should never take food at all, if we do not wish to be shut out from the kingdom of God. But, I imagine that, on his admission, we do belong somewhat religiously to the Church on Sundays even when, by his permission, we dine.

'Why,' he says, 'do we grumble at offering to a more powerful Lord a precious sacrifice, which the spirit desires and the angel praises?' Then he adds the testimony of the angel,[32] when he said: 'Prayer is good, with fasting and alms.'[33] Why he said: 'to a more powerful Lord,' I have no idea, unless, perhaps, the scribe made a mistake which escaped your notice, and you did not correct what you sent me to read. Therefore, by a sacrifice precious to the Lord, he intends us to understand fasting, as if this argument were about fasting and not about fasting on Saturday. Certainly, Sunday is not passed without a sacrifice which is precious to the Lord, but it is not the sacrifice of fasting. He goes on further and piles up testimony for the case which he has undertaken to defend—thoroughly irrelevant testimony. 'Offer to God,' he says, 'the sacrifice of praise,'[34] and trying, somehow or other, to connect that expression of the divine psalm to the argument he is building up, he continues: 'Assuredly it is not the banquet of blood and drunkenness, in which no praise is paid to God, but blasphemies run wild, with the

---
32 Raphael.
33 Tob. 12.8.
34 Ps. 49.14.

assistance of the devil.' O unimaginable presumption! Then, the sacrifice of praise is not offered to God on Sunday, because there is no fasting that day, but a 'banquet of drunkenness' is celebrated and 'blasphemies run wild, with the assistance of the devil.' If that is wrong to say, let him understand that fasting is not what is meant by the words, 'Offer to God a sacrifice of praise.' Indeed, on certain days, and especially on feast days, fasting is not practised, but on all days the sacrifice of praise is offered by the Church all over the world. Otherwise—and this is something no insane person would venture to say, much less any Christian—the fifty days between Easter and Pentecost, during which there is no fasting, would be deprived, according to him, of the sacrifice of praise, yet it is only on those days, in many churches—indeed in almost all—that the Alleluia[35] is sung. And none but an extremely ignorant Christian would fail to know that that is the very word of praise.

Nevertheless, he admits that he himself dines on Sunday, not in drunkenness, but in joy of heart, when he says that we few, chosen by the faith of the Christian name from among Jews and many Gentiles, ought to offer our fast instead of victims of animals, as something pleasing to God, with our praises at the time of the evening incense on Saturday, and by our fervor our sinful deeds will be burned up and destroyed. 'And in the morning,' he says, 'He will be heard by us and He will hear us, and we shall have houses to eat and drink in, not in drunkenness but in joy of heart, when Sunday has been duly celebrated by us.' So, now it is a *eulogia* —a praise—not an *alogia*, as he said above, which is celebrated. But, why Saturday, a day which God has sanctified, is a stumbling-block to him, I do not know, or why he should

---

35 The phrase, 'Praise the Lord,' is added to all antiphons, versicles, and responses during the Easter Season.

think it impossible to eat and drink on that day, with such joy of heart as to avoid excess, since we are as able to fast on the day before Saturday as he says we can on the day before Sunday. Perhaps he thinks it is wrong to dine two days in succession? Let him note how he thereby insults the Roman Church itself, where fasting in observed on the fourth, sixth and seventh days of the week, but there are three successive days—namely, Sunday, Monday and Tuesday—on which it is customary to dine.

'It is certain', he says, 'that the life of the sheep depends on the will of the shepherds. But woe to you that call evil good, and darkness light and light darkness, and bitter sweet and sweet bitter.'[36] I do not quite understand what he means by these words. For, if you write them, as your city friend says, then the people depending on the will of their shepherd fast with their bishop on Saturday; but, if he wrote such things to you because in your letter you had said something of the sort yourself, do not let him so influence you to praise the Christian city for fasting on Saturday as to force you to condemn the Christian world for not fasting. For, when he says: 'Woe to those who call evil good, and darkness light and light darkness, and bitter sweet and sweet bitter'—meaning, by good and light and sweet, fasting on Saturday, and, by evil and darkness and bitter, dining on Saturday—what else is he doing but condemning the universal world of Christians who do not fast on Saturday? But, he does not see himself as others see him, nor does he notice to whom he speaks, so as to restrain himself in his writing from such headlong boldness. He thereupon adds: 'Let no man therefore judge you in meat or in drink'[37]—which he himself certainly does when he so charges those who take food and drink. How far

---
36 Cf. Isa. 5.20.
37 Col. 2.16.

he was from recalling this other admonition which the same Apostle utters elsewhere: 'Let not him that eateth despise him that eateth not; and he that eateth not, let him not judge him that eateth.'[38] In that way he would hold the balance, by which scandals are averted, between those who fast on Saturday and those who do not; so that the one who eats would not despise the one who does not eat, and the one who fasts would not judge the one who eats.

'Even Peter,' he says, 'head of the apostles, doorkeeper of heaven, and foundation of the Church, upon the death of Simon,[39] who was a figure of the devil, impossible to cast out except by fasting, taught this same thing to the Romans, whose faith is preached to the whole world.' So, then, the other Apostles, contrary to Peter, taught the Christians throughout the world to dine? And, likewise, as Peter and his fellow Apostles lived together in harmony, so the fasters-on-Saturday, whom Peter planted, live harmoniously with the diners-on-Saturday, whom the other Apostles planted. The following opinion is held by many—although a number of Romans claim that it is false—that the Apostle Peter, intending to debate with Simon the Magician on a Sunday, fasted the day before to guard against the great danger of temptation, and that the Church in the same city fasted with him. After his famous and outstanding victory, he continued this custom, and some of the Churches of the west imitated him. But, if, as that one says, Simon the Magician was a figure of the Devil, who is not exclusively a Saturday or a Sunday tempter, but a daily one, still, we do not fast against him every day, since we do not fast on any Sunday, nor in the fifty days after Easter, nor, in different places, on the solemn feasts of the martyrs and other feasts. And the

---
38 Rom. 14.3.
39 Simon Magus; cf. Acts 8.18-24.

Devil is overcome, notwithstanding, if 'our eyes are ever towards the Lord, that He may pluck our feet out of the snare,'[40] and if, 'whether we eat or drink or whatever we do, we do all to the glory of God,'[41] and if, as far as in us lies, 'we be without offense to the Jews and to the gentiles and to the Church of God.'[42] Those persons have too little regard for these thoughts who eat with offense or fast with offense, and by either excess stir up scandals, whereby the Devil is not defeated, but delighted.

But, if the answer is made that James taught this at Jerusalem, and John at Ephesus, as Peter did at Rome, namely that one should fast on Saturday, but that the other lands fell away from this teaching, while Rome remained steadfast; and if the other side retorts that it was rather certain localities in the west, including Rome, which did not hold the tradition of the Apostles, while the lands of the east, where the Gospel was first preached, remained firm without any variation in the tradition handed down by all the Apostles as well as by Peter himself, namely that one should not fast on Saturday, then this is an interminable quarrel, begetting contention and endless argument. Let there be one faith of the universal Church, which is spread abroad everywhere, just as within the Church among the members, even if that same unity of faith is manifested by divers practices, what is true in the faith is nowise hindered by that diversity. 'All the glory of the king's daughter is within.'[43] But, those observances which are differently practised are prefigured by her garment, of which it is said: 'In golden borders, clothed round about with varieties.'[44] Let

---
40 Cf. Ps. 24.14.
41 Cf. 1 Cor. 10.31.
42 Cf. 1 Cor. 10.32.
43 Ps. 44.14.
44 Ps. 44.15.

that garment also be so varied by diver observances, but not so as to be rent by contradiction and controversy.

'Finally,' he says, 'if a Jew denies the sabbath by observing Sunday, why does a Christian observe the sabbath? Either we are Christians and we observe Sunday, or we are Jews and we observe the sabbath, for "no man can serve two masters." '[45] Does he not say this as if there were one lord of the sabbath and another of Sunday? Or does he not recall what he himself quoted: 'The Son of man is Lord also of the sabbath'?[46] In wishing us to be opposed to the sabbath as the Jews are opposed to Sunday, he is so far from the truth that he could even say that we ought not to accept the Law and the Prophets, just as the Jews do not accept the Gospel and the Apostles. You surely understand who it is that knows, and what wrong things he knows. 'But,' he says, 'all the old things are passed away and are made new in Christ.'[47] This is true, and therefore we do not rest on the sabbath as the Jews do, even if, to indicate the rest which is signified by that day, we relax the obligation of fasting by a duly Christian moderation and simplicity. And, if some of our brethren think that the sabbath rest ought not to be signalized by a relaxation of fasting, we argue to no purpose about the variety of the royal garment. But, let us not trouble the inner members of the queen herself, when we hold the same belief about the day of rest. Although, with the passing of the old things, the carnal rest of the sabbath has also passed, still, in dining on both sabbath and Sunday without superstitious observance, we are not thereby serving two masters, because the Lord of the sabbath and of Sunday is one.

But, he who says that the old things have passed away,

---
45 Matt. 6.24.
46 Luke 6.5.
47 Cf. 2 Cor. 5.17.

so that in Christ altar yields to altar,[48] fire to prayers, animal victims to bread, blood to the chalice, does not know that the word *'altare'* is used quite often in the Law and the Prophets, and that an altar [*altare*] was first raised to God by Moses in the Tabernacle,[49] while the word *'ara'* is also found in the writings of the Apostles, where the martyrs cry out under the altar [*ara*].[50] He says that the sword has yielded to fasting, forgetting that two-edged sword of both Testaments, with which the soldiers of the Gospel are armed.[51] He says that fire has given place to prayers, as if prayers were not then offered in the Temple, and fire is not now cast by Christ upon the world.[52] He says that animal victims have been replaced by bread, as if he did not know that even then the loaves of proposition were placed upon the table of the Lord,[53] and that now he partakes of the Body of the immaculate Lamb.[54] He says that blood has given place to the chalice, not thinking that he now receives the Blood in the chalice.[55] How much more truly and more appropriately could he say that the old things are passed away and are made new in Christ, so that altar yields to altar,[56] sword to sword, fire to fire, bread to Bread, victim to Victim, blood to Blood. Surely, we see by this that the carnal old things give place to spiritual newness. This, then, is what we have to understand—whether we dine on that changeable seventh day or whether some fast on that day—that the carnal sabbath

---

48 Urbicus uses two words for altar: *ara* and *altare,* implying that *ara* was used in the old dispensation, *altare* in the new. Augustine disposes of this assumption.
49 Exod. 40.24.
50 Apoc. 6.9,10.
51 Eph. 6.17; Heb. 4.12.
52 Luke 12.49.
53 Exod. 25.30.
54 1 Peter 1.19.
55 Matt. 26.26,27; Mark 14.22,23; Luke 22.17; 1 Cor. 11.23-25.
56 He uses *altare* both times.

has been transformed into the spiritual one, and that a true and eternal rest is looked for in the latter, while a merely physical rest is now despised in the former as a superstitious observance.

The other points which follow in the conclusion of his disputation as well as some interspersed with the others, I have not thought worthy of comment, because they have nothing to do with the question of fasting or not fasting on Saturday. I leave those to be noted and criticized by you, especially if you have been helped somewhat by what I have said. I think I have made an adequate answer to him, to the limit of my ability, but, if you want my opinion on this matter, I see, as I turn it over in my mind, that fasting is commanded in the Gospel and apostolic writings, and in the whole book which is called the New Testament. I do not find anything prescribed in the teachings either of the Lord or of the Apostles about the days when it is proper to fast and those when it is not. For this reason, then, I think that relaxation rather than the austerity of fasting is more fitting: not to obtain what faith obtains, and justice, in which is the glory of the king's daughter within,[57] but rather to symbolize that eternal rest which is the true sabbath.

Truly, in this question of fasting or not fasting on Saturday, it seems to me that we can hold safely and peaceably to these words: 'Let not him that eateth despise him that eateth not; and he that eateth not, let him not judge him that eateth,'[58] for, 'neither, if we eat, shall we have the more, nor, if we eat not, shall we have the less,'[59] with all due regard, of course, in these things not to hurt the fellowship of those among whom we live and with whom we live for

---
57 Ps. 44.14.
58 Rom. 14.3.
59 1 Cor. 8.8.

God. For, just as, according to the Apostle, it truly is 'evil for that man who eateth with offense,'[60] so it is evil for a man to fast with offense. Let us, then, not be like those who saw John not eating or drinking and said: 'He hath a devil,'[61] nor yet like those who saw Christ eating and drinking and said: 'Behold a man that is a glutton and a wine-drinker, a friend of publicans and sinners.'[62] The Lord made a truly necessary addition to these words when He said: 'And wisdom is justified by her children.'[63] If you ask who those children are, read what is written: 'The sons of wisdom are the church of the just.'[64] These are the ones who, when they eat, do not despise those who eat not, or when they eat not do not judge those who eat, but who certainly either despise or judge those who eat not or eat unto offense.

The case of fasting on Saturday is an easier question, because the Roman Church fasts on that day and so do some others, both near and far. But it is a great scandal to fast on Sunday, especially since the spread of the detestable heresy of the Manichaeans, so openly opposed to the Catholic faith and the Divine Scriptures, for they have selected that day for their adherents to fast, as if it were the proper day. The consequence of this is that fasting on Sunday is considered utterly revolting, except, of course, in the case of one who was prolonging his fast beyond the week, so as to approximate a forty-day fast, as far as he might be able, taking no food at all—as we have known some to do, for we have been assured by brethren most worthy of credence that a certain one did attain to that number forty. Just as, in the times of the ancient fathers, Moses and Elias did noth-

---

60 Rom. 14.20.
61 Matt. 11.18.
62 Matt. 11.19; Luke 7.33,34.
63 Matt. 11.19.
64 Eccli. 3.1.

ing contrary to the sabbath when they each fasted forty days, so, if anyone has been able to pass seven days without eating, he has not chosen Sunday as a fast day, but he happened to find it among the several days, which he had vowed to pass without eating. However, if a continuous fast is to be ended in a week, there is no day more fitting than Sunday to bring it to an end. But if the body is refreshed after the lapse of a week, then, surely, Sunday is not chosen as a fast day, but is included among those during which one had promised to fast.

Do not be disturbed by the fact that the Priscillianists[65] —quite like the Manichaeans—are accustomed to produce a text from the Acts of the Apostles as evidence for fasting on Sunday—the one when the Apostle Paul was in Troas. For it is written: 'And on the first day of the week when we were assembled to break bread, Paul discoursed with them, being to depart on the morrow, and he continued his speech until midnight.'[66] Then, when he had gone down from the upper room where they were gathered together, to restore to life the youth who, oppressed with sleep, had fallen from the window and was carried in dead, the Scripture speaks thus of the Apostle himself: 'Then going up and breaking bread and tasting, and having talked a long time to them until daylight, so he departed.'[67] Far be it from us

---

65 A heretical sect originating in Spain at the end of the fourth century, which preached a Gnostic-Manichaean dualism of Light and Darkness. Human souls, intended to conquer the kingdom of Darkness, fell and were imprisoned in bodies. Our Lord's death was said to be only apparent, and released men from the influence of the material. They rejected some of the Scriptures, and interpreted others in an unliteral sense. They had an indecent system of asceticism and peculiar liturgical observances, such as fasting on Sundays and on Christmas day. They permitted lying for a holy end. Augustine wrote his *De mendacio* against them.
66 Acts 20.7.
67 Acts 21.11.

to interpret this as meaning that the Apostles were accustomed to fast solemnly on Sunday. For, what was then called the first day of the week is not called Sunday, the Lord's day, as it is found clearly in the Gospels. In St. Matthew the day of the Resurrection of the Lord is called '*prima sabbati*,'[68] the first day of the week, and the other three evangelists have '*una sabbati*,'[69] similarly the first day of the week, which means that day which was afterwards called the Lord's day, Sunday. It is one of two things then: either they were gathered together at the beginning of the night, after the completion of the sabbath, which certainly was the night leading into Sunday—that is, it belonged to the first day of the week—and so, in that night he was about to break bread, as it is broken in the Sacrament of the Body of Christ; and he prolonged his talk until midnight, so that, after administering the Sacrament and again addressing the gathering (because time pressed) he might set out at the dawn of Sunday. The other interpretation would be that they were gathered together on the first day of the week, not during the night but through the day from the first hour of Sunday, and that the words, 'Paul discoursed with them, being to depart on the morrow,' explain the reason for his prolonging his discourse, because he was about to depart, and he wished them to be sufficiently instructed. Therefore, they did not regularly fast on Sunday, but it seemed to them that his impelling sermon, which they were listening to with eager attention, should not be interrupted for the sake of bodily nourishment, especially when the Apostle was about to leave them; as he visited them but rarely because of his other journeys in various places; and most especially because he was going away from that country, and, as sub-

---

68 Matt. 28.1.
69 Mark 16.2; Luke 24.1; John 20.1.

sequent events showed, he would never see them again in the flesh. Another point which shows even more clearly that they were not accustomed to fast on Sundays, is that the writer of the book took care to explain the reason for the prolonging of the discourse, to let us know that, if need arose, food was not to be preferred to a more important activity. So, then, they listened to him with the greatest eagerness, drinking in without sating their deep thirst—not of water, but of the Word—all that flowed from that fount, which they remembered was soon to leave them. And it was not only the breaking of their fast that they forgot, but they scorned even the chief meal of the day.

Although fasting on Sunday was not customary at that time, it was not offensive to the Church, if some emergency, such as the Apostle Paul experienced, kept them from taking bodily refreshment for the whole of a Sunday, that is, until midnight, or even until the next morning. But, now, in this later time, when impious heretics are making a point of fasting on Sunday, without any pressing emergency such as the Apostle had, and are beginning to teach it as a matter of canonical legislation, and to propagate it among Christian peoples, I think we should do what he did, lest the evil incurred by scandal should be greater than the good resulting from preaching. So, then, if any case of necessity arises which forces a Christian man to fast on Sunday, as we find in the Acts of the Apostles, where the Apostle himself, voyaging and in danger of shipwreck, had fasted for fourteen days,[70] which included two Sundays, we still ought to hold that Sunday is not to be included among the days of fasting, unless one has made a vow to fast for more than seven days continuously.

As to why the Church fasts on the fourth and especially

---
70 Acts 27.33.

on the sixth day, this seems to be the reason given, that, according to the Gospel, that fourth day of the week which is commonly called the fourth feria [Wednesday] was the day when the Jews took counsel how they might put the Lord to death. On the evening of the intervening day— that is, the end of the day which we call the fifth of the week—the Lord ate the Pasch with His disciples, and then was betrayed on the night which leads to the sixth of the week, the manifest day of His Passion. This day, beginning with the evening, was the fifth day of unleavened bread.[71] But the Evangelist Matthew says that the fifth day of the week was the first of the Azymes, because the paschal supper was to take place on the evening which followed it, and at this supper they began to eat unleavened bread with the lamb which had been sacrificed. From this it may be inferred that it was the fourth day of the week when the Lord said: 'You know that after two days shall be the Pasch, and the Son of man shall be delivered up to be crucified.'[72] And that is why this day is selected for fasting, because, as the Evangelist continues and says: 'Then were gathered together the chief priests and ancients of the people into the court of the high priest, who was called Caiphas: And they consulted together that by subtilty they might apprehend Jesus and put Him to death.'[73] But when one day had intervened, of which the Gospel says: 'And on the first day of the Azymes, the disciples came to Jesus, saying, Where wilt Thou that we prepare for Thee to eat the Pasch?'[74]—when this day had intervened, the Lord suffered on the sixth day of the week, a fact which no one calls in question. For this reason that sixth day is rightly set aside for fasting, because fast-

---

71 Matt. 26.17.
72 Matt. 26.2.
73 Matt. 26.3,4.
74 Matt. 26.17.

ing signifies humiliation, according to the saying: 'And I humbled my soul with fasting.'[75]

There follows, then, Saturday, the day on which the Body of Christ rested in the tomb, just as in the first labor of creation God rested on that day from all His works.[76] From this has arisen that variety in the royal garment that some peoples, especially oriental ones, prefer to omit fasting on that day to mark it as a day of rest; while others, like the Roman and some occidental Churches, fast only on that single day on which the Pasch is celebrated, to call to mind what was done when the disciples gave way to human grief for the death of the Lord, and this fast is so observed by all that even those who do not fast on Saturdays throughout the year keep this fast most religiously. Doubtless, the twofold signification of this is the grief of the disciples on the one anniversary day, and the blessedness of rest on the other Saturdays. Certainly, there are two things which make us hope for the bliss of the just and the end of all suffering: death and the resurrection from the dead. In death is rest, as the Prophet says: 'My people, enter into thy chambers, hide thyself a little until the indignation of the Lord pass away';[77] but in the resurrection there is perfect happiness in the whole man, that is, in flesh and spirit. Consequently, we are not to think that both of these are to be marked by the labor of fasting, but rather by the rejoicing of refreshment, except that one paschal Saturday, on which, as we said, the grief of the disciples over what had been done is to be commemorated by a more rigorous fast.

But, since, as I said above, I have not found, either in the Gospels or in the apostolic writings which directly refer

---
75 Ps. 34.13.
76 Gen. 2.2.
77 Cf. Isa. 26.20.

to the revelation of the New Testament, any definite precept regarding the observance of fasting on any special days, and this matter, like several others too difficult to enumerate, finds its place in the variegated garment of the king's daughter, that is, of the Church, I will tell you what the venerated Ambrose, Bishop of Milan (who baptized me) answered when I asked him about it. When my mother was with me in that city, and we catechumens were still untroubled about it, she was worried about whether it was better to fast on Saturday, according to the custom of our city,[78] or to dine in accordance with the Church in Milan. To free her from this anxiety, I consulted the above-mentioned man of God. He said: 'What better can I teach you than what I do myself?' And when I thought that his answer meant that we should dine on Saturday, he continued and added: 'When I am here, I do not fast on Saturday; when I am at Rome, I do fast on Saturday. To whatever church you come, keep its custom, if you do not wish either to receive or to give scandal.' I took this answer to my mother, who was satisfied and had no qualms about obeying it. And we, also, have followed this. But, since it happens, especially in Africa, that one church, or the churches of one region, have some who fast and some who do not fast on Saturday, it seems best to me to follow the custom of those to whom the charge of those same people has been entrusted. Therefore, if you willingly accept my advice, which I have given with more emphasis than was needed, because of your urgent request, do not resist your bishop in this matter, but follow what he himself does without any scruple or misgiving.

---

[78] Tagaste.

37. Augustine gives greeting in the Lord to the most blessed lord and father, Simplicianus,[1] ever to be embraced in the most sincere charity (397)

I have received the letters sent by the kindness of your Holiness, letters full of good joys, because you are mindful of me, and love me, as you are wont, and because it is a personal satisfaction to you that the Lord has deigned in His mercy to confer on me something of His gifts, through no merits of my own. In these letters I have drunk deep of your fatherly affection for me, not a new or sudden thing for your loving heart, but something I have tried and known intimately, most blessed lord, worthy to be embraced by the most respectful and sincere charity.

But, whence comes this great good fortune for my literary labor—and I have truly toiled over the writing of some of my books—that my works should be read by your Worthiness, except that the Lord to whom my heart is subject has wished to comfort my troubles and free me from fear? Truly, in such works I must needs be anxious, lest I stumble in the open field of truth through my lack of learning or attention. When what I write pleases you, I know whom it pleases, because I know who dwells in you. It is, indeed, the same Giver and Bestower of all spiritual gifts who has strengthened my obedience through your words. If any of my writings has deserved to give you pleasure, it is because in regard to my ministry God said: 'Let it be done, and it was done'; but, in regard to your approval: 'God saw that it was good.'[2]

The points of controversy which you have been so kind as to bid me solve, with the help of your merits I will try

---
[1] An old priest of Milan who had instructed both St. Ambrose and St. Augustine. Cf. *Conf.* 8.1.
[2] Cf. Gen. 1.3,4.

to explain, although I do not understand them, weighed down as I am by my own slowness of comprehension. I ask only one thing, that you pray God to make up for my weakness, and that you not only read carefully, but also apply the censure of correction to whatever I do, whether it be this task which your fatherly kindness wishes me to undertake, or any other works of mine which may fall into your holy hands, because I do not distinguish between my own errors and the inspirations of God.

38. Augustine to his brother, Profuturus[1] (397)

In spirit, as far as it pleases the Lord and as He deigns to give me strength, I am well; but, in body, I am in bed, for I can neither walk nor stand nor sit because of the pain and swelling of hemorrhoids and chafing. Even so, since it pleases the Lord, what else is to be said but that I am well? If we do not will what He wills, we must blame ourselves, not Him, who does and permits only what is for our good. You know all this, but because you are my other self, I delight in saying to you what I say to myself. Therefore, I commend to your holy prayers both my days and my nights; pray for me that I may not waste the days, that I may bear the nights with patience, and, 'though I should walk in the midst of the shadow of death,' that the Lord may be with me 'so that I may fear no evils.'[2]

I am sure you have heard of the death of the elder Megalius.[3] The day I am writing is almost the twenty-fourth since his burial. We wish to know whether you will now

---
[1] Profuturus (cf. Letter 28) was now bishop of Cirta or Constantina.
[2] Ps. 22.4.
[3] Bishop of Calama, and primate of Numidia, who had consecrated Augustine bishop.

look to a successor for his see, if possible, for you have been putting it off. If there are scandals, there is also a remedy; if there are griefs, there is comfort. Meantime, we must be on guard lest hatred for anyone should seize our innermost heart and prevent us from 'praying to God in our chamber, having shut the door';[4] for you know well, excellent brother, that hatred would close the door against God Himself. Anger creeps in so subtly that everyone deems his own anger just, and habitual anger becomes hatred. And the mingled sweetness of a just resentment is like a trace of perfume in a vial, remaining too long until the whole becomes sour and the vial unfit for use. Therefore, it is better for us not to harbor even a just anger against anyone, because it is only too easy to fall unperceived from just anger into hatred. In receiving unknown guests we are wont to say that it is better to put up with a bad one than unknowingly to shut out a good one, through our very desire not to receive a bad one. But, with the passions of the heart, it is just the opposite. It is unquestionably safer not to open the guest chamber of the heart to the knocking of anger, even just anger, than to admit a guest not easy to get rid of, and likely to grow from a twig to a tree. Indeed, it is not ashamed to grow more quickly than it is pruned, and it does not blush in the darkness when the sun had set upon it.[5] You recall, I am sure, with what care and anxiety I write this, if you recall what you said to me lately on a certain journey.

We send greetings to brother Severus[6] and those who are with him. We might have written to them if the courier had not been in such haste. I ask, however, that you be helpful to this same brother Victor[7] of ours, to whom I send

---
4 Cf. Matt. 6.6.
5 Cf. Eph. 4.26.
6 Cf. Letter 31 n. 16.
7 Cf. Letter 36.

thanks through your Holiness for letting me know when he was passing through Constantina, and that you ask him not to make a difficulty about going back through Calama,[8] as he promised me. For I bear a very heavy burden—and he knows the affair—with Nectarius the older begging earnestly to be let off this business.

39. Jerome gives greeting in Christ to the truly holy lord and blessed prelate, Augustine (397)

Last year, I sent to your Worthiness by our brother Asterius, the subdeacon, a letter paying my respects to you; and I believe you received it. Now, I am again sending a message through my holy brother Praesidius, a deacon, asking you, first, to be mindful of me; second, to receive the approved bearer of my letter, and know that he is most dear to me; and, finally, to cherish and support him in any need he may have. With Christ as his Giver, he does not lack anything, but he has a most eager desire for the friendship of good men, and, when he has attained that, he thinks he has gained the greatest benefit. You will hear from him in person why he is making this trip to the west.[1]

We who are settled in the monastery are tossed this way and that by waves of change, and we endure all the troubles of a pilgrimage. But we trust in Him who said: 'Have confidence, I have overcome the world,'[2] because by His help and protection we win the victory over our enemy, the Devil. I ask you to greet in my name our holy and venerable brother, Bishop Alypius. The holy brethren, who make haste to

---

8 A town in Numidia.

---

1 From the Holy Land, where Jerome was living.
2 John 16.33.

serve the Lord in the monastery with us, send you hearty greetings. May Christ, our almighty God, keep you safe and ever mindful of us, truly holy lord and father ever to be cherished.

40. Augustine to his fellow priest and brother, Jerome, most beloved lord, worthy of the honor and embrace of the most sincere charity (397)

I thank you for sending me, according to the greeting mentioned below,[1] a full answer, although a much shorter one than I should like from a man like you, because no word of yours is superfluous, however much time it consumes. Therefore, although I am beset by the monstrous cares of irrelevant and secular business, I would not easily forgive the brevity of your letter except on the ground that it can be answered with fewer words. Come, then, at my request, and undertake a written debate with me, for I should not like the silence and inactivity of our pens to complete the separation caused by physical absence, since we are joined in the Lord by the unity of the spirit.[2] Indeed, the books which you have garnered from the granary of the Lord give us almost a perfect picture of you. If the reason we do not know you is that we have not seen your actual face, then for the same reason you do not know yourself, because you do not see it either. But, if you are otherwise known to yourself through your knowledge of your own mind, then we also know you quite well through your writings, and we bless the Lord because He has given such a one as you to yourself and to all of us, your brothers, who read your writings.

---

[1] A reference to an apparently lost letter.
[2] Eph. 4.3.

One book of yours among other things came into our hands not long ago, but we do not yet know its title, because the copy did not have a title page, as books usually do. The brother who first had possession of it said that it is called an obituary notice. We could believe that this is the name you wished it to have, if we read in it the lives or writings of men who are dead; but since it mentions the works of many who were living at the time it was written, and even of many who are still living, I wonder why you gave it that name or are believed to have given it that name. However, we fully approve of the same book since it is written by you.

In the explanation of the Epistle of the Apostle Paul to the Galatians, we also find something which disturbs us profoundly. For, if the validity of the polite lie[3] be admitted in the Holy Scriptures, how will their authority be maintained? How can one use the Scriptures to give weight to a verdict by which the dishonesty of deliberate deceit is condemned? If you have once made that admission, then the one who is arguing against you, and who thinks otherwise, will say that the text which you quote is an example of the writer making use of the polite lie. If this can be believed and asserted in that narrative with which the Apostle begins where he says: 'Now the things which I write to you, behold before God, I lie not,'[4] why can he not be said to be lying when he says of Peter and Barnabas: 'When I saw

---

[3] Catholic theology, as formulated by St. Augustine and St. Thomas Aquinas, distinguishes three kinds of lies: (1) injurious, or malicious; (2) officious, or polite, or 'white'; (3) jocose. No. 1 does harm and is intended to deceive; it is therefore always wrong. No. 2 does nobody harm; it may be a lie of excuse or one told to benefit somebody. For this reason some theologians justify the officious lie, but St. Augustine held unequivocally that all lying, including this kind, is morally wrong. No. 3 is told to afford amusement, and is not truly a lie, because it does not deceive anybody.

[4] Gal. 1.20.

that they walked not uprightly unto the truth of the Gospel'?[5] If they were walking uprightly, then he lied; but, if he lied there, where did he speak the truth? Or shall he seem to speak the truth when he says something the reader knows to be true, but shall be impugned of a polite lie when he says something contrary to the thought of the reader? There will be no lack of reasons for thinking that he both could and ought to lie, if this rule be once admitted. There is no need of many words to plead this case in your court; a word to the wise is sufficient for one as far-seeing as you. Indeed, I should never presume to attempt to enrich with my pennies that genius of yours, divinely gifted with pure gold; and there is no one better fitted than you to annotate that work.

Again, you are not to be taught by me[6] how that passage is to be understood where he says: 'I became to the Jews as a Jew that I might gain the Jews,'[7] and other things which are there said through mercy and compassion, not through deceit and deception. For, a person who nurses a sick man becomes, in a sense, sick himself, not by pretending to have fever, but by thinking sympathetically how he would like to be treated if he himself were sick. Certainly, he was a Jew, and, on becoming a Christian, he had not given up those practices of the Jews which they had lawfully adopted as being in accord with their times. Thus, he undertook to keep up those observances even after he became an apostle of Christ, but he taught that they were not dangerous to the conscience of those who wished to keep them, as they had received them from their parents under the Law, even after they had come to believe in Christ. However, they were not to put their hope of salvation in them, because the salvation which was

---
5 Gal. 2.14.
6 In Letter 75, Jerome quotes this passage to answer it.
7 1 Cor. 9.20.

typified by those mysteries had come through the Lord Jesus. For that reason he judged that they were not to be required of the Gentiles, since their calling to the faith had relieved them of a heavy and unnecessary burden to which they had not been accustomed.

Consequently, he did not rebuke Peter for observing his ancestral traditions,[8] which he could do without deceit or inconsistency if he wished—they might be superfluous, but they were not harmful—but because he 'compelled the gentiles to live as do the Jews.'[9] This he could not do unless he regarded these practices as necessary for salvation even after the coming of the Lord. Truth, as set forth by Paul's apostolate, proved this to be wrong. Peter knew this, but he acted as one 'fearing them who were of the circumcision.'[10] Thus, he was himself truly corrected, and Paul told the truth. Otherwise, the Holy Scripture, which has been given to preserve the faith in generations to come, would be wholly undermined and thrown into doubt, if the validity of lying were once admitted. It is not possible or desirable to put into writing what great and unforeseen evils would result if we granted this point, but, in a personal conference, it could be dealt with more appropriately and more safely.

Paul had given up this evil belief of the Jews, therefore; first because, 'they not knowing the justice of God and seeking to establish their own have not submitted themselves to the justice of God.'[11] Next, because after the Passion and Resurrection of Christ, when the sacrament of grace[12] had been given and made known, 'according to the order of Melchise-

---

8 Quoted in Letter 75.
9 Gal. 2.14.
10 Gal. 2.12.
11 Rom. 10.3.
12 The Holy Eucharist which, in the Mass, replaced the sacrifices of the Old Law.

dech,'[13] they still thought the old ceremonies should be celebrated, not through respect for their traditional value, but as if necessary for salvation. This is not to say that they had never been necessary; otherwise, the martyrdom of the Macchabees[14] in their defense would have been vain and fruitless. Finally, he condemned them because the Jews persecuted the Christian preachers of grace as enemies of the Law. It is these errors and wrong practices which, he says, 'he counted as loss . . . and dung that he might gain Christ,'[15] not the observances of the Law when kept through ancestral custom, as he kept them, without any implication of their being necessary for salvation. The Jews held this latter view, and what he rebuked in Peter was a deceitful pretense to the same view. For, if he took part in those ceremonies because he was pretending to be a Jew, in order to win them, why did he not also sacrifice with the Gentiles, putting himself outside the Law as they were outside it, in order to win them? Doubtless, he did the former as one who was a Jew by birth, and he said what he did, not to pretend falsely to be what he was not, but to declare his own need of mercy, as if he were involved in the same error with them. In this he was evidently moved by a feeling of compassion, not by a crafty intent to deceive. So he asserted in the same place, in a general sense: 'To the weak I became weak, that I might gain the weak,' so that the following statement—'I became all things to all men that I might gain all,'[16]—might be understood to mean that he pitied each one's weakness as if it were his own. Certainly, when he said: 'Who is weak and I

---

13 Heb. 6.20.
14 2 Mach. 7.
15 Cf. Phil. 3.8.
16 Cf. 1 Cor. 9.22; the Douay version reads: 'that I might save all.'

am not weak?"¹⁷ he did not mean that he was counterfeiting their weakness, but that he sympthized with it.

I ask you, then, to gird yourself with a sincere and truly Christian severity, tempered with charity, and proceed to correct and revise that work of yours. Sing us a palinode, as they say in Greek.¹⁸ Indeed, the truth of the Christians is incomparably more beautiful than the Helen of the Greeks. For the former, our martyrs fought more valiantly against this Sodom¹⁹ than those famous heroes fought for the latter against Troy. I do not say this as asking you to regain the eyes of your heart—may you never lose them!—but that you turn them back, strong and watchful, from that deceitful averted glance which prevented you from noticing what disadvantages would arise if once it could be believed that the writer of the Sacred Books could lawfully and justly lie in any part of his work.

Sometime ago I wrote you a letter, but it was not delivered because the bearer to whom I entrusted it never set out.²⁰ Something I added to it was called to my mind while I was dictating this letter, and I ought not to pass it over; namely, that you pardon my timidity, if your opinion is different from mine, and better. If you think otherwise, and your opinion is true—for it could not be better unless it were true—then my mistake, which is not a fault, or at least not a great one, will serve the cause of truth if truth can rightly serve falsehood in anything.

---

17 2 Cor. 11.29.
18 Isocrates 10.64. Palinode is a recantation; e.g., Horace, *Epode* 17.
19 By Sodom, Augustine seems to mean paganism or pagan Rome.
20 Profuturus, who was prevented from making his journey by being elected and consecrated bishop.

By what you were so good as to answer about Origen,[21] I am now sure that not only in Church literature, but in general literature, you approve and praise what is true and right, but detest and repudiate what is false and wicked. But I needed this help of your experience and learning, and I still need it, namely, that you point out the erroneous ideas by which such a great man is convicted of departing from the true faith. In the book in which you treat of all the ecclesiastical writers and their writings, as far as you could recall them, it would be more useful, I think, if, when you have named those whom you know to be heretical—since you thought fit to include them, although you have omitted some —you would indicate also wherein they are not to be followed. What I should like to know is whether there were some way of bringing out in a small volume, briefly summarized, all the false teachings of the heretics who have tried, up to the present time, to destroy the purity of the Christian faith by their arrogance and intransigence. This could be done, in case you did not wish to lengthen your present book too much, by adding to it the notes on the heretics and the points on which Catholic authority has condemned them. My brotherly love makes this suggestion in all humility, with the proviso that your duties allow it, and that it should not be too heavy an addition to your literary work, which, by the grace of our Lord, has done not a little to enkindle and encourage studies of the saints in the Latin tongue. This would be a help to those who have no time for such studies because of other duties, or whose lack of knowledge of a foreign tongue prevents them

---

21 Origen (185-255) was one of the most brilliant and voluminous of early Christian writers. He unfortunately fell into error on some doctrinal points and in his Scriptural commentaries he frequently neglected the literal sense and made exaggerated use of allegorical exegesis. Notwithstanding his errors, he loved Christian truth devotedly and spent his life and energies in its service.

from reading and learning many things. I could keep on asking you this for a long time, but that would be to take advantage of friendship. Meanwhile, I commend to your kindness in Christ our brother Paul,[22] and I testify before God that he is held in high esteem in our country.

41. Alypius and Augustine send greetings in the Lord to the blessed lord Aurelius,[1] their venerable brother ever to be cherished with sincere affection, and their fellow priest and prelate (c. 397)

'Our mouth was filled with gladness and our tongue with joy'[2] when we learned from your letters that your holy plan, with the help of the Lord who inspired it, had been put into effect, regarding all the brethren in Orders and especially the priests who had preached to the people in your presence.[3] Thus, by the Lord's help, the language of your Charity sounds in their hearts more loudly than the voices of the preachers in their ears. What better prayer can we think in our mind, or utter with our tongue, or express with our pen than 'Thanks be to God!' Nothing can be said more briefly than this, or heard more joyfully, or used more fruit-

---

[22] Augustine's messenger. He did not make this trip to Palestine, because he was afraid of the perils of the sea; instead of returning this letter to Augustine, he let it circulate in Italy before it reached Jerome, who was much displeased. This could have caused a breach of friendship between the two saints and scholars, but Augustine's humble explanations soothed the rather peppery temper of Jerome.

[1] Bishop of Carthage.
[2] Ps. 125.2.
[3] This was not customary in the churches of Africa, and we read that Valerius, Augustine's bishop, had been criticized for allowing Augustine, while still a priest, to preach in his presence. But Augustine's preaching had such good effect that other bishops imitated Valerius, among whom Aurelius seems to have been one of the first.

fully. Thanks be to God, who enriched you with a heart so faithful toward your sons, and who brought to light what you carried in the secret of your breast, where human eye does not see, by granting you not only this good intention, but also the opportunity of making it manifest. So be it, so be it, utterly! May these good works shine before men,[4] may they see, rejoice and glorify their Father, who is in heaven. May you rejoice in the Lord in such men. May he deign to hear you praying for them, as you do not refuse to hear Him speaking through them; may they go, walk and run in the way of the Lord; may the humble be blessed with the great, rejoicing in those who say to them: 'We shall go into the house of the Lord';[5] may they go before, and the rest follow as imitators of them, as they are of Christ.[6] May the way of the sacred ants glow with activity; may the work of the sacred bees give forth fragrance; may they bear fruit in patience, persevering unto the end, unto salvation; 'and may the Lord not permit us to be tempted above that which we are able to bear, but may He make with temptation issue that we may able to bear it!'[7]

You who deserve to be heard, pray for us, since with such a great sacrifice[8] you draw near to the God of most pure love, as also in your works for His glory. May these works shine before us, also, since He to whom you pray knows with how great gladness they shine before you. These are our prayers; these 'the multitude of comforts, according to the multitude of our sorrows in our heart, give joy to our soul.'[9] Thus it is, because thus it was promised; thus will it be in

---

4 Matt. 5.16.
5 Ps. 121.1.
6 Cf. 1 Cor. 11.1.
7 Cf. 1 Cor. 10.13.
8 The Sacrifice of the Mass.
9 Cf. Ps. 93.19.

the future, because it was so promised. We beg you by Him who has granted you this, and who has endowed the people whom you serve with this blessing through you, that you order such of their sermons as you direct to be written and corrected and sent to us. On my part, I am not forgetting what you asked about the Seven Rules or Keys of Tyconius,[10] and, as I have written many times, I am waiting to hear what you think if it.

We strongly recommend to you brother Hilarinus, chief physician and magistrate of Hippo. We know that you are arranging about brother Romanus and we ask nothing except that the Lord help you in his behalf.

42. Augustine gives greeting in the Lord to the estimable lords and most holy brothers in Christ, Paulinus and Therasia (397)

Surely, this was not to be looked for or expected, that we should wait so long and so eagerly for the answer sent by your Charity but not delivered by brother Severus. How does it happen that we are forced to thirst here in Africa these two summers? Oh, you who give your substance daily in alms, pay what you owe. Was it, perhaps, because I had heard that you were writing a book against demon-worshippers and I had shown how much I wanted that work that you put off for so long writing a letter in order to finish your book and send it to me? Would that you might at least receive me at your rich table, starving this whole year for your writing! If it is not yet ready, I shall not stop complaining unless you give me some refreshment before you finish your book.

---

10 A Donatist writer, contemporary of Augustine, who was excommunicated by the Donatists, but never returned to the Catholic fold. His *Liber regularum* or *De septem regulis,* an exposition of the general principles of hermeneutics, was greatly appreciated by Augustine.

Greet our brethren Romanus and Agilis in particular. Those who are with us here share too little in our annoyance if they love too little.

43. *Augustine to the most beloved lords, and deservedly praiseworthy brothers, Glorius, Eleusius, the Felixes, Grammaticus and others to whom this may give pleasure*[1]
(397 or early 398)

The Apostle Paul said: 'A man that is a heretic, after the first admonition, avoid, knowing that he that is such a one is subverted and sinneth, being condemned by himself,'[2] But, those who maintain their own opinion, however false and perverted, without obstinate ill will, especially those who have not originated their own error by bold presumption, but have received it from parents who had been led astray and had lapsed, those who seek truth with careful industry, ready to be corrected when they have found it, are not to be rated among heretics. Therefore, if I did not believe you to be such, I would probably not send you any letters. However, although we give warning that the heretic himself, swollen with hateful pride and with the self-assertion of evil contradiction, is to be avoided like a madman, lest he deceive the weak and the little ones, still we do not shrink from correcting him in whatever way we can. Thus it happened that we wrote to some of the leading Donatists; not such letters as we address to our fellow communicants, which they have not received for a long time now, by reason of their turning away from Catholic unity, of world-wide extent, but such private

---

1 Donatists of Augustine's time; probably more open to conviction than some of their brethren.
2 Cf. Titus 3.10,11.

letters as we might exchange with pagans. And, although they read them some time ago, they either would not, or more probably could not, answer them. Thereupon, it seemed to us that we had satisfied the obligation of charity, which the Holy Spirit teaches us is owed not only to our own but to all men, when He speaks to us through the Apostle: 'And may the Lord multiply you and make you abound in charity towards one another and towards all men.'[3] He also warns us in another place that those who differ from us are to be corrected with moderation, 'Lest peradventure God may give them repentance to know the truth and they may recover themselves from the snares of the devil by whom they are held captive at his will.'[4]

I have made this introductory explanation[5] to prevent any-

---

3 1 Thess. 3.12.
4 Cf. 2 Titus 2. 25,26
5 As Augustine presupposes a knowledge on the part of his correspondents of the happenings in question, a brief summary is essential here. The Donatist schism began in Carthage after the 'great' or last persecution. In 311, Caecilian, an archdeacon, was elected bishop to succeed Mensurius. He was unpopular because of his harshness, and a group of disaffected, unable to dispute his election, challenged his ordination. Some bishops of Numidia, including Donatus, were among them, and they assembled in Carthage. They declared Caecilian's ordination invalid because it had been conferred by Felix of Aptunga, who was accused of being a *'traditor,'* or one who had surrendered or betrayed the Holy Scriptures to the persecutors. This was regarded as a grave sin, and the argument was that Felix, no longer possessing the Holy Spirit, could not transmit it to Caecilian. There were here two points, one of fact and one of doctrine. The dissidents chose Maiorinus to replace Caecilian, and, on his death in 315, they chose Donatus. Meantime, the government recognized Caecilian as the lawful bishop. The Donatists asked for an investigation by 'overseas' bishops, appealed from them to the emperor, who permitted another trial at Arles, and who later acted as arbitrator between Caecilian and his accusers. The result of all these investigations was the same—Caecilian was declared properly ordained. But the Donatists refused to accept the decision. The quarrel was carried on for more than a hundred years, with bitterness and violence; the Donatists set up rival churches in most of the cities and towns of Africa. Augustine entered the lists against them at the end of the fourth century, but was forced to admit that they had been suppressed rather by coercion than by free discussion.

one from thinking that I had written to you too freely or without due prudence, wishing to deal with you about the business of your soul, even though you are not of our communion. Whereas, if I were writing you about the business of a farm or of quashing a financial law suit, probably no one would object. So dear is this world to men, and so cheap are they to themselves! This letter, then, will be a witness in my defense at the judgment of God, who knows with what motive I have acted and who has said: 'Blessed are the peace-makers, for they shall be called the children of God.'[6]

Therefore, you will kindly call to mind that, when we were in your city[7] and were treating some questions about the nature of Christian unity, certain public records were produced by your partisans, in which it was related that about seventy bishops had condemned Caecilan at one time, a bishop of the church of Carthage of our communion, together with his colleagues and consecrators. There the case of Felix of Aptunga[8] also was trumpeted about much more violently and more objectionably than the others. When these records had been read, we answered that it was no wonder if the men who were responsible for that schism, as well as for the correctness of the records, should think that the absent were to be rashly condemned without a hearing, roused as they were against them by envious and abandoned men. But, we have other records of the church, in which Secundus of Tigisis,[9] who then held the primacy in Numidia, left proved and avowed traitors to the judgment of God and even allowed them to occupy their episcopal thrones. And their names are listed among the accusers of Caecilian.

---

6 Matt. 5.9.
7 Carthage.
8 A city in Numidia.
9 Also in Numidia.

Then we said, sometime after the ordination of Maiorinus, whom they wickedly raised up against Caecilian, setting altar against altar, and rending the unity of Christ with frightful divisions, that they had requested Constantine, then emperor, to appoint bishops[10] as judges to arbitrate the differences that had arisen to break the bond of peace in Africa. But, when this was granted, in the presence of Caecilian and those who had gone abroad to appear against him, Melchiades, Bishop of Rome,[11] acting as judge, with his colleagues whom the emperor had sent at the request of the Donatists, had decided that nothing could be proved against Caecilian, that he was thereby confirmed in his bishopric, and that Donatus, who had appeared against him, was censured. After this development, it was noted that, when all of them persisted obstinately in their detestable schism, the emperor made provision for examining the same case more carefully and for concluding it at Arles,[12] but they appealed from the ecclesiastical verdict and asked for a hearing by Constantine. After this meeting, with both sides present, Caecilian had been declared innocent and they had returned defeated, but perversely determined not to give in. Nor was the case of Felix of Aptunga passed over; by order of the same prince his record was cleared in the proconsular archives.[13]

But, because we were only saying all this and not even reading it, we seemed to you to be accomplishing less than you expected of our urgency. So, when we noticed this, we did not delay to send it to you in writing. All of which came after a lapse of not quite two days, while we were travel-

---

10 They demanded as judges bishops from Gaul, on the ground that they were pure of the taint of the *traditores*. Three bishops, from Cologne, Arles, and Autun, were chosen to go to Rome and meet with fifteen Italian bishops.
11 I.e., he was Pope.
12 This was the Council of Arles in 314.
13 By the emperor, at Milan, in 316.

ing to the Church at Geliza,[14] intending to return to your town, and, as you know, the following points were read in one day, as far as time allowed: first, the case of Secundus of Tigisis, who did not venture to remove from his suite those who were avowed betrayers, with whom he dared to condemn Caecilian, absent and not confessing, as well as his other colleagues; then, the proconsular archives where Felix, after a searching inquiry, was proved innocent. You remember that these were read to you before noon, and in the afternoon we made public the petitions to Constantine, the judges appointed by him, the ecclesiastical proceedings at Rome, in which they were censured but Caecilian confirmed in his episcopal office, and finally the letters of emperor Constantine, which proved all this with explicit testimony.

What more, fellow men? What more do you want? There is no question of your gold and silver; not your land or your farms, or even the health of your body is put in danger; we are calling on your soul to grasp everlasting life and avoid everlasting death. Arouse yourselves at last! We are not concerned with some obscure question, we are not peering into deeply hidden secrets which scarcely a single human mind can penetrate. This matter is out in the open. What more obvious? We say that innocent men were condemned in their absence by a presumptuous council. We prove this by the proconsular archives, according to which he was pronounced free of all charge of betrayal, while the report published by your council shouted aloud that he was supremely guilty. We say that sentence was passed against those who were accused of betrayal by avowed betrayers. We prove this by the ecclesiastical records, where the guilty are mentioned by name. Among them, Secundus of Tigisis condoned what he knew to be wrong, as if he connived at

---

[14] A town in Numidia.

it in the interests of peace; but, in concert with men whom he did not know, he gave judgment to the detriment of peace. From this it was clear that he was not primarily thinking of peace, but was concerned for his own safety. For, Purpurius of Linia[15] charged that, when he was imprisoned by the overseer and the troop, to make him betray the Scriptures, he was let go, and surely not gratuitously, unless he either betrayed or ordered some one else to do so. Fearing this very probable suspicion, and warned by the younger Secundus, his relative, and other advisers, who were with him, he dismissed these charges which were very evident to the bishops, and left the judgment to God. Thus, he seemed to be acting in the interests of peace, which was untrue, because he was acting in his own interest.

For, if the thought of peace dwelt in his heart, he would not afterwards, at Carthage, in company with betrayers whom he had acquitted, have condemned of betrayal men who were absent and whom none had convicted. All the more should he have feared to break the peace of unity, because Carthage was a great and famous city, whence the evil might spread from the head through the whole body of Africa. Besides, it was in touch with the overseas countries, and enjoyed widespread fame. Certainly, it had a bishop of no ordinary authority, who was able to pay no attention to a crowd of hostile conspirators, when he saw that he was united by pastoral letters to the Church of Rome, where the primacy of the apostolic chair has always flourished, and to those other countries from which the Gospel came to Africa, itself, and when arrangements were made for him to plead his case if his opponents should try to win over those churches from him. But, since he would not accept the hospitality of his colleagues because he thought or suspected,

---

15 Linia or Lima, a town in Numidia.

untruly, that they had been won over from his side to his enemies—or so he pretended, according to their assertions—there was all the more reason for Secundus, if he was to be the true guardian of peace, to make sure that men should not be condemned in their absence for refusing to have anything to do with this trial. For, there was here no question of priests or deacons or clerics of minor orders, but of equals[16] who had the right to reserve their case intact for the judgment of their peers, especially those of the apostolic churches. Consequently, the verdict pronounced against them in their absence had no validity at all, especially as they had not first accepted the authority of these men and then denied it, but had never been willing to submit to it in the first place, because they had always held it suspect.

This circumstance ought to cause great anxiety to Secundus, who was then primate; if he was presiding over the synod in the interests of peace only, perhaps he might easily have restrained those tongues raging against the absent and made them mild and submissive, by saying: 'See, brothers, how, after the great violence of persecution, by the mercy of God, peace has been granted by the rulers of the world; we Christians and bishops ought not to shatter the unity of Christendom, which our pagan enemy no longer assails. Therefore, let us leave all these cases, which the disorder of a most unbridled age has inflicted on the Church, or if there are some among us who have evidence so certain that they can easily persuade and convince their opponents, yet fear to have dealings with such persons, let them have recourse to our brothers and colleagues, the bishops of the overseas Churches. There, let them make their complaints of the actions and insubordination of such persons as refuse, through lack of confidence in themselves, to submit to the

---

16 I.e., of bishops.

judgment of their African colleagues. But, let it be so done that the accused may come and reply to the charges which these others allege against them. If they will not do this, let their dishonesty and perversity be published in synodal letters, sent out to report on them through the whole world wherein the Church of Christ has now spread, and let them be cut off from communion with all those churches, lest any error arise in the government of the Church at Carthage. Only then shall we feel safe in ordaining another bishop for the people of Carthage, when that faction has been cut off from the whole Church. There might be danger, perhaps, that, when another has been ordained, some overseas Church would refuse to have anything to do with him, on the ground that the other had not been duly removed from office after his ordination had been recognized, and pastoral letters had been sent to him. Thus, the great scandal of schism in the unity of Christ might arise in times of peace, and we should, by our too hasty decisions, dare to erect another altar, not against Caecilian, but against the whole world, which might accept him without knowing the facts.'

If anyone should be so misguided as to refuse to yield to such sound and reasonable advice, what would he do or how could he condemn any of his absent colleagues, without having the proceedings of the council as authority, and despite the opposition of the primate? But, if such rebellion should arise against the chief bishopric and some should wish to condemn while the bishop wished to delay, how much better for division to occur among men planning such disturbing and subversive tactics than in the universal Church! But, because there were no charges that could be proved in the overseas trial of Caecilian and his consecrators, they were therefore unwilling either to postpone their sentence against him or to make provision, after they had pronounced it, for giving notice of it to the Church overseas, since they would be bound to avoid communication with the betrayers who had been condemned in Africa. If they had tried to do that, Caecilian and the others would be at hand to disprove the charge made by their lying prosecutors and to clear themselves by cogent arguments before the overseas ecclesiastical judges.

This, then, was the malicious and extremely wicked device—believed to be the trick of betrayers themselves who had confessed and been pardoned by Secundus of Tigisis—that, when the report of betrayal became public, they could turn suspicion from themselves by incriminating others. Thus, when men all over Africa, who believed false accusations against innocent bishops, said that betrayers had been condemned at Carthage, the real betrayers would hide behind a cloud of false rumor. Hence you see, dearly beloved, how something could happen which some of you said was improbable, namely, that those who had confessed their own betrayal and had won their point of a suspended sentence had afterwards sat in judgment to prosecute alleged betrayers who were not even present. More than that, they had embraced an occasion by which they could blacken others by false charges, and in this way turn against them the tongues of men who might have inquired into their own crimes. Otherwise, if it could not happen that anyone should judge in another the very wrongs he himself had committed, the Apostle Paul would not have said to certain persons: 'Wherefore thou art inexcusable, O man, who judgest. For wherein thou judgest another, thou condemnest thyself, for thou dost the same thing which thou judgest.'[17] These words of the Apostle completely and precisely fit those who have done just that.

---
17 Rom. 2.1.

Therefore, Secundus was not acting in the interest of peace and unity when he left their crimes to God; if so, he would rather have taken measures at Carthage to prevent schism, where no one was at hand with an avowed record of betrayal to whom he had to give acquittal. On the other hand, it would have been the easiest thing in the world to preserve peace intact by refusing to condemn the innocent. Thus, they were doing an injury to the innocent even if they had wished to acquit them, since they had not confessed nor been convicted nor even been present. He indeed receives pardon whose guilt is most incontestable. How great, then, the cruelty and blindness of those who thought they could condemn acts which they could not even acquit because they were untried! But there, known acts were condoned to prevent examination into other matters; here, unproved acts were condemned to cover up others. Someone will say: 'They did know.' If I grant this, I maintain that, even so, the absent should have been protected. They had not run away from a trial, when they had never stood for one at all. The African bishops were not the whole Church, that that refusal to submit to their judgment should be considered an attempt to avoid trial entirely. There still obviously remained any number of overseas colleagues before whom they could be examined, since they seemed to hold their African or Numidian colleagues in distrust. Where is the case which Scripture cites: 'Before thou inquire blame no man: and when thou hast inquired, reprove justly?'[18] If, then, the Holy Spirit did not wish anyone to be blamed or reproved unless he had been examined, how much more reprehensible for men to be, not blamed or reproved, but entirely condemned when they were absent and unable to make any answer to the charges brought against them!

---
18 Eccli. 11.7.

Yet, those[19] who say they have pronounced sentence on the known charges against men who, though absent, were not running away from investigation—because they had never appeared there and claimed that they had always distrusted that faction—I ask you, my brothers, how did they know the truth of the charges? You answer: 'We do not know, because that set of facts is not included in their report.' I will show you how they knew. Listen to the case of Felix of Aptunga and read, first of all, how very bitter they were against him. That is how they knew about the others, the same way they knew about him—and he was afterward proved completely innocent after a searching and terrible examination! How much more justly and safely and quickly ought we to think them innocent who are so much less rigorously condemned, when he was proved innocent whom they had attacked so savagely!

Or, perhaps, as someone said—and this offended some of you when it was said, but it cannot be passed over—someone did say: 'A bishop ought not to have been cleared by a governor's sentence,'[20] as if he had arranged this for himself; whereas the emperor had ordered the examination, since the matter concerned him very closely and he was accountable for it before God! They[21] had made him arbiter and judge of a case of betrayal and schism; they had sent their petition to him and afterwards appealed to him; yet they would not abide by his decision. Therefore, if anyone is to be blamed whom a secular judge acquitted, although he had not asked this favor for himself, how much more blameworthy are

---

19 The Donatists who held the first meeting at Carthage.
20 The point of the reproach was that a bishop was not supposed to be subject to a civil court, but only to an ecclesiastical one. If he appealed himself to the civil authorities, he diminished the prestige of the ecclesiastical tribunal.
21 The Donatists.

they who wished to have a secular ruler as judge of their case! If it is not wrong to appeal to an emperor, it is not wrong to be heard by an emperor, and, therefore, not wrong to be heard by an emperor's delegate. That friend[22] even wished to incriminate a witness who had been stretched on the rack in the case of Bishop Felix, and wanted him torn with iron hooks.[23] Could Felix object to this searching and cruel examination, when the examiner was seeking information against him? Objection to this inquiry would have been taken for confession of guilt. Yet, the governor himself, with the dread summons of heralds and the bloody hands of torturers at his disposal, would never have condemned an absent colleague, who had refused to submit to his judgment, unless he had some other evidence; or, if he did condemn, he would pay the just and due penalty according to his own secular laws.

If the proconsular records displease you, turn to the ecclesiastical ones. All the facts are set out in order for you. But, perhaps Melchiades, Bishop of the Church of Rome, with his colleagues, the overseas bishops, should not have taken over the jurisdiction of a case which had been concluded by seventy Africans under the primacy of Tigisis? The emperor, when requested, sent bishop-judges to sit with him and decide what seemed just to them about the whole affair. We prove this by the petition of the Donatists and the emperor's own records. You recall that both were read to you and you now have the liberty of examining and transcribing them. Read them all and weigh them well. See how carefully all the discussions were carried on with a view to preserving or restoring peace and unity; how the character of

---
22 Probably an ironic reference to Donatus.
23 It was standard procedure under Roman law to question unreliable witnesses under torture. It is clear that the Christian emperor had not yet brought about an abolition of this procedure.

the accusers was treated, and, in the case of some of them, how it was degraded when it became clear by the evidence of those present that they had nothing to say against Caecilian. They wanted to transfer the whole case to the people who favored Maiorinus, a turbulent crowd, hostile to the peace of the Church, with the idea, no doubt, that Caecilian would be accused by that mob by popular outcry alone, with no documents for proof, no inquiry into the truth; and they imagined that they could sway the opinion of the judges to their side. Of course, such an ungoverned mob, drunk with the wine of error, could make true charges against Caecilian, when, as happened to Felix of Aptunga, seventy bishops could so rashly and irrationally condemn absent and innocent colleagues! That kind of crowd they agreed with in pronouncing sentence against innocent and unheard men, that same they wanted to use again in accusing Caecilian. They certainly found such judges as they could win over to that madness!

In your prudent way you can observe both their malice and the conscientiousness of the judges; how they could not be induced to take the final measure of allowing Caecilian to be charged by the mob of the Maiorinus faction, which had no definite standing. Note, also, how prosecutors or witnesses or any sort of hangers-on of the case, who had come with them from Africa, were hunted out by them and how it was reported that they had been present, but had been withdrawn by Donatus. The same Donatus promised that he would produce them. But, after he had made this promise, not once but many times, he no longer wanted to attend that trial where he had made so many admissions, and this unwillingness of his to be present gave the impression that he feared to be condemned himself if he appeared. In fact, the points that had to be adversely decided had been brought out by his presence and interrogation. An additional fact is that a bill of indictment against Caecilian was offered by a certain group. After this, what shall I say about the revival of the judicial examination, and the character of those who gave in the indictment? You have heard it all, and you can read it as often as you like.

Concerning the number of the seventy bishops, when their supposedly weighty authority was contested, you remember what was said. Nevertheless, these very influential men preferred not to indulge their investigation in an endless questioning which bound them with a sort of unbreakable chain. They did not care how many bishops there were or from where they had been gathered, when they saw them blinded by such folly that they dared to pronounce an unconsidered verdict against absent colleagues, without any inquiry. Yet, what kind of final verdict was given by blessed Melchiades! How blameless, how upright, how far-seeing and peaceful! By it he did not try to remove from his flock colleagues who had nothing against them, but, when he had laid the blame on Donatus alone, whom he found to be the cause of all the trouble, he gave the rest full opportunity to recover spiritual health. He was even ready to send pastoral letters to those who were admittedly ordained by Maiorinus, with the provision that, wherever there were two bishops, because dissension had doubled the office, he would confirm the one who had been ordained first. For the other, another flock would be found over whom he could rule. O excellent man! O son of Christian peace and father of Christian people! Compare now that small group,[24] with their great number of bishops, and do not set number against number, but weight against weight: on this side moderation, on that recklessness; on this side watchfulness, on that blindness;

---

24 The Pope and the bishops from overseas.

here mercy did not diminish justice, nor justice contend with mercy; there fear was concealed under fury and fury aroused by fear; one side had met to repel false charges by revealing the truth; the other to conceal the truth by a false incrimination.

Was Caecilian to trust himself to their hearing and judgment when he had other judges, if the case were tried, before whom he could demonstrate his innocence with the greatest ease? He would not trust them at all, nor would a foreigner if he had suddenly been ordained bishop of the Church at Carthage, and did not know what power a very wealthy woman, named Lucilla,[25] had to corrupt the minds of depraved or inexperienced men. But he, by reproving her, in accord with ecclesiastical discipline, had offended her when he was a deacon. This misfortune was added to fill up the measure of the injustice. For, in that council when innocent men were condemned in their absence by avowed betrayers, there were a certain few who wished to cover their own wrong-doing by accusing others, and by false reports to turn men away from the search for the truth. They who were particularly involved in this business were few, but they had greater influence because of their association with Secundus, who had been frightened into pardoning them. The rest were reported to have been bought by Lucilla's money, and so instigated violently against Caecilian. The minutes of the proceedings before the consul Zenophilus are available; as far as is known from them, a certain deacon named Nundinarius,[26] who had been silenced by Silvanus of Cirta, his bishop, had tried to gain favor with this group by

---

25 A rich lady to whose 'household' Maiorinus belonged. She had been rebuked by Caecilian for insisting on kissing an unauthenticated relic of a 'martyr.'
26 This word has also a common adjective meaning: pertaining to market-day or public fair.

means of letters from other bishops; failing that, he had revealed many things in anger, and had appealed to a public trial. Among other details, it is related that certain bishops in the Church at Carthage, capital of Africa, had been bribed by Lucilla's money, and that altar had been raised against altar.[27] I know that we did not read these minutes to you, but you remember that time did not allow. There was involved some resentment arising from pride because they had not ordained a bishop for Carthage.

For all these reasons, when Caecilian recognized that they had not met as true judges, but as enemies who had been bribed, how could it be possible that either he should be willing or the people of his flock should permit him to leave his church and go into a private house, not to be examined by the scrutiny of colleagues, but to be slain by a factional mob and a woman's hatred? And especially how could he do it when he saw a Church overseas, free from personal feuds and unbiassed toward either side, ready to afford him an impartial and thorough investigation? If his opponents did not wish to press the case there, they would cut themselves off from the most guiltless communion in the world; but, if they tried to accuse him, he would be present and could defend his innocence against their contrivances. This did happen afterwards, as you have learned, when they demanded an overseas trial, but too late, because they were then guilty of schism and stained with the horrible crime of setting up another altar. They should have done that first, if they had had any reliance on the truth of their case, but when false reports had been strengthened by the lapse of time, and the old story was being taken for granted, they were then willing to come to trial. What is more likely is that, if Caecilian were condemned first, as they wanted, they would come, seemingly

---

27 I.e., they set up rival churches and hierarchies.

free of apprehension, relying on their numbers, yet not daring to present so bad a case in any other place where truth could be discovered without any chance of bribery.

But, when they had learned by this experience that Caecilian was in union with the rest of the world and that pastoral letters from the overseas Churches had recognized him, but not the one whom they had wrongfully ordained, they were ashamed of their silence, because they could not answer the objection that a Church, unknown in so many countries, was in communion with condemned men, but they had cut themselves off from communion with all the rest of the blameless world. By their silence they were consenting to non-recognition by the rest of the world of a bishop whom they had ordained for the Carthaginians. To meet these two objections they chose, according to report, to take their case against Caecilian to the overseas Churches, ready for either contingency; if they could triumph over him by some crafty trick of false charges, they would get full satisfaction for their ambition; if they could not, they would remain fixed in the same obstinacy, as if they really had what they claimed, namely, that they had to endure biassed judges—and this is the excuse of all crooked litigants. But, in fact, they were overwhelmed by absolutely truthful evidence, and it could most justly be said to them: 'Look! are we to think that the bishops who were judges at Rome were not good judges?' There still remained in reserve a general conference of the whole Church[28] where the case could be taken up with the judges themselves, and, if it could be proved that their decision was wrong, their sentence could be revoked. Let them show what they will do; we can easily prove that nothing was done from the fact that the world is not in a state of unity with them. But, if

---

28 This was finally held at Carthage, in 411.

anything was accomplished, they were beaten even there because their separation from the Church is evident.

What they did afterward is very plainly shown from the emperor's letter. They presumed to criticize, on the grounds of false verdict, the ecclesiastical judges—bishops of such influence, by whose judgment the innocence of Caecilian and their own malice was published—and this, not to their colleagues but to the emperor. He gave them another trial at Arles, doubtless with other bishops, not because it was necessary, but by way of yielding to their obstinacy and wishing by all means to restrain their excessive boldness. Yet, as a Christian emperor, he did not venture to sustain their disorderly and unfounded complaints by giving a judgment on the court of bishops which had sat at Rome, but, as I said, he appointed other bishops. And even from these they chose to appeal to the emperor in person. In this affair, you have heard how he despised them; would that by his decision he at least had made an end of their senseless rivalries! And, as he yielded to them by taking up the question after the bishops had decided, with an apology to the holy prelates, it could be wished that they, too, having nothing more to say, yet unwilling to give in to his verdict to which they had appealed, might at length yield to truth. He ordered that both sides come to him at Rome to try the case. But, when Caecilian, for some reason or other, did not go there, notified by them, the emperor instructed them to follow him to Milan. Then, some of them began to withdraw, angered because Constantine had not followed their example by instantly and speedily condemning the absent Caecilian. When the wise emperor learned this, he forced the rest of them to come to Milan under guard, and, as he wrote, when Caecilian also arrived, he had him appear, heard his case, and with the care, precaution and foresight manifested in his letters, he declared him completely innocent, and his accusers guilty of base injustice.

And still they baptize outside the Church, and, when they can, they rebaptize the Church; they offer the sacrifice[29] in a state of disunion and schism, and greet people in the name of peace whom they cut off from the peace of salvation. The unity of Christ is blasphemed, the baptism of Christ is scorned, and they refuse to be corrected of those sins by common human authority, through temporal penalties, which would ward off the eternal chastisement due to their great blasphemies. We reproach them with the violence of schism, the madness of rebaptism, the sinful separation from the inheritance of Christ, which is spread abroad among all peoples. Not only from our own documents, but even from theirs, we can list churches whose names they read today, but with which they are not in communion. When these names are read in their places of assembly, they say to their readers: 'Peace be to thee!' but they do not share peace with the peoples to whom those epistles were written. And they bring against us the false charges of dead men, not realizing that, even if they were true, they would have nothing to do with our complaints against them; or that they are rated as chaff, especially in the objections they bring against us; and that they are rebuked as the cockle[30] of the Lord's harvest. They do not see that this reproach does not apply to the good grain, because those who take pleasure in partaking of evil share the lot of the evil-minded, but those whom evil displeases cannot make them better; nor do they dare to root up the cockle before the time of the harvest, 'lest they root up the wheat also together with it.'[31] These have no part in their misdeeds,

---

29 The Sacrifice of the Mass.
30 Matt. 13.24-30.
31 Matt. 13.30.

but in the altar of Christ. And so they are so far from being contaminated by them that they deserve to be praised and spoken of in the divine words, because they bear for the sake of unity what they hate for the sake of justice, to prevent the name of Christ from being blasphemed by vile schism.

'If they have ears, let them hear what the Spirit saith to the Churches.'[32] Thus we read in John's Apocalypse: 'Unto the angel,' he says, 'of the Church of Ephesus write: These things saith he who holdeth the seven stars in his right hand, who walketh in the midst of the seven golden candlesticks: I know thy works and thy labor and thy patience and how thou canst not bear them that are evil; and thou hast tried them who say they are Apostles and are not; and hast found them liars: and thou hast patience and hast endured for my name and hast not fainted.'[33] But, if he meant this to be understood of the angels of the heavens above, he would not go on to say: 'But I have somewhat against thee, because thou hast left thy first charity. Be mindful therefore from whence thou art fallen: and do penance and do the first works or else I come to thee and will move thy candlestick out of its place, except thou do penance.'[34] This cannot be said of the angels above who keep their charity forever, but from which the Devil and his angels have departed and fallen.[35] Therefore he says first charity, because he endured the false apostles, and he orders him to seek it again and to do the first works. But it is the evil deeds of wicked men that are imputed to us, not our own; something foreign and even unknown to us. Even if we saw these defects true and present, we should endure them for the sake of unity, sparing the cockle because of the wheat; and anyone who hears the Holy Scriptures with open

---
32 Cf. Apoc. 2.7.
33 Apoc. 2.1-3.
34 Apoc. 2.4-5.
35 Matt. 25.41; Apoc. 12.9.

heart would say that we are not only undeserving of blame, but even worthy of no slight praise.

Aaron bore with the people dragging out and making and adoring an idol;[36] Moses bore with so many thousands of them murmuring against God and so often offending His holy Name;[37] David bore with Saul his persecutor, who by his wicked deeds forsook heavenly aims, and by magic arts sought out the lower regions; he defended him after he was killed, and even called him the Lord's anointed, because of the rite of religious unction.[38] Samuel bore with the wicked sons of Heli, his debased sons whom the people would not bear,[39] and who were thereupon accused by divine truth or disciplined by divine wrath; finally he bore with the people themselves in their pride and rejection of God. Isaias bore with them against whom he uttered so many true charges; Jeremias bore with them from whom he suffered so much; Zacharias bore with the Pharisees and the scribes, and the Scripture bears witness what kind of men they were. I know that I have passed over many examples. Let them read who wish, and who can, the heavenly language; they will find that all the saints have held as servants and friends of God those from whom they had to suffer among their own people. When they shared the religious rites of that time with them, they were not defiled, but even deserved praise for their support, 'Careful,' as the Apostle says, 'to keep the unity of the spirit in the bond of peace.'[40] Let them note the time after the coming of the Lord, when we should find many more examples of this toleration all over the world, if it were possible to write them all and authenticate them.

---

36 Exod. 32. 1-6.
37 Exod. 14.11; 15.24; 16.2,8; 17.2,3; Num. 14.2,3; 16.2,3.
38 1 Kings 18.10-24;23; 26.1-12; 28.7-14; 2 Kings 1.116.
39 1 Kings 2.12-26; 8.1-22.
40 Eph. 4.3.

However, note those which we have: the Lord Himself bore with Judas, a devil, a thief and His betrayer;[41] He permitted him to receive, among the innocent Apostles, what the faithful know as their reward;[42] the Apostles bore with false apostles,[43] 'seeking the things that are their own and not the things that are Jesus Christ's';[44] and Paul, not seeking the things that were his own but those of Jesus Christ, dealt with them with most magnificent toleration. Finally, as I recalled a little while ago, a bishop of the Church, under the name of angel, is praised by the Word of God because, although he hated those who were evil, he endured them for the name of the Lord, even after he had tried and found them out.

Finally, let them examine themselves. Do they not tolerate the massacres and burnings of the Circumcellions,[45] the veneration of corpses of the self-destroyed, the groans of all Africa for many years, under the unbelievable cruelty of Optatus?[46] I forbear to speak of the tyrannical powers and public thefts of individual regions, and cities and estates. It will be better for you to speak of this to yourselves either privately or publicly, as you wish. Wherever you turn your eyes, you will meet what I say, or, rather, what I do not say. We on our side do not accuse those whom you love on your side. It does not displease us that they bear with evil men, but that they are unbearably evil themselves because of schism, because of setting up a rival altar, because they are separated from the inheritance of Christ spread through-

---

41 John 12.4-6; Matt. 26.14-16.
42 Judas received the Body and Blood of Christ at the Last Supper, which the faithful receive in Holy Communion.
43 2 Cor. 11.13.
44 Cf. Phil. 2.21.
45 Cf. Letter 23 n. 13.
46 Donatist bishop of Thamugada.

out the world, as was long ago promised.[47] We bewail and lament the breaking of peace, the rending of unity, the repetition of baptism, the mockery of the sacraments, things which are sacred even to abandoned men. If they make light of these, let them look at the instances which show how much God makes of them. Those who made an idol were cut off by the common death of the sword,[48] the leaders of those who tried to create a schism[49] were swallowed up by the earth opening, and the people who agreed with them were destroyed by fire. By the difference in punishments is shown the difference in guilt.

The holy books are betrayed in time of persecution; the betrayers confess and are left to God; the innocent are condemned by unscrupulous men without examination; one is judged blameless by selected judges, who is indicted much more violently than the rest in the midst of men condemned in their absence; there is a trial by bishops; there is an appeal to the emperor; the emperor is chosen as judge; the emperor's verdict is repudiated. You have read what was done at that time; you see what is going on now. If you have any doubt about the previous happenings, look at these. Let us not deal now with ancient documents, or public records, or minutes of civil or ecclesiastical courts. Our book is the larger one of the world; in it I read the fulfillment of the promise I find in the book of God: 'The Lord,' it says, 'hath said to me, Thou art my son, this day have I begotten thee. Ask of me, and I will give thee the Gentiles for thy inheritance, and the utmost parts of the earth for thy possession.'[50] Whoever does not share in this inheritance, whatever books he has, let him know that he is disinherited; whoever attacks

---

47 Ps. 2.8.
48 Exod. 32.1-28.
49 Num. 16.1-35;41-49.
50 Ps. 2.7,8.

this inheritance shows plainly that he is not a member of the family of God. Certainly, there is question of handing over the divine books in which that inheritance is promised. Therefore, he that goes to law against the will of the testator should be considered to have consigned the testament to the flames. What did the Church of the Corinthians do to you, faction of Donatus; what did it do to you? And what I say of that Church I mean to be applied to all that are like it, however remotely situated. What did they do to you, those Churches which could not know at all either what you did or what men you defamed? Was it, perhaps, because Caecilian offended Lucilla in Africa that the world lost the light of Christ?

Let them finally realize what they have done; their work has been spread out before their eyes for a considerable period of years. Inquire what woman caused Maximian,[51] said to be a relative of Donatus, to cut himself off from communion with Primian,[52] and how, with a group of dissident bishops, he condemned Primian in his absence, and was ordained bishop in his stead; just as Maiorinus, urged by Lucilla, gathered a group of dissident bishops, condemned

---

51 Donatist deacon of Carthage.
52 Like many other schisms, that of Donatus bred schisms within itself. Primian, Donatist bishop of Carthage, excommunicated the deacon, Maximian, who thereupon secured the support of a hundred bishops in a synod, and Primian was deposed. Maximian was consecrated bishop in his place, and ordered all Primianists to forsake their bishop and come over to him under severe penalties. Primian, however, allied 310 bishops on his side, and condemned Maximian and his followers under similar penalties. Maximian's church was razed to the ground, and his sectaries severely persecuted. But with great inconsistency to their own principle of requiring rebaptism for all returning Maximianists, the Primianists did not require rebaptism for Praetextatus of Assur and Felician of Musti, two of the consecrators of Maximian, who simply refused to be ousted from their churches, and had to be reinstated on their own terms by the Primianists. Augustine uses this inconsistency as a telling argument against them in later letters.

Caecilian in his absence, and was ordained bishop against him. Or are you, perhaps, willing to uphold the fact that Primian was cleared by the rest of the African bishops of his communion against the faction of Maximian, but unwilling to uphold the fact that Caecilian was cleared by the overseas bishops in union with the Church against the faction of Maiorinus? I ask you, my brothers, what great favor am I seeking? Am I asking you to understand something difficult? If a comparison were made on the basis of influence or numbers, there would be a great difference between the African church and the other parts of the world, and it would fall very far short of them; yet it is less—even if there were unity here—far less, in comparison with all the other Christian peoples, than the faction of Maximian is compared with that of Primian. I ask, however, and I think it a just request, that the synod of Secundus of Tigisis, which Lucilla stirred up against the absent Caecilian, and the Apostolic See, and the whole world on the side of Caecilian, be worth as much as the synod of the Maximian supporters, which some woman or other stirred up against the absent Primian and all the rest of the people in Africa on Primian's side. What is more obvious? What more reasonable to ask?

You see all this, and you know it and you bewail it; yet God sees that nothing forces you to remain in that pestilential and sacrilegious state of schism, if, for the sake of gaining a spiritual kingdom, you would overcome a worldly attraction, and if, for the sake of avoiding eternal punishments, you would not fear to offend the friendships of men, which will profit you nothing in the judgment of God. Go, then, consult together, discover what they can answer to these arguments of ours. If they bring out documents, we bring out documents; if they say ours are spurious, they cannot resent our saying the same of theirs. No one blots out of heaven the ordinance of God; no one blots from the earth the Church of God. He promised the whole earth: she has filled the whole earth, and she includes both bad and good; but she loses none on earth but the bad, and admits to heaven none but the good. This will be our word to you, by the gift of God; and He knows how we have uttered it out of our love of peace and of you: for your correction, if you wish it; but for a witness, whether you like it or not.

44. Augustine to the beloved lords and estimable brothers, Eleusius, Glorius, and the Felixes (late 397 or early 398)

On our recent visit to Tubursicum,[1] as we passed through quickly on our way to the church in Cirta,[2] we found Fortunius, your bishop there, to be quite what you always promised he would be. Indeed, he did not belie the account you gave of him, when we sent him word that we wished to see him. So, we went to him rather than expect him to come to us first, because we thought his age required that consideration. We traveled with a fairly large company, which the occasion[3] had gathered together, but, when we sat down with Fortunius, another good-sized crowd collected, as the report had gone round. However, there were very few in that entire gathering who wanted the case to be dealt with practicably and profitably, or who wished a question of such great importance to be discussed with prudence and mutual respect. Most of them had come, as they go to the theatre, to witness the stage play of a quarrel between us, rather than to receive with Christian eagerness an instruction on salva-

---
1 A town in Numidia.
2 A large Numidian town.
3 He was on his way to ordain a bishop for Cirta.

tion. Therefore, they did not give us the tribute of silence, nor were they able to argue with us with attention or any sort of moderation or order; with the exception, as I said, of a few whose religious and unprejudiced interest was evident. Consequently, everything was in disorder, with the confusion of people speaking freely and without restraint, each one according to his own bent; and neither he nor we could succeed, by request or even by strong appeal, in securing for ourselves a respectful silence.

However, we carried on the debate for several hours, as it had begun, with alternate speech, whenever we could get a hearing in the intervals of their shouting. But, when we saw, at the very beginning of the discussion, that what was said slipped from our memory or theirs—and our concern was for their salvation—and so that our handling of the question might be more considered and restrained, and also that you and other brothers, who were absent, might learn by reading what was settled between us, we asked that our words be taken down by stenographers.[4] There was prolonged opposition by him and those on his side, but at length he gave in. But the stenographers who were present and able to write that quickly, for some reason or other did not want to take down the proceedings. We succeeded at length in getting some brothers who were with us to take down what was said, although they were rather slow at it, promising to leave duplicate records behind us. They agreed to this. Our words began to be recorded, and also some other things, said on each side for the record. Then, our stenographers stopped, not able to keep up with the disorderly interruptions of the shouters, or even with our own more agitated arguments. We

---

4 There was a system of shorthand in use among the Romans, known as *notae tironianae,* its origin attributed to Tiro, Cicero's secretary. One who took down notes was a *notarius.* The use of such notaries or secretaries must have been widespread in Augustine's time.

did not stop, however, but went on saying much more, whenever chance allowed. I have not wanted to deprive your Charity of the account of the whole affair, as far as I have been able to recall something of all that I said. You can read my letter to him,[5] so that he may either admit that I have written the truth or may straightway suggest something else to you, if his recollection is better than mine.

In the first place, then, he was so kind as to commend our life, which he said he had heard you describe—with more politeness than truth, perhaps—adding how he had told you that we could accomplish everything which you had told about us, if we acted within the Church. Thereupon, we began to inquire which Church that was where one should so live; whether it was the one which was spread throughout the world, as the Holy Scripture had foretold so long ago, or that other one which was confined to a small group of Africans or a small part of Africa. Here, he tried at first to claim that his sect was world-wide. I asked whether he could give letters of authentication, which we call *formate,* anywhere he wished; and I asserted that the question could very easily be settled by that proof, which was evident to all. I was ready, if he agreed, for the test of sending such letters from our Churches to those which, as we read, were founded by apostolic authority in apostolic times.

But, because this claim was obviously unfounded, we quickly left that topic with a great mixture of words. Among these words he recalled that warning of the Lord, when He said: 'Beware of false prophets: many will come to you in the clothing of sheep but inwardly they are ravening wolves. By their fruits you shall know them.'[6] When we said that the same words could be quoted by us about them, he turned

---
5 Fortunius, their bishop.
6 Cf. Matt. 7.15,16.

to making much of persecution which he said his sect had often suffered, wishing from this to show that his people were Christians because they suffered persecution. When I was about to reply to these words by others from the Gospel, he took up first the chapter where the Lord said: 'Blessed are they that suffer persecution for justice sake: for theirs is the kingdom of heaven.'[7] Delighted with this text, I broke in at once with the objection that the question to be asked was whether they suffered persecution for justice sake. I was anxious to have that point discussed—it was clear to everybody—whether the time of Macarius[8] had found them in union with the Church or even then separated by schism, because anyone who wanted to know whether they suffered persecution for justice sake should note whether they had been right in separating themselves from the unity of the universal Church. If they had not been right, it would be evident that they had suffered persecution for the sake of injustice rather than justice, and therefore they could not be included in the number of the blessed of whom it was said: 'Blessed are they that suffer persecution for justice sake.' Then the question came up of betraying the [sacred] books, a matter based more on rumor than on truth. And our side answered that, if they could not accept our records on that point, they had no right to force us to accept theirs.

However, when that doubtful question had been set aside, I asked how they could rightly have separated themselves from the pure body of Christians, who had been organized in the most ancient Churches, guarding the order of succession all over the world, yet completely unaware who were the betrayers in Africa, since they could communicate only with those whom they knew to occupy the bishop's see. He answer-

---

7 Matt. 5.10.
8 See Letter 23 n. 12.

ed that the Churches in overseas countries had remained pure until they had shared the guilt of bloodshed in what he called the Macarian persecution. I could have said that the purity of the overseas Churches could hardly be tainted by the ill-repute of Macarian times, since it could not be proved that they had any responsibility for what had been done; but I preferred to inquire, in short, if the overseas Churches lost their purity from the time when they had approved the cruelty of Macarius, could it at least be proved that the Donatists had remained in unity up to that time with the eastern Churches and those of other parts of the world?

Then he brought out a certain book in which he wanted to point out to me that the Council of Sardis[9] had sent letters to African bishops of the sect of Donatus. When this was read, we heard the name Donatus among other bishops, and we began to ask for information whether he was the Donatus whose name had been given to their sect; for it could have been that they were writing to some other Donatus, a bishop of another sect. This was especially likely, because no mention of Africa was made among those names. How could he prove that the Donatus, bishop of the Donatist sect, was to be indentified by that name when it could not even be proved that the letters in question had been sent specifically to bishops of African churches? For, although Donatus is usually an African name, it would not be inconsistent with truth to suppose that someone in that part of the world was called by an African name, or that some African had been set up as bishop out there. Moreover, in that record we found neither date nor consul to give us light on any definite time. Certainly, sometime ago we heard that, when the Arians had broken away from the Catholic communion, they tried to get the Donatists in Africa to join them—

---

9 Sofia, in Bulgaria.

brother Alypius whispered this in my ear. Then I took the book and examined the proceedings of that same council, and I read that Athanasius, Catholic Bishop of Alexandria, whose bitter dispute with the Arians had reached a climax of conflict, and Julius,[10] an indisputably Catholic bishop of the Church of Rome, had been condemned at that Council of Sardis. Hence it was clear to us that the council was an Arian council, and that those Catholic bishops were in violent opposition to it. We wanted to take the book away with us for a more careful discussion of those happenings, but he would not give it to us, saying that we had it there when we wanted to look at anything in it. I then asked to be allowed to make some notes from it in my own hand, because I feared that, if I asked for it, in the heat of discussion another might be substituted for it. But he would not allow this, either.

Then he began to insist that I should answer his questions briefly, asking me which one I thought a just man: the persecutor or the one who suffered persecution. I answered that this was not a fair question, for it could be that both were wicked men, and it could be that the more just persecuted the more wicked one. Besides, it did not necessarily follow that anyone was more just because he suffered persecution, although this commonly happens. Then, when I saw that he lingered long on this point, so as to stress the justice of his sect on the ground that it had suffered persecution, I asked him whether he thought that Ambrose, Bishop of Milan, was a just man and a Christian. He was certainly forced to deny that he was a Christian and just, because, if he admitted it, we should straightway object that he [the Donatist] would require him [Ambrose] to be rebaptized. When he was forced to the admission that Ambrose could

---

[10] Pope Julius.

not be considered a Christian and a just man, I recalled how great a persecution he had suffered when even his church was surrounded by soldiers.[11] I asked further, whether he thought Maximian, who had seceded from his schism at Carthage, was a just man and a Christian. He could not but deny it. Then I reminded him that he had suffered such a persecution that his church was razed to the foundations. By these examples, I tried, if possible, to induce him to give up saying that the suffering of persecution is the surest proof of Christian justice.

He also related how, at the very beginning of the schism, his predecessors, while they were considering the guilt of Caecilian, wanted to adopt some kind of palliative measure to prevent schism, so they appointed someone, called an *interventor*,[12] to be temporarily in charge of the people of his communion gathered in Carthage, before Maiorinus was ordained to displace Caecilian. He said that this interventor had been killed in his own place of worship by our people. I confess that I had certainly never heard this before, although many charges were made by them and refuted by ours, and more and even greater crimes were alleged against them. However, after this, he again began to ask insistently whom I considered just—the one who killed or the one who was killed, as if he had proved that it had happened as he related it. I said that in the first place we must inquire whether it

---

[11] This occurred in a contest between St. Ambrose, Bishop of Milan, and Empress Justina, mother of Valentinian II. Justina was an Arian, and demanded for the Arians the new basilica of Ambrose. He refused, and was firmly supported by his people. During the offices of Holy Week, Justina sent soldiers to seize the basilica and the bishop. The congregation resisted firmly, barricaded themselves inside for several days, and the services continued. The soldiers, most of whom were not Arians, soon joined in the services, and the empress was forced to yield. Eventually, peace was restored, and the basilica remained in the possession of the Catholics.

[12] This name was given to one who ruled over a diocese during a vacancy.

was true, for it is not fitting to believe whatever is said without proof; nevertheless, it could have happened that both were equally wicked or even that the less wicked had killed the more wicked of the two. In fact, it can happen that a rebaptizer of the whole man is more guilty than the slayer of his body alone.

What he asked me afterwards was not to be taken up then, for he said that even an evil man ought not to be killed by Christians and just men, as if we call those good in the Catholic fold who do such things. But they commonly say things like that to us more easily than they prove them, especially when they continually allege against us so many violent murders and massacres. Moreover, those who allege them are bishops and priests and clerics of various grades, with mobs made up of the most savage kind of men, not Catholics, but sometimes of their own adherents, when possible. In spite of this he pretended not to know their infamous deeds—which he knows better than anyone—and he kept insisting that I should tell him who among good men had ever killed a bad man. Although this had nothing to do with the question, I admitted that, when such things were done under Christian auspices, they were not done by good men. Then, to warn him what question should be asked, I replied by inquiring whether Elias seemed to him a good man, and he could not deny it. We then added how many false prophets he had killed with his own hand.[13] He saw the point clearly, that certain things were allowable to good men at that time, and that they acted by prophetic impulse under the authority of God, who knew without doubt those to whom death would be an advantage. But he kept insisting on my telling him what good man in New Testament times had killed any person, even a wicked and impious one.

---

13 3 Kings 18.40.

Then we returned to the previous argument by which we wished to demonstrate that we ought not to blame them for the crimes of their followers, nor should they blame us if any such deeds were found among ours. From the New Testament I showed that is was not possible for a just man to kill anyone, for, indeed, it was proved by the example of our Lord that wicked men had been endured by the innocent. He suffered His very betrayer,[14] who had already received his price, to remain with Him among the innocent until the last kiss of peace. Although He did not conceal from them that a man stained with such crime was in their midst, He gave the first sacrament of His Body and Blood to all of them, without excluding the traitor. When almost all had been impressed by this example, Fortunius tried to claim that before the Passion of the Lord such communication with a criminal had not harmed the Apostles, because they had not yet received the baptism of Christ, but only that of John. At this, I began to ask him how it was written that: 'Jesus baptizeth more than John, though Jesus Himself did not baptize but His disciples.'[15] How, then, did they give what they had not received?—an argument which is a great favorite of theirs: 'Did Christ then baptize with the baptism of John'?[16] I was going on to ask many questions along this line: how, when John was asked about the baptism of the Lord, he answered that He had the bride and He was the bridegroom. Was it fitting, then, that the Bridegroom should baptize with the baptism of a friend or a servant? Besides, how could they receive the Eucharist if they were not yet baptized? Or how could He reply to Peter wishing to be washed all over: 'He that is washed once,

---

14 Matt. 26.14-16; 20-28; 48,49.
15 John 4.12.
16 John 3.22-29.

needeth not to be washed again but is clean wholly?'[17] Therefore, the perfect cleansing is not the baptism in the name of John, but in the name of the Lord, if he that receives it proves worthy of it. But, if he proves unworthy, the sacraments will remain in him, not for his salvation but for his damnation. Just as I was about to ask these questions, he saw for himself that he had better not ask about the baptism of the Lord's disciples.

We then turned to another point, with much arguing back and forth on both sides as best we could. Among other things, it was said that ours intended to persecute them, and he told us he would like to see how we would behave in that persecution; whether we would agree to such cruelty or whether we would disapprove of it. We said that God sees our hearts—which they could not—and that they were fearing something without good reason, but, if it befell, it would be at the hands of evil men, and they had worse ones themselves. But that was no reason for us to separate from the Catholic communion, if, perhaps, something was done against our will or even against our protest, if we were strong enough to protest. On our part, we had learned peaceable endurance from the Apostle, when he said: 'Supporting one another in charity, careful to keep the unity of the Spirit in the bond of peace.'[18] We said that they who had caused schism had not kept peace and patience, but that those among them who are more peaceable now tolerate greater evils to prevent schism from the schismatic than they had borne to preserve unity in the first place. We said that in ancient times the peace of unity and forbearance had not been preached with such persuasiveness as it was by the example of the Lord and the charity of the New Testament, yet those

---
17 Cf. John 13.10.
18 Eph. 4.2,3.

prophets and holy men who were accustomed to denounce the crimes of the people did not try to separate themselves from the unity of their people or from participation with them in such religious rites as were then in use.

Then, somehow or other, we came to the recollection of Bishop Genethlius[19] of blessed memory, because he had suppressed some ordinance issued against them, and had not allowed it to take effect. They all praised him and spoke kindly of him. In the midst of their praises, we interrupted to ask whether, if he had fallen into their hands, they would have obliged him to be rebaptized. We said this standing up, because it was time to leave. There, the old man said frankly that it was an established practice that, if any of the faithful went over from us to them, he was baptized, but it was clear that he said it unwillingly, and even with such regret as he could show. Certainly, since he so openly lamented and pointed out the many wicked excesses of his followers—and it was proved by the testimony of the whole city how far he was himself from such doings—and since he uttered with restrained complaint what he is accustomed to say to his people, we on our side would recall that passage of the Prophet Ezechiel where it is openly written that the guilt of the son is not to be imputed to the father, nor the guilt of the father to the son,[20] as it says: 'As the soul of the father so also the soul of the son is mine, for whatsoever soul shall sin, it alone shall die.'[21]

So it was agreed among all of us that in such discussions there should be no mutual recriminations about the cruel deeds of wicked men. There remained the question of schism, and we exhorted him again and again to side with us in a

---
19 Migne adds: 'bishop of Carthage before Aurelius.'
20 Ezech. 18.20.
21 Cf. Ezech. 18.4.

spirit of peace and unity, to the end that the inquiry should end with a careful examination. When he said mildly that I alone sought that end, but that our side did not want these things looked into, we parted with the promise that we should produce for him several colleagues of ours, at least ten, who had the same desire for this conference in a kindly and calm and charitable spirit, such as he had noticed and approved in us. And he promised the same number from his side.

So, then, I urge and beseech you by the Blood of the Lord to remind him of his promise and to strive valiantly to bring this beginning to the end which you see is now near at hand. As far as I can see, you will have great difficulty in finding among your bishops so open a mind and such good will as we noted in this old man. The next day he came to us and we began to go over the same ground again, but, because we had to ordain a bishop[22] and time was hurrying us on, we were unable to stay longer with him. Besides, we had sent for the Elder of the Heaven-dwellers[23] to have a talk with him, as far as the limits of our time allowed, because we heard that he had set up an advocate of new baptism[24] among them, and had led many astray by that sacrilege. So, when Fortunius heard that he was coming, and that we had taken up another task, alleging pressing business, he took leave of us cordially and quietly.

It seems to me, therefore, that we should meet at some small country place, so as to avoid altogether the noisy crowds, which are more hindrance than help, and there continue, in a friendly and peaceable spirit, this very im-

---

22 Fortunatus, successor to Profuturus, who died after a brief term in office.
23 This name occurs in several laws of Honorius, which threatened heretics with certain penalties unless they were converted to the worship and Christian veneration of God.
24 The rebaptism of Catholics who went over to the Donatists.

portant business which we have undertaken with the help of the Lord. This should be a place where neither of us has a church, yet a place owned jointly by his people and ours, as for example, Villa Titiana. If, then, such a place can be found at Tubursicum or at Tagaste, either the one I have mentioned or any other, let us have at hand canonical books and documents from both sides, if such can be produced. Then, setting all else aside, with no importunate interruptions, if God so wills, let us spend as many days on this task as we can, each of us praying God under his own roof, and with His help, to whom Christian peace is so pleasing, let us bring to a successful end this important inquiry, which has been begun with such good will. Write me, please, what you and he think of this proposal.

45. Alypius and Augustine give greetings to their intimately beloved lords, praiseworthy in Christ, Paulinus and Therasia (398)

Your unexplained silence, in which we have received no letters from you, lo! these two years, since those sweetest of brothers, Romanus and Agilis, left us to go to you, has not made us slothful in writing to you. For, although in other things the more one is loved, the more worthy he seems of imitation, in this matter it is just the opposite. So, the more ardently we love you, the less easily we bear your not writing to us, and we have no wish to imitate you in that. Behold us, then, sending you greetings, if not in answer to letters of yours, not one of which has come to us, at least in protest, and with no slight regret. Doubtless, your Charity would likewise complain if you knew that letters sent by you had not reached us, and, contrariwise, that ours had been sent but not delivered to you. If that is the case, let us turn our complaints into prayers to the Lord that He may not refuse us such comfort.

We heard that you were writing a book against the pagans. If it is finished, please do not delay to send it by the bearer of this letter. He is dear to us and we can testify freely to his good reputation in this country. He requests your Sanctity, through us, to be so kind as to recommend him to those with whom he has business. He is afraid his good cause may be opposed by them. It will be better for him to tell you what he is engaged to do, and you can question him about the details, which perhaps disturb his mind. We shall esteem it a favor and we shall give thanks through the Lord our God to your most sincere kindness, if, through your help, we can rejoice in the safety of a brother Christian.

46. *Publicola*[1] *to the beloved and venerable bishop and father, Augustine (398)*

It is written: 'Ask thy father and he will declare to thee; thy elders and they will tell thee.'[2] Therefore, I have decided that I must seek out the law from the mouth of the priest in such matter as I am explaining by letter. And that I may at the same time be instructed on various points, I have planned out separate questions and noted them under various heads, which I ask you to be so kind as to answer.

I. In Arzuges, as I heard, the barbarians are accustomed to swear by their demons to the overseer or tribune in charge of the boundary. Those who have been hired to escort bag-

---

1 The writer is evidently one whose native language is not Latin. He handles the language awkwardly, constructs his sentences clumsily, and moves uneasily within the circle of a restricted vocabulary.
2 Deut. 32.7.

gage, or others to guard the harvest, the various land-owners and stewards are accustomed to receive, to guard the harvest, as if they were of the faithful, on receipt of a letter written by the overseer. And the same is true of individuals passing through, who have to pass through. A doubt has arisen in my heart whether that property-owner who received a barbarian, whose fidelity is vouched for by his oath to the demons, is defiled, either himself or the things which are guarded, or the one who is escorted by a barbarian guide. But you should know this, that the barbarian who takes the oath receives money from the property-owner for guarding his harvest, or the guide receives it from the traveler, and with this pay which is given by the property-owner or traveler, that deadly oath is given publicly to the overseer or tribune. What disturbs me is, lest it defile him who received the oath of the barbarian, or the things which the barbarian guards. For, on any condition, by giving money and hostages, as I have heard, an oath, even sinful, guarantees public credit. Please give a clear and not long-drawn-out answer, because, if you write doubtfully, I can fall into doubts greater than those I had before I asked you.

II. I have heard that the stewards themselves who have charge of my property receive from barbarians for guarding the harvest an oath sworn by demons. Please tell me if those who swear by their demons to guard my crops do not defile the crops themselves and if a Christian who knowingly eats of the crops, or makes use of the price of them, is defiled.

III. Likewise, I heard from another that the oath is not given to the steward by the barbarian and another says that he has sworn to the steward. If he has lied to me who said the oath had been given to the steward, ought I not to use the crops or the price of them on this mere hearsay, because it is written: 'If any man say: this has been sacrificed to idols: do not eat of it for his sake'?[3] Is this the same case as the case of food sacrificed to idols? If so, what ought I to do with the crops or the price of them?

IV. If I ought to inquire about both of them, the one who said to me that the oath is given to the steward, or the one who said that the oath is not given to the steward, and prove the word of each one by witnesses, [to find out] who spoke the truth of those two, and not to touch anything of those crops or of the price, so long as it shall be proved to me if he spoke the truth who said that the oath is not given to the steward?

V. If the barbarian who swears wrongly through his oath shall make that Christian steward or tribune, who is in charge of the boundary, swear to him to keep faith with him in guarding the crops, by the same wicked oath, by which he swears himself, if the Christian alone is defiled? If not also those things on account of which he swears? Or if a pagan who is in charge of the boundary swears to a barbarian to keep faith with him by a wicked oath, if he does not defile that for which he swears? If I send someone to Arzuges, if it is allowed him to receive from a barbarian that pagan oath, and if a Christian who receives such an oath is not defiled?

VI. If from a threshing floor there is some wheat or beans or something from the wine-press of which some has been offered to the demon, if it is allowed a Christian to eat of it knowingly?

VII. If it is allowed a Christian knowingly to take wood from a grove[4] for his own use?

VIII. If anyone going to the market buys meat which has

---
[3] 1 Cor. 10.27.
[4] Many groves were held sacred by pagans, who peopled them with dryads and such creatures.

not been offered to idols, and has two thoughts in his heart, that it was offered and that it was not, and he holds to that thought by which it was not immolated, if he eats of it, does he sin?

IX. If anyone does a good action, about which he doubts whether it is good or bad, because he thinks it good, although he could have thought it bad, if sin is imputed to him?

X. If anyone says that something has been offered to idols and afterward says again that he lied, and he truly lies to affirm the truth, if it is allowed a Christian to eat of it, or to sell it and use the price of it on the score of what he heard?

XI. If a Christian walking along suffers need and is overcome by hunger for one day or two days or many days, so that he can no longer bear it, and it shall so happen that the hunger in that necessity in which he sees himself near death, finds food placed before an idol, where there are no men around and he cannot find other food, ought he to die or to eat of it?

XII. If a Christian should see a barbarian or a Roman wanting to kill[5] him, ought the Christian kill them himself so as not to be killed by them? Or if it is allowed without killing to fight them and chase them off, because it is said: 'not to resist evil'?[6]

XIII. If a Christian ought to make a wall for his property because of an enemy, if that Christian does not become a cause of murder because from behind it some enemies may begin to fight and kill?

XIV. If it is allowed to drink from a spring or a well where something has been thrown from a sacrifice? If it is from a well that is in a temple and is now deserted, ought

---

5 The writer has, literally: 'should see himself being wanted to be killed.'
6 Matt. 5.39.

a Christian to drink of it? If in a temple of an idol there should be a well or a spring and nothing is done to it, if a Christian ought to draw water from it and to drink of it?

XV. If a Christian ought to bathe in the baths or hot baths in which sacrifice is made to images?[7] If a Christian ought to bathe in baths in which pagans bathe on their feast day, either with them or without them?

XVI. If in a sitting-bath in which the pagans have gone down, coming on their feast day and there in the sitting-bath they perform some of their sacrilege, if the Christian knows it, if he ought to go down into the same sitting-bath?

XVII. If a Christian, invited out by someone, shall have meat set before him for food, of which it is said to him that it has been offered to idols, and he does not eat it; but afterwards, invited out by someone else, he shall find that same meat carried off some way or other and offered for sale, and he [the host] shall buy it and have it served, and he [the Christian] does not know it and eats it, if he sins?

XVIII. If from a garden or property of idols or their priests a Christian ought knowingly to buy vegetables or fruits and eat of them?

Certainly, I wanted to set before your eyes this matter about oaths or idols, how we have found it, so that you would not have the trouble of inquiring what the Lord has given; but, if you find something clearer or better in the Scriptures, please point it out to me. Here is some of what we have found: where Laban said to Jacob: 'The God of Abraham and the God of Nachor,'[8] but Scripture does not indicate what god; again, Abimelech, when he came to Isaac, where he swore and those who were with him,[9] but the Scripture does not indicate what sort of oath; again, about idols, where

---

7 Many of the large Roman pleasure-palaces, which incidentally housed places to bathe, also had shrines or altars of the gods.
8 Gen. 31.53.

it was said to Gideon by the Lord in the Book of Judges that he should offer a holocaust of a heifer which he had killed;[10] and in Josue, son of Nun, of Jericho that all the gold, silver and vessels of brass should be laid up in the treasures of the Lord,[11] and it was called holy from that city which was anathema;[12] and what is that which is placed in Deuteronomy: 'Thou shalt not bring an abomination into thy house and thou shalt be an anathema, as itself is.'[13]

May the Lord keep you; I salute you. Pray for me.

47. Augustine gives greeting in the Lord to his honorable and beloved son, Publicola (398)

The anxieties of your mind became mine also as soon as I had learned of them from your letter, not because the same things disturb me as you have declared disturb you, but because, I admit, I was concerned to know how I could remove your uneasiness, especially as you ask me to answer you clearly, lest you fall into greater doubts than you had before you consulted me. Something may seem absolutely certain to me, but, if I do not put it in such a way as to convince you, you will undoubtedly be more confused than ever. I have not the same facility for convincing that others have, but, after a little reflection, I decided I should answer you so as not to refuse my poor help to your affection.

You are uncertain whether one should rely on the trustworthiness of a man whose surety is an oath sworn by demons. I want you to consider in the first place whether a

---

9 Gen. 26.26-31.
10 Judges 6.26.
11 Jos. 6.19,16,17.
12 A person or thing accursed.
13 Cf. Deut. 7.26.

man does not seem to you to have sinned twice, if he swears by false gods to keep his word and does not keep it. But, if he kept his word, pledged by such an oath, he would be deemed to have committed only one sin, that of swearing by such gods; surely no one rightly blames a man for keeping his word. Now, then, because he swore by such gods, as he should not have done, and acted contrary to his pledged word, as he should not have done, he certainly sinned twice. Therefore, he who makes use of his word, which, it is clear, has been sworn by false gods, and makes use of it, not for a bad purpose, but for a good and legitimate one, does not share in the sin by which he swore by demons, but in the good act by which he kept his faith. Here I am not speaking of that faith being kept by which those who are baptized in Christ are called faithful, for that faith is very different and far removed from the faith of human contracts and agreements. But, without any doubt, it is less a sin to swear truly by false gods than to swear falsely by the true God. For, the more sacred is that by which one swears, the more culpable is it to swear falsely. Therefore, it is another question whether one sins who obliges some one else to swear to him by false gods, when the one who swears worships the false gods. In fact, there is evidence bearing on that question, such as you recalled yourself, Laban and Abimelech, if, however, Abimelech swore by his gods as Laban did by the God of Nachor.[1] But that, as I said, is another question, about which I might properly be concerned, except that the examples occur of Isaac and Jacob,[2] and some others that might be found; although what does now concern me is what is written in the New Testament that we should not swear at all.[3] And

---

[1] Gen. 31.53.
[2] Gen. 26.26-31.
[3] Matt. 5.34-36.

it seems to me that this was said, not because it is a sin to swear truly, but because it is a heinous sin to swear falsely, and so He warned us not to swear at all because He wished to keep us far from that sin. I know that this seems to you a different point, about which there is now no discussion, and that we should rather get on to what you wanted solved. Therefore, just as you do not swear, so you do not force another to swear, if you agree to this; but, although it is said that we should not swear, I do not remember reading anywhere in the Holy Scriptures that we should not receive an oath from another. Truly, it is another question whether we should profit by a peace which has been sanctioned by a mutual oath among others. If we do not wish to do so, I do not know whether we can find anywhere on earth to live, for peace is secured by the oath of barbarians, not only for a single boundary but for whole provinces. It will follow from this that not only the crops which are protected by those who swear by false gods, but everything else which is safeguarded by the same agreement, confirmed by that kind of oath, would be defiled. If it is utterly absurd to say that, then do not be disturbed by that scruple.

Likewise, if something is taken from a threshing floor or a wine press for use in sacrifices to demons, and a Christian knows it, he sins if he allows it when he has power to prevent it. But, if he finds out that it has happened, or he had no power to prevent it, he uses without defilement the rest from which some has been taken, just as we use springs from which we know very certainly that water has been drawn for use in sacrifices. The same principle holds for bathing. For, we do not cease to draw breath from the air into which we know the smoke rises from all the altars and incense of the demons. From this it is clear that it is forbidden to make use of any object for the honor of strange gods, or to be thought to do so by receiving such object; for, although we despise them interiorly, we might make others, who do not know our mind, think that we are honoring them. And when temples, idols, groves, and other things of the sort are authorized to be torn down, although it is evident when we do this that we are not honoring but despising them, still we should not take away anything for private, or at least personal, use so that our purpose in tearing down must be manifest as devotion, not cupidity. However, when such things are turned over for public, not private or personal use, as when they are used to honor the true God, that same holds true for things as for people, when they turn from sacrilege and impiety to the true religion. God is understood to have taught this by those texts which you quoted, as when He ordered wood from the grove of foreign gods to be brought for a holocaust, and ordered that all the gold, silver and brass vessels be carried into the treasury of the Lord.[4] Therefore, that which is written in Deuteronomy: 'Thou shalt not covet the silver and gold of them, neither shalt thou take to thee any thing thereof, because it is an abomination to the Lord thy God, and thou shalt not bring an accursed thing into thy house and thou shalt be an anathema like it, and thou shalt offend with its offense and shalt be defiled by that abomination because it is anathema.'[5] It is quite clear that private use of such things is forbidden, and also the carrying home of any of them to honor them; that is where the abomination and execration lie, not in overturning such sacrilegious worship by complete destruction.

Concerning food offered to idols, be assured that we are not obliged to observe more than what the Apostle prescribes. Recall his words on this point, and in case they are not clear,

---
4 Judges 6.19.
5 Cf. Deut.7.25.26.

I shall do my poor best to explain them. He does not sin who afterward unwittingly eats food which he had previously refused as belonging to idols. Vegetables and any kind of fruit grown in any field are His who created them, because 'The earth is the Lord's and the fulness thereof'[6] and 'Every creature of God is good.'[7] But, if that which grows in the fields is consecrated to an idol or offered in sacrifice, then it must be considered idolatrous. But, if we believe we should not eat vegetables which grow in the temple garden of an idol, we must guard against thinking that the Apostles ought not to have eaten any food at Athens, because that city is dedicated to Minerva and her worship. I would also make this answer about a well or spring which is in a temple. It is a more serious matter if the remains of sacrifices are thrown into the well or the spring. But, the same reasoning applies to the air which receives all the smoke of which we spoke above, if it seems to make a difference because the sacrifice whose smoke is mingled with the air is not offered to the air, but to some idol or demon, yet sacrifices sometimes are thrown into the waters as an act of worship of the waters. But, surely, we do not stop using the light of the sun because idolators are continually offering sacrifice to it when they can. Sacrifices are even offered to the winds, which we use nevertheless to our great advantage, although they seem to drink and swallow the smoke of the same sacrifices. If anyone doubts whether meat was offered to idols, and it was not so offered, if he holds to the view that it was not offered and eats it, he certainly does not sin, because it neither was offered nor is it now thought to have been offered, even if previously he thought it was. Obviously, it is not forbidden to correct a false idea by a true one. But, if anyone thinks some-

---
6 Ps. 23.1; 1 Cor. 10.26.
7 1 Tim. 4.4.

thing is good, whereas it is bad, and does it, he certainly sins in thinking that. All these are sins of ignorance, when anyone thinks a bad act is a good act.

In regard to killing men so as not to be killed by them, this view does not please me,[8] unless perhaps it should be a soldier or a public official. In this case, he does not do it for his own sake, but for others or for the state to which he belongs, having received the power lawfully in accord with his public character. Even to those who are deterred from doing evil by some fear, perhaps some help is offered. Hence it was said: 'We are not to resist evil,'[9] lest we take pleasure in vengeance which nourishes the soul on another's wrong, but we are not to fall short in correcting men. He is not guilty of another's death who builds a wall around his property, if some one is struck and killed by its fall.[10] Neither is a Christian guilty if his cow kills someone by tossing him, or his horse by kicking. If that were so, a Christian's cow should not have horns, nor his horse hooves, nor his dog teeth. Or, again, if this were so, since the Apostle Paul acted correctly when it was brought to the notice of the tribune that a trap was being laid for Paul by certain desperate men, and for this reason he accepted an armed escort,[11] if the desperate men had fallen afoul of those arms, he should have acknowledged his own guilt in the shedding of their blood. Far be it from us to be considered blameworthy if the things which we do or have for a good and lawful purpose cause harm to anyone without our consent. Otherwise, we could have neither household nor farm utensils of iron; lest someone should use them to kill himself or another; nor should we have a tree or

---

8 Augustine treats of this problem at more length in his *De libero arbitrio* 1.5.
9 Matt. 5.39.
10 The Vienna text indicates a lacuna here; Migne adds *ex ipsius ruinis,* if it falls.
11 Acts. 23.17-24.

a rope, lest anyone should hang himself; nor should a window be made, lest anyone jump out of it. What further examples should I use, when there is no end of examples? Or what object used by man for a good and lawful purpose cannot be misused for destructive purposes?

It remains, if I mistake not, to say something about that Christian traveler whom you described as overcome by the extremity of hunger, finding no other food except some placed before an idol, and with no other human being at hand. Is it better for him to die of hunger, or to eat the said food? In this question, since it is not logically required that the food should belong to the idol, inasmuch as it could have been left there by accident or design, or for some other reason, by travelers who had turned aside from the road at that point to refresh themselves, I shall answer briefly. Either it is certain that the food belonged to the idol, or it is certain that it did not, or it is not known whether it did or not. If it is certain, it is better to refuse it with Christian fortitude; if it is known not to be idolatrous or if there is doubt, it may be used in this extremity without any scruple of conscience.

48. Augustine and the brethren who are with me give greetings in the Lord to the beloved lord and most desired brother and fellow priest, Eudoxius[1] (398)

When we think of the quiet life which you have in Christ, even we, who are involved in many hard tasks, find rest in your Charity. We are one body under one head, so that you

---

[1] Abbot of a monastery on the Island of Capraria, northeast of Corsica. Two of his monks, Eustace and Andrew, crossed over to Africa in the retinue of a Roman general who had been sent to oppose the pretensions of Gildo, Count of Africa. The latter had usurped tyrannical power and was upholding the Donatists. Eustace died before this letter was written.

are care-worn in us and we are carefree in you, because, 'if one member suffer anything, all the members suffer with it; or if one member glory, all the members rejoice with it.'[2] We warn you, therefore, and we beg and pray and beseech by the most deep humility and most merciful sublimity of Christ, that you remember us in your prayers, in which we believe you are more watchful and careful, whereas ours are often wounded and weakened by the fog and confusion of worldly affairs. And as if we did not have affairs of our own, we are loaded with the troubles of those who 'force us to go a mile' and we are ordered 'to go with them other two,'[3] so that we can scarcely breathe, but we believe that He 'in whose sight the sighing of prisoners comes in'[4] will, with the help of your prayers, free us by his promised reward from our anguish, if we persevere in the ministry in which He has deigned to place us.

But, brethren, we exhort you in the Lord to keep your resolution and persevere to the end, and, if mother Church has need of your help, do not accede to her request with eager pride, nor refuse it with slothful complacence; rather, obey God with meek heart, and bear with submission the one who rules over you: 'he who guides the mild in judgment, will teach the meek his ways.'[5] And do not prefer your peaceful retirement to the needs of the Church; otherwise, you would find no way of being born, if there were no good men to minister to her. Just as a man has to pick his way between fire and water, so as to be neither burned nor drowned, so we should steer our way between the pinnacle of pride and the whirlpool of sloth, as it is written, 'turning

---

2 1 Cor. 12.26.
3 Cf. Matt. 5.41.
4 Cf. Ps. 78.11.
5 Cf. Ps. 24.9.

neither to the right nor to the left.'⁶ For, there are some who, through fear of being carried up to the heights on the right, slip and are drowned on the left, and others who fear to be sucked in by the soft ease of sloth on the left, and are ruined and destroyed by the ostentation of boasting on the other side, and vanish into smoke and ashes. So, then, dearly beloved, you must so love your quiet peace that you continue to withdraw yourselves from all worldly pleasure; that you remember that there is no place where he whom we judge to be the enemy of all the good, whose captives we have been, cannot spread his snares, fearing, as he does, lest we fly away to God; and, finally, that you consider that there is no perfect rest for us, 'Until iniquity pass away, and justice be turned into judgment.'⁷

Likewise, when you perform a task with strength and readiness, and strive manfully, whether in prayers or in fasting or in almsgiving, by distributing something to the needy, or 'forgiving injuries, even as God hath forgiven you in Christ,'⁸ or conquering your evil habits, 'chastising your body and bringing it into subjection,'⁹ or suffering tribulation, and, above all, suffering each other in charity—for who suffers who does not suffer his brother?—or forestalling the craftiness and snares of the tempter, and 'repelling and extinguishing his fiery darts with the shield of faith,'¹⁰ or 'singing and making melody in your hearts to the Lord,'¹¹ with voice and hearts in harmony—'do all to the glory of God,'¹² 'Who worketh all in all'¹³ and so be 'in spirit fervent'¹⁴ that 'in

---

6 Deut. 17.11; Prov. 4.27.
7 A composite of Ps. 56.2 and Ps. 93.15.
8 Cf. Eph. 4.32; Col. 3.13.
9 Cf. 1 Cor. 9.27.
10 Cf. Eph. 5.16.
11 Cf. Eph. 5.19.
12 Cf. 1 Cor. 10.31.
13 Cf. 1 Cor. 12.6.
14 Cf. Rom. 12.11.

the Lord your soul may be praised.'[15] This is the direction of the right road, 'which has its eyes ever towards the Lord, for He shall pluck [your] feet from the snare.'[16] This course of life is not parched by activity, nor cooled by sloth, nor stormy, nor withered, nor bold, nor timid, nor headlong, nor faint-hearted. 'These things do ye, and the God of peace will be with you.'[17]

Let your Charity not think me unmannerly because I have wished to speak with you by letter. I have not urged this upon you because I supposed you were not already doing it, but because I believe I should be commended to God by you more often if, what you do in His service, you do with a remembrance of my words. Sometime ago rumor brought us the good odor of Christ of your manner of life, and now the brothers, Eustace and Andrew, who have come from you, have brought it even more. Of them, Eustace has gone before us into that rest which is buffeted by no waves as his island was. No, he no longer sighs for Capraria, because he no longer seeks to be clothed in sackcloth.[18]

49. Augustine, bishop of the Catholic Church, to Honoratus, bishop of the Donatist sect (398)

That plan of yours pleases me greatly, which you were so kind as to confide to brother Eros, a praiseworthy man and very dear to us, that we should carry on our argument by

---
15 Cf. Ps. 33.3.
16 Cf. Ps. 24.15.
17 Cf. Phil. 4.9.
18 There is an obscure pun in this causal clause. Capraria was an island named from the prevalence of wild goats there at its discovery (*caper*, a goat). Sackcloth, *cilicium*, was a penitential garment, so named because it was originally woven of Cilician goat hair. Thus, Eustace in heaven no longer sighs for his goat-island because he no longer needs his goat-cloth.

letter Thus, no interruption of crowds can disturb our debate, which should be undertaken and carried on with all peace and quietness of mind, as the Apostle says: 'But the servant of the Lord must not wrangle, but be mild towards all men, apt to teach, patient, with modesty admonishing those who differ in opinion.'[1] Thus we indicate briefly what we wish answered by you.

Since we see His Church, which is called Catholic, spread throughout the world, as was prophesied of it, we think we should not doubt of the manifest fulfillment of the holy prophecy, which the Lord even confirmed in His Gospel, and the Apostles, also, by whom the same Church was spread abroad according to prophecy. For, at the head of the holy psalter it is written of the Son of God: 'The Lord hath said to me: Thou art my son, this day have I begotten thee. Ask of me and I will give thee the Gentiles for thy inheritance and the utmost parts of the earth for thy possession,'[2] and the Lord Jesus Christ Himself says that His Gospel will be preached to all nations.[3] The Apostle Paul, also, before the word of God had come to Africa, at the very beginning of the Epistle which he writes to the Romans, says: 'By whom we have received grace and apostleship for obedience to the faith in all nations for His name.'[4] Then he himself, 'from Jerusalem round about,' through all of Asia, 'as far as unto Illyricum,'[5] preached the Gospel and set up and founded churches, 'yet not he, but the grace of God with him,'[6] as he testifies. What greater proof could there be than the names of places and cities which we find in his letters? He

---
1 Cf. 2 Tim. 2.24,25.
2 Ps. 2.7,8.
3 Matt. 24.14.
4 Rom. 1.5.
5 Rom. 15.19.
6 1 Cor. 15.10.

writes to the Romans, to the Corinthians, to the Galatians, to the Ephesians, to the Philippians, to the Thessalonians, to the Colossians: and John also writes to the seven Churches[7] which he mentions as established in those places, by all of which we understand that the Church is commended by the number seven: Ephesus, Smyrna, Sardis, Philadelphia, Laodicea, Pergamus, Thyatira. It is clear that we today are in communion with all those Churches, as it is clear that you are not in communion with those Churches.

We ask, then, that you do not refuse to answer us—you doubtless know the reason—how it happened that Christ lost His world-wide inheritance, and that suddenly it existed only among the Africans, and not all of them. The Catholic Church does exist even in Africa, because God wished and foretold that it should be in all lands. But your sect, which is called Donatist, is not found in all those places to which the epistles and preaching and acts of the Apostles penetrated. But, lest you say that our Church is not called Catholic but Macarian,[8] as you call it, you ought to know—as you very easily can—that in all those regions from which the Gospel of Christ spread to these lands, neither the name of Donatus nor that of Macarius is known. But you cannot deny, and it is known to all wherever your communion exists, that your sect is called Donatist. Please write to us, so that we may know how it could happen that Christ lost His Church through the whole world and began to have it among you alone. The burden of this proof is on you, because it is enough for our side that we see the prophecy and the Holy Scriptures fulfilled throughout the world. I, Augustine, have dictated this because I have wished for a long time to talk to you, for it seems to me that, because of our nearness, we

---
7 Apoc. 1.11.
8 Cf. Letter 23 n. 12.

can, at need, converse on this question by letter, with the help of God, without any disturbance.

50. Augustine, bishop, to the leaders and chiefs or elders of the colony of Sufes[1] (399)

The infamous crime and unspeakable cruelty of your savagery shakes the earth and strikes the heavens, when blood flows and murder cries aloud in your streets and shrines. By you Roman law is buried, respect for upright judges is trampled under foot; and among you there is surely neither respect nor fear for the emperors. The innocent blood of sixty brothers has been shed among you, and, if anyone killed more, he enjoyed praise and held high position in your government. Let us come, now, to the chief cause. If you say Hercules is yours, we will restore him; there is bronze, there is no lack of stone, there are several kinds of marble, and a supply of artisans is at hand. So, then, your god is carved carefully, he is smoothed off, and adorned; we add red clay to paint him red,[2] so that your prayers may have the true ring of sacredness. For, if you say that Hercules is your god, we can take up a collection from everybody and buy you a god from the stone-cutter. You give us back the lives which your fierce hand wrested from us, and your Hercules will be restored to you exactly as the lives of so many are given back by you.

---

[1] Emperor Honorius had issued an edict in 399 against idols. In the colony of Sufes, in northern Africa, a statue of Hercules had been pulled down and broken up by the Christians. In revenge, the pagans attacked them and killed sixty, who are honored in the Roman Martyrology as martyrs on August 30.

[2] This painting of statues red or vermilion seems to have been a Roman custom, whereby an imitation of archaic statues was achieved. Early statues were of terra cotta and, hence, naturally red.

51. Augustine urges Crispinus, Donatist bishop of Calama, to reply by letter to a few brief propositions (late 399 or early 400)

Since your people despise our lowliness, I preface my letter in this fashion,[1] trusting that I may not seem to belittle you; if not, I expect to be answered in the same way. There is not much for me to say about your promise of a meeting at Carthage, or of my insistence on it. Whatever arrangements we made have gone by, but let them not stand in the way for the time that remains. With the Lord's help, there is now no excuse—if I am not wrong about it; we are both in Numidia, and we are in places where we are near each other. A report has reached me that you wish to examine into this question by debating on what has sundered our communion. See how quickly all ambiguity is swept away! Answer this letter, if it pleases you, and perhaps it will satisfy not only us but those also who are longing to hear us; or, if this is not enough, let the writings go back and forth until all are satisfied. What could offer us more convenience than the close proximity of the cities where we are staying? I have decided to treat of this matter between us by letter only, so that what is said may not be forgotten by any of us, and also so as not to deprive of their share of such important discussions those who are interested, but not able to be present. You are accustomed to make false boasts, when it pleases you, about your records of the past, probably through misinformation rather than deliberate falsehood. Therefore, if you agree, let us measure them against the present. Doubtless, you are not unaware that in the early history of the chosen people the sacrilege of idolatry was

---

[1] There is no salutation at the beginning of the Letter; the descriptive title is from Migne.

committed² and a prophetic book burned by a scornful king;³ but the crime of schism would not be punished more severely than either of these acts unless it were considered more grievous. Surely you remember how the earth opened and swallowed up alive the authors of schism, and how fire coming down from heaven destroyed those who followed them.⁴ But not such vengeance did the making and adoring of an idol or the burning of a sacred book deserve to meet.

You habitually make a charge against us which is not proved about our people, but is proved about yours; namely, that some persons, driven by fear of persecution, gave up the sacred books to be burned. But how is it that you, by the 'sacred utterance of a plenary council,'⁵ condemned of the crime of schism—as it is there written—men whom you received back into the same bishopric from which you expelled them? I mean Felician of Musti and Praetextatus of Assur. They were not, as you tell the ignorant, included among those for whom you adjourned your council and set a date before which they were to return to your communion, or be subject to the same sentence; but they were among those whom you condemned without delay on that same day on which you granted a delay to the others. If you deny it, I will prove it: your council speaks, we have the proconsular records in our possession, and not once did you make that statement in them. Get ready another line of defense, if you can, so as not to waste our time by denying what I shall

---

2 Exod. 32.1-6.
3 Jer. 36.23.
4 Num. 16.31-35.
5 This Donatist council, attended by 310 bishops, was called to condemn the followers of Maximian, at Bagai, a Numidian town. Cf. Letter 43 n. 51. Felician of Musti and Praetextatus of Assur were condemned because they had taken part in the ordination of Maximian, but they could not be expelled from their dioceses even by the civil power, and in the end, had to be reinstated.

prove. If, then, Felician and Praetextatus were innocent, why were they thus condemned? If they were guilty, why were they reinstated? If you prove them innocent, why should we not believe that innocent men could have been incriminated on the false charge of betrayal by a much smaller number of your predecessors, when three hundred and ten of their successors could condemn innocent men on the false charge of schism, as is emphatically written in the 'sacred utterance of a plenary council'? But, if you prove that they were justly condemned, what argument have you left to justify their being reinstated in their bishoprics, except to show, by magnifying the necessity and desirability of peace, that things like that must be tolerated to preserve the bond of unity? Would that you might deal with this question with strength of heart rather than of voice! Doubtless, you would see at once how inadmissible it is to break the peace of Christ by false charges, if it is allowed, in order to keep the peace of Donatus, to receive condemned men back to their bishoprics.

You also continually object to us that we persecute you through the secular powers. In this matter I do not assert either what you deserve for such monstrous sacrilege or how much Christian mildness restrains us. I do say this: if it is a crime, why did you pursue the same followers of Maximian, summoned before judges by the emperors themselves, men whom our communion begot by the Gospel, harried from the basilicas which they held at the time schism overtook them, and why did you torture them with the clamor of controversy, the commands of authority, and the violence of civil guards? In that conflict there is contemporary evidence of what they suffered in several places: public documents affirm the orders given; the lands themselves cry out what was done, those lands where the holy memory of Optatus, that great tribune of yours, is praised.[6]

You also keep saying that we have not the baptism of Christ, and that it is found nowhere outside your communion. Starting from this point, I could argue at considerable length, but against you that is not necessary, since, along with Felician and Praetextatus, you even received the baptism of Maximianists. For as many as they baptized when they were in communion with Maximian—when you were trying, by the long-drawn-out contest of judges, to expel them from their basilicas, namely Felician and Praetextatus, as the records show—that many whom they baptized at that time they now have with them and with you, not only in time of difficulty but even through the paschal solemnities, in so many churches belonging to their cities, and in such great cities, and they keep men baptized in the crime of schism,[7] and do not require them to be rebaptized. Would that you could prove that those whom Felician and Praetextatus baptized outside, as it were invalidly, and in the crime of schism, had been baptized again validly after they had been received back. For, if the former had to be baptized again, then the latter had to be ordained again; separating from you, they lost their character of bishop if they could not baptize outside

---

6 Donatist bishop of Thamugada (modern Timgad), known as Gildonianus, because he shared with Gildo the tyrannical power over Africa which the latter had usurped. Cf Letter 48 n. 1. Augustine is here speaking in pure sarcasm.

7 That is, schism from schism. Augustine is here driving home by a neat dilemma his theme that the validity of baptism does not depend on the character of the baptizer, but only on his intention of baptizing. It is probable that he is not here attacking the validity of Orders of the schismatic bishops, and it is noteworthy that when he is addressing any of them he gives them their proper titles.

your communion; but, if they lost it, they would have to be ordained at their return in order to recover what they had lost. But, do not fear: as it is certain that they came back with the same episcopal power with which they went out, so it is sure that all those whom they baptized in the schism of Maximian rejoined your communion without any repetition of baptism.

Shall we ever find tears enough to bewail the fact that the baptism of Maximianists is accepted and that of the worldwide Church despised? Whether you condemned Felician, whether you condemned Pratextatus heard or unheard, justly or unjustly, tell me: what bishop of the Corinthians did any one of you either hear or condemn? what bishop of the Galatian, of the Ephesians, of the Colossians, of the Philippians, of the Thessalonians, and of all those other cities of which it is said: 'All the kindreds of the Gentiles shall adore in his sight'?[8] Therefore, your baptism is acceptable and theirs is despised; yet, it is neither yours nor theirs but His, of whom it is said: 'He it is that baptizeth.'[9] But, I am not going back over that; turn your attention to what is at hand, something to strike even blind eyes. Look! the condemned have true baptism and the unheard have not! Those who were rejected and expelled on the charge of schism have it, and the unknown, strangers from afar, men never accused and never judged, have it not! Those who were cut off a second time from the cut-off part of Africa have it, and those from whom the very Gospel came into Africa have it not! Why pile up arguments? Answer these! Give heed to the sacrilege of schism, magnified for the Maximianists by your council; give heed to the persecutions which you called down on them through the power of the courts; give heed to their baptism

---
8 Ps. 21.28.
9 John 1.33.

which you receive with them whom you condemned, and answer, if you can, whether you have any way of clouding the issue for the uninstructed, as to why you are cut off from the rest of the world by a far greater crime of schism than that which you boast of having condemned in the followers of Maximian. May the peace of Christ prevail in your heart!

52. Augustine to the much-desired lord and very dear brother, Severinus[1] (c. 400)

I have received with joy the letter of your Fraternity, though very late and beyond what I had hoped. But I was filled with much deeper joy when I learned that your messenger had come to Hippo for the sole purpose of bringing me your Fraternity's letter. I thought that there was good reason why you should recall our kinship, doubtless because you saw—and I know the strong quality of your prudence—how sad a thing it is that we are brothers according to the flesh, but we do not live in the same relationship in the Body of Christ. Moreover, it is especially easy for you to note and see the 'city seated on a mountain' of which the Lord said in the Gospel that 'it cannot be hid.'[2] It is the Catholic Church itself, called in Greek *katholiké*, because it is spread through the whole world. No one can fail to know it and, therefore, according to the word of our Lord Jesus Christ, it cannot be hid.

But, the sect of Donatus, restricted to Africa alone, is an object of scorn to the rest of the world, and does not perceive that, by its sterility which refuses to bring forth fruits of peace and charity, it has been cut off from the root of the eastern

---
1 Apparently a Donatist bishop.
2 Matt. 5.14.

Churches from which the Gospel came into Africa. If that land should be offered to them, they would adore, but if one of the faithful should come from there, they would even scorn and rebaptize him. The Son of God, who is Truth, foretold this: He is the vine, His Son the branches, and His Father the husbandman. 'The branch in me that beareth not fruit, my Father will take away, but the branch in me that beareth fruit, He purgeth it that it may bring forth more fruit.'[3] It is then no wonder if from that vine which has grown and 'filled all lands,'[4] those branches have been cut off which refused to bring forth the fruit of charity.

If their predecessors, when they effected the schism, had made true charges against their colleagues, they would have won their case in the Church overseas,[5] whence authority spread to those parts of the Christian faith; and those against whom the charges were made would be outside. But, now, when these latter are found to be in communion with the apostolic Churches, whose names they have and recite in the sacred books, while the former are outside and are severed from that communion, who does not understand that the ones who had the good case were those who were able to win it before impartial judges? Or, if they had a good case and could not prove it to the overseas Churches, why did the world injure them when bishops could not rashly condemn colleagues who had not been convicted of the charges brought against them? Therefore, the innocent are rebaptized and Christ is despised among the innocent. But, if the same Donatists knew any true accusations against their African colleagues and neglected to disclose them and to prove them to the overseas Churches, they cut themselves

---
3 Cf. John 15.1,2.
4 Cf. Ps. 79.10.
5 Cf. Letter 43 n. 6.

off from the unity of Christ by a most accursed schism, and they have no excuse. But you know, especially since so many wicked men[6] came to prominence among them and they bore with them so many years, so as not to wreck the sect of Donatus. By hurling their false suspicious during that time they did not shrink from rending the peace and unity of Christ. You see this.

But, some worldly habit holds you there, brother Severinus, and I have grieved over it for a long time; long have I mourned, recalling especially your prudence, and long have I wished to see you to talk this over with you. For, what good is well-being or temporal kinship, if in our relations we overlook the eternal inheritance of Christ and eternal well-being? I shall have to be satisfied with writing this much for the present—little and almost nothing to unloving hearts, but to yours, which I know well, much and very significant. The words are not mine, who am nothing, except that I hope for the mercy of God, but of that almighty God who will show Himself at the end a judge to those who have despised Him as a Father in this world.

53. *Fortunatus, Alypius, Augustine give greeting in the Lord to their well-beloved and honorable brother, Generosus[1] (400)*

As you wished to show us the letter sent you by the Donatist priest, which you, of course, repudiate with a truly Catholic mind, we are writing you an answer to send him,

---

[6] This is the language ordinarily used by Augustine when referring to the ten-year reign of terror under Gildo and Optatus.

[1] A Catholic of Constantina (Cirta)

so as to set him right, if he is not hopelessly far gone in folly. He writes that an angel ordered him to win you over to the form of Christianity of your city, whereas your form of Christianity is not only that of your city, or even of Africa and the Africans, but of the whole world, which has been and is being preached to all peoples. And they[2] are so far from shame at being cut off and at taking no measures to rejoin the root, when it is possible for them, that they try to cut others off and to doom them, like dry wood, to the fire. Therefore, if an angel had really stood beside you, as he, with crafty deceit, according to my way of thinking, pretends that one stood beside him, on your account, and if the angel had said those same things which he says he suggested to you at an angel's bidding, it would be your duty to recall the Apostle's words, when he said: 'But though we or an angel from heaven preach a Gospel to you besides that which we have preached to you, let him be anathema.'[3] It has been preached to you by the voice of the Lord Jesus Christ Himself: 'that His Gospel shall be preached . . . to all nations, and then shall the consummation come';[4] it has been preached to you by prophetic and apostolic writings that: 'to Abraham were the promises made and to his seed . . . which is Christ,'[5] when God said to him: 'In thy seed shall all the nations . . . be blessed.'[6] If, therefore, while you hold to these promises, an angel from heaven should say to you: 'Give up the Christianity of the world, and lay hold of the sect of Donatus, whose origin is explained for you in a letter of a bishop of your city,' he ought to be anathema, because he is trying to cut you off from the whole and to

---

2 The Donatists.
3 Gal. 1.8.
4 Matt. 24.14.
5 Gal. 3.16.
6 Gen. 22.18.

push you into a part, and to make you a stranger to the promises of God.

For, if the order of succession of bishops[7] is to be considered, how much more surely, truly and safely do we number them from Peter, to whom, as representing the whole Church, the Lord said: 'Upon this rock I will build my church and the gates of hell shall not prevail against it.'[8] For, to Peter succeeded Linus, to Linus Clement, to Clement Anacletus, to Anacletus Evaristus, to Evaristus Sixtus, to Sixtus Telesphorus to Telesphorus Hyginus, to Hyginus Anicetus, to Anicetus Pius, to Pius Soter, to Soter Alexander, to Alexander Victor, to Victor Zephyrinus, to Zephyrinus Calistus, to Calistus Urban, to Urban Pontian, to Pontian Antherus, to Antherus Fabian, to Fabian Cornelius, to Cornelius Lucius, to Lucius Stephen, to Stephen Sixtus, to Sixtus Dionysius, to Dionysius Felix, to Felix Eutychian, to Eutychian Gaius, to Gaius Marcellus, to Marcellus Eusebius, to Eusebius Melchiades, to Melchiades Sylvester, to Sylvester Marcus, to Marcus Julius, to Julius Liberius, to Liberius Damasus, to Damasus Siricius, to Siricius Anastasius. In this order of succession not a Donatist bishop is found. On the other hand, they ordained and sent somebody from Africa who wielded authority over a few Africans in Rome and who gave out the names of Montenses or Cutzupitae.[9]

Even if in that succession of bishops which comes down from Peter to Anastasius, now occupying the throne, there had happened to be a betrayer, there would still be no harm to the Church and to innocent Christians, to whom the Lord, foreseeing it, said, of evil rulers: 'Whatsoever

---

7 The Popes.
8 Matt. 16.18.
9 The small Donatist sect in Rome was known by these two names. Montenses is explained by the fact that they built their first church on a hill, or else that they met in a cave in a hill. Cutzupitae could be a Numidian name, or it may be a manuscript corruption.

they say to you, . . . do, but according to their works, do ye not, for they say and do not.'[10] Thus He made sure that a faithful hope, founded not on man but on the Lord, should never be scattered by the storm of sacrilegious schism, as those are scattered who read the names of churches in the holy books which the Apostles wrote, but they have not a single bishop in them. What could be more erroneous or more absurd than for their readers, when they read those Epistles, to say, 'Peace to thee!' and to be separated from the peace of those Churches to which the Epistles were written?

However, lest he fool you with the succession of bishops of Constantina, that is, of your city, quote for him from the archives of Munatius Felix, the perpetual flamen[11] and caretaker of your city, that in the eighth consulship[12] of Diocletian and the seventh of Maximian, on the eleventh day before the Kalends of June,[13] it is abundantly clear that Bishop Paul was a traditor, that Silvanus, then his deacon,[14] was one also, and with him betrayed the sacred vessels, even some that had been carefully concealed—a silver box and a silver lamp—because a certain man named Victor said to him: 'You were a dead man if you had not found them!' Your correspondent makes great account of this Silvanus, a most evident traditor, and in the letter which he wrote to you, he calls him a bishop ordained by Secundus of Tigisis, bishop of the primal see. Then let their proud tongue fall silent and let them recognize their own crimes before they speak so madly of those of others. Quote to him, also, if he

---

10 Matt. 23.3.
11 A priest of some particular deity; priests frequently were repositories of public records.
12 Even under the emperors, the Romans continued the clumsy and inconvenient method of noting time by consulships.
13 May 22.
14 Cf. Letter 43.

is willing, the ecclesiastical records on that same Secundus of Tigisis, of a meeting held in the house or Urban, a Donatist, where he reserved avowed betrayers to the judgment of God,[15] namely, Donatus of Mascula, Marinus of Aquae Tibilitanae, Donatus of Calama, with which avowed betrayers he assisted in the ordination as bishop of the above-mentioned traditor, Silvanus. Quote him the records of the transactions before Zenophilus, the consular official, where Nundinarius[16] a certain deacon, angered by Silvanus because he had been excommunicated by him, revealed all this to the court. All these facts, clearer than daylight, are found in trustworthy documents, together with the interrogations of witnesses, the action taken and quotations from numerous letters.

There are many other facts which you can quote to him if he is willing to listen carefully and not act belligerently: the appeals of the Donatists to Constantine that he put an end to the controversy among the African bishops by submitting it to the judgment of bishops from Gaul; the letters of the same emperor when he sent bishops to Rome; also, the decisions taken at Rome, where the case was heard and argued. There are other letters, too, in which the above-mentioned emperor declares that they[17] had protested to him against the verdict of their own colleagues—that is, the bishops whom he had sent to Rome—and, when he wished other bishops to judge the case at Arles, they appealed from this judgment to the personal decision of the emperor. Finally, when he heard the case between them, he declared emphatically that they had no case against the innocence of Caecilian. If your correspondent will listen to all this, he will keep silent hereafter and will stop laying snares for truth.

---

15 This is an expression taken from early Church Law. A bishop was not amenable to public penance, and was said to be 'reserved to God.
16 Cf. Letter 43 n. 25.
17 The Donatist bishops.

However, we do not rely so much on those documents as on the Holy Scriptures, where the inheritance of Christ is promised to all peoples, to the uttermost parts of the earth.[18] But they, separated by a wicked schism, scatter their charges among the grain of the Lord's harvest, which must remain intermingled there until the whole threshing-floor is winnowed at the Last Judgment.[19] From this it is evident that those charges, whether true or false, have nothing to do with the Lord's grain, which must grow in the whole field of this world, until the end of time. Thus speaks the Lord in the Gospel, not a false angel of the Donatist's wrong teaching. Therefore, God has treated as they deserved these wretched Donatists, scattering their many false and vain charges among the innocent Christians, who are mingled with bad Christians throughout all the world, as His grain is mixed with cockle. He has made them condemn in their general council the Maximianist secessionists at Carthage; those who condemned Primian; those who baptized outside Primian's flock; those who rebaptized after Primian. And sometime afterwards, at the insistence of Optatus Gildonianus,[20] they reinstated some of their number, Felician of Musti and Praetextatus of Assur, in the full dignity of their episcopate, and with them all those whom they had baptized while under condemnation. But, if they are not defiled by communion with men reinstated in their positions, men whom they had condemned with their own mouth as accursed and sacrilegious, whom they had compared to those first of all schismatics, who were swallowed up by the earth,[21] let them reflect on the great blindness and folly with which they declare the

---
18 Ps. 2.8.
19 Matt. 13.30; 3.12.
20 Cf. Letter 51 n. 8.
21 Num. 16.21-23.

whole world defiled by the obscure accusations of Africans, and assert that the inheritance of Christ, manifestly displayed among all nations, according to promise, has been destroyed by communion with men whose known misdeeds they had judged.

Therefore, since the Apostle Paul again says that: 'Satan himself transformeth himself into an angel of light,' it is no wonder if 'his ministers be transformed as the ministers of justice,'[22] and if that correspondent of yours really saw an angel as a messenger of error, and, desirous of separating Christians from Catholic unity, he then experienced the angel of Satan transforming himself into an angel of justice. But, if he lies, and saw no such thing, he himself is the minister of Satan, transforming himself into a minister of justice. However, considering all this, if he does not insist on being perverse and persistent, he will be able to free himself from evil enticement, either his own or another's. We have agreed on this in your regard, without any hatred, observing toward him what the Apostle says: 'But the servant of the Lord must not wrangle, but be mild towards all men, apt to teach, patient; with modesty admonishing them that think differently, lest peradventure God may give them repentance to know the truth and they may recover themselves from the snares of the devil, by whom they are held captive at his will.'[23] If we have said anything harsh, let him know that its intent is not the bitterness of dissension, but the correction of charity. May you live safely in Christ, most beloved and honorable brother. Amen.

---

22 2 Cor. 11.14,15.
23 2 Tim. 2.24-26.

54. Augustine gives greeting in the Lord to his most beloved son, Januarius[1] (c. 400)

Book I,[2] in answer to the Inquiries of Januarius

I should prefer to know beforehand what answer you would give to the questions you have asked me; in that way I could answer much more briefly by approving or correcting your answers, as it would be very easy for me to agree with you or set you right. This, as I said, is what I should prefer. But, in answering you now, I have preferred to make my answer longer than my delay. In the first place, I want you to hold as the basic truth of this discussion that our Lord Jesus Christ, as He Himself said in the Gospel, has subjected us to his yoke and His burden, which are light.[3] Therefore, He has laid on the society of His new people the obligation of sacraments, very few in number, very easy of observance, most sublime in their meaning, as, for example, baptism, hallowed by the name of the Trinity, Communion of His Body and His Blood, and whatever else is commended in the canonical writings, with the exception of those burdens found in the five books of Moses,[4] which imposed on the ancient people a servitude in accord with their character and the prophetic times in which they lived. But, regarding those other observances which we keep and all the world keeps, and which do not derive from Scripture but from tradition,

---

1 Januarius: a notarius, or stenographer.
2 In *Retractions* 2.20, Augustine says: 'Two books, with the title "Answer to the Inquiries of Januarius," contain many disputed points about the sacraments; of these books, the first is a letter and has at the head who writes to whom, but is numbered among the books; whereas the second, which does not carry our names, is much fuller and treats many more topics.'
3 Matt. 11.30.
4 The Pentateuch, or first five books of the Bible.

we are given to understand that they have been ordained or recommended to be kept by the Apostles themselves, or by plenary councils, whose authority is well founded in the Church. Such are the annual commemorations of the Lord's Passion, Resurrection and Ascension into heaven, the descent of the Holy Spirit from heaven, and other such observances as are kept by the universal Church wherever it is found.

As to other customs, however, which differ according to country and locality, as the fact that some fast on Saturday, others do not; some receive daily the Body and Blood of the Lord, others receive it on certain days; in some places no day is omitted in the offering of the Holy Sacrifice, in others it is offered only on Saturday and Sunday, or even only on Sunday; and other such differences as may be noted, there is freedom in all these matters, and there is no better rule for the earnest and prudent Christian than to act as he sees the Church act wherever he is staying. What is proved to be against neither faith nor morals is to be considered optional and is to be observed with due regard for the group in which he lives.

I believe you heard this some time ago, but I am nevertheless repeating it now. My mother, who had followed me to Milan, found that the church there did not fast on Saturday. She began to be anxious and uncertain as to what she should do. I was not then concerned with such things, but for her sake I consulted on this matter that man of most blessed memory, Ambrose. He answered that he could teach me nothing but what he himself did, because, if he knew anything better, he would do it. When I thought that he wished to impose his views on us, solely by his own authority, without giving any reason, he followed up and said to me: 'When I go to Rome, I fast on Saturday, but here I do not. Do you also follow the custom of whatever church you attend, if you do not want to give or receive scandal.' When I told this to my mother, she willingly accepted it. And, recalling this advice over and over again, I have always esteemed it as something given by a heavenly oracle. For, I have often experienced with grief and dismay that the weak are deeply disturbed by the aggressive obstinacy or superstitious fears of certain brethren, who stir up such controversial questions, that they think nothing is right except what they do themselves. And these are things of such sort that they are not prescribed by the authority of Holy Scripture nor by the tradition of the universal Church, and they serve no good purpose of amending one's life, but they are insisted on simply because somebody thinks out a reason for them, or because a man was accustomed to do so in his own country, or because he saw things done somewhere on a pilgrimage, and he esteemed them to be more correct because they were further from his own usage.

Someone will say that the Eucharist is not to be received every day. You ask: 'Why?' 'Because,' he says, 'those days are to be chosen on which a man lives with greater purity and self-restraint, so as to approach so great a sacrament worthily. "For he that eateth . . . unworthily, eateth and drinketh judgment to himself." '[5] Another, on the other hand, says: 'Not at all, if the wound of sin and the onset of disease are so great that such remedies are to be postponed, then everyone should be debarred from the altar by the authority of the bishop, in order to do penance[6] and to be

---

5 1 Cor. 11.29.
6 Penance: this refers to the public penance imposed on notorious sinners in the early Church. It was a sort of temporary excommunication, and the sinner had to be publicly reconciled before he could again enter a church. The argument implies that, if one was not fit to receive the Sacrament of the Eucharist, he was a subject for public penance. The argument is refuted in the next sentence.

reconciled by the same authority; for, this is to receive unworthily, if one receives at a time when he ought to do penance; but he should not deprive himself of Communion or restore it to himself at his own wish and will. But, if his sins are not so great that a man is judged fit for excommunication, he ought not to cut himself off from the daily remedy of the Lord's Body.' With good reason, perhaps, does someone break off the quarrel by exhorting them to remain, first of all, in the peace of Christ. Let each one do what he thinks he ought to do according to his faith and devotion. Let neither of them dishonor the Body and Blood of the Lord, but vie with each other in honoring this life-giving sacrament. For, there was no quarrel between Zachaeus and the centurion, nor did one set himself above the other when one, rejoicing, received the Lord into his house,[7] and the other said: 'I am not worthy that Thou shouldst enter under my roof.'[8] Both honored the Saviour in diverse and even contrary manner; both were weighed down with sins; both found mercy. There is force in the comparison of the manna: as among the ancient people it tasted to each one according to what he liked,[9] so in the heart of each Christian is that sacrament by which the world is brought into subjection. This one honors Him by not daring to receive the sacrament daily, that one by not daring to let a day go by without receiving it. But, that Food is not to be despised, as the manna was not to be disliked. Thus, the Apostle says it is unworthily received by those who do not distinguish it from other food, and do not render it the veneration eminently due; therefore, when he says: 'he eateth and drinketh judgment to himself,' he adds: 'not

---

7 Luke 19.6.
8 Matt. 8.8.
9 Wisd. 16.21.

discerning the Body.'¹⁰ This is very clear if all that passage of the first Epistle to the Corinthians is carefully read.

Suppose someone is traveling in a place where, in the continuous observance of Lent, people do not bathe or relax their fast on the fifth day of the week, and he says: 'I will not fast today.' He is asked why, and he says: 'Because it is not done in my country.' What is he doing but trying to make his own custom superior to another's custom? He will not quote me this from the Book of God, nor assert it with the full voice of the universal Church which is published everywhere; nor will he show that the other acts against the faith, but he in accordance with it; nor will he prove that the other violates good morals, while he preserves them. To be sure, they both violate the peace and quiet of the Church by quarreling about a foolish question. I should prefer that each one would not repudiate the custom of the other's country, but each do what the others do. If someone is traveling in a strange country, where the people of God are more numerous, more assiduous and more devout, and there, for example, he sees that the Sacrifice is offered twice on the last Thursday of Lent,¹¹ at morning and at evening, and coming back to his own country where it is customary to offer the Sacrifice at the end of the day, he should claim that it is wrong and unlawful because he saw it done differently elsewhere, that childish way of thinking must be avoided for ourselves, but we must bear with it and correct it among our people.

Therefore, take note to which of these three classes your question belongs, which you set down first in your memorandum. You ask in these words: 'What ought to be done

---
10 1 Cor. 11.29.
11 Holy Thursday, when it is now the custom of the Church to celebrate only one Mass in each church, in the morning.

on the Thursday of the last week of Lent? Is the Sacrifice to be offered in the morning and again after supper, because it is said, "In like manner after He had supped,"[12] or is one to remain fasting and offer it only after supper, or is one to fast and then to sup after the offering as we are used to doing?' To this, therefore, I make the answer that, if the authority of the Divine Scripture prescribes which of these is to be done, there is no doubt that we should do as we read, and that our discussion should turn not on how it is to be administered, but on how the sacrament is to be understood; likewise, if any of these customs is common to the whole Church throughout the world, it is the most unheard of madness to doubt that such custom is to be followed. But, what you ask belongs to neither of these suppositions. It follows, then, that it is of that third sort which varies according to locality and country. Let each one, then, do what he finds in that church which he attends. For, none of these usages is contrary to the faith, nor do morals become better by one or other of them. For these reasons, that is, because of faith or morals, what is wrongly done should be corrected, and what is not done should be begun. But, the mere change of custom, though it may be helpful, may also be disturbing because of novelty. Therefore, what is not helpful is a source of fruitless and, consequently, harmful disturbance.

We are not to think that the reason for the custom in many places of offering the Sacrifice on that day after the meal is because it is written: 'In like manner, the chalice also, after he had supped, saying,'[13] for He could have called that supper their having now received the Body, in order thereafter to receive the Chalice. As to his saying elsewhere: 'When you come therefore together into one place, it is not

---
12 Luke 22.23.
13 Luke 22.20; 1 Cor. 11.25.

now to eat the Lord's Supper,'[14]—calling this reception of the Eucharist the Lord's Supper—that could rather induce men to offer or receive the Eucharist after the meal of that day, because it says in the Gospel: 'Jesus took bread and blessed,'[15] even though he had said above: 'But when it was evening he sat down with the twelve . . . and whilst they were eating, he said that one of you is about to betray me,'[16] but afterward he gave them the Sacrament. And it is quite clear that, when the disciples first received the Body, they did not receive it fasting.

Is the whole Church, then, to be unjustly blamed because the Sacrament is always received fasting? From this time it has pleased the Holy Spirit that, in honor of so great a Sacrament, no other food should enter into the mouth of a Christian before the Lord's Body; that custom, therefore, is observed throughout the world. If the Lord gave the Sacrament after the taking of food, that is no reason for the brethren to assemble to receive it after having dined or supped, or to mingle it with their own meals, as those did whom the Apostle rebuked and corrected. Our Saviour commended the sublimity of that mystery with special emphasis, because He wished to impress this last gift on the hearts and memory of the disciples, whom He was about to leave to enter on His Passion. Therefore, He did not give directions on the manner of its reception afterwards, in order to leave this sacred charge to the Apostles, through whom He was about to institute the Churches. If He had so ordained that the Sacrament should always be received after other food, no one, I believe, would have changed the custom. But, when the Apostle, speaking of this Sacrament, says:

---
14 1 Cor. 11.20.
15 Matt. 26.26.
16 Matt. 26.20,21.

'Wherefore, my brethren when you come together to eat, wait for one another; if any man be hungry, let him eat at home, that you come not together unto judgment,' and straightway he subjoins: 'And the rest I will set in order when I come,'[17] we are given to understand by this that it was too much for him to set forth in a letter the whole manner of proceeding to be observed by the universal Church, and that what he set in order personally is subject to no variation of custom.

A certain probable explanation has appealed to some: on one fixed day of the year, when the Lord held His Supper, it should be allowed to offer and receive the Body and Blood of the Lord, after taking food, as a special form of commemoration. However, I think it came about more naturally, so that anyone who had been fasting might be able to assist at the offering of the Sacrifice after the meal which is taken at the ninth hour.[18] But, we do not, for that reason, oblige anyone to sup before that Banquet of the Lord, nor do we venture either to hinder anyone from doing it. I think this custom originated because many or almost all persons in many places were in the habit of bathing on that day, and, because many were keeping the fast, the Sacrifice was offered in the morning for the benefit of those who would dine—since they could not stand bathing and fasting at the same time—but it was offered at evening for the sake of those who remained fasting.

If you ask how the custom of bathing arose, no more reasonable explanation occurs to me than that the bodies of those to be baptized had become foul during the observance of Lent, and they would be offensive if they came to the

---
17 1 Cor. 11.33,34.
18 About 3 P.M., the usual hour for taking the one meal allowed on fast days.

font without bathing on some previous day. This day was especially chosen for it, on which the Lord's Supper is annually commemorated, and, because it was permitted for those about to be baptized, many others wished to join with them in bathing and relaxing the fast.

I have discussed these points to the best of my ability, and I advise you to observe what I have hitherto said, as far as you are able, and as befits a prudent and peaceable son of the Church. If the Lord wills, I shall answer at another time the other questions you asked.

55. [Augustine to Januarius, regarding the celebration of Easter] (c. 400)

Book II of the Inquiries of Januarius

After reading your letter in which you reminded me of the debt I owe you in solving the rest of the difficulties which you submitted to me a long time ago, I could no longer bear to put off your eager desire, so pleasant and so dear to me, and, although I am swamped with duties, I put this one, of answering what you asked, ahead of the others. But, I do not want to keep talking about your letter, since that delays me in paying what I owe.

You ask why it is that the annual commemoration of the Lord's Passion does not come around on the same day of the year, as does the day on which He is said to have been born, and then you add that, if this happens because of the sabbath and the moon, what does this observance of sabbath and moon mean? Here you must know, first of all, that the day of the Lord's birth does not possess a sacramental character,¹ but is only a recalling of the fact that He was born, and so it was only necessary to mark the day of the year, on which that event occurred, by devout festivity. But, there is a sacrament in any celebration when the commemoration of the event is so made that it is understood to indicate something which must be reverently received. In that manner, therefore, we celebrate Easter, so as not only to call to mind what happened—that is, that Christ died and rose again— but we do not pass over the other things about Him which bear witness to the significance of sacraments. Because, as the Apostle says: 'He died for our sins, and rose again for our justification,' a certain passage from death to life is consecrated in that Passion and Resurrection of the Lord. Even the word itself, which is called *pasch,* is not Greek, as it commonly seems, but those who know both languages say that it is Hebrew. For, it does not come from *passio,* since the Greek *páschein* is the same as *pati* (suffer), but, as I said, it is derived from a Hebrew word meaning that which passes over, from death to life. In that language, *pasch* signifies passing over, as those say who know these things. And this the Lord Himself wished to convey when He said: 'He that believeth . . . in me . . . is passed from death to life.'³ And the same Evangelist very evidently wished this to be understood, for, when the Lord was about to celebrate the pasch with His disciples, at which He gave them the mystic Supper, he says: 'Jesus saw that the hour was come that He should pass out of this world to the Father.'⁴ Therefore, the

---

1 In its broadest sense, Sacrament means a sign of something sacred and hidden (in Greek *musterion,* mystery); this mysterious thing being divine grace. It is commonly used in this sense by St. Augustine and other Fathers. In this Letter it has most frequently the meaning of mystery.
2 Cf. Rom. 4.25.
3 John 5.24.
4 Cf. John 13.1.

passing from this mortal life to another immortal life, that is, from death to life, is commended to us in the Passion and Resurrection of the Lord.

This passing is accomplished in us only by faith, which works in us for the remission of sin, with the hope of eternal life to those who love God and their neighbor, because 'Faith worketh by charity'[5] and 'the just shall live in his faith,'[6] but 'hope that is seen is not hope, for what a man seeth why doth he hope for? But if we hope for that which we see not, we wait for it with patience.'[7] According to this faith and hope and love, by which we begin to be subject to grace, we are now dead with Christ[8] and 'buried together with him in baptism,'[9] as the Apostle says: 'because our old man is crucified with him,'[10] and we have risen again with Him, and 'He hath quickened us together and hath made us sit together in heavenly places.'[11] From this he exhorts us: 'Mind the things that are above, not the things that are upon the earth.'[12] And, because he continues and says: 'For you are dead and your life is hid with Christ in God; for when Christ shall appear, who is your life, then you also shall appear with him in glory,'[13] he shows clearly what he wishes to express, that now our passing from death to life which is accomplished by faith is perfected by hope of a future resurrection at the end, and of glory when 'this corruptible,' that is, the flesh in which we now groan, 'shall put on incorruption and this mortal shall put on immortality.'[14] Now, indeed, we have

---

5 Gal. 5.6.
6 Hab. 2.4.
7 Rom. 8.24,25.
8 2 Tim. 2.11
9 Rom. 6.4; Col. 2.12.
10 Rom. 6.6.
11 Eph. 2.5,6.
12 Col. 3.2.
13 Col. 3.3,4.
14 1 Cor. 15.53.

by faith 'the first-fruits of the spirit,' but we still 'groan within ourselves, waiting for our adoption, the redemption of our body, for we are saved by hope.'[15] When we are in this hope, 'the body indeed is dead because of sin, but the spirit liveth because of justification.'[16] But, see what follows: 'If the spirit of him,' he says, 'that raised up Christ from the dead dwell in you, he that raised up Christ from the dead shall quicken your mortal bodies, because of the spirit that dwelleth in you.'[17] Therefore, the universal Church, which is now in the pilgrimage of mortal life, awaits at the end of time what was first shown in the body of our Lord Jesus Christ, who is 'the first-born from the dead,'[18] because the Church is His body, of which He is the head.

Some, examining into the words which the Apostle speaks with exactness, that 'We are dead with Christ,'[19] and we are risen with Him, not understanding how far these words are to be taken, have thought that the resurrection is already accomplished and that there is no further one to be hoped for at the end of time, 'Among whom,' he says, 'are Hymeneus and Philetus, who have erred from the truth, saying that the resurrection is past already, and have subverted the faith of some.'[20] The same Apostle censures and denounces these men, yet he says that we have risen with Christ.[21] But how does he say that this is accomplished in us according to the 'first-fruits of the spirit,'[22] except by faith and hope and love? But, because 'hope that is seen is not hope,' therefore, if 'we hope for that which we see not, waiting for it with patience,'[23]

---

15 Rom. 8.23,24.
16 Rom. 8.10.
17 Cf. Rom. 8.10,11.
18 Col. 1.18.
19 Rom. 6.8; Col. 2.20; 2 Tim. 2.11.
20 2 Tim. 2.17,18.
21 Col. 3.1.
22 Rom. 8.23.
23 Rom. 8.24,25.

there remains the redemption of our body, which we await, groaning within ourselves. Hence, that saying: 'rejoicing in hope, patient in tribulation.'[24]

Therefore, this renewal of our life is in a sense a passing from death to life, which begins by faith, that we may rejoice in hope and be patient in tribulation, while still 'our outward man is corrupted, yet the inward man is renewed day by day.'[25] Because of this very beginning of new life, because of the new man which we are ordered to put on, and to put off the old,[26] 'purging out the old leaven, that we may be a new paste, for Christ our Pasch is sacrificed,'[27] because of this newness of life, the first month among the months of the year[28] is selected for this celebration. It is called the month of the new corn,[29] because, truly, in the whole time of the world, the third period has now come, and therefore the Resurrection of the Lord happened on the third day. For, the first period was before the Law, the second under the Law, the third under grace, where we have now the revealing of a mystery previously hidden in prophetic obscurity. This is also signified in the lunar number: because the number seven in Scripture commonly has a mystic connection with some sort of perfection, the pasch is celebrated in the third week of the moon, that is, a day which falls between the fourteenth and the twenty-first.

There is here another mystery, and, if it is obscure to you because you have less experience in such investigations, do not be sad and do not think that I am better than you because I have learned these things in my youthful studies: 'But let him that glorieth, glory in the Lord that he under-

---

24 Rom. 12.12.
25 2 Cor. 4.16.
26 Col. 3.9,10.
27 Cf. 1 Cor. 5.7.
28 The ancients considered March the first month of the year.
29 Exod. 23.15.

standeth and knoweth, for I am the Lord.'[30] Many, then, who were interested in such things delved deeply into numbers and the movement of stars, and those who reasoned them out more subtly figured out the waxing and waning of the moon from the revolution of its sphere; not that any matter is added to it when it increases or any taken away when it decreases. This is what the Manichaeans, in their insane ignorance, said: that it was filled as a ship is filled with an overflowing part of God, and they do not hesitate to believe and to say, with sacrilegious heart and mouth, that this is intermingled with the princes of darkness and defiled with their filth. With this, then, they say the moon is filled up, and, when that part of God, with great effort, is purged of defilement, and, flowing from the whole world and all its sewers, is restored to a weeping god, then it reappears; but it is filled during half of the month, and during the other half is poured back into the sun, as into another ship. But, among those accursed blasphemies of theirs, they were never able to explain why, when it is increasing or diminishing, it shines with crescent light, or why it begins to wane from the middle of the month and does not come at the full to that pouring back.

Those, however, who search into these things by numerical calculations, so that they predict a long time ahead, not only why eclipses of the sun and moon occur, but even when they are to occur, and who figure them out at regular intervals by rules of computation, and write them down, so that those who only read and understand, predict them, also, just as and when they happen—such as these 'are not to be pardoned,' as the Holy Scripture says, 'because, if they were able to know so much as to make a judgment of the world,

---

30 Cf. Jer. 9.24.

they did not more easily find out the Lord thereof.'[31] From those very horns of the moon which are turned away from the sun, either waxing or waning, they reasoned that either it was illumined by the sun, and, the further it receded from that body, the more it received its rays on the side which is visible to the earth, and the nearer it approached the sun, by the other side of its orbit, after the middle of the month, the more that side, illumined from above, which it shows to the earth, is unable to receive the rays, and therefore it seems to decrease; or, if it had its own light, it had it on one side of its sphere, which part it shows to the earth as it moves away gradually from the sun, until it shows the whole; and this it shows as an increase; not that what was missing is added, but what is there is displayed; and again it conceals what was visible and so it seems to decrease. Whichever of these it is, it is certainly evident and easily understood by anyone noticing it that the moon is not increased to our sight except by moving away from the sun, nor diminished except by approaching the sun from the other side.

Notice, now, what we read in proverbs: 'A wise man continueth as the sun, but a fool is changed as the moon,'[32] and who is that wise man who continueth but that Sun of Justice of whom it is said: 'The sun of justice is risen to me?'[33] But the impious to whom He has not risen shall say, weeping, on the last day: 'The light of justice hath not shined into us, and the sun . . . hath not risen upon us.'[34] For, God has made the Sun visible to fleshly eyes, 'to rise upon the good and bad,' who also 'raineth upon the just and the unjust.'[35]

31 Cf. Wisd. 13.9.
32 Cf. Eccli. 27.12.
33 Cf. Mal. 4.2.
34 Wisd. 5.6.
35 Matt. 5.45.

But, appropriate comparisons of invisible things are often drawn from visible ones. Who, then is that fool who is changed as the moon but Adam, 'in whom all have sinned?'[36] Doubtless, the human mind, turning away from the Sun of Justice, I mean from that interior contemplation of unchangeable truth, diverts all its energies to earthly things, and is thereby more and more blinded to things within and things above; but, when it begins to return to that immutable wisdom, the nearer it draws to Him by devout affection, the more 'the outward man is corrupted, but the inward man is renewed day by day.'[37] Then, all that light of his mind which was directed to lower aims is turned to higher ones, and, in a sense, is removed from earthly objects, so that more and more he dies to this world, and his life is hidden with Christ in God.[38]

Therefore, the one who turns toward outward things is changed for the worse, and 'while he liveth casting away his bowels';[39] in this he appears better to the world, that is, to those 'who mind earthly things,'[40] when 'the sinner is praised in the desires of his soul, and the unjust man is blessed.'[41] He is changed for the better when he gradually turns his attention from earthly things which appear in this world, and puts his glory in the higher and inner things; in this, he seems worse to the world, that is, to those who mind earthly things. Consequently, the impious, repenting vainly at the end, will say this, among many things: 'These are they whom we had sometime in derision, and for a parable of reproach: we fools esteemed their life madness.'[42] Thus,

---

36 Rom. 5.12.
37 2 Cor. 4.16.
38 Col. 3.3.
39 Eccli. 10.10.
40 Phil. 3.19.
41 Ps. 9.24 (10.3).
42 Wisd. 5.3,4.

the Holy Spirit, drawing a comparison from visible to invisible, and from corporal to spiritual mysteries, has wished that passing over from one life to another, which is called pasch, to be observed from the fourteenth day of the moon —and this not only because of the third period, which I mentioned above, since the third week begins from there, but also because of that conversion from exterior to interior things, whence a parable is to be drawn from the moon— up to the twenty-first day, because of that number seven, which is used to signify perfection, and is attributed to the Church because it is a figure of perfection.

Therefore, the Apostle John in the Apocalypse writes to the seven churches.[43] But the Church, as yet constituted in that mortality of the flesh, is referred to in the Scriptures by the name of the moon, because it is subject to change. Whence this saying: 'They have prepared their arrows in the quiver to shoot in the dark of the moon the upright of heart.'[44] But, before that can happen, the Apostle says: 'When Christ shall appear, who is your life, then you also shall appear with him in glory,'[45] the Church seems hidden during the time of her pilgrimage, groaning amid many iniquities, and then many snares of deceitful tempters are to be feared, which he wishes to be understood under the name of arrows. Therefore, in another passage, because of the most faithful messengers of truth whom the Church begets everywhere, it is said: 'the moon . . . faithful witness in heaven';[46] and, speaking of the kingdom of the Lord, the psalm says: 'In his days shall justice spring up, and abundance of peace, till the moon be taken away,'[47] that is,

---

43 Apoc. 1.4.
44 Cf. Ps. 10.3. The Douay text has 'in the dark,' not 'in the dark of the moon.'
45 Col. 3.4.
46 Ps. 88.38.
47 Ps. 71.7.

the abundance of peace shall increase until it supplants all that is transitory in mortality. Then, 'the enemy death shall be destroyed last,'[48] and whatever offers resistance from the weakness of the flesh, hindering perfect peace in us, shall be entirely destroyed, when 'this corruptible shall put on incorruption, and this mortal shall put on immortality.'[49] So the walls of that city, called Jericho, which in the Hebrew tongue is said to mean moon, fell when they had been encircled seven times by the Ark of the Covenant.[50] What, then, does the announcement of the kingdom of heaven portend—signified by the encircling of the Ark—except that all the battlements of mortal life, that is, all the hope of this world, which is opposed to the hope of the world to come, will be destroyed by the sevenfold gift of the Holy Spirit, working through the free will? For, those walls fell of their own accord, not by any violent push of the Ark in its circuit. There are other references in Scripture which suggest the Church to us under the symbolism of the moon, as she makes her pilgrimage in this mortal life, amid toils and labors, far from that Jerusalem whose citizens are the holy angels.

Nevertheless, fools who do not wish to change for the better are not to suppose that those luminaries are to be adored because they are used as a parable to symbolize divine mysteries—such comparisons are drawn from all created things. Neither are we to include ourselves in that sentence of condemnation, which was uttered by the mouth of the Apostle concerning some 'who worshipped and served the creature rather than the Creator, who is blessed forever.'[51] For, just as we do not adore domestic animals, although He

---
48 1 Cor. 15.26.
49 1 Cor. 15.53.
50 Jos. 6.16.
51 Rom. 1.25.

is called lamb[52] and calf,[53] nor wild beasts, because He is called 'Lion of the tribe of Juda,'[54] nor stones, because 'the rock was Christ,'[55] nor Mount Sion, because it is a figure of the Church, so neither do we adore the sun or the moon, although from that celestial creation, as from many an earthly one, symbols of mysteries are drawn to increase our mystical knowledge.

Therefore, the ravings of the Manichaeans are to be treated with scornful laughter. When we have exposed their vain imaginings, made to cast men into the same error into which they have first fallen, they seem to babble when they say to us: 'Why do you also celebrate as the pasch the computation of the sun and moon?' As if we were condemning the phases of the stars and the changes of seasons, set up by the high and excellent God, and not their evil-mindedness which perverts a most wisely ordered creation to the futile theories of their folly. For, if a mathematician should object to our using the stars and the luminaries of heaven to symbolize sacramental mysteries, the soothsayers[56] also could object to its being said to us: 'Be ye simple as doves,'[57] and the Marsians[58] to the saying, 'wise as serpents'; the actors could object to our naming the harp in our psalms,[59] or, because we make use of these things as comparisons to illustrate the mysteries of the word of God, they could say, if they liked, that we took auspices, or compounded poisons, or indulged in the extravagances of the theatre—which it would be utterly ridiculous to say.

---

52 John 1.29.
53 Ezech. 43.19.
54 Apoc. 5.5.
55 1 Cor. 10.4; 1 Peter 2.4,6.
56 Augurs read auspices from the flight of birds.
57 Matt. 10.16.
58 Famous as snake-charmers.
59 Music was a usual accompaniment to drama.

We do not forecast the outcome of our acts, then, by the sun or the moon, or by yearly or monthly periods, lest we be shipwrecked in the most dangerous storms of human life, cast by our free will onto the rocks of a wretched slavery; but we make use of parables, formulated with reverent devotion, to illustrate our religion, drawing freely in our speech on the whole creation, the winds, the sea, the earth, birds, fishes, flocks, trees, men; just as, in the administration of the sacraments, we use with Christian liberty, but sparingly, water, wheat, wine, oil. Many observances were imposed on the ancient people under the yoke, which are transmitted to us merely for our understanding. Therefore, we do not 'observe days and years and month and times,'[60] so as not to hear from the Apostle: 'I am afraid of you lest I have labored in vain among you.'[61] He was blaming those who say: 'I will not start on my journey because it is an unlucky day,' or 'because the moon is in such a quarter,' or 'I will start because the position of the stars guarantees luck.' 'I will not carry on business this month, because that star works against me,' or 'I will carry on because it favors the month,' or 'I will not plant a vineyard this year because it is leap year.' On the other hand, no sensible man thinks it blameworthy to observe the weather, as when someone says. 'I shall not set out today because it is stormy,' 'I should not set sail because there are still some vestiges of winter left,' or 'It is time to sow, because the ground is soaked by the autumn rains.' Nor is it wrong to note that certain natural phenomena, such as movements of the air and moisture, are connected with the ordered motions of the stars in bringing about different kinds of weather, and of these it was said when they were created: 'Let them be for signs, and for seasons, and

---

60 Cf. Gal. 4.10.
61 Gal. 4.11.

for days and for years.'[62] If, however, these allegories, taken not only from heaven and the stars, but even from the lower creation, are adapted to the dispensation of the sacraments, they become a sort of eloquence of redemptive doctrine, fit to win the affection of its disciples from visible to invisible, from corporal to spiritual, from temporal to eternal things.

No one of us adverts to the fact that, at the time when we celebrate Easter, the sun is in Aries, as they call that certain arrangement of stars where the sun is actually found in the month of new corn. But, whether they want to call that part of the sky Aries or something else, we have learned from the Holy Scriptures that God created all the stars and set them in their places in the sky as He wished. They may divide these places, marked and distinguished by the stars, into whatever zones they like, and signalize them by any names they please, but, wherever the sun was in the month of new corn, there this celebration would find it, because it is a symbol of the mystery of renewal of life, as we have amply demonstrated. But, if, by some appropriate analogy, that grouping of stars could be called Aries, the Divine Word would not fail to use that term, to point out some mystery, as it has used other names, not only of the celestial but also of the terrestrial creation, as, for example, Orion, the Pleiades, Mount Sinai, Mount Sion, or the rivers which are called Geon, Phison, Tigris, Euphrates, and the Jordan itself, so often ennobled by assimilation with sacred mysteries: all these figures are mystically used to describe reality.

Everyone understands that there is a great difference between observing the stars as natural phenomena, in the way that farmers and sailors do, either to verify geographical areas, or to steer their course somewhere, as pilots of ships do, and travelers, making their way through the sandy wastes

---

62 Gen. 1.14.

of the south with no sure path; or to explain some point of doctrine by mentioning some of the stars as a useful illustration —as I said, there is a great difference between these practical customs and the superstitions of men who study the stars, not to forecast the weather, or to find their way, or for spiritual parables, but to peer into the predestined outcome of events.

Let us now see, in the second place, why that calculation is made to ensure that a sabbath occurs when we celebrate Easter, for that is peculiar to the Christian religion—the Jews only figured the month of new corn and the moon from the fourteenth to the twenty-first day. Because their pasch, on which the Lord suffered, so fell that there was a sabbath between His death and resurrection, our fathers have seen fit to make the additional requirement that our feast should be distinguished from the Jewish feast. As we must believe that His action was not without meaning, who is before time, and by whom time was created, and who came in the fullness of time,[63] and who had power to lay down His life and to take it up again;[64] therefore He awaited His hour, not a chance one, but one appropriate to the mystery which He ordered to be observed when He said: 'My hour is not yet come,'[65] so that the memory of His Passion might be kept by posterity in a yearly observance.

Because, then, as I said above, we pilgrims make our way by faith and hope, and strive to reach our end by love, there is a certain holy and eternal rest from all toil and all trouble. Into it we pass from this life, as our Lord Jesus Christ deigned to show the way and to hallow it by His Passion. In that rest there is no slothful idleness, but a certain indescribable tranquility of serene activity. The rest from the toils of this life,

---

63 Gal. 4.4.
64 John 10.18.
65 John 2.4.

which comes at the end, becomes the joy of action in the other life. But, because this activity is the praise of God, entailing no effort of the limbs, no anxiety of care, we do not attain to it through rest, as labor succeeds rest—that is, the act does not begin as a cessation of rest, nor is there any return to toils and cares—but we are maintained in the action which belongs to rest, without toiling at work or wavering in thought. Therefore, because we return through rest to the original life from which the soul fell into sin, for that reason rest is signified by the sabbath. That original life which is restored to those returning from their wandering and receiving the first robe[66] is symbolized by the first day of the week, which we call the Lord's Day. Seek out the seven days; read Genesis; you will find the seventh day without an evening,[67] which signifies rest without end. That first life was not eternal for the sinner, but the last rest is eternal, and for this reason the eighth day will have eternal blessedness, because that rest which is eternal is taken up from the eighth day and it has no setting; otherwise, it would not be eternal. Thus, the eighth shall be as the first, so that the first life may be restored to immortality.

It was enjoined on the ancient people to keep the sabbath by bodily repose that it might be a figure of the sanctification which becomes the repose of the Holy Spirit. For, we do not read that all the preceding days were made holy; only of the sabbath was it said: 'And God sanctified the seventh day.'[68] Both holy and wicked souls love rest, but mostly they do not know how to attain to what they love, for bodies do not tend to anything by their physical mass, except what souls aim at by their love. For, as a body strains

---
66 Luke 15.22; a reference to the parable of the Prodigal Son.
67 Gen. 2.2,3.
68 Gen. 2.3.

by its weight, whether carried up or down until it comes to rest in its place of balance, as a quantity of oil falls down if dropped in the air, but rises if dropped in water, so souls strive after what they love, so as to find rest in accomplishment. And many things give pleasure in the body, but there is in them neither eternal nor even long-lasting rest; therefore, they rather defile the soul and weigh it down, hindering its pure weight from being carried upward. But, when a soul takes pleasure in itself, it does not enjoy unchanging bliss and, therefore, it is proud because it is supreme to itself, whereas God is supreme. But, it is not left unpunished in such a sin, because 'God resisteth the proud but giveth grace to the humble.'[69] But, when He delights in God, he finds a true, sure, eternal rest, which he sought in other things but did not find. Therefore, the psalm admonishes: 'Delight in the Lord and he will give thee the requests of thy heart.'[70]

But, 'because the charity of God is poured forth in our hearts by the Holy Spirit who is given to us,'[71] sanctification is therefore attributed to the seventh day when rest is enjoined. Indeed, we can do no good work unless helped by His gift, as the Apostle says: 'For it is God who worketh in you, both to will and to accomplish, according to his good will,'[72] neither shall we be able to rest, after all the good works which we perform in this life, unless by His gift we are sanctified and perfected for eternity. Therefore it is said of God Himself that, when He had done all his works, exceedingly good, 'He rested on the seventh day from all his works which he had made.'[73] Thus, He foreshadowed the rest to come, which He was to give men after their good works. For, just as when we

---

69 James 4.6; 1 Peter 5.5.
70 Ps. 36.4.
71 Rom. 5.5.
72 Phil. 2.13.
73 Gen. 1.31; 2.2.

do a good work, He is said to work in us, by whose gift we perform our good work, so, when we rest, He is said to rest in us by whose gift we rest.

Hence it is that in the first three commandments of the Decalogue, which refer to God—for the other seven refer to the neighbor, that is, to man, because, 'on [these] two commandments dependeth the whole law'[74]—the third of them bears on the observance of the sabbath. As in the first commandment we recognize the Father, when we are forbidden to worship any image of God made to the likeness of man, not because God has no image, but because no image of Him should be worshipped, except that which He is, and not the image instead of Him, but with Him; and, because created nature is variable, it is said: 'Every creature was made subject to vanity,'[75] since the nature of the whole is shown even in the part. But, lest anyone should think that the Son of God, the Word, 'by whom all things were made,'[76] is a creature, there follows another commandment: 'Thou shall not take the name of the Lord, thy God, in vain.'[77] The Holy Spirit, through whom that rest is granted to us, which we universally crave but do not find except by loving God, since 'His charity is poured forth in our hearts by the Holy Spirit Who is given to us,'[78] because God sanctified the seventh day in which He rested,[79] has enjoined on us in the third commandment, which is written about the observance of the sabbath, not that we are to expect to rest now, in this life, but that all good works which we perform should have no other intention but that eternal rest to come. Remember

---
74 Matt. 22.40.
75 Rom. 8.20.
76 John 1.3.
77 Exod. 20.7; Deut. 5.11.
78 Rom. 5.5.
79 Gen. 2.3.

especially what I said above: 'For we are saved by hope, but hope that is seen is not hope.'[80]

But, all those truths which are presented to us in figures tend, in some manner, to nourish and arouse that flame of love by the impulse of which we are carried upward and inward toward rest, and they stir and enkindle love better than if they were set before us unadorned, without any symbolism of mystery. It is hard to explain the reason for this; nevertheless, it is true that any doctrine suggested under an allegorical form affects and pleases us more, and is more esteemed, than one set forth explicitly in plain words. I believe that the soul makes its response slothfully as long as it is involved in earthly things, but, if it is borne along to corporeal representations and from them to spiritual ones, which are symbolized by those figures, it gains strength by that transition, it is enkindled like fire shaken in a torch, and by that more ardent love it is carried on to rest.

Therefore, among all those ten commandments, only when it is question of the sabbath is a figurative observance required, and we recognize that we must understand the figure and not observe it by a merely physical abstinence from work. Although spiritual repose is signified by the sabbath, of which it is said in the psalm: 'Be still and see that I am God,'[81] and to which men are called by the Lord Himself, saying: 'Come to me all you that labor and are burdened and I will refresh you: Take up my yoke upon you and learn of me because I am meek and humble of heart, and you shall find rest to your souls,'[82] still, we keep all the other commandments literally, as they are given, without any figurative meaning. We have learned plainly not to worship

---

80 Rom. 8.24.
81 Ps. 45.11.
82 Matt. 11.28,29.

idols, not to take the name of the Lord our God in vain, to honor father and mother, not to commit adultery, not to kill, not to steal, not to bear false witness, not to covet our neighbor's wife, not to covet anything that is his.[83] These do not express one thing figuratively and mean something else mystically, but they are taken for just what they say. We are not ordered to keep the sabbath day by a literal corporal abstinence from work, as the Jews observe it—and, indeed, that observance of theirs, because it is so commanded, is considered ludicrous unless it signifies some other spiritual rest. From this we understand that all the truths which are expressed figuratively in the Scriptures are appropriately designed to arouse love, by which we attain to rest, since only that commandment is given figuratively by which rest is enjoined; rest which is universally loved, but found pure and entire in God alone.

However, the Lord's day was not made known to Jews but to Christians by the Resurrection of the Lord, and from that event it began to acquire its solemnity. Doubtless, the souls of all the saints prior to the resurrection of the body enjoy repose, but they do not possess that activity which gives power to risen bodies. It is the eighth day which symbolizes that activity, which is also the first, because it does not destroy that rest but glorifies it. The limitations of the body do not rise with the body, which is free from corruption: 'For this corruptible must put on incorruption, and this mortal must put on immortality.'[84] And so, before the Resurrection of the Lord, although this mystery of the eighth day by which the Resurrection is symbolized was not concealed from the holy Patriarchs, filled as they were with the spirit of prophecy, it was locked up and hidden and taught only

---

83 Exod. 20.4,5,7,12-17; Deut. 5.8; 9.11,16-21.
84 1 Cor. 15.53.

as the sabbath observance. As examples we have the psalm written 'for the octave,'[85] and children circumcised on the eighth day;[86] in Ecclesiastes it is used to signify the two Testaments: 'Give a portion to seven and also to eight.'[87] Before the Lord's Resurrection there was rest for the departed but resurrection for none: 'Rising from the dead he dieth no more, death hath no more dominion over him';[88] but after such Resurrection had taken place in the Lord's Body, so that the head of the Church might foreshadow what the body of the Church hopes for at the end, then the Lord's day—that is the eighth, which is also the first—began to be observed. The reason also is understood why, in observing the pasch, they were ordered to kill and eat a sheep, since it plainly prefigured the Passion of the Lord, but they were not commanded to see that a sabbath coincided with the month of new corn and with the third week of the moon: so that the Lord might signalize that same day by His Passion, who had also come to announce the Lord's day, the eighth, which is also the first.

Note, therefore, the three sacred days of His Crucifixion, Burial and Resurrection. Of these three, the Cross signifies what we do in this present life, but the Burial and Resurrection what we perform by faith and hope. In this present time it is said to man: 'Take up thy cross and follow me.'[89] The flesh, then, is crucified when our members are mortified on earth destroying fornication, uncleanness, intemperance, avarice, and other such vices, of which he says: 'For if you live according to the flesh, you shall die, but if by the spirit

---

85 This is the direction given at the head of Psalms 6 and 11. It seems to be a musical note calling for a harp of eight strings.
86 Gen. 17.12.
87 Eccle. 11.2.
88 Rom. 6.9.
89 Matt. 16.24.

you mortify the deeds of the flesh, you shall live.'[90] Hence, he even says of himself: 'The world is crucified to me and I to the world,'[91] and in another place: 'Knowing this,' he says, 'that our old man is crucified with him, that the body of sin may be destroyed, to the end that we may serve sin no longer.'[92] As long, therefore, as our works aim at this, 'that the body of sin may be destroyed,' as long as 'our outward man is corrupted that the inward man may be renewed day by day,'[93] so long we live in the time of the Cross.

But, there are good works, toilsome indeed as yet, whose reward is rest. Therefore it is said: 'Rejoicing in hope,'[94] that we may look forward to the rest to come, and so conduct ourselves cheerfully in the midst of our toils. This cheerfulness is signified by the width of the cross along its transverse beam, where the hands are fastened; by the hands we understand works, and by width the cheerfulness of the worker, because sadness has a straitening effect. The height of the cross, on which the head rests, symbolizes the expectation of reward or punishment from the exalted justice of God, who 'will render to every man according to his works: to them indeed who, according to patience in good work, seek glory and honor and incorruption, eternal life.'[95] And the length, along which the whole body is stretched, signifies that same patience, whence those who are patient are called long-suffering. But the cavity in the earth in which the cross is planted foreshadows the secret of the sacrament. You recall, I am sure, those words of the Apostle, on that meaning of the cross, which I am explaining, where he says: 'Rooted and founded

---
90 Rom. 8.13.
91 Gal. 6.14.
92 Rom. 6.6.
93 2 Cor. 4.16.
94 Rom. 12.12.
95 Rom. 2.6,7.

in charity, that you may be able to comprehend, with all the saints, what is the length and breath and height and depth.'[96] Those things which we do not yet see, and do not yet hold, but which we grasp by faith and hope, are shown forth in the other two days. However, those things which we now perform, fastened as if by the nails of His commandments, to the love of God, as it is written: 'Pierce thou my flesh with thy fear,'[97] are reckoned among our obligatory actions, not among those which are chosen and desired for their own sake. Therefore, he says that he desires this excellent thing; 'to be dissolved and to be with Christ; but to abide still in the flesh,' he says, 'is needful for you.'[98] When he says 'to be dissolved and to be with Christ,' this is the beginning of rest, which is not interrupted, but made glorious by resurrection; however, it is now held back by faith, because 'the just man liveth by faith.'[99] 'Know you not,' he says, 'that all we who are baptized in Christ Jesus, are baptized in his death? For we are buried together with him by baptism into death.'[100] And how is this except by faith? This is not yet accomplished in us, groaning as we are and awaiting our adoption, the redemption of our body, 'for we are saved by hope, but hope that is seen is not hope, for what a man seeth why doth he hope for? But if we hope for that which we see not, we wait for it with patience.'[101]

Remember how often I remind you of this, and let us not think that we ought now, in this life, to be happy and free from all trials; let us not sacrilegiously murmur against God in the straits of our temporal affairs, as if He were not giving

---

96 Cf. Eph. 3,17,18.
97 Ps. 118.120.
98 Phil. 1.23,24.
99 Rom. 1.17. (Hab. 2.4); Gal. 3.11; Hab. 10.38.
100 Rom. 6.3,4.
101 Rom. 8.23-25.

us what He has promised. For, He promised what we need for this life, but the comforting of the sad is one thing, the joys of the blessed something quite other. 'Lord,' he says, 'according to the multitude of my sorrows in my heart, thy comforts have given joy to my soul.'[102] Let us not, then, murmur in our trials, lest we lose the wideness of good cheer, of which it is said: 'Rejoicing in hope,' followed by: 'patient in tribulation.'[103] Therefore, the new life begins now by faith, and is carried on by hope, but then will come the time when death shall be swallowed up in victory,'[104] when that 'enemy, death, shall be destroyed last,'[105] when we shall be changed and shall become like the angels, 'For we shall all indeed,' he says, 'rise again, but we shall not all be changed.'[106] And the Lord said: 'They will be equal to the angels of God.'[107] We have now been mastered in fear by faith, but then we shall have the mastery in love by vision. 'For as long as we are in the body, we are absent from the Lord, for we walk by faith and not by sight.'[108] Thus, the Apostle himself, when he says: 'That I may apprehend, as I am apprehended,' confesses openly that he has not apprehended; 'Brethren,' he says, ' I do not count myself to have apprehended.'[109] Nevertheless, because that hope, according to the promise of truth, is assured to us, when he has said: 'We are buried with him by baptism into death,' he continues and says: 'That as Christ is risen from the dead by the glory of the Father, so we also may

---

102 Ps. 93.19.
103 Rom. 12.12.
104 1 Cor. 15.54.
105 1 Cor. 15.26.
106 1 Cor. 15.51.
107 Luke 20.36.
108 2 Cor. 5.6,7.
109 Phil. 3.12,13. In the translation of the New Testament by Monsignor Ronald Knox, apprehend is given the meaning of 'gaining the mastery.'

walk in newness of life.'[110] We walk, therefore, in the act of laboring, but in the hope of rest, in the oldness of the flesh, but in the newness of faith. For he says: 'The body indeed is dead because of sin, but the spirit is life because of justice; and if the Spirit of him that raised up Jesus Christ from the dead dwell in you, he that raised up Christ from the dead shall quicken also your mortal bodies, because of his Spirit that dwelleth in you.'[111] These are the truths which by the authority of the Divine Scriptures and the consent of the universal Church, which is spread throughout the world, are commemorated by the yearly celebration of Easter, truly a great sacramental observance, as you now understand. In the Old Testament, no other time is prescribed for keeping the pasch, except the month of new corn and the days between the fourteenth and the twenty-first of the moon. Since it is clear from the Gospel on what days the Lord was crucified and rested in the tomb and rose again, there is added, through the councils of the fathers, the requirement of retaining those same days, and the whole Christian world is convinced that the pasch should be celebrated in that way.

The forty-day fast of Lent draws its authority from the Old Testament, from the fasts of Moses[112] and Elias,[113] and from the Gospel, because the Lord fasted that many days,[114] showing that the Gospel is not at variance with the Law and the Prophets. The Law is personified by Moses, the Prophets by Elias, between whom the Lord appeared transfigured on the mountain,[115] making manifest what the Apostle said of Him: 'being witnessed by the law and the

---
110 Rom. 6.4.
111 Cf. Rom. 8.10,11.
112 Exod. 34.28.
113 3 Kings 19.8.
114 Matt. 4.2.
　Matt. 17.2-5.

prophets.'[116] In what part of the year, then, could the observance of Lent be more appropriately instituted than that adjoining, so to speak, and touching on the Lord's Passion? In it is portrayed this toilsome life, with its need of self-conquest, to be achieved by withdrawing from the friendship of the world, a deceitful and flattering friendship, always displaying and strewing about its counterfeit enticements. And I think that life itself is represented by the number forty, because the number ten, in which is the perfection of our happiness—as with eight, which is a return to one, so in this because the creature, expressed under the number seven, clings to the Creator, in whom is revealed the unity of Trinity—this ten, then, is made known in time to the world, because the world is divided by four winds, made up of four elements, and goes through the changes of four seasons annually; but four times ten makes forty, and forty, composed of its parts, is added to ten and becomes fifty, which is the reward of labor and self-restraint. Not without reason did the Lord Himself remain on this earth forty days after His resurrection, when He conversed with His disciples in this life, and when He had ascended into heaven, after a space of ten days, He sent the promised Holy Spirit on the perfected day of Pentecost. There is another mystery connected with the fiftieth day, in the fact that seven times seven makes forty-nine, and when there is a return to the beginning, which is the octave, identical with the first, fifty is complete; and these days after the Lord's Resurrection form a period, not of labor, but of peace and joy. That is why there is no fasting and we pray standing, which is a sign of resurrection. This practice is observed at the altar on all Sundays, and the Alleluia[117] is sung, to indicate that our future occupation is

---
116 Rom. 3.21.
117 'Praise the Lord.'

to be no other than the praise of God, as it is written: 'Blessed are they that dwell in thy house: they shall praise thee for ever and ever.'[118]

But, the fifty-day period is also praised in Scripture, not only in the Gospel, because the Holy Spirit came on the fiftieth day, but even in the Old Testament. Therein, fifty days are numbered from the celebration of the pasch by the killing of a lamb, to the day on which the law was given on Mount Sinai to the servant of God, Moses.[119] This law was 'written with the finger of God,'[120] and this finger of God the New Testament explicitly identifies with the Holy Spirit. For, when one Evangelist has: 'By the finger of God, I cast out devils,'[121] another says this same thing thus: 'By the spirit of God, I cast out devils.'[122] Who would not have this joy in the divine mysteries, when the redemptive doctrine shines with so clear a light, rather than all the powers of this world though they be infused with unwonted peace and happiness? Do not the Seraphim cry to each other, singing the praises of the Most High: 'Holy, holy, holy, the Lord God of hosts'?[123] Thus the two Testaments agree faithfully in proclaiming the sacred truth. A lamb is slain, the pasch is celebrated, and after fifty days the law, written with the finger of God, is given in fear: Christ is slain, who was led 'as a sheep to the slaughter,'[124] as the Prophet Isaias testifies, the true pasch is celebrated, and after fifty days the Holy Spirit, who is the finger of God, is given in love. He is opposed to men who seek their own, who therefore bear a hard yoke and a heavy burden, who do not find rest to their

---
118 Ps. 83.5.
119 Exod. 12.16; 19.1-25.
120 Exod. 31.18.
121 Luke 11.20.
122 Matt. 12.28.
123 Isa. 6.3.
124 Isa. 53.7.

souls, because 'charity seeketh not her own.'[125] That is why
the enmity of heretics is always restless, such men as the
Apostle declares to be like the magicians of Pharaoh,[126] in
their striving, saying: 'Now as Jannes and Mambres resisted
Moses, so these resist the truth, men corrupted in mind, reprobate concerning the faith: but they shall proceed no
further, for their folly shall be manifest to all men, as theirs
also was.'[127] Because their corruption made them so uneasy
in mind, they failed in the third sign,[128] confessing that the
Holy Spirit who was in Moses was against them. For, at
their failure they said: 'This is the finger of God.'[129] Just as
the Holy Spirit, won over and appeased, gives rest to the
meek and humble of heart, so, when He is contradicted and
opposed, He goads the choleric and the haughty with unrest.
Those small flying insects signified unrest, and forced the
magicians of Pharaoh to admit their failure with the words:
'This is the finger of God.'

Read Exodus, and see how many days after the celebration
of the pasch the law was given. God spoke to Moses in the
desert of Sinai on the third day of the third month. Notice,
therefore, one day after the beginning of that same third
month, and see what He says, among other things: 'Go down,
testify to the people and sanctify them today and tomorrow
and the third day, and let them wash their garments, and
let them be ready against the third day, for on the third day
the Lord will come down in the sight of all the people upon
Mount Sinai.'[130] The Law, then, was obviously given on the
third day of the third month. Now count the days from the

---

125 1 Cor. 13.5.
126 Exod. 7.11.
127 2 Tim. 3.8,9.
128 The third plague in Egypt, a plague of small flying insects.
129 Exod. 8.19.
130 Cf. Exod. 19.10,11.

fourteenth of the first month, when the pasch was kept, to the third day of the third month: you will have seventeen of the first month, thirty of the second, three of the third, which makes fifty. The Law in the Ark is sanctification in the Body of the Lord, through whose Resurrection future rest is promised to us, to be attained by the charity breathed into us by the Holy Spirit. But, 'as yet the Spirit was not given, because Jesus was not yet glorified.'[131] Hence, that prophecy was sung: 'Arise, O lord, into thy resting-place, thou and the ark which thou hast sanctified.'[132] Where there is rest, there is also sanctification. So, we have now received a pledge that we may love and desire it. To the repose of the other life, to which we pass over from this life—according to the meaning of pasch—all are called 'in the name of the Father and of the Son and of the Holy Ghost.'[133]

Therefore, the number fifty multiplied by three, and with that same three added, to exalt the mystery, is found in those 'great fishes,' which the Lord, showing His new life after the Resurrection, commanded to be drawn up from the right side, 'and the net was not broken,'[134] because, then, there will be no unrest of heretics. Then, man, perfected and at rest, purified in soul and body by 'the words of the Lord, pure as silver tried by the fire, purged from the earth, refined seven times,'[135] shall receive as his reward the penny,[136] that there may be ten and seven. In this number, as in others having a variety of aspects, a marvellous mystery is revealed. With

---

[131] John 7.39.
[132] Ps. 131.8.
[133] Matt. 28.19.
[134] John 21.6,11.
[135] Ps. 11.7.
[136] A denarius was a Roman coin of silver valued at ten asses, the *as* being the lowest Roman coin. The value of the denarius was about sixteen cents, American money. In the parable of the laborers in the vineyard they received 'every man a penny', i.e., a denarius. Matt. 20.2,9,10,13.

good reason is the seventeenth psalm alone found intact in the Book of Kings,[137] because it signifies that kingdom in which we shall have no enemies. For its title is: 'In the day that the Lord delivered him out of the hand of his enemies and out of the hand of Saul.'[138] But, of whom is David a figure if not of Him who came, 'According to the flesh, of the seed of David'?[139] And He still manifestly suffers enemies in His Body, which is the Church. So, when He had struck down that persecutor with His word, and after drawing him into His Body, He as it were devoured him, He called from heaven: 'Saul, Saul, why persecutest thou me?'[140] But, when will this body of His be delivered from the hand of all His enemies except when that 'enemy death shall be destroyed last'?[141] To that time belongs the number of fishes, one hundred and fifty-three. For the number seventeen, erected into a triangle, completes the sum of one hundred fifty three. Starting from one and going up to seventeen, add all the intermediate numbers and you will find it so: to one add two and make it three; add three, it makes six; add four, it makes ten; add five, it makes fifteen; add six, you get twenty-one; add all the others in order, including seventeen, and it comes to one hundred and fifty three.

Easter and Pentecost are feasts with the strongest Scriptural authority. The observance of forty days before Easter rests on the decree of the Church, and by the same authority the eight days of the neophytes[142] are distinguished from other

---

137 2 Kings 22.2-51.
138 2 Kings 22.1.
139 Rom. 1.3.
140 Acts 9.4.
141 1 Cor. 15.26.
142 The newly baptized. Baptism was usually administered on Holy Saturday, and the neophytes remained in a group for eight days, wearing their white robes and attending services together. On the octave of Easter they laid these robes aside and returned to family life.

days, so that the eighth harmonizes with the first. It is not a universal custom that Alleluia should be sung in the Church on those fifty days only, for the custom of singing it on other days varies from one place to another. However, on those days it is sung everywhere. I am not sure whether it is a general custom to pray standing on those days and on all Sundays. I have told you to the best of my ability what practice the Church follows in that matter, and I think it is clear.

Concerning the washing of feet, although the Lord commended it as a form of the humility which He had come to teach, as He later explained, the question is raised about the time when such a great practice should best be taught by example, and it coincided with that time at which His teaching made a deeper religious appeal. Many have been unwilling to accept it as a custom, lest it should seem to be a part of the sacrament of baptism. Some have not even shrunk from abolishing it as a custom. But others, in order to promote it at a less conspicuous time, and to separate it from the sacrament of baptism, have chosen to do it either on the third day of the octave—because the number three has such pre-eminence in many sacraments—or on the octave day itself.

I wonder why you wanted me to write you some comments on customs which vary in different places, since there is no obligation about them, and there is one completely safe rule to be followed in such things, namely, when they are not contrary to faith or morals, and they have some effect in encouraging us to a better life, wherever we see them in use, or know that they are used, we do not censure them, but support them by our approval and imitation—all this, of course, unless they might cause harm to others whose faith is weak. But, if this obstacle is such that more gain for the devout is to be hoped for than harm from the evil-minded is to be feared, then the custom should be followed without scruple, especially the sort of thing that can be supported from Scripture, such as singing hymns and psalms, of which we have the example and teaching of both the Lord Himself and His Apostles. Of this practice, which is so effective for rousing the mind to piety and enkindling the sentiment of divine love, there are varieties of performance, and many members of the Church in Africa are somewhat slothful about it. Consequently, the Donatists reproach us because we sing the divine songs of the Prophets too plainly in church, whereas they increase their orgies by singing psalms composed by human genius, which excite them as by trumpet calls. But, is not any time appropriate for singing sacred hymns when the brethren gather in the church, except when there is reading or discussion or praying aloud by the bishop, or prayer in common, led by the voice of the deacon?

In the other intervals of time, I do not know of anything better or more profitable or more holy for Christians to do when they are gathered together. I cannot approve what is established outside the common custom, and observed almost as if it were a sacrament, but I do not venture to disapprove too freely, even though many things of this sort are to be avoided so as not to scandalize certain holy or troublesome people. I regret deeply that so many very wholesome practices, which are taught in the Sacred Books, are too little esteemed, while all around are others so full of superstition that it is harder to correct a man who touches the earth with his bare foot for eight days than one who stupefies his mind with drink. All such things should, I think, be cut out ruthlessly, where opportunity allows; such as are not authorized by the Holy Scriptures, nor found among those decreed by the councils of bishops, nor sanctioned by the custom of the universal Church, but which are so endlessly varied by the circumstances of different places that the original ideas which men had in starting them can scarcely be discovered. Even if it cannot be proved that they are contrary to faith, they still weigh down with servile burdens a religion which the mercy of God wished to be free, with only a very few and very well-chosen sacramental obligations. By comparison they make the status of the Jews more bearable, who, though they did not know the time of liberty, were subject to the obligations of the Law, not those of human contrivance. The Church of God, established in the midst of much chaff and much cockle, tolerates many things, yet those that are contrary to faith and good living it neither approves, nor accepts in silence, nor practices.

Therefore, what you wrote of certain brethren refraining from flesh meat because they believe it to be unclean is very clearly against faith and sound doctrine. If I wanted to carry on the discussion from this point, it could be deduced by some that the Apostle was obscure in his teaching, although he has much to say about this matter, and shows his detestation of the impious theories of the heretics in these words: 'Now the Spirit manifestly saith that in the last times some shall depart from the faith, giving heed to spirits of error and doctrines of devils; speaking lies in hypocrisy and having their conscience seared; forbidding to marry; to abstain from meats; which God hath created to be received with thanksgiving by the faithful and by them that have known the truth. For every creature of God is good, and nothing to be rejected that is received with thanksgiving: for it is sanctified by the word of God and prayer.'[143] And in another place he speaks of these things: 'All things,' he says, 'are clean to the clean, but to them that are defiled and unbelievers, nothing is clean, but both their mind and their

---
143 1 Tim. 4.1-5.

conscience are defiled.'¹⁴⁴ Do you read the rest and quote it to others, when you can. Let them not make the grace of God void for themselves, for we 'are called unto liberty, only let them not make liberty an occasion to the flesh,'¹⁴⁵ and therefore let them not, for the sake of taming carnal concupiscence, refrain altogether from any kinds of food, because it is not permitted them to act through superstition or unbelief.

Now, regarding those who draw lots from the pages of the Gospel, although it could be wished that they would do this rather than run around consulting demons, I do not like this custom of wishing to turn the divine oracles to worldly business and the vanity of this life, when their object is another life.

If you do not think I have covered adequately all the points you inquired about, then you have no idea of either my physical strength or my duties. Certainly, I am so far from knowing everything, as you think, that I found no part of your letter more disagreeable reading than that, because it is so obviously false. I wonder at your not knowing that there are innumerable things of which I am ignorant, and even in the Holy Scriptures themselves my ignorance is greater than my knowledge. Therefore, I cherish a sure hope in the name of Christ, because not only do I believe on the authority of my God that in those two commandments depend the whole Law and the Prophets,¹⁴⁶ but I have even experienced and do daily experience it; and never is a mystery or some word hitherto obscure to me laid open from the Sacred Letters that I do not find the same commandments: 'Now the end of the commandment is charity from a

---
144 Titus 1.15.
145 Gal. 5.13.
146 Matt. 22.40.

pure heart and good conscience, and an unfeigned faith,'[147] and: 'love is the fulfilling of the law.'[148]

Therefore, do you also, dearly beloved, so read these and other texts, and so learn them that you remember the true saying: 'Knowledge puffeth up,'[149] but 'charity envieth not, is not puffed up.'[150] So, then, use your knowledge as a sort of tool, to build the edifice of charity, which remains forever, even when 'Knowledge shall be destroyed.'[151] For, knowledge which is used to promote love is useful, but in itself and separated from such an objective it turns out to be not only useless but even harmful. I know the kind of holy meditation which gives you protection 'under the shadow of the wings'[152] of the Lord our God. And that is why I have given you this brief warning, since I know that the same charity of yours, which envieth not, will give and read this letter to many.

56. Augustine to his beloved son, Celer,[1] excellent lord, worthy of honor, greeting (c. 400)

I am not forgetting my promise and your desire. But, as I had to set out on a round of visits to the churches which are under my care, and as I could not at once pay my debt to you personally, and I did not want to owe any longer what could be paid from what I have, I therefore commissioned my very dear son, the priest Optatus, to read with you what I promised, at the times that you would find most convenient.

---

147 1 Tim. 1.5.
148 Rom. 13.10.
149 1 Cor. 8.1.
150 1 Cor. 13.4.
151 1 Cor. 13.8.
152 Ps. 16.8.

---

1 Celer was proconsul or governor of Africa in 429.

When he sees that this task can be wholly completed, your Excellency will except it gratefully, and so he will persuade you to act quickly and willingly. I think you know quite well how much I love you and how I wish to see you rejoice in and pursue these profitable studies and this knowledge of divine and human truths.

If you do not despise the charity of my service, I hope that you will make such progress in Christian faith and morals as is consistent with your established position, so that you may await the last day of this smoke or vapor of time[2] which is called human life (a day which it is granted to no mortal to escape), and that you may await it with eagerness or resignation, or at least not in frantic anxiety, on the solid ground of truth, not in the vanity of error. As sure as you are of your own existence, so sure must you be, by the saving doctrine, that the life which is passed in temporal pleasures is not to be considered life but death, in comparison with the eternal life which is promised to us through Christ and in Christ. I will have no doubt about your ability, because you will very easily extricate yourself from that intimacy with the Donatists, if you will not underestimate Christian purity with due regard for religion. It is not a great achievement for even the dull-witted to perceive, if only they listen patiently and carefully, with what unshaken[3] foundation of authorities that error is propagated. To break the bonds of a habitual and familiar aberration in order to follow a course of unaccustomed uprightness is a mark of greater strength. And it is not to be despaired of by the help and inspiration of the Lord, our God, acting on your naturally free and certainly manly heart. May the mercy of the Lord our God preserve you, excellent lord, deservedly honored and beloved son.

---
2 Cf. James 4.15.
3 This is obviously said in sarcasm, because Augustine himself had more than once shaken the foundations on which this schism rested.

*57. Augustine gives greeting in the Lord to Celer,
his most beloved and deservedly honored lord,
and son worthy of being cherished (c. 400)*

I believe there was no good reason why the sect of Donatus should sever itself from the rest of the world wherein the Catholic Church is spread, according to the promises of the Prophets and the Gospel, a fact which your Prudence has easily grasped upon further consideration. If there is need of more detailed argument on this point, I remember that I gave your Benevolence a book[1] to read, when my dear Caecilius, your son, hinted to me that you wanted it. This book remained in your hands for some time. If in your desire to know about this matter, you were willing or able to read it, even in the midst of your duties, I am sure your Prudence discovered that they have nothing to offer as a probable rebuttal. If you are still interested, as far as God grants or permits it, perhaps we shall be able to answer your questions or give you something else to read, beloved sir, justly honored and cherished son.

Therefore, I ask you to support Catholic unity among your people in the region of Hippo, especially with Paternus and Maurusius. I know your conscientious watchfulness and I think there is no need to write more, since you can easily find out, if you wish, about the cares and anxieties of others on your estates, and also what is going on in your own household. It has been represented to me very strongly that there is a friend[2] in your employ with whom I am anxious to have a conference. I ask you to give your support to this matter, and so you will have great praise from men and great mercy from God. He has now sent me his message by someone

---
1 One of his treatises against the Donatists.
2 This friend was a Donatist, 'subject to' Celer, probably in his employ.

named Carus, whom he uses as a go-between, through fear of certain turbulent characters whom he will not have to fear in your household and with your protection. Indeed, what you ought to dislike in him is not his constancy, but his obduracy. For to change one's belief is shameful when it is true and right, but praiseworthy and meritorious when it is foolish and harmful. Just as constancy keeps a man from being perverted, so obduracy keeps him from being corrected; therefore, as the former is to be praised, so the latter is to be amended. The priest whom I have sent will confide the rest to your Prudence in greater detail. May the mercy of God keep you safe and happy, beloved lord, son deservedly honored and cherished.

58. Augustine gives greeting in the Lord to the excellent and estimable lord, his son, intimately loved in Christ, Pammachius[1] *(401)*

Your good works, springing up by the grace of Christ, have made you honorable and widely known, and greatly to be loved by us among His members. You would not be better known to me, if I saw your face every day, than you are since I have beheld the inner beauty of your peaceful soul, lovely and shining with the light of truth, with the splendor of this one deed of yours—I have beheld and recognized, I have recognized and loved. To this dear friend I now speak, to him I now write, who is well known to me though we are separated in the flesh, one from another. Truly we are together, and we have been living together under one Head, for, if you had not been rooted in His love, Catholic unity

---

[1] A Senator who had converted some Donatist tenant farmers of his to Catholicism.

would not be so precious to you, and you would not with such enthusiasm have roused those African tenant farmers of yours who were settled in that part of the land where the Donatist madness began, that is, in the middle of the consular district of Numidia. You would not have stirred them to such heat of fervor that they chose with instant devotion to follow you, because they realized that such a man as you would follow nothing but recognized truth; and because, though far distant from you in terms of space, they would be counted with you forever among His members, since by His ordinance they serve you in this life.

Having acquaintance with you, then, by this deed of yours, I embrace you with joy, I congratulate you in Christ Jesus, our Lord, and I send you this letter of felicitation as a token of my heart-felt love for you—there was nothing else I could do. But, I ask you not to measure by this how much I love you. When you have read this letter, use it as an invisible bridge to cross over and proceed in thought into my heart, and see what goes on there concerning you. There will be laid open to the eye of love the inner chamber of love, which we close against the troublesome trifles of the world when we adore the Lord. There you will see the ecstasy of my joy in that good deed of yours, which I cannot utter in my speech nor express with my pen, burning and glowing as it is in the sacrifice of praise of Him by whose inspiration you willed it and by whose help you carried it out. 'Thanks be to God for His unspeakable gifts.'[2]

Oh, how we wish there were many senators and many sons of holy Church to perform such good works in Africa as we rejoice at in you! It is dangerous to exhort them, but safe to congratulate you. They will probably not do anything, and the enemies of the Church, as if they had already triumphed

---
[2] 2 Cor. 9.15.

over us in mind, will set snares to deceive the weak, but you have done something that confuses the enemies of the Church by freeing the weak. Therefore, it seems to be enough for you to read this letter in friendly confidence to any of those you can reach by your Christian authority. Thus, from you, indeed, they will believe that can happen which, perhaps, they thought could not happen; in consequence of which they would remain inert. But, I do not want to write about the snares which the heretics contrive; I only laugh at their thinking that they could contest your soul with the possession of Christ. You will hear all this from my brethren[3] whom I earnestly recommend to your Excellency, and I ask you, in the midst of this great and unexpected conversion of so many, which brings such joy to Mother Church, that you do not disdain them, even if their fears are unnecessary.

59. *Augustine gives greeting in the Lord to the most blessed lord and venerable father and fellow priest, Victorinus[1] (401)*

The synodal summons reached me on November 9, at the end of the day, and it found me altogether unprepared, so that I was not able to go. But, whether it disturbed me because of my inexperience, of whether I was disturbed with good reason, it is for your Holiness and Dignity to decide. I read in the same summons that it had been addressed even to the Mauretanias, although we know that those provinces have their own primates. And, if any of them were summoned to a council held in Numidia, then it was certainly proper to

---

[3] Delegates to a council held at Carthage in the middle of September, 401.

[1] Primate of Numidia.

put in the summons the names of some other Maurish bishops who have precedence there, and I was much surprised at not finding them there. In the second place, even the notice to the Numidians was in so mixed and disorderly an arrangement that I found my name in the third place, and I know how much more recently I became bishop than many others. This is unjust to others and unfair to me. Moreover, our venerable brother and colleague, Xanthippus of Tago,[2] says that the primacy belongs to him, that he is recognized as such by many and he sends out letters in that capacity. No doubt, this mistake can easily be recognized and settled between your Holinesses; still, his name should not have been passed over in the summons which your Reverence sent out. I should have been much surprised if he had been listed half-way down and not at the head of the list, but it is much more surprising that no mention is made of him at all, since he had the best claim to come to the council, so that the question of his rank as primate might be treated first of all before the bishops of all the Numidian churches.

For these reasons I would have hesitated to come, fearing that the summons in which such mistakes occur might have been forged, although the emergencies of the time and other pressing necessities would doubly prevent me. Consequently, I ask your Beatitude to pardon me and to deign to insist first of all on harmonious agreement between your Holiness and the aged Xanthippus, on the question of which one of you should summon a council; or at least—which I think would be better—that you both convoke our colleagues, especially those that are near you in age in the episcopacy, who would easily distinguish which one of you speaks the truth. Let the

---

2 A small country place in Numidia. There were so many bishops in Africa at the time of the Council of Carthage—567 in all—that many of them lived in small hamlets not found on the map.

controversy be settled among the few of you, and, when the mistake is rectified, let the younger ones be summoned by the others, since they neither can nor ought to trust anyone in this matter but you, their elders, and at present they do not know which one of you they are to believe unquestionably. I have sent this letter sealed with a ring which has a head of a man looking to one side.

60. Augustine gives greeting in the Lord to the most blessed lord, worthy of respect and veneration, his most sincerely loved brother and fellow priest, Bishop Aurelius[1] (401)

I have received no letters from your Reverence since we parted from each other in the flesh, but now I have read the letters of your Benignity about Donatus[2] and his brother and I have wavered a long time over the answer I should make. After thinking it over again and again, trying to see what is useful for the best interests of those whom we shepherds have to feed in Christ, I can reach no other conclusion than that we should not open that road to the servants of God, so that they could too easily think themselves called to something better, whereas they become worse. For, then, it is easy for them to fall back, and at the same time a very grave injustice is done to the regular clergy, if deserters of

---

1 Cf. Letter 24 n. 15.
2 Not the founder of the Donatists. This man and his brother had left their monastery, in Augustine's diocese, without permission, had gone to Aurelius, and Donatus had been ordained and admitted among his clergy. Augustine objected to this on the ground of its demoralizing effect on both monks and clerics.

monasteries are chosen to fill their ranks.[3] Moreover, of those who remain in the monastery, we are accustomed to admit to the clergy none but the well-tried and the better ones; otherwise, as the common saying has it, 'A poor flute player makes a good chorister'—so the common people might be able to jest about us, saying: 'A poor monk makes a good cleric.' It would be too lamentable to raise monks to such a dangerous degree of pride, and to think clerics—in whose ranks we belong—worthy of such insult. Sometimes, a good monk hardly makes a good cleric, for, even if he observes celibacy, he may lack the necessary education or the requisite integrity of character.

But, I believe your Beatitude has thought that these monks left the monastery with our sanction, and so as to be of use to their fellow countrymen. That is not true; they went away of their own accord; of their own accord they deserted us, although we strove to the best of our ability to hold them back, out of consideration for their salvation. Since Donatus has already been ordained, before we have had a chance in the council to make a decision about this matter, your Prudence will have to do what you wish about him, always supposing he has been cured of his pride and insubordination. But, about his brother, who was the principal reason for Donatus' leaving the monastery, since you understand how I feel, I do not know what answer to make. I do not venture to oppose your Prudence, Honor and Charity, but I earnestly hope you will do what you see is beneficial to the members of the Church. Amen.

---

[3] It must be remembered that monks at that time were not priests. and that, in order to be ordained, they had to be accepted by a bishop to whose jurisdiction they were to be subject. As the monastery was in Augustine's diocese, it was irregular for Donatus to apply to another bishop.

61. Augustine to his beloved brother, Theodore[1] (401)

When your Benevolence was speaking to me about our receiving clerics from the Donatist sect, if they wanted to be Catholics, I decided to set forth in this letter which is being despatched to you the answer which I then made to you, so that, if anyone asks you what we think of this matter, you can show him this, written by my own hand. You should know, then, that we do not hate anything in them except that separation by which they became schismatics or heretics, since by not holding to the unity of the Catholic Church they neither enjoy the peace of the people of God, who are dispersed throughout the whole world, nor do they recognize the baptism of Christ, among men. We therefore condemn the wicked error which they hold because it is their own, but the good name of God, which they hold, and His sacrament, we acknowledge in them, and we venerate and embrace it. For that reason, we grieve over their wandering and we long to win them for God, through the charity of Christ, so that the holy Sacrament[2] which they receive outside the Church to their destruction, they may have in the peace of the Church for their salvation. If, then, the wicked ways of men are removed from their midst, and the good ways of God are honored among men, there will be brotherly agreement and sweet peace, so that the charity of Christ may overcome in the hearts of men the temptations of the Devil.

So, then, when they come to us from the Donatist sect, we do not receive their aberrations, that is, their dissension and error, for these are to be removed from their midst as obstacles to agreement, but, standing with them, we embrace

---
1 Probably an African bishop, but his exact dignity is not known.
2 The Eucharist.

them as brothers, as the Apostle says: 'In the unity of the Spirit in the bond of peace.'[3] We recognize in them the gifts of God, either holy baptism, or the blessing of ordination, or the profession of celibacy, or the consecration of virginity, or belief in the Trinity, or anything else, all of which, even if present to them, profited them nothing, since charity was not there.[4] For, who can say truly that he has the charity of Christ when he does not accept His unity? Therefore, when they come into the Catholic Church they do not receive here what they had, but in order to begin to profit by what they had, they receive what they had not. Here they find the root of charity in the bond of peace, and they share in unity, and so all the mysteries of truth which they have may now avail them, not to damnation but to deliverance. The branches ought not to boast[5] that they are not the wood of thorns, but of the vine. For, if they do not live in the root, they shall be cast into the fire, whatever their appearance. Of certain broken branches the Apostle said: 'God is able to graft them in again.'[6] Therefore, dearest brother, whenever you see any of them doubting of their standing when received by us, show them this handwriting of mine, which you know well, and, if they wish to have it, let them have it, because I call God to witness, on my soul, that I will so receive them that they may not only keep the baptism of Christ which they have received, but even the rank of religious life and celibacy.[7]

---
3 Eph. 4.3.
4 1 Cor. 13.3.
5 Rom. 11.8.
6 Rom. 11.23.
7 It had been decided at the Council of Carthage, held in September, 401, that the individual bishops could use their own discretion in receiving Donatists into the Church, in the same rank and standing they had held. This proved that Donatist baptism and Orders were to be considered valid, and apparently the same consideration was extended to religious vows.

62. *Alypius, Augustine, Samsucius,*[1] *and the brethren who are with us give greeting in the Lord to the most blessed lord and venerated and sincerely beloved brother and fellow priest, Severus*[2] *and the brethren who are with you (401)*

When we arrived at Subsana[3] and were inquiring about what had been done there against our will and in our absence, we heard that some things had been done differently, and all of them matters of regret, but having to be tolerated; so we corrected them, as far as we could with the Lord's help, partly by remonstrance, partly by warning and partly by prayer. But, what saddened us most after the departure of your Holiness was that the brethren were sent away from there without a guide for their journey, and we ask you to pardon us and be assured that this was the result of over-cautiousness rather than of ill-will. For, although they thought that they were being sent by our son, Timothy,[4] for the special purpose of rousing the anger of your Charity against us, and they wished to keep everything intact for our arrival, which they hoped would coincide with yours, they thought they were not likely to set out if they did not obtain a guide for the road. Now, anyone would know that there was something wrong, and, as a result, Fossor[5] was told that Timothy had already started with the brethren. This was clearly a mistake, but it was not a priest who said it, and we have been informed very definitely, in the way such things usually

---
1 Bishop of Turres. Cf. Letter 34. At the beginning of Augustine's episcopate, he is spoken of as a bishop of established reputation.
2 Bishop of Milevis. Cf. Letter 31.
3 A town in the diocese of Hippo.
4 A young cleric who should have been ordained in Augustine's diocese, but had received the subdiaconate in that of Severus.
5 Apparently, one of the guides mentioned.

get around, that your brother Carcedonius knew nothing whatever about it.

But, why prolong this any further? Timothy, the abovementioned son of ours, was greatly troubled and he told us that he had experienced a most disagreeable and unexpected doubt, because, while you were arranging for him to serve God at Subsana, he burst forth and swore that he would not, under any circumstances, leave you. When we inquired what he wanted to do, he answered that he was prevented by his oath from being where we had previously wanted him to be, whereas now, especially, he was free from care regarding any exercise of his liberty. And we made it clear to him that he would not be guilty of perjury, if it was not by his responsibility but yours—and for the avoidance of scandal—that he could not be with you, especially as he could not bind your will with an oath, but only his own. As he admitted that you had not sworn anything to him in return, he finally said what a servant of God and a son of the Church ought to say, that he would carry out unfalteringly whatever might be decided about him between your Holiness and us. Therefore, we beg and beseech your Prudence, by the charity of Christ, to remember all that we have said and to rejoice us by your answer. 'Now that we are stronger,'—if we dare to say this in the midst of such dangers and temptations—as the Apostle says, 'we ought to bear the infirmities of the weak.'[6] Brother Timothy has not written to your Holiness because your holy brother has related all that has happened. Remember us, and glory in the Lord, most blessed lord, reverend and sincerely loved brother.

---
6 Rom. 15.1.

63. Augustine and the brethren who are with me give greeting in the Lord to the most blessed lord and sincerely cherished brother and fellow priest, Severus (401)

If I say what the case in hand forces me to say, where is the respect for charity? But, if I do not say it, where is the freedom of friendship? After wavering awhile, I have decided to excuse myself rather than blame you. You wrote that you were surprised at our being willing to tolerate, with sorrow, what could have been remedied by correction, as if one ought not to grieve over wrong-doing even when it is corrected, as far as possible afterwards, or as if there were not the greatest need of toleration when something which was evidently wrong cannot be undone. Cease to be surprised, dearest brother. For, against my advice and without my consent, Timothy was ordained subdeacon at Subsana, while the question of what to do with him was still unsettled between our opposing opinions. See, then, how I still grieve, although he has now returned to you, and I regret that we did not obey your will regarding him.

Hear, then, what we corrected by remonstrance, by warning, by prayer, so that he may not seem, before he left us, to have been uncorrected, because he had not yet returned to you. First, we corrected him by remonstrance, because he did not obey you, but went out to your Holiness without consulting your brother Carcedonius beforehand, and this was the beginning of all our trouble. Next, we corrected the priest and Verinus, through whom we learn that the ordination was contrived. But when, upon our remonstrance, they all confessed that all this was not right, and begged to be forgiven, there would be too much pride in our failing to believe that they had been corrected. It is true, they could not undo what was done, but neither did we achieve anything by our remonstrance, except to make them realize that they had done wrong and regret it. By warning we corrected all of them in the first place, so that they would not dare such things again, to avoid drawing down the wrath of God; next and especially, we corrected Timothy, who kept saying that he was obliged by his oath alone to go over to your Charity. If, as we hope, your Holiness would recall what we said together and if, out of regard for the scandal of the weak for whom Christ died, and of the discipline of the Church which they neglect to their peril, you would refuse to have him with you—since he had already been a lector[1] with us—he would now, with a tranquil mind, free from the obligation of his oath, serve God to whom we have to give an account of our deeds. By our warning, also, we brought brother Carcedonius to the point of receiving with the utmost patience whatever might have to be done about him as a necessary measure of Church discipline. And by prayer, we corrected ourselves, so as to commend to the mercy of God our measures and the outcome of our decisions; and by taking refuge under His healing right Hand to find our cure, in case our indignation has wounded us. See how many abuses we corrected, partly by remonstrance, partly by warning and partly by prayer.

And, now, having regard for the bond of charity, 'that we may not be overreached by Satan, for we are not ignorant of his devices,'[2] what else should we do but yield to your will, since you did not think that what has been done could be set

---
[1] One of the Minor Orders, whereas subdeacon is one of the Major Orders. The Council of Milevis had ruled that if anyone had exercised the office of lector once in a church, he should not be admitted as a cleric by any other church. As Augustine does not appeal to this canon, it seems clear that it had not yet been promulgated when the letter was written.
[2] 2 Cor. 2.11.

right unless he was returned to your jurisdiction, inasmuch as you complained of the injustice done to you through him? Brother Carcedonius himself has acted thus, seeing Christ in you, although it was with no slight disturbance of mind that he did so, and I ask you to pray for him. For, while I was still thinking over whether I should send any more letters to your Fraternity, as long as Timothy was staying with us, he feared your fatherly wrath, and cut short my delay by not only allowing but even insisting that Timothy should be returned to you.

So, then, Brother Severus, I submit my case to your judgment; I am certain that Christ dwells in your heart; and I beg you through Him to consult Him who rules over your mind to know whether a man who had begun to exercise the office of lector in a church under my jurisdiction, not once but two or three times, at Subsana as attendant to the priest of Subsana, and also at Turres, at Cizau and at Verbalis,[3] can cease to be a lector or should be considered to have done so. And as we, at God's command, corrected what was afterward done against our will, so do you equally correct what was previously done without your knowledge. I do not fear that you will fail to understand how widely a door is opened which may lead to a breakdown of ecclesiastical discipline, if a cleric of one church can make an oath to someone else that he will not leave him, and if he can thereupon be allowed to stay with that one because he protests that he acts so as not to be responsible for perjury. Assuredly, the one who does not allow this and does not permit such a one to stay with him, because the oath can bind only the maker of it and not another, that one keeps the rule of peace without any blame.

---

[3] Small Numidian towns in the diocese of Hippo.

64. Augustine gives greeting in the Lord to his beloved brother and fellow priest, Quintianus[1] (401)

We do not disdain to look on bodies which are not beautiful, especially since our own souls are not yet beautiful, as we hope they will be when He, the indescribably beautiful one, 'shall appear,' in whom we now believe without seeing Him, 'then we shall be like to Him, because we shall see Him as He is.'[2] We exhort you also to feel thus about your soul, if you are willing to take this in a brotherly spirit, and do not assume that it is beautiful, but, as the Apostle enjoins, that you rejoice in hope and do what follows from that, for he says: 'Rejoicing in hope, patient in tribulation.'[3] 'For we are saved by hope,' as he says again, 'but the hope that is seen is not hope, for what a man seeth why doth he hope for? But if we hope for that which we see not, we wait for it with patience.'[4] May this patience not fail you, but, with a good conscience, 'Expect the Lord, do manfully, and let thy heart take courage and wait thou for the Lord.'[5]

It is clear, however, that if you should come to us by breaking off relations with the venerable Bishop Aurelius, you could not become a member of our clergy, but we should act with that charity which we do not doubt that he would show. Your coming would not be burdensome to us, because you have an obligation to act with due consideration for the discipline of the Church, and, above all, according to your conscience, as you know, and God knows. At the same time, he[6] has delayed the settlement of your case, not through any

---
1 A priest of the diocese of Aurelius, Bishop of Carthage, who had fallen out with his bishop and wanted to join the diocese of Augustine.
2 1 John 3.2.
3 Rom. 12.12.
4 Rom. 8.24,25.
5 Ps. 26.14.
6 Aurelius; cf. Letter 41.

ill will toward you, but because of his own pressing duties, and if you knew his problems as well as you know your own, you would be neither surprised nor distressed. Please believe the same about mine, which you cannot know in the same way. There are bishops older than I am and more worthy of the episcopal dignity, as well as nearer to you geographically, through whom you could more easily push on the ecclesiastical cases that arise among your flock. I have not failed to mention your trouble and the complaint in your letter to the aged Aurelius, my venerable brother and honorable colleague, who deserves my support, and I have made it my duty to use your letter to establish your innocence. I received your letter two or three days before Christmas, when you hinted that he would probably come to the church at Badesilta[7] where you fear that the people of God are disturbed and led astray. For this reason, I do not dare to address your flock in writing: I could answer those who write to me, but how could I write to a flock that is not entrusted to my care?

However, what I say to you personally, since you wrote to me, you can share with those who have need of it. First of all, do not scandalize the Church by reading to the people scriptures which ecclesiastical law has not authorized; by such means heretics, and especially the Manichaeans, are wont to lead the unwary astray—and I hear that they like to hide in your territory. I am surprised that your Prudence should request me not to authorize our monastery to receive those who come to us from you—this in order to carry out what was decided by us in the council[8]—and you do not remember what was laid down by another council[9] regarding the canonical scriptures which alone ought to be read

---

7 A town too small for maps.
8 At Carthage, September, 401.
9 Council of Hippo, 393; of Carthage, 379.

to the people of God. Recall this council to your mind and commit to memory all that you read of it: there you will find that this decree concerned clerics only, not laymen.[10] By it, clerics coming from anywhere at all are not to be received into a monastery—not that mention was made of monasteries, but it was prescribed that no one should receive a strange cleric. But, in the recent council,[11] it was decreed that those who leave or are expelled from any monastery are not to become clerics or superiors of monasteries elsewhere. If, then, you are somewhat alarmed about Privation,[12] be assured that he has not yet been received by us into the monastery, but I have submitted his case to the venerable Aurelius, and whatever he decides about it I will do. I wonder whether he can be appointed lector, since he has more than once read uncanonical scriptures. If he is validly a lector, then surely the scripture he read is canonical, but if the scripture is not canonical, then whoever read it, even in church, is not validly a lector. However, in the case of this young man, I must carry out whatever seems good to the aforementioned bishop. If the people of Vigesilita,[13] as dear to us as to you in the vitals of Christ, will not receive a bishop who has been deposed by a plenary council of Africa,[14] they will act with good sense, and they neither can nor ought to be coerced. Whoever tries to force them will show what kind of man he is, and will betray what sort he was, since he does not want anything detrimental to be believed about him. No one is so clearly shown up, in the kind of case he has, as the one who tries by his trouble-making and complaining to recover,

---

10 Many monks at that time were laymen, i. e., did not receive Holy Orders.
11 Carthage, 401.
12 Also spelled Privatian; evidently, one of Quintianus' monks.
13 Another small hamlet or town.
14 Carthage, 401.

with the help of the secular power or by violent means, an honor which he has lost. His object is not to serve the willing Christ, but to lord it over unwilling Christians. Brothers, be on your guard: the Devil is very crafty, but Christ is the wisdom of God.[15]

65. Augustine gives greeting in the Lord to the blessed, venerable and cherished father and fellow priest, the elder, Xanthippus[1] (402)

I salute your Worthiness, I earnestly recommend myself to your prayers, and I give notice to your Worthiness that a certain Abundantius has been ordained priest in the hamlet of Strabonia, which belongs to our diocese. As he did not walk the ways of the servants of God, he began to acquire an unfavorable reputation. Alarmed by this, while unwilling to believe anything without proof, but growing more anxious, I took steps to secure, if possible, some direct proofs of his wrong behavior. First, I discovered that he had diverted the money of a certain farmer from the religious purpose intended, so that he could give no proper account of it. Then, when this was proved against him and he admitted it, on Christmas Eve, a day when even the Church at Gippe,[2] as well as others, fasted, he said good-bye to his colleague, the priest of Gippe, about the fifth hour,[3] as if he intended to go to his church, and, without any cleric for companion, he stopped in that hamlet and stayed at the house of a woman of evil fame, where he lunched and dined. In this place, a

---
15 1 Cor. 1.24.

1 Primate of Numidia. Cf. Letter 59.
2 Gippa, or Gibba, a Numidian town.
3 In winter, before 11 A.M.

certain cleric of ours, removed from Hippo, was staying, and because the culprit knew this very well, he could not deny being there, for what he denied I left to the judgment of God, and he was not permitted to conceal it. I feared to entrust a church to him, especially one surrounded by ravening heretics. So, when he asked me to send a letter, with a statement of his case, to the priest of the hamlet of Armenia[4] in the territory of Bulla[5]—he had come to us from that place—and also to allow him to live there, if possible, without the duties of the priesthood, for his amendment, and to ward off evil rumors about him, I was touched with compassion and I granted his request. I felt that I owed a special account of this to your Prudence, to forestall any false report that might reach you.

I heard his case when there were still a hundred days to Easter—which will be on April 6. Because of the council[6] I have taken pains to notify your Reverence, and I did not conceal from the man himself what had been decreed—on the contrary I gave him a true account of it. If within a year he fails to plead his case—if he thinks he has any case to plead—no one is to give him a hearing thereafter. As far as I am concerned, most blessed lord, venerable and cherished father, when it is a case of proved evil conduct on the part of clerics, especially when a bad reputation accompanies them, I think that they should be punished only in the manner prescribed by the council, but I find myself forced to try to discuss things which cannot be known, and either to condemn on insufficient evidence or to dismiss them as quite unknown. I certainly think that a priest who goes so far as to say good-bye to his colleague, a priest of that place, on

---
4 A hamlet in Numidia.
5 Also in Numidia.
6 At Carthage, 401

a fast day, when the church of that place is fasting, and goes to stay in the house of a woman of evil fame, with no cleric for companion, and who lunches and dines and sleeps in that house, ought to be suspended from his priestly duties, and I would fear to entrust the Church of God to his care hereafter. But, if it seems otherwise to the ecclesiastical judges —and it was decided in the council[7] to submit the case of a priest to six bishops—let anyone who wishes give this priest a church which has been entrusted to his own care. I confess that I fear to entrust any flock to such men, especially those whose reputation does not speak in their defence, so as to win them indulgence. I should blame myself for inaction if anything worse came out of this.

66. Book[1] of Augustine, the Catholic Bishop, against the schismatic Crispinus (c. 402)

Surely, you should have feared God, but, since you wished to be feared as a man when you rebaptized the citizens of Mappala, why should a royal decree not prevail in a province, if a provincial one had such weight in a hamlet? If you compare the respective roles, you are the owner, he the emperor; if you compare territories, you rule over a country estate, he over a realm; if you compare objectives, his is the healing of division, yours the rending of unity. We could make

---

7 An earlier Council of Carthage, 348 or 349.

1 This Letter has no salutation, but several MSS entitle it 'The treatise of St. Augustine, the Catholic bishop, against Crispinus the schismatic.' This Crispinus was a Donatist bishop of Calama, who had rebaptized eighty persons at Mappala. These were tenant farmers on an estate which he had bought. Calama was a Numidian town; Mappala a hamlet.

you pay ten pounds of gold² by imperial command, but we are not trying to make you fear a man. Or, perhaps, you have not the wherewithal to pay it because the rebaptizers were ordered to give it up when you demanded so much, in order to buy those whom you rebaptize? But, as I said, we are not trying to make you fear a man; Christ is rather the one to fear. I wonder what you would answer if He were to say to you: 'Crispinus, you paid a high price for the fear of the people of Mappala, and was My death a cheap price to pay for the love of all men? Was that which was paid out of your life for the rebaptism of your tenants worth more than the Blood from My side, poured out for the baptism of My people?' I know that you can hear even more, if you lend your ear to Christ, and that you will be reproached by that estate of yours for the impious things you speak against Christ. If you rely on human law to assure your possession of what you bought with your own money, how much more validly does Christ own, by divine law, what He bought with His Blood! And He, indeed, has undisputed possession of everything, as it is written: 'He shall rule from sea to sea, and from the river unto the ends of the earth.'³ But, how are you sure of not losing what you seem to have bought in Africa, when you say that Christ has lost the rest of the world, and has only Africa left?

Is there any more to be said? If the people of Mappala went over to your communion voluntarily, let them hear us both; let what we say be written down, and let what is written down by us be translated for them into Punic.⁴ Then, when they are free from the fear of coercion, let them choose according to their own will. From what we say, it will be clear

---

2 The fine imposed on Crispinus' bishop as a penalty for heresy. It was remitted by the Catholic bishop, Possidius.
3 Ps. 71.8.
4 Latin was evidently not universally used in northern Africa.

whether they are remaining in falsehood under compulsion or holding to the truth by their own choice. If they do not understand these arguments, what rashness you showed in forcing their ignorance! But, if they do understand, let them hear us both, as I said, and act with free will. If there are some people who have come over to us, under the compulsion of their masters, let the same thing be done there as here; let them hear us both and choose what pleases them. If, however, you do not want this to be done, it would be clear to anybody that you do not rely on the truth. Beware of the wrath of God, both here and in the world to come. I adjure you by Christ to answer this.

67. *Augustine gives greeting in the Lord to Jerome, most dear lord, most cherished and honored brother and fellow priest (402)*

I have heard that my letter has reached you, but, as I have not deserved an answer, I do not blame this on your lack of love—no doubt there has been something to prevent it. I realize that I must beg the Lord to give you the inclination and opportunity of sending what you write, for He has already given you the ability to write, and, when you wish, you can do it with ease.

It is a fact that I was not sure whether to believe the report which was brought to me, but I did not doubt at all whether I should write to you about it. This is it, in brief. I have been told that it was intimated to your Charity by some nameless brethren that I had written a book[1] against you and sent it to Rome. You know that this is not true. I call God to witness that I did not do it. If some chance

---
1 Cf. Letter 28.

statements are found in some of my writings, in which I am found to have views different from yours, that is nothing against you. As I see it, you ought to know that I wrote what seemed true to me, or, if you could not know it, you should believe it. And this also I will say, that not only am I most ready to receive in a brotherly spirit any contrary opinion you may have to anything in my writings to which you take exception, but I ask and insist that you do so, and I will take pleasure in my own correction and your goodness.

Oh, if it were only possible for me—if I cannot live with you as a neighbor—at least to enjoy you in the Lord, in sweet and frequent converse! But, since this is not granted to us, I ask this, that you also may wish our being together in Christ to be, as far as possible, preserved and increased and perfected, and that you do not scorn to answer us, however seldom.

Give my kind greetings to your holy brother, Paulinian,[2] and to all the brethren who rejoice in the Lord with you and for you. May your every holy prayer for us be heard by the Lord, beloved lord, most desired and honored brother in Christ.

68. Jerome gives greeting in the Lord to the truly holy lord and most blessed prelate, Augustine (402)

Our holy brother Asterius, the subdeacon, was just on the point of starting out when the letter of your Beatitude reached me, the one in which you make clear that you did not send a book against my lowliness to Rome.[1] I had not heard that you did this, but copies of a certain letter supposedly writ-

---

[2] Jerome's own brother, whom he had sent back to Italy to sell some inherited property; he had just returned to Bethlehem, where Jerome was.

---

[1] A title of self-depreciation.

ten to me came to me through our brother Sisinnius, the deacon, and in it you exhort me to sing my palinode[2] on a certain chapter of the Apostle, and to imitate Stesichorus[3] who wavered between abuse and praise of Helen, and who lost his eyes by criticizing her and recovered them by praising her. I admit frankly to your Worthiness, although they seemed to me to be your writing and your arguments,[4] still I did not want to put too much trust in copies of letters, lest you be justly hurt and upbraid me for not proving that the letter was yours before I answered it. The long illness of the holy and venerable Paula[5] has added to my delay. For, while we were attending her in her prolonged weakness, we almost forgot your letter, or whoever it was who wrote in your name, mindful of the verse, 'A tale out of time is like music in mourning.'[6] Therefore, if the letter is yours, write openly or send a more exact copy, so that we may engage in a debate over the Scriptures without any personal feeling, and may either correct our mistake or learn that someone else made a heedless remonstrance.

I could never go so far as to attack anything from the works of your Beatitude. It is enough for me to approve of my own and not to criticize those of others. But, your Prudence knows very well that everyone abounds in his own sense,[7]

---

2 Cf. Letter 41.
3 A famous Greek lyric poet of Himera, in Sicily, 630-550 B.C. He wrote narrative lyrics on the Fall of Troy, Helen and other characters of the epic cycle. The legend about him mentioned by St. Jerome is found in Plato, *Phaed.* 243A; Isocrates, *Encom. Hel.*; Pausanias 3.19.11; and some of the scholiasts.
4 Epichirema: a special form of syllogism, in which the reason or proof is added immediately to one or both of the premises.
5 A Roman lady who followed St. Jerome to the Holy Land, with her daughter, Eustochium, and other patrician women. She there founded a convent near the monastery for men founded by Jerome in Bethlehem. She was a scholar as well as a noble lady, and encouraged Jerome in his work on the Scriptures.
6 Eccli. 22.6.
7 Rom. 14.5.

and it is a mark of childish boastfulness to act as boys are wont to do, and to seek credit for one's own name by depreciating famous men. I am not so foolish as to think myself injured if your interpretations differ from mine, any more than you are injured if my views differ from yours. But, that is truly a friendly reprehension, if as Persius says,[8] we look at the shoulder-bag of others without seeing our own wallet. It comes to this, that you love the one who loves you, and in the field of the Scriptures you do not youthfully challenge an old man.[9] We have had our time and have run our race as best we could; and now, while you run and cover long distances, we deserve rest. I say this with all due respect for you: do not imagine that you are the only one who can quote from the poets; remember Dares and Entellus,[10] and the popular proverb about the tired ox setting his foot down more heavily. I have dictated this with sorrow. How I wish I might deserve to embrace you, and that we might teach or learn something by mutual conversation!

Calpurnius, with his usual effrontery, has sent me, under the pseudonym of Lanarius, his accursed writings, which I hear have made their way into Africa by some effort of his.[11]

---

8 Persius, *Sat.* 4.24; also, Phaedrus, *Fab.* 4.10; Catullus, *Car.* 22.21; Horace, *Serm.* 2.3.299. According to the fable, each one carries his faults in a bag slung over his shoulder, and as we march along we see the bag of the one in front of us, while the one behind us sees ours. Another version has it that we carry a double pack, the part in back with our own faults, the one in front with our neighbor's.
9 Jerome was seven years older than Augustine; at this time he was 55 to Augustine's 48. Hardly the difference between youth and age!
10 Vergil, *Aen.* 5.368-484. In the funeral games celebrated by Aeneas in Sicily in honor of his dead father Anchises, Dares, a famous Trojan boxer, fought Entellus, an equally famous Sicilian one. The contest was called off after a long struggle, to prevent the death of Dares.
11 Calpurnius Rufinus had been a close friend of Jerome in his youth. They had lived the monastic life together for awhile in Aquileia, and had been close confidantes. The translation by Rufinus of Origen's *De principiis* caused an irreparable break in their friendship, and Jerome felt obliged to attack an opponent who did not answer him.

I have answered them briefly and partially, and have sent you a copy of this book.[12] I shall send the fuller work at the first opportunity. In it I have been careful not to injure the Christian esteem of anyone, but only to refute the unbridled falsehood of ignorant raving. Remember me, holy and venerable prelate. See how much I think of you that I do not wish to answer a challenge, or to believe anything of you which I would blame in another. Brother Communis salutes you humbly.

69. Alypius and Augustine give greetings in the Lord to the justly beloved lord, their worthy, honored and cherished son, Castorius[1] (402)

The enemy of Christians[2] has contrived to cloud over with dark sadness the sweetness of our joy, which had come to us through the boon of your acquaintance, trying, by means of your brother, our most dear and sweet son, to stir up a dangerous scandal for our Catholic mother, who received us, with loving embrace, into the inheritance of Christ, when we were escaping from the state of the disinherited and the cast-off. But, the 'Lord, our God, compassionate and merciful,'[3] consoling the afflicted, feeding the little ones, curing the sick,[4] has permitted him to do something so that we might rejoice much more over a situation set right than we had grieved over our distressing loss. Indeed, it is a far

---
12 His *Apologia* against Rufinus.

---
1 Brother of Maximian, Bishop of Bagai, who was permitted by the synod of Milevis to lay down the burden of his episcopate. This is obviously not the schismatic Maximian mentioned in Letter 43. It would seem that this one found his right to the office challenged, and, rather than force the issue and risk causing a schism in his flock, had abdicated.
2 Satan.
3 Ps. 85.15; 102.8; 110.4; 111.4; 144.8; James 5.11.
4 Matt. 10.8.

greater thing to lay down the burden of the episcopate in order to ward off dangers from the Church than it is to take the helm for the sake of the power. He certainly shows that he could have received the honor worthily if some peaceful way were found, since he refuses to claim it by unworthy means. Therefore, God has wished to show to the enemies of His Church, through your brother, our son Maximian, that there are in His vitals those who 'seek not the things that are their own, but the things that are Jesus Christ's.'[5] For he has not abandoned that ministry of dispensation of the mysteries of God through the attraction of any worldly passion, but he has laid it down because of his love of peace, to prevent dissension over his position from arising, a dissension which could be shameful, dangerous or possibly even destructive for the members of Christ. Indeed, what could be more misguided and more worthy of execration than to forsake schism for the sake of the peace of the Catholic Church, and to disturb that same Catholic peace by a quarrel about his position? But, what more praiseworthy and more fit to promote Christian charity than to leave the mad pride of the Donatists and to cling to the inheritance of Christ, and thus give proof of humility by his love of unity? So, as far as he is concerned, we both rejoice that he has been found such that no storm of temptation can overthrow what the divine word has raised up in his heart, and we beg and pray the Lord that he may show forth more and more clearly in his future life and conduct how well he would have administered what he undoubtedly would have administered, if it had been expedient. May the eternal peace which was promised to the Church be granted to him, since he has understood that what did not conduce to the peace of the Church was not fitting for him.

---
5 Cf. Phil. 2.21.

But you, dearest son, our no slight joy, are hindered by no such necessity from undertaking the episcopate, and it is proper that your natural ability should manifest to Christ, who is in you, what He has given you. For, your mental gifts, your prudence, eloquence, dignity, self-control, and the other qualities with which your character is endowed are truly the gifts of God. To whose service can you better devote them than to His, since they come from Him, so that they may be preserved and increased and perfected and rewarded? Do not spend them on this world; they would merely fade and vanish with it. We know that we need not press this argument further with one who can so easily observe the empty hopes and unsatisfied desires and precarious life of men. Drive from your mind, then, whatever anticipations it has formed of earthly and false happiness; labor in the field of God where the harvest is sure; where so many things, promised so long before, are realized, and those which remain are madly despaired of. By the divinity and humanity of Christ, by the peace of that heavenly city from which we pilgrims purchase eternal rest at the price of earthly labor, we beg you to succeed to the episcopacy of the Church of Bagai, which your brother has not basely abandoned in failure, but has laid aside to his own renown. We hope for that flock a rich increase through your mind and tongue, endowed and adorned by the gifts of God. May they learn from you that your brother did what he did, not through love of his own ease, but for the sake of their peace. We have given orders that this letter is not to be read to you, unless they possess you to whom you are indispensable. We possess you by the bond of spiritual love, because you are our absolutely indispensable colleague. You shall know later why we do not show ourselves in person.

70. Alypius and Augustine to the beloved lord and honorable brother, Naucellio[1] *(402)*

When you had brought us back word what your bishop, Clarentius,[2] answered about Felician of Musta,[3] namely, that he did not deny either that he had been condemned by them or that he had been afterward reinstated in his diocese, but that he claimed that the condemnation was wrong because the condemned was not present—a fact which he had proved —we say this by way of answer, that it was not lawful for anyone to be condemned unheard, even if they who condemned him now declared him innocent. Surely, an innocent man ought not to be condemned, nor should a guilty one be reinstated; if he was innocent when reinstated, he was innocent when he was condemned; if he was guilty when he was condemned, he was guilty when reinstated. If those who condemned him did not know whether he was innocent or not, they are to be charged with foolhardiness, because they dared to condemn unheard an innocent man of whom they knew nothing. And we understand from the present case that they acted with the same lack of consideration in condemning those earlier victims whom they charged with the infamy of betrayal.[4] If it was possible for them to condemn an innocent man, it was equally possible for them to call men betrayers who were not betrayers.

In the next place, the same Felician, condemned by them, was in communion with Maximian[5] for a long time. If he was innocent when he was condemned, why did he later,

---

1 A Donatist cleric who apparently had been circulating the old calumnies against Catholics: that they had surrendered the sacred books to the pagans.
2 A Donatist bishop.
3 Cf. Letter 51.
4 Of the sacred books.
5 Cf. Letter 51.

in communion with the accursed Maximian, baptize many outside their own communion? The witnesses of this are those who brought the matter before the governor, so that the same Felician was expelled from the basilica, as being with Maximian. It was not enough to condemn an absent man, to condemn him without a hearing, to condemn, as they say, an innocent man, but, over and above that, the governor is approached against him, so as to expel him from his church. Perhaps, when they were expelling him from his church, they admit that they included him among the condemned and wicked Maximianists—but, when he gave baptism while he was in communion with Maximian, did he give a true or a false baptism? If he gave a true baptism when he was in communion with Maximian, why is the baptism of the rest of the world repudiated? But, if he gave a false baptism when he was in communion with Maximian, why are they thus reinstated with him whom he baptized in the schism of Maximian, and why did no one in your sect rebaptize them?

71. Augustine gives greeting in the Lord to the venerable lord, his holy and esteemed brother and fellow priest, Jerome (403)

From the time when I began to write to you and to long for your replies, never have I had a better opportunity of sending my letter to you than through this servant and most faithful minister of God, one most dear to me, our son, the deacon Cyprian. Through him I have a strong hope of letters from you, stronger than any hope I could have in matters of this sort. For, this son of ours will not be lacking in eagerness to secure your answer, nor in gratitude to deserve it, nor in care in guarding it, nor in readiness in carrying it, nor in trustworthiness in delivering it. Only, if I deserve it in any way, may the Lord help you and further your inclination and my longing, so that no opposing will may stand in the way of this brotherly will.

As I have sent two letters,[1] then, but have received no answer, I have decided to send them again, in the belief that they have not reached you. If they have reached you and it is perhaps yours to me that have not been able to get through, send me those same ones again, which you have sent before, if you have kept copies. If you have not, then dictate again something for me to read, but do not begrudge me an answer to this, because I have been waiting so long a time. The first[2] letter, which I had made preparations to send you by our brother Profuturus,[3] could not be delivered by him in person, because, while he was getting ready to set out, he shortly afterward became our colleague and has now departed from this life. He was bowed down under the weight of the episcopate and discharged it for a short time only. I should now like to send that letter again, to let you know how long I have sighed after your conversation, and how I suffer violence because your bodily senses, through which my mind might make contact with your mind, are so far from me, my sweetest brother, worthy of honor among the members of our Lord.

In this letter I add what I have since learned, that you have translated the Book of Job from the Hebrew, although we have had for some time your translation of that Prophet, rendered into Latin from the Greek tongue, wherein you have

---

[1] Nos. 40 and 67. Augustine had evidently not yet received Jerome's letter sent through Asterius (No. 68).
[2] Letter 28, the one which was not delivered and which aroused Jerome's resentment.
[3] Cf. Letters 28 and 38.

marked by asterisks[4] what is found in the Hebrew version but not in the Greek and by obelisks[5] what is found in the Greek but not in the Hebrew, with such extraordinary care that in some places we see stars appended to single words, indicating that these words are in the Hebrew but not in the Greek version. But, in this later translation, which is made from the Hebrew, there is not the same authority for the words, and it rouses no little disquiet when one wonders why in the former translation the asterisks are placed with such care as to show even the most insignificant parts of speech which are lacking in the Greek texts, but are found in the Hebrew, while in the later one, taken from the Hebrew, less care is shown in assigning these particles to their places. I should like to give you an example of this, but at the moment I have no text from the Hebrew. However, as you surpass me in quickness of mind, I think you understand not only what I say, but even what I want to say, and you can clear up what troubles me as if the case had been presented.

For my part, I would rather you translated the Greek Scriptures to us as they are presented in the Septuagint. It will be very difficult if they begin to read your translation more commonly in many churches, because the Latin churches will differ from the Greek, and especially because an objector is easily refuted by producing a Greek book, as that is the best known language. But, if anyone is disturbed by an unusual passage translated from the Hebrew, and claims that it is wrong, seldom or never is there an appeal to the Hebrew to sustain the passage challenged. Even if there were, who would allow so many Latin and Greek authorities to be overruled? In addition to this, Hebrew experts could conceivably give different answers, and you would then seem to

---

4 The asterisk (*) was generally used by classical editors to indicate something missing.
5 The obelisk (†) was used to indicate suspected passages.

be the sole indispensable critic to convince them, and I doubt that you could find any experts with that judge.

There was a certain brother bishop of ours who decided to read your translation in the church over which he presided, and he caused a sensation by some passage from the Prophet Jonas,[6] which was very different from the version enshrined in the memory and hearing of all and sung for so many generations. There was such a disturbance made among the people by the Greeks arguing and stirring up passions with the charge of falsity, that the bishop—it was in the city of Oea[7]—was forced to call on the testimony of the Jews. Was it through ignorance or malice that they answered that what the Greeks and Latins said and maintained was found in the Hebrew texts? To make a long story short, the man was forced to correct an apparently wrong statement, not wishing to run the great risk of remaining without a flock. After this, it seems to us that you, also, among others, can be wrong, and you see the sort of thing that can happen when a text cannot be corrected by comparison with the familiar languages.

Therefore, we give no slight thanks to God for your work of translating the Gospel from the Greek, because there is scarcely ever objection made by anyone when we consult the Greek. So, if anyone persistently clings to a long-standing error, he can easily be enlightened or refuted by a presentation and comparison of texts. And if some very rare passages rightfully cause controversy, who is so harsh as not to be indulgent toward such a useful piece of work, and to pay it the due meed of praise? But, I wish you would be so kind as to explain what you think about the difference of author-

---

6 Jonas 4.6. The question seems to have been whether Jonas sat down under an ivy or a gourd-vine.
7 A city in Tripolitania.

ity in many places between the Hebrew texts and the Greek, which is called the Septuagint. Surely, that version has no little weight which was duly published abroad and which experience shows was used by the Apostles—a fact which you asserted, as I recall. In this you would perform a great service if you would put into correct Latin the Greek translation which the Seventy made,[8] for our Latin Scriptures vary so from text to text that it is almost unbearable, and they are so doubtful that we hestiate to quote them or prove anything by them, lest it be different in Greek. I intended this letter to be short, but somehow or other I find great sweetness in going along as if I were talking to you. But, I beseech you by the Lord not to disdain to answer all this and to lend me your presence as far as that may be.

72. Jerome to the truly holy lord and blessed prelate, Augustine (403 or 404)

You send me frequent letters, and you often insist that I answer one of your letters, of which, as I wrote you before, copies were brought by the deacon Sisinnius without your signature, and which you say that you sent first by brother Profuturus,[1] and a second time by somebody else. You say that Profuturus was interrupted when about to set out, was made a bishop and was carried off by a speedy death: and the other, whose name you do not mention, was frightened by the perils of the sea and gave up the idea of sailing.[2] With that set of circumstances I need not be surprised that the

---

8 The Septuagint version, so called because it was made by seventy translators.

1 Cf. Letter 71.
2 A cleric named Paul; cf. Letter 40 n. 22.

letter in question was reported to be circulating at Rome and in Italy, and the only one it did not come to was the one to whom it was addressed. Over and above that, the same brother Sisinnius said that he had found it among other treatises of yours, not in Africa, not in your house, but on an island of the Adriatic, at least five years ago.³

Friendship should be free of all suspicion and one should speak to a friend as to another self. Some of my intimates, servants of Christ, of whom there are many at Jerusalem and in the holy places, have been suggesting that your conduct was not single-minded, but that your motive was a desire of praise and small renown and cheap popularity; that you wished to gain credit at my expense, so that many might know that you challenged, but I feared; that you, the learned one, were writing, but I, the unlettered one, had nothing to say; and that at last someone had appeared to put a stop to my chattering. However, I admit frankly I would not answer your Worthiness at first, because I was not fully convinced that the letter was yours, and, as the popular proverb has it of such things, the sword was not dipped in honey. Later, I was on my guard against seeming to be disrespectful in answering a bishop of my own communion, or in taking issue with any points in a letter of reproof, especially as I considered some things in it heretical. Finally, I did not want you to have grounds for reproaching me and saying: 'What? you saw my letter and you recognized the handwriting of a signature known to you, and you would so easily injure a friend and turn the ill will of another to my heart?' Therefore, as I wrote before, either send me the same letter signed by your own hand, or cease to harass an old man⁴ who has retired to a cell. If you want to show off or practise

---
3 It was written in 397.
4 Cf. Letter 68 n. 9.

your learning, seek out young, fluent, well-known men—they say Rome abounds in them—men who can or dare contest with you and can carry their weight with a bishop in a discussion on the Holy Scriptures. A former soldier, but now a veteran, I ought to be praising your victories and those of others, and not to be re-entering the lists myself, with a worn-out body; otherwise, if you push me too hard into writing, I might recall the story of Quintus Maximus who broke down, by his endurance, the youthful ardor of Hannibal.[5] 'Time carries all away, even the mind. How often I recall that, as a boy, I whiled away the long, sunny days with song. Now, so many songs have passed into forgetfulness; even voice itself now fails Moeris.'[6] And, to quote more properly from the Scriptures, Berzellai the Galaadite, declining all the favors of King David and all his delights in favor of his young son, showed that old age ought not to desire these things nor accept them when offered.[7]

As to your swearing that you did not write a book against me, nor send to Rome one you did not write, and your asserting that, if it happened that some things were found in your writings which differed from my views, I was not thereby injured by you, but that you wrote what seemed correct to you, I ask you to listen to me patiently. You did not write the book. And how was your writing, with its criticism of me, brought to me by others? Why does Italy possess what you did not write? How can you ask me to answer what you say you did not write? I am not so silly as to think myself injured if you have views different from mine. But, if you attack my writings with knockout blows, and question the authority of writers, and urge me to correct

---

5 Livy 22.12-18. This was Quintus Fabius Maximus, surnamed Cunctator.
6 Vergil, *Ec.* 9.51-54.
7 2 Kings 19.31-39.
8 Cf. Letter 67.

what I have written, and challenge me to a palinode⁹ and restore me my eyes,¹⁰ then by that conduct friendship is injured and the bonds of intimacy are broken.

I write this that we may not seem to be engaging in a childish contest, and may not give grounds of contention to our mutual supporters or detractors, because I wish to love you with a pure, Christian love, and I would not keep in my heart anything that differs from my words. It is not fitting for one who has lived a life of toil with holy brethren, in a monastery, from his youth to this age, to dare to write anything against a bishop of my communion, and a bishop whom I began to love before I knew him, who first invited my friendship, and at whose growing skill in the Scriptures I rejoiced, as he followed in my footsteps. Do you, then, either deny your own book if it happens not to be yours, and cease to torment me with requests for an answer to what you did not write; or, if it is yours, admit it frankly. Then, if I write something in my own defense, the blame would be yours who challenged me; not mine, who was obliged to reply.

You add, besides, that you are ready to take it in a brotherly spirit, if I object to anything in your writings, or if I wish to correct anything in them, and that you will not only be glad of such kindness, but you beg me to show it. I say again what I think: you are harassing an old man; you are goading a silent one to speech; you seem to make a show of your learning. It is not in keeping with my age to be considered envious of one to whom I ought rather to show favor. And if, in the Gospels and the Prophets, evil-minded men find something on which to exercise their critical faculties, are you surprised, if in your books and especially in your explanation of Scripture, some points of which are very

---
9 Cf. Letter 40.
10 This is the reference to Stesichorus found in Letters 40 and 68.

obscure, there are statements that seem to deviate from the straight line of truth? I am not saying this because I now think there is anything to object to in your works, for I have not applied myself to reading them; I have no copies of them, except the books of your Soliloquies and some short commentaries on the Psalms. If I wished to discuss these I would not say that they differ from my views—since I am nothing—but I would show that they are at variance with the interpretations of the ancient Greeks. Farewell, my very dear friend, my son in years, my father in dignity, and please note this request: that, whatever you write to me, you see that it comes to me first.

73. Augustine gives greeting in the Lord to the venerable lord and most cherished brother and fellow priest, Jerome (404)

Although I think that my letter—the one which I sent by our son, the servant of God, deacon Cyprian—came into your hands before you undertook that one in which you recognized that it was my letter, of which you said copies had reached you, I now feel, from your answer, as if I were beginning to be battered and knocked about, as bold Dares was, by the great, heavy boxing gloves of Entellus.[1] But, I now am answering that same letter of yours which you were so kind as to send me by our holy son, Asterius, in which I find many marks of your most kindly charity, and also some indications that I have offended you. So, then, I was charmed, as I read, and likewise constantly shocked, but most of all I wondered at your saying that you did not think you should too easily accept copies of a letter as mine, lest I should be

---

1 Cf. Letter 68. The reference is to Vergil, *Aen.* 5:368-484.

hurt at your answering it and should justly reproach you because you ought to have proved it was mine before you answered it. But, after that, you bid me, if the letter is mine, to admit it openly or to send you a more correct copy, so that we can engage in a discussion of the Scriptures without any personal feeling. But, how can we engage in this discussion without personal feeling if you are getting ready to hurt me? Or, if you are not, how can I, hurt by you—although you are not hurting me—reasonably protest that you should have proved that the composition was mine before you answered it, that is, before you hurt me? For, if you had not hurt me by answering, I should not be able to make a reasonable protest. Thus, when you answer so as to hurt me, what chance is left us of carrying on a discussion of the Scriptures without personal feeling? I hope I am far from being hurt if you have the wish and ability to show with unquestioned proof that you have a truer understanding than I have of that passage from the Epistle of the Apostle, or of any other part of Scripture. What is more, I hope I can thankfully count it as gain to be enlightened by your teaching and set right by your correction.

On your side, my dearest brother, you would not think I could be hurt by your reply, if you did not yourself feel hurt by my writing. I would never have thought this of you, that, considering yourself not hurt, you should nevertheless so write as to hurt me. Or, if I was thought capable of being hurt, without your so writing, by reason of my own foolishness, then you do me a great injury in thinking so of me. But, you should never believe me to be such as you had never found me to be, when you would not believe that copies of my letter were mine, even though you knew my writing. You saw well enough that I would have had reason for reproaching you if you had believed groundlessly that a letter was mine which was not mine, but how much reason for reproach I would have had, at being thought to be such as the one who thought it knew me not to be? Therefore, you will not achieve anything by saying that you did not write so as not to hurt me, if you go on thinking that I am such a fool as to be hurt by such an answer of yours.

It remains, then, for you to proceed to hurt me by answering, if you know by sure proof that the letter is mine. Yet, because I do not believe that you should think me a subject of unjust injury, it remains for me to acknowledge my sin of offending you first in that letter of mine, which I cannot disavow. Why, then, do I struggle against the current, and why not preferably ask pardon? Therefore, 'I beseech you by the mildness of Christ[2] to forgive me if I have hurt you, and not to return evil for evil by hurting me in turn. But, you will hurt me if you pass over in silence the mistake which you have perhaps noticed in my deeds or in my words. For, if you reprove in me things which are not reprehensible, you harm yourself rather than me. This is something which should be foreign to your character and to your holy calling, to act with the intention of hurting, by carping with envious tooth, at what you know, in the truth of your own mind, is not blameworthy in me. So, then, with kind heart, you will either object to what you think objectionable, even if there is no guilt involved, or you will soothe with fatherly affection the one whom you cannot approve. It can even happen that a thing appears different to you from the way truth has it, so long as it does not become by your treatment different from the way charity has it. I will most gratefully receive a truly friendly reproof, even if it is a matter which cannot rightly be defended, but which still does not deserve reproof; or else I will ac-

---
2 2 Cor. 10.1.

knowledge both your kindness and my fault, and, as far as the Lord grants me to do so, I shall come out grateful in one case, corrected in the other.

Why should I fear your possibly hard, but certainly salutary words, as if they were the boxing gloves of Entellus? He was beaten, not cured; therefore, he was defeated, not healed. If I receive your medicinal correction with peaceful mind, I shall not suffer; if, through a human weakness which is also mine, I feel some sadness at being put in the wrong with good reason, it is better for the swelling of the head to suffer while it is being cured than to be spared pain and not be healed. That is what he[3] saw so clearly when he said that enemies who find fault with us are generally more useful than friends who fear to criticize us: the former often speak the truth in their ill will, and we amend our conduct; but the latter give less freedom than they should to truth, because they fear to embitter the sweetness of friendship. Therefore, if you seem to be an ox,[4] wearied with age of body, perhaps, but still, with active mind, laboring with fruitful toil on the Lord's threshing-floor, here I am; if I have said anything wrong, set your foot down strongly. The weight of your age should not be burdensome to me so long as the chaff of my mistake is threshed out.

That sentence you wrote at the end of your letter, I read and recall with deep sighs of longing. You say: 'How I wish I might deserve to embrace you, and that we might teach or learn something by mutual conversation!'[5] But I say: 'How I wish we lived in places nearer to each other, so that, even if we could not converse together, at least we could have letters more often!' At present, we are so far

---
3 Cicero, *Lael. de Amicitia* 24.90.
4 Cf. Letter 68.
5 Cf. Letter 68.

removed from actual communication with each other that I remember writing in my youth[6] to your Holiness on those words of the Apostle to the Galatians,[7] and here I am an old man and I haven't yet been rewarded with an answer. Meantime, copies of my letter reach you by chance opportunity more easily than the letter itself, which I took such care to send; for the man[8] who took charge of it neither delivered it to you nor returned it to me. That letter has acquired such apparent importance in your letters which have succeeded in reaching me that I would willingly give up all my studies to be able to live in your company. But, since this cannot be, I am thinking of sending one of our sons in the Lord to be instructed by you for us, if I deserve an answer from you even on this matter. For I neither have nor can have as much knowledge of the Divine Scriptures as I see abounds in you, and, if I have any ability in this field, I must spend it on the people of God. Because of my duties as bishop, I cannot spend more time and effort on the training of students than on preaching to the people.

We did not know that any blasphemous writings had come over your name into Africa, but we did receive what you were so kind as to send, in answer to those blasphemies.[9] When I had read it, I confess that I felt deep grief that such a great evil of discord had arisen between two such dear and intimate persons, united by a bond of friendship, so well known to almost all the churches. In your letters there is evidence of how strongly you controlled yourself, and how you withheld the sharp darts of your wrath, so as not to render evil for evil. But, if, when I read them, I was stricken

---
[6] Letter 28, written in 394 or 395.
[7] Gal. 2.11-14.
[8] Profuturus, who became Bishop of Cirta.
[9] The writings of Rufinus and Jerome's answer to them, mentioned in Letter 68.

with grief and frozen with fear, what would have been the effect on me if what he wrote against you had happened to fall into my hands! 'Woe to the world because of scandals!'[10] And now it is happening; now we see the fulfillment of what Truth says: 'Because iniquity shall abound, the charity of many shall grow cold.'[11] What faithful hearts can now pour themselves out in safety? Into whose breast can love exhaust itself without risk? And, finally, what friend is not to be feared as a future enemy, if that which we mourn could come about between Jerome and Rufinus? A sad and pitiable state of affairs! How unreliable is knowledge based on the sentiments of present friends, when there is no foreknowledge of what they will be in the future! But, why should I think this a matter of grief to one about another, when a man's future conduct is not known even to himself? Of a truth, a man hardly knows what he is like now; of what he will be in the future he knows nothing.

If the saints and the blessed angels possess not only this knowledge of what each one is, but also the foreknowledge of what he will be, then I do not see at all how the Devil could have been happy at any time, even when he was still a good angel, knowing his own future fall and eternal punishment. I should like to hear what you think about this matter, if it is something that needs to be known. Look what land and sea are doing, keeping us physically apart! If I were this letter which you read, you would now be telling me what I ask; but, as things are now, when will you write? When will you send your answer? When will it come? When shall I receive it? I greatly wish it may be sometime, while I bear with what patience I can its not coming as quickly as I wish. So I fall back on those most

---
10 Matt.18.7.
11 Cf. Matt. 24.12.

sweet words in your letter, so full of holy longing, and I make them my own, saying in my turn: 'How I wish I might deserve your embraces, and that we might teach or learn something by mutual converse!'—if it could ever be that I could teach you!

With these words, now no longer yours only, but mine also, I cheer and refresh myself, and also in no small measure, comfort myself, while this longing of both of us remains in suspense and unfulfilled. But, there again, I am pierced with the sharpest darts of grief when I think that the calamity of such great bitterness stole upon you two,[12] to whom God gave in full and generous measure what each of us has prayed for, namely, that in the closest and most intimate union you should together sip the honey of the Holy Scriptures. When and where and by whom is this not to be feared, when it befell men of mature age, dwelling, like you, in the word of the Lord, when, after laying down the burdens of the world, and sacrificing your possessions, you were following the Lord and living together in that land where the Lord walked with human feet. 'My peace,' He said, 'I give you, my peace I leave you.'[13] Truly, 'The life of man upon earth is a warfare.'[14] Woe is me that I cannot find you together anywhere at all! If I could—moved with fear and grief as I am—I would kneel at your feet, I would weep, and with all the strength and all the love I have I would beg each one of you, in the name of your own and your mutual welfare and that of others, especially the weak ones 'for whom Christ hath died,'[15] who look at you on the stage of this life to their own great peril, not to publish in writing statements about each other which would make it

---
12 He refers to Jerome's former friendship with Rufinus.
13 John 14.27.
14 Job 7.1.
15 1 Cor. 8.1.

impossible for you to be friends again. I mean such things as you could not retract, even if you were subsequently reconciled, or which you could not read without fearing that the reconciliation might turn again to enmity.

Truly, I assure your Charity that nothing made me tremble more than this instance, when I read in your letter those signs of your displeasure. I do not mean the reference to Entellus and the tired ox, which I took to be an amusing jest rather than an angry threat, but what you seem to have meant seriously when you said: 'Lest you should be hurt and should justly reproach me.'[16] Perhaps I have previously said more than I should on this, but not more than I feared. I ask you, if it can be done, that we inquire into and discuss some point, on which our souls may feed without any bitterness of dissension. But if I cannot mention what seems to me faulty in your writings, nor you in mine, without suspicion of jealousy or injury to our friendship, then let us drop this for the sake of our lives and salvation. That[17] which 'puffeth up' would then not ensue, while that[18] which 'edifieth' would not be offended. For myself, I feel that I am far from that perfection of which it is written: 'If any man offend not in word, the same is a perfect man.'[19] But, certainly, I think that by the mercy of God I can easily ask your pardon if I have offended you. And you should grant this to me so that, when I hear you, 'You will gain your brother.'[20] If you cannot act thus between us because of the distance between us, you still ought not to leave me in error. Henceforth, in those points which refer to the things which we wish to know, if I know or believe or think that

---

16 Cf. Letter 68.
17 Knowledge. Cf. 1 Cor. 8.1.
18 Charity.
19 James 3.2.
20 Matt. 18.15.

I hold the true view, where you think otherwise, I will try to make my position clear, as far as the Lord grants me to do so without doing you a wrong. But, in what touches your displeasure, when I feel that you are angry, I shall do nothing but beg your pardon.

I do not at all think that you could be angry unless I either said what I should not, or did not say what I should, because I am not surprised that we do not know each other as well as we are known by our closest and dearest friends. I confess that I readily throw myself entirely upon their charity, especially when I am wearied with the scandals of the world, and I rest in that without anxiety. Indeed I feel that God is there, and I cast myself upon Him and rest in Him without care. And in that carefree state I do not in the least fear the uncertain tomorrow of human frailty, which lately I lamented. Whenever I feel that a man burning with Christian charity and love for me has become my friend, when I entrust any of my plans and thoughts to him, I am entrusting them not to a man, but to Him in whom he abides, so as to be like Him, 'for God is charity, and he that abideth in charity, abideth in God.'[21] But, if he deserts Him, he inevitably causes as much sorrow as he caused joy by abiding in Him. Let the one who from an intimate friend has been turned into an enemy seek rather for himself what he may craftily contrive, but let him not find what he may angrily betray. This is something easily attained by anyone, not by concealing what he has done, but by not doing what he wishes to conceal. The mercy of God allows the good and faithful to move with ease and freedom among those, whoever they be, who are likely to be their enemies; they do not reveal the sins of others made known to them; they do not commit sins which they fear to have revealed. So,

---

21 1 John 4.16.

when any false rumor is made up by a traducer, it is either discredited outright, or the mere circulation of it is censured without its doing any essential harm. But, when an evil deed is committed, the enemy is within, even if it is not bruited about by any familiar gossip or spite. Therefore, any observant man can see how patiently you bear the unbelievable present enmities of one who was formerly your dearest and most intimate friend, because you have the support of your conscience, and how you estimate the attacks he makes—or is, perhaps, believed by some to make—as among the weapons on the left hand, which, as well as those on the right,[22] are used in the conflict with the Devil. Truly, I would rather have him as a milder adversary than you with that armament! It is a matter of deep and sad perplexity that such enmity can come out of a friendship of that sort. But it will be a much greater joy to bring about a return from such estrangement to former intimacy.

74. *Augustine gives greeting in the Lord to the most blessed lord, and deservedly revered brother and fellow priest, Praesidius*[1]

Following up what I said in person to your Sincerity, I urge you now again not to fail to send my letter to our holy brother and fellow priest, Jerome. As your Charity knows what an obligation you have to write to him yourself in my behalf, I have sent copies of my letter to him and of his

---

[22] The weapon of the left, defensive, was the shield; those of the right, of attack, were sword, spear or javelin.

[1] Praesidius is either to carry or forward Augustine's letter to Jerome, No. 74. He was evidently a bishop, probably the one whom Jerome commends to Augustine in Letter, 39, calling him at that time (397) a deacon.

to me. When you have read them, in accordance with your holy prudence, you may easily see both the moderation which I have thought fit to observe, and his irritation which I have good reason to fear. If I have written anything which I ought not to write or if I have not written the right way, then do not write to him about me, but rather send me an exhortation with brotherly love, so that I may be corrected and may beg his pardon when I have realized my own fault.

75. *Jerome gives greeting in Christ to the truly holy lord and most blessed prelate, Augustine (404)*

I have received at one time through Deacon Cyprian three letters, or, rather, three brief treatises[1] of your Worthiness, containing what you call inquiries, but which I consider criticisms of my works. If I wanted to answer them, it would take a large book. But, I shall try as best I can not to exceed the limits of a rather long letter, and not to delay a brother who is in a hurry to start, but who asked me for letters only three days before his departure. As a result, I am forced to babble something or other, almost in the fashion of a quick engagement, and to answer in random speech what I should weigh as I write, but have to dictate in haste. So, what I say may serve for trouble rather than for enlightenment, in the way that sudden wars upset even the bravest soldiers, and they are put to flight before they can snatch up their weapons.

However, Christ is our armor, and the injunction of the Apostle who wrote to the Ephesians: 'Take unto you the armor of God, that you may be able to resist in the evil day,' and again: 'Stand having your loins girt about with truth, and having on the breast-plate of justice and your feet shod

---
[1] Letters 28, 40 and 71.

with the preparation of the Gospel of peace; in all things taking the shield of faith by which you may be able to extinguish all the fiery darts of the most wicked one. And take unto you the helmet of salvation and the sword of the spirit, which is the word of God.'[2] With these weapons King David once went out to battle, and, taking 'five smooth stones out of the brook,'[3] he showed that there was in his senses none of the cruelty and filthiness of this world; in the midst of its storms, 'drinking of the torrent in the way and therefore lifting up his head,'[4] he most appropriately overthrew the overweeningly proud Goliath with his own weapon, striking the blasphemer on the forehead, and wounding him in that part of the body, in which Ozias, presuming to act as priest, was struck with leprosy.[5] And the saint glories in the Lord, saying: 'The light of thy countenance, O Lord, is signed upon us.'[6] Let us therefore also say: 'My heart is ready, O God, my heart is ready, I will sing, and will give praise with my glory; arise psaltery and harp, I will arise early,'[7] that we may see fulfilled in us the words, 'Open thy mouth wide and I will fill it,'[8] and 'The Lord shall give the word to them that preach good tidings, with great power.'[9] Of you, also, I venture to make this prayer, that, in this struggle of ours, truth may prevail. For, you are not seeking your own glory, but Christ's,[10] and, when you win the victory, I also shall win it if I recognize my own error, and, contrariwise, you prevail when I win, 'for neither ought the children to lay up

---

2 Eph. 6.13-17.
3 1 Kings 17.40-51.
4 Cf. Ps. 109.7. The tense is changed from future to present in the quotation.
5 2 Par. 26.19.
6 Ps. 4.7.
7 Ps. 56.8-9.; 107.2-3.
8 Ps. 80.11.
9 Ps. 67.12.
10 John 7.18.

for the parents, but the parents for the children.'[11] And in the Book of Paralipomenon we read [12] that the sons of Israel went out to fight with peaceful heart, in the very midst of swords and blood-shedding and the corpses of the slain, because they were thinking of the victory of peace, not their own. Let us therefore answer all these objections, and, if Christ shall so order, let us resolve them with brief speech. I pass over the greetings and compliments with which you anoint my head; I say nothing of the flattery with which you try to make up to me for your reproof of me; I shall come to the actual points.

You say[13] that you received from a certain brother a book of mine which had no title, in which I had listed ecclesiastical writers, both Greek and Latin; and when you asked him, to quote your own words, why the first page had no title, or by what name it was to be called, he answered that is was called an obituary notice; and you objected that it would rightly be called so if you read therein the lives or writings of those who are already dead, but that many works were listed there of men who were living at the time the book was written, and are still living, and you wondered why I had given the book such a title. I think your Prudence knows that you can understand the title from the work itself, for you have read both Greek and Latin authors who have related the lives of illustrious men, but who never used the word obituary notice for works of this sort, but they called them, 'Of Illustrious Men,' as, for instance, military leaders, philosophers, historians, epic, tragic and comic poets. The word funeral notice is properly used of the dead, as, indeed, I know I once used

---
11 2 Cor. 12.14.
12 1 Par. 12.17.18.
13 Cf. Letter 40.

it in the obituary notice of the priest Nepotian, of holy memory. This book, then, is to be called 'Of Illustrious Men,' or, more properly, 'Of Ecclesiastical Writers,' even though it is said to be entitled 'Of Authors' by a number of unskilled commentators.

In the second place, you ask why I said in the Commentaries on the Epistle to the Galatians that Paul could not have reproved in Peter what he himself had done, nor rebuke in another a deceit of which he himself was held guilty, and you add that the reproof of the Apostle was not a mere question of discipline, but a true correction, and that I ought not to teach a lie, but that all the things that are said should mean what they say. To this, I answer, first, that your Prudence should have remembered the little Prologue to my commentaries in which I said of myself:[14] 'But what? am I so stupid or so thoughtless as to promise what he could not? Not at all! On the contrary, it seems to me that I am too careful and fearful, because, knowing the deficiency of my own strength, I followed the commentaries of Origen. For, that famous man wrote five special volumes on the Epistle of Paul to the Galatians, and he ended the tenth book of his Miscellany with an additional explanation, word by word. He also composed different treatises and abstracts, which ought to be enough authority. I pass over my Didymus the Seeing,[15] and the Laodicean[16] recently gone out of the Church,

---

14 Jerome, on *Epistle to Galatians, prologue,* Migne, *PL* 26.307.
15 Didymus the Blind (313-398), a prolific exegete, who followed Origen and was involved in his condemnation. Jerome calls him my 'seeing' Didymus, perhaps because his loss of sight did not prevent him from seeing into the meaning of Scripture.
16 Apollinaris of Laodicea (*c*.310-*c*.392), a gifted and erudite scholar who fell into the error of the monophysites, and was condemned by Pope Damasus in 377.

and Alexander[17] the ancient heretic, and Eusebius of Emesa,[18] and Theodore of Heraclea,[19] who have left several commentaries on this text. If I took only a few extracts from these, the result would be something not entirely worthy of condemnation. In fact, to make a frank admission, I read all of them and I had many of them jumbled together in my mind when I called a secretary and dictated both my own and others' thoughts without regard to arrangement, and sometimes without recalling the exact meaning of the words. And now it is a mark of the Lord's mercy if these well-worded sayings of others do not lose their force through my uncouthness and fail to have their effect among strangers such as they have among their own.' If, then, you thought anything in my commentary was worthy of criticism, with learning like yours, you should have examined whether what we wrote was found in the Greek sources, and, if it was not theirs, then you could validly object to my opinion, especially when I had freely admitted in the Prologue that I had followed the commentaries of Origen, and that I had dictated both my own and the quoted opinions. Besides, at the end of that same chapter to which you object, I wrote: 'If anyone does not like the interpretation by which it is shown that Peter did not sin and Paul did not disrespectfully rebuke his elder, he ought to show how inconsistent it would be for Paul to reprove in another what he himself had done.'[20] By this I showed that I was not precisely defending what I had read in the Greek authors, but that I had merely set down

---

17 Bishop in Cappadocia or Cilicia (c.160-216), who ordained Origen to the priesthood, and was probably involved in his errors.
18 Bishop of Emesa (c.341-359), an Arian whose exegetical writings were much quoted.
19 Another Arian bishop, who died c.355, and was the author of commentaries on Gospels, Epistles and Psalms.
20 Jerome, on *Epistle to Galatians* 1.2.14, Migne, *PL* 26.308-309.

what I had read, leaving my reader to judge for himself whether it was to be approved or disapproved.

But you, instead of doing what I asked, hunted up a new argument, claiming that the Gentiles who believed in Christ were free of the burden of the Law, whereas the Jews who were converted were subject to the Law, and thus, in the person of one or other of them, Paul, the doctor of the Gentiles, could rightly rebuke those who observed the Law, and Peter could be justly rebuked, because, as the apostle of circumcision, he had imposed on the Gentiles what the Jewish converts alone were obliged to observe.[21] If this is your idea, in fact, because it is your idea, that Jewish converts 'are debtors to do the whole Law,'[22] then you, as a bishop of world renown, ought to publish this opinion and get your fellow bishops to agree with that interpretation. As for me, in my poor little hut, with the monks, that is, with my fellow sinners, I do not venture to decide about such great matters; I only admit openly that I read the writings of my betters, and in my commentaries I put down, according to universal custom, different interpretations, so that, out of many, each one may follow what he likes. And I think that in secular literature as well as in the divine books you read and choose in the same way.

Many other commentators have since followed this explanation which Origen first set forth in the tenth book of his Miscellany, where he annotates the Epistle of Paul to the Galatians, and they bring it in for the special purpose of refuting the blasphemy of Porphyry,[23] who accused Paul of disrespect in daring to rebuke Peter, the Prince of the Apostles,

---
21 Gal.2.7,8.
22 Gal. 5.3.
23 A Neo-Platonist (233-303), follower of Plotinus, noted for the bitterness of his attacks on Christians. He attempted to use historical criticism against the Old Testament.

and to accuse him to his face, and to prove that he did wrong, that is, that he was in the same error in which Paul himself was, while he was calling another to task for his wrong-doing. And what shall I say of John,[24] who long ruled the Church at Constantinople in the pontifical rank, and who, on this chapter, produced a very extensive book, in which he followed the opinion of Origen and the ancients? If, then, you charge me with error, allow me, please, to err with men like these, and, when you see that I have so many companions in my error, you will have to stand forth as at least one propagator of your own truth. All this about an explanation of a single chapter of the Epistle to the Galatians!

Now, lest I seem to rely on the number of my witnesses against your argument, and the support of such illustrious men, and so as not to hide from the truth or shrink from the combat, I shall propose a few examples from Scripture. In the Acts of the Apostles, 'There came a voice to Peter, saying, Arise, Peter, kill and eat,' that is, 'of all manner of four-footed beasts, and creeping things of the earth, and fowls of the air.'[25] By this saying it is shown that no man is unclean according to nature, but that all are equally called to the Gospel of Christ. To which Peter answered: 'Far be it from me, for I never did eat anything that is common and unclean. And the voice spoke to him again the second time, That which God hath cleansed, do not thou call common.'[26] He then went to Caesarea and entered in to Cornelius, 'and opening his mouth, he said: 'In very deed I perceive that God is not a respecter of persons, but in every nation, he that feareth him and worketh justice, is acceptable

---

24 John of Constantinople, better known as St. John Chrysostom, Bishop of Constantinople, 397-404. His 'extensive book' was probably a collection of his homilies on Galatians.
25 Acts. 10.13,12.
26 Acts 10.14,15.

to him.'[27] Then, 'The Holy Ghost fell on them, and the faithful of the circumcision, who had come with Peter, were astonished, for that the grace of the Holy Ghost was poured out upon the Gentiles also. Then Peter answered: Can any man forbid water, that these should not be baptized, who have received the Holy Ghost as well as we? And he commanded them to be baptized in the name of Jesus Christ.'[28] 'And the apostles and brethren, who were in Judea, heard that the Gentiles also had received the word of God. And when Peter was come up to Jerusalem, they that were of the circumcision contended with him, saying: Why didst thou go in to men uncircumcised, and didst eat with them?'[29] And when he had set forth in its entirety his reason, he ended his speech to them thus: 'If then God gave them the same grace as to us also who believed in the Lord Jesus Christ, who was I, that could withstand God? Having heard these things, they held their peace, and glorified God, saying, God then hath also to the Gentiles given repentance unto life.'[30] And when again, much later, Paul and Barnabas had come to Antioch, 'and had assembled the church, they related what great things God had done with them, and how he had opened the door of faith to the Gentiles.'[31] 'And some, coming down from Judea, taught the brethren and said that, except you be circumcised after the manner of Moses, you cannot be saved. And when Paul and Barnabas had no small contest with them, they determined that they themselves who were accused and those who accused them should go up to the apostles and priests at Jerusalem, about this question. And when they were come to Jerusalem, there arose some

---

27 Acts 10.34,35.
28 Acts 10.44,45,47,48.
29 Acts 11.1-3.
30 Acts 11.17,18.
31 Acts 14.26.

of the sect of the Pharisees that believed in Christ, saying: they must be circumcised and be commanded to observe the law of Moses. And when there had been much disputing about this word, with his customary freedom, Peter said: Men, brethren, you know that in former days God made choice among us, that by my mouth the Gentiles should hear the word of the gospel and believe. And God, who knoweth the hearts, gave testimony, giving unto them the Holy Ghost as well as to us, and put no difference between us and them, purifying their hearts by faith. Now, therefore, why tempt you God, to put a yoke upon the necks of the disciples, which neither our fathers nor we have been able to bear? But by the grace of our Lord Jesus Christ, we believe to be saved, in like manner as they also; and all the multitude held their peace,'[32] and the Apostle James and all the priests with him yielded to his opinion.

These things ought not to cause trouble to a reader, but should be useful both to him and to me, to prove that, before Paul came, Peter was not ignorant; he was rather the prime mover of this decree that the Law was not to be imposed, once the Gospel had been established. Finally, Peter's authority was so great that Paul wrote in his epistle: 'Then after three years, I went to Jerusalem to see Peter, and I tarried with him fifteen days,'[33] and again, in a subsequent passage: 'Then after fourteen years I went up again to Jerusalem, with Barnabas, taking Titus also with me, and I went up according to revelation: and communicated to them the gospel which I preach among the Gentiles,'[34] proving that he did not feel sure of his preaching of the Gospel, until it had been confirmed by the opinion of Peter and the others

---
[32] Cf. Acts 15.1,2,4,5,7-12.
[33] Gal. 1.18.
[34] Gal. 2.1,2.

who were with him; and he continues at once: 'but apart with them who seemed to be something, lest perhaps I should run or had run in vain.' Why apart and not in public? Lest a scandal should arise among the faithful who had been Jews, who thought that the Law should be observed along with belief in the Lord as Saviour. Therefore, at the time 'When Peter was come to Antioch,' although the Acts of the Apostles do not write this, it is to be believed on the assertion of Paul, who writes: he 'withstood him to the face, because he was to be blamed. For before that some came from James, he did eat with the Gentiles, but when they were come, he withdrew and separated himself, fearing them who were of the circumcision. And . . . the rest of the Jews consented, so that Barnabas also was led by them into that dissimulation. But when I saw,' he says, 'that they walked not uprightly unto the truth of the gospel, I said to Peter before them all, If thou, being a Jew, livest after the manner of the Gentiles, and not as the Jews do, how dost thou compel the Gentiles to live as do the Jews?'[35] and the rest. No one can doubt that the Apostle Peter was the first advocate of this opinion, which he is now accused of trying to evade. The cause of his evasion was fear of the Jews, for the Scripture says that he formerly ate with the Gentiles, but, when some came from James, he withdrew and separated himself, fearing those who were of the circumcision. He feared that the Jews whose apostle he was would leave the faith of Christ because of the Gentiles, and the follower of the Good Shepherd might lose the flock entrusted to him.

As we have shown, then, that Peter understood perfectly about the abrogation of the Mosaic Law, but was driven by fear to a pretense of its observance, let us see whether Paul himself did the same thing that he blamed in another. We

---

35 Cf. Gal. 2.11-14.

read in the same book: But Paul 'went through Syria and Cilicia, confirming the churches . . . And he came to Derbe and Lystra. And behold there was a certain disciple there named Timothy, the son of a Jewish woman that believed, but his father was a Gentile. To this man the brethren that were in Lystra and Iconium, gave a good testimony. Him Paul would have to go along with him: and taking him he circumcised him, because of the Jews who were in those places. For they all knew that his father was a Gentile.'[36] O blessed Apostle Paul, who blamed in Peter an evasion whereby he withdrew himself from the Gentiles through fear of the Jews, who had come from James; why did you, against your own conviction, force circumcision on Timothy, the son of a Gentile father, and himself a Gentile—for he was not a Jew if he was not circumcised? You will answer me: 'because of the Jews who were in those places.' Since, then, you pardon yourself for the circumcision of a disciple of Gentile origin, pardon Peter your superior, also, for having acted in some cases through fear of the faithful who were Jewish. Again, it is written: 'But Paul, when he had stayed yet many days, taking his leave of the brethren, sailed thence into Syria (and with him Priscilla and Aquila), having shorn his head in Cenchrae, 'for he had a vow.'[37] Granted that there he did what he did not wish to do, through the compelling fear of the Jews: why did he let his hair grow in consequence of a vow, and afterward cut it at Cenchrae in obedience to the law, because the Nazarites who vowed themselves to God were accustomed to do this according to the commands of Moses?[38]

But, these instances are trifling in comparison with the

---

[36] Acts 15.41;16.1-3.
[37] Acts 18.18.
[38] Num. 6.18.

one which follows. Luke, the author of the sacred history,[39] relates that 'When we were come to Jerusalem, the brethren received us gladly,' and, on the following day, James and all the ancients who were with him, after commending his ministry said to him: 'Thou seest, brother, how many thousands there are among the Jews that have believed in Christ, and they are all zealous for the law. Now they have heard of thee that thou teachest those Jews who are among the Gentiles, to depart from Moses: saying that they ought not to circumcise their children, nor walk according to the custom. What is it therefore? the multitude must needs come together; for they will hear that thou art come. Do therefore this that we say to thee: we have four men, who have a vow on them. Take these and sanctify thyself with them: and bestow on them that they may shave their heads: and all will know that the things which they have heard of thee are false, but that thou thyself also walkest, keeping the law. Then Paul took the men, and the next day being purified with them, entered into the temple, giving notice of the accomplishment of the days of purification, until an oblation should be offered for every one of them.'[40] O Paul, again I ask you about this: why did you shave your head; why did you take part in a barefoot procession of the Jews; why did you offer sacrifices, and allow victims to be offered for you according to the Law? Doubtless, you will answer: 'In order not to scandalize the believers who were Jews.' You played the part of a Jew, then, to win the Jews, and James and the other priests taught you this dissimulation. In spite of this, you were not able to escape, for, when a disturbance arose and you were due to be killed, you were seized by a tribune, and sent by him under the close guard

---
39 The Acts of the Apostles.
40 Cf. Acts 21.20-24.26.

of soldiers to Caesarea, to prevent the Jews from killing you as a deceiver and destroyer of the Law. From there you went to Rome and in lodgings which you had hired you preached Christ to the Jews and Gentiles; and your sentence was concluded by the sword of Nero.

We have learned that both Peter and Paul equally, through fear of the Jews, made pretence of observing the precepts of the Law. With what assurance, with what boldness, can Paul rebuke that in another which he himself has practised? I, or, rather, others before me, have set forth what they think is the reason, not by way of excusing the officious lie, as you write,[41] but showing that it was an honorable course of action, one which manifests the prudence of the Apostles, and at the same time restrains the impudent blasphemy of Porphyry, who claims that Peter and Paul engaged in a childish contest with each other, or, rather, that Paul was violently jealous of Peter's virtues, and he wrote boastingly either what he had not done, or if he had, it had been done recklessly, reproving in another what he himself had practised. They explained it as they could: but, how do you elucidate that passage? No doubt, you will have something better to say, since you repudiate the opinion of the ancients.

You write me in your letter: 'For, you are not to be taught by me, how that passage is to be understood where he says: "I became to the Jews as a Jew that I might gain the Jews,"[42] and the other things which are there said through mercy and compassion, not through deceit and deception. For, a person who nurses a sick man becomes, in a sense, sick himself, not by pretending to have fever, but by thinking sympathetically how he would like to be treated if he were sick himself. For, certainly he was a Jew, and, on becoming a Christian, he

---
41 Letter 40.
42 1 Cor. 9.20.

had not given up those practices of the Jews which they had lawfully adopted as being in accord with their times. Thus, he undertook to keep up those observances even after he became an apostle of Christ, but he taught that it was not dangerous to conscience for those who wished to keep them as they had received them from their parents under the Law, even after they had come to believe in Christ. However, they were not to put their hope of salvation in them, because the salvation which was typified by those mysteries had come through the Lord Jesus.' The whole tenor of this passage of yours, which you have developed with a very long-drawn-out argument, is that Peter was not wrong in thinking that the Law should be kept by the Jewish converts, but that he was not right in obliging the Gentiles to live like the Jews, even though he did not enforce this by his teaching authority, but by the example of his conduct, and that Paul was not speaking against what he had done himself, but was asking why Peter obliged the Gentiles to live like the Jews.

The sum and substance of this question, then, or, rather, of your opinion, is that the Jewish believers do well after they have accepted the Gospel, if they keep the requirements of the Law; that is, if they offer sacrifices, as Paul offered them, if they circumcise their children, if they keep the sabbath, as Paul acted toward Timothy, and as all the Jews do. If this is true, then we fall into the heresy of Cerinthus[43] and Ebion,[44] who, though believing in Christ, were con-

---

43 A Gnostic-Ebionite heretic, contemporary with St. John the Evangelist, who is believed to have written the Fourth Gospel against the errors of Cerinthus on the divinity of Christ.
44 Ebionites or Ebioneans, literally, 'poor men,' because they followed the early Christians in giving up their property, were originally orthodox Jewish-Christians of Palestine who continued to observe the Mosaic Law. Surviving the destruction of Jerusalem, they were cut off from contact with the apostolic Church, and were condemned as heretics. The name Ebion is probably an invention.

demned by the fathers for this reason alone, that they mingled the ceremonies of the Law with the Gospel of Christ, and made confession of the new faith without giving up the old. What shall I say of the Ebionites who claim to be Christians? Until this very day there is a heresy called the Minaeans, among the Jews, through all the synagogues of the east, and it is still condemned by the Pharisees. These are popularly called Nazareans, and they believe in Christ, the Son of God, born of the Virgin Mary, and they say that He is the one who suffered under Pontius Pilate, and rose from the dead, the One in whom we believe also. But, by wishing to be both Jews and Christians, they are neither Jews nor Christians. You think to heal a little wound of mine, as if it were caused by the prick, or rather by the piercing, of a needle, but you had better try to heal the wound made by this opinion of yours, a wound made by a lance or a phalaric missile.[45] For, there is a difference between setting down various opinions of our predecessors in interpreting the Scriptures and introducing a most accursed heresy again into the Church. However, if we are faced with this necessity of receiving the Jews with their obligations of the Law, and if they are to be allowed to observe in the churches of Christ what they practised in the synagogues of Satan—I will say what I think—they will not become Christians, but they will make us Jews.

What Christian would willingly accept what is contained in your letter: 'Paul was a Jew, but, on becoming a Christian, he had not given up those practices of the Jews which they had lawfully adopted in accord with their times. Thus, he undertook to keep up those observances even after he became an apostle of Christ, but he taught that they were not dangerous to conscience for those who wished to keep them as they

---

45 A missile wrapped with tow and pitch and thrown by a catapult.

had received them from their parents under the Law.' Again I ask you, with your good leave, to hear my grievance. Paul kept the ceremonies of the Jews even after he had become the apostle of Christ, and you say that it is not harmful to those who wish to keep them as they have received them from their parents. On the contrary, I will say, and I will insist with unfettered speech against the opposition of the world, that the ceremonies of the Jews are harmful and deadly to Christians, and that whoever keeps them, whether Jew or Gentile, is doomed to the abyss of the Devil. 'For the end of the law is Christ, unto justice to every one that believeth'[46] —namely, to Jew and Gentile; but it will not be an end unto justice to every one that believeth, if exception is made of the Jew. And we read in the Gospel: 'The law and the prophets were until John, the Baptist,'[47] and in another place: 'Hereupon therefore, the Jews sought the more to kill him; because he did not only break the sabbath, but also said that God was his Father, making himself equal to God,'[48] and again: 'And of his fullness we all have received, and grace for grace; For the law was given by Moses; grace and truth came by Jesus Christ.'[49] For the grace of the Law, which has passed away, we have received the abiding grace of the Gospel, and, instead of the shadows and figures of the ancient covenant, truth has come by Jesus Christ. Jeremias also prophesies in the person of God: 'Behold the days shall come, saith the Lord, and I will make a new convenant with the house of Israel, and with the house of Juda: Not according to the covenant which I made with their fathers, in the day that I took them by the hand, to bring them out of the land

---

46 Rom. 10.4.
47 Luke 16.18.
48 John 5.18.
49 John 1.16,17.

of Egypt.'⁵⁰ Notice what He says, that it is not to the people of the Gentiles, with whom He had not previously made a covenant, but to the people of the Jews, to whom He had given the Law by Moses, that He promises the new convenant of the Gospel, so that they might no longer live according to the ancient letter, but in the newness of the Spirit. And Paul, too, around whose name this tempest has blown up, sets down several pronouncements of this sort, of which, for the sake of brevity, I shall add only a few: 'Behold I, Paul, tell you: that if you be circumcised, Christ shall profit you nothing,'⁵¹ and again: 'You are made void of Christ, you who are justified in the law: you are fallen from grace,'⁵² and, further on: 'But if you are led by the spirit, you are not under the law.'⁵³ From this it is evident that he who is under the Law, not for form's sake, as our elders admitted, but truly, as you understand it, such a one does not possess the Holy Spirit. Let us learn, from the teaching of God, the nature of the obligations of the Law: 'I,' He says, 'gave them statutes that were not good, and judgments in which they shall not live.'⁵⁴ We do not say this to destroy the Law, as Manichaeus and Marcion⁵⁵ do, for we know it to be holy and spiritual, according to the Apostle;⁵⁶ but because, with the advent of faith, 'when the fulness of the time was come, God sent his Son, made of a woman, made under the law, that he might redeem them who were under the law, that we might receive the adoption of sons,'⁵⁷ and that we should no

---

50 Jer. 31.31,32.
51 Gal. 5.2.
52 Gal. 5.4.
53 Gal. 5.18.
54 Ezech. 20.25.
55 Marcion (d. 170) was the leader of a heretical sect based on the opposition between the Law, work of a just God, and the Gospel, work of a good God.
56 Rom. 7.12,14.
57 Gal. 4.4,5.

longer live under a pedagogue,[58] but under a grown man, the lord and heir.[59]

You continue thus in your letter: 'Consequently, he did not rebuke Peter for observing his ancestral traditions, which he could do without deceit or inconsistency, if he wished'—and you, I repeat, are a bishop and a teacher of the churches of Christ. To prove the truth of what you assert, take any Jew who has become a Christian, who circumcises the son born to him, who keeps the sabbath, who refrains from eating foods 'which God hath created to be used with thanksgiving,'[60] who at evening on the fourteenth day of the first month sacrifices a lamb, and, when you have done this—but you will not do it, for I know that you are a Christian and that you will not commit a sacrilege—then, whether you like it or not, you will repudiate that opinion of yours, and you will learn that, in practice, it is harder to prove one's own argument than to object to another's. Lest we should not believe, as we certainly do not understand what you say—for an argument that is long-drawn-out frequently becomes unintelligible, but is not criticized by the ignorant because they do not notice this—you insist, and repeat: 'This evil belief of the Jews, therefore, Paul had given up.' Why had Paul given up the evil belief of the Jews? Doubtless, because of what follows: because, 'they not knowing the justice of God and seeking to establish their own, have not submitted themselves to the justice of God.'[61] Next, because after the Passion and Resurrection of Christ, when the sacrament of grace had been given and made known, 'according to the order of Melchisedech,'[62] they still thought the old ceremonies should be

---

58 Gal. 3.25.
59 Gal. 4.1.
60 Cf. 1 Tim. 4.3.
61 Rom. 10.3.
62 Heb. 6.20.

celebrated, not through respect for their traditional value, but as if necessary for salvation. However, if they had never been necessary, the martyrdom of the Macchabees in their defense would have been vain and fruitless. Finally, he condemned them because the Jews persecuted the Christian preachers of grace as enemies of the Law. It is these errors and wrong practices which, he says, 'he counted as loss . . . and dung that he might gain Christ.'[63]

We have learned from you what evil practices of the Jews Paul gave up; let us learn in turn from your teaching what good practices of theirs he kept. 'The observances of the Law,' you say, 'which they kept through ancestral custom, as they were kept by Paul, without any implication of their being necessary for salvation.' What do you mean by 'necessary for salvation'? I do not quite understand. If they do not conduce to salvation, why are they practised? If they are to be practised, then they surely conduce to salvation, especially when their observance leads to martyrdom. If they were not aids to salvation, they would not be practised. Moreover, they are not indifferent, between good and bad, as the philosophers distinguish things. For example, continence is good, self-indulgence is bad: between the two is the indifferent act, as to walk; to evacuate the excrement of the bowel, to discard the secretions of the nasal passages, to spit out the mucus of a cold—these actions are neither good nor bad; it is not a matter of good or bad conduct to do them or not to do them. On the other hand, to carry out the ceremonies of the Law cannot be an indifferent act; it is either bad or good. You say it is good; I insist that it is wrong, and wrong not only for believers who were Gentiles, but also for those who were Jews. In this position, unless I mistake, you fall into one difficulty while trying to

---
[63] Phil. 3.8.

avoid another; fearing to agree with the blasphemy of Porphyry, you fall into the snare of Ebion by declaring that the Law is to be observed by Jewish converts. Then, because you understand how dangerous your statement is, you again try to tone it down with superfluous words: 'Without their being necessary for salvation, as the Jews thought they should be observed, or by a deceitful pretense, which he rebuked in Peter.'

So, then, Peter pretended to keep the Law, but that reprover of Peter boldly kept the Law. Your letter continues: 'If he took part in those ceremonies because he was pretending to be a Jew, in order to win the Jews, why did he not also sacrifice with the Gentiles, putting himself outside the Law, as they were outside it, in order to win them? Doubtless, he did the former as one who was a Jew by birth, and he said what he did, not to pretend falsely to be what he was not, but to declare his own need of mercy, as if he were involved in the same error with him. In this he was evidently moved by a feeling of compassion, not by a crafty intent to deceive.' You make a good defense of Paul, that he did not pretend to accept the error of the Jews, but was truly in error; and that he would not imitate Peter in his lie by hiding what he was through fear of the Jews, but that he fully and frankly said he was a Jew. A new kind of apostolic kindness! Wishing to make Christians of the Jews, he became a Jew himself. Obviously he could not bring the self-indulgent to sobriety without showing himself to be self-indulgent, nor show mercy toward the wretched without feeling the wretchedness himself, as you say. But, of a truth, those poor things are to be pitied, who, out of love for an abrogated Law, set up an argument to make a Jew out of the apostle of Christ. There is not much difference between my opinion and yours, for I say that both Peter and Paul practised the

Law of the Jews, or, rather, pretended to observe its requirements, through fear of the Jewish Christians; but you assert that they did this out of kindness, 'moved by a feeling of compassion, not by a crafty intent to deceive.' That is satisfactory to me, so long as it is granted that they pretended to be what they were not, either through fear or through favor. As for that argument which you use against me that he ought to have become a Gentile to the Gentiles, if he became a Jew to the Jews, it works for my side of the case better than for yours. For, just as he was not truly a Jew, so he was not truly a Gentile, and as he was not truly a Gentile neither was he truly a Jew. In one point, however, he is an imitator of the Gentiles, because he does not require circumcision in the faith of Christ, and he allows foods to be used freely, such as the Jews avoid, but not, as you think, because of the worship of idols: 'For in Christ Jesus, neither circumcision availeth anything, nor uncircumcision,'[64] but obedience to the commandments of God.

I ask you, therefore, and I beg of you again and again, to pardon this little debate of mine, and, if I have gone beyond bounds, lay the blame on yourself for forcing me to answer you, and for taking away my eyes with Stesichorus.[65] And do not go on thinking that I am a master of lies, for I follow Christ, who says: 'I am the Way and the Truth and the Life,'[66] and a lover of truth cannot bend under the yoke of falsehood. And do not stir up against me a mob of ignorant people, who respect you as a bishop and receive you with priestly honor when you preach in the church, but who have little use for a man like me, old and almost feeble, and living an obscure life in a country monastery. In other words,

---
64 Gal. 5.6.
65 Cf. Letter 68 n. 3.
66 John 14.6.

find yourself some other people to teach or criticize. The sound of your voice hardly reaches us, separated from you as we are by such expanses of sea and land; if, by any chance, you write more letters, before Italy and Rome gets them, see that they are delivered to me to whom they are addressed.

As to that question in your other letter,[67] why my first translation of the canonical books has asterisks and other critical marks, and the one I did later is without these, I would say, with your good leave, that you seem not to understand what you ask. The former translation is from the Septuagint, and, wherever there are commas or obelisks, it indicates that the Septuagint has something more than is found in the Hebrew; but, where there are asterisks, that is, little stars, it marks an addition made by Origen, taken from the edition of Theodotion.[68] The former translation we made from the Greek; in the latter, we expressed what we understood from the Hebrew source, preserving at times the true meaning rather than the order of words. I am surprised that you read the Septuagint version—not in the form in which it was originally issued, but in the corrected or corrupted version of Origen, with its obelisks and asterisks—when you will not accept the poor version of a Christian man, especially when he has removed those additions which were made from the edition of a Jew and a blasphemer after the Passion of Christ. You wish to be a true lover of the Septuagint, but you do not read what is under the asterisks: you should erase them if you would show your appreciation of the ancients. But, if you do that, you will be forced to condemn all

---

67 Letter 71.
68 An Ephesian Jew or Ebionite, who made a Greek translation of the Old Testament, sometime in the second century. This version supplied some parts missing in the Septuagint, and was used by Origen in his *Hexapla*, or six-column edition of the Old Testament, containing Greek and Hebrew texts in parallel columns.

the libraries of the churches, for you can scarcely find one or two books without them.

Continuing, you say that I ought not to have used the old texts in my translation, and you make use of a novel argument:[69] the version made by the Seventy is either clear or it is not clear; if it is not clear, you run the risk of falling into their mistake; if it is clear, then they obviously get the credit for trustworthiness. I answer you in your own words. There are many ancient commentators who have gone before us to the Lord and who have interpreted the Holy Scriptures, and these interpretations are either obscure or they are clear. If they are obscure, how do you dare, after them, to explain what they could not elucidate? And, if they are clear, it is useless for you to want to explain what was no mystery to them. This is especially true in the commentary on the Psalms, which several among the Greeks have treated in many volumes: first, Origen; second, Eusebius of Caesarea;[70] third, Theodore of Heraclea; fourth, Asterius of Scythopolis;[71] fifth, Apollinaris of Laodicea; sixth, Didymus of Alexandria. There are also said to be some short works on separate psalms, but we now are speaking of the whole collection of the Psalms. Among the Latins, Hilary of Poitiers[72] and Eusebius,[73] Bishop of Vercellae, translated Origen and Eusebius,[74] while

---

69 Taken from Letter 28.
70 Bishop of Caesarea (c.265-c.340), a follower of Origen, a man of wide erudition, best known for his work on Church history.
71 An Arian of the time of the Emperor Constantius; his commentaries, mentioned by St. Jerome, are known only through citations.
72 Bishop of Poitiers (315-368), a convert from paganism, chief defender of orthodoxy in the West. Of his Commentary on the Psalms, written in 365, which follows the Septuagint version, only part remains.
73 St. Eusebius of Vercellae, an opponent of Arianism, who, like St. Hilary, suffered exile for his orthodoxy. He preached much more than he wrote, but Jerome credits him with a translation of a commentary on the Psalms by Eusebius of Caesarea.
74 Eusebius of Caesarea.

our Ambrose followed the first-named in some of his works. Your Prudence must tell me why you hold views different from those of such great and eminent commentators on the Psalms. If the Psalms are obscure, we must believe that you could be wrong about them, too; if they are easily understood, no one would believe that these scholars could fall into error about them. Either way, your interpretation will be unnecessary, and, according to this principle, no one will dare to write after his predecessors; but, whatever ground one writer has covered, no other writer will have the right to encroach on it. You, with your reputation for kindness, should grant to others the same indulgence which you claim for yourself. As for me, I have not tried so much to do away with the old texts, which, with their emendations, I translated from Greek into Latin for men of my own tongue, but rather to bring out that evidence which was passed over or corrupted by the Jews, so that our people might know what the Hebrew text really contained. If anyone does not wish to read my version, he will not be forced to do it against his will. Let him drink the old wine, which is sweet, and scorn our new, unfermented vintage, which is offered in explanation of the old, with the purpose of making clear what was unintelligible. As to what method of interpretation is to be followed in dealing with the Holy Scriptures, that is set forth in the book which I wrote on the best kind of interpretation and in all the short prologues to the divine books which I have added to my edition, and I think the experienced reader should be referred to them. If, as you say, you approve of my translation of the New Testament, and you give as your reason for that approval that many, with knowledge of the Greek tongue, can judge of the correctness of my work, you ought to attribute the same authenticity to the Old Testament, which I did not compose as something of my own, but I translated the divine texts as I found them among the Hebrews. If you have any doubt, ask the Hebrews.

You will say: but suppose the Hebrews either will not give an answer, or they deliberately give a wrong one? Is the whole throng of Hebrews in my translation reduced to silence, if nobody can be found with knowledge of the Hebrew tongue, or will they all imitate the Jews mentioned by you —those in some small African town who joined a conspiracy to put me in the wrong? You tell a tale of this sort in your letter:[75] 'There was a certain brother bishop of ours who decided to read your translation in the church over which he presided, and he caused a sensation by some passage from the Prophet Jonas, which was very different from the version enshrined in the memory and hearing of all, having been sung for so many generations. There was such a disturbance made among the people by the Greeks arguing and stirring up passions with the charge of falsity, that the bishop—it was in the city of Oea—was forced to call on the testimony of the Jews. Was it through ignorance or malice that they answered that what the Greeks and Latins said and maintained was found in the Hebrew texts? To make a long story short, the man was forced to correct an apparently wrong statement, not wishing to run the greak risk or remaining without a flock. After this, is seems to us that you, also, among others, can be wrong.'

You say that in the Prophet Jonas I made an unfortunate translation, and that a bishop almost lost his pastorate because of the violent outcry of the people against the unfamiliar sound of one word. You fail to mention what mistranslation I made, thereby robbing me of a chance to defend myself, and securing yourself against correction by my answer. Probably, you mean that time some years ago, when the gourd

---
[75] Letter 72.

came into prominence, on the assertion of Cornelius and Asinius Pollio[76] that I put 'ivy' instead of 'gourd.' As I have answered that objection at length in my commentary on the Prophet Jonas, I shall deal with it briefly here. In that place where the Septuagint has 'gourd' and Aquila[77] and the others have 'ivy,' that is *'kittón,'* the Hebrew version has *'ciceion,'* which the Syrians commonly call *'ciceiam'*: it is a sort of shrub with broad leaves like the vine, and when planted it springs up quickly into a bush, supporting itself with its own trunk, without need of the props and poles which gourds and ivies need. Explaining this word, if I had wanted to put *'ciceion,'* no one would have understood me; if I put 'gourd', I would say what was not in the Hebrew; so, I put 'ivy' to agree with other translators. But, if your Jews, as you declare, through malice or ignorance, said that the Hebrew texts have the same terms that the Greek and Latin versions have, it is obvious either that they do not know Hebrew literature or that they deliberately lied in order to make fun of the gourd-planters. At the end of my letter, I ask you not to force me to imperil my life again, now that I have found the quiet life of old age, and have long since retired from military service. You are still young, and have reached the heights of episcopal dignity; teach your people, and enrich Roman homes with new African fruits. I am satisfied to whisper to a single hearer and reader in a poor little corner of the monastery.

---

76 Under these two names, Jerome refers to a certain Canthelius, who claimed to be a descendant of these two ancient patrician families of Rome. He is mentioned in Jerome's treatise on Jonas 4.6.
77 A Greek proselyte (95-135) to Judaism, who made a literal translation of the Old Testament into Greek. Favored more by Jews than by Christians, it also was used by Origen in his *Hexapla.*

76. [Augustine to the Donatists] (404)

To you, Donatists, the Catholic Church says: O ye sons of men, how long will you be dull of heart? Why do you love vanity and seek after lying?[1] Why do you separate yourselves from the unity of the whole world, by the wicked sacrilege of schism? You listen to falsehoods spoken to you by men who either are deliberately lying, or are in error concerning the betrayal of the sacred books, and as a result you will die in your schismatic separation; but you do not listen to what the same sacred texts say to you, so that you may have the life of Catholic peace. Why do you open your ears to the words of men who have never been able to prove what they say, yet are deaf to the word of God saying: 'The Lord hath said to me: Thou art my son, this day have I begotten thee. Ask of me and I will give thee the Gentiles for thy inheritance, and the utmost parts of the earth for thy possession.'[2] 'To Abraham were the promises made and to his seed. He saith not: And to his seeds, as of many; but as of one: And to thy seed, which is Christ.'[3] 'In thy seed,' He says, 'shall all nations . . . be blessed.'[4] Lift up the eyes of your heart and consider the whole extent of the earth, how, in the seed of Abraham, all nations are blessed. What was not seen was then believed by one; you now see, and you still refuse belief. The Passion of the Lord is the price paid for the world; He redeemed the whole world, and you do not agree with the world, which would be your gain; but you prefer to carry on strife in one part of the world to your own destruction, and so lose the whole. Hear, in the words of the psalm, at what price we were redeemed: 'They have dug,' He says, 'my hands and

---
1 Ps. 4.3.
2 Ps. 2.7,8.
3 Gal. 3.16.
4 Gen. 22.18.

feet; they have numbered all my bones. And they have looked and stared upon me. They parted my garments amongst them, and upon my vesture they cast lots.'[5] Why do you will to be dividers of the garments of the Lord, and why will you not, with the rest of the world, keep whole that tunic of charity, woven from the top throughout,[6] which even His persecutors did not divide? In that same psalm we read that the whole earth holds to it: 'All the ends of the earth,' he says, 'shall remember, and shall be converted to the Lord: and all the kindreds of the Gentiles shall adore in his sight; for the kingdom is the Lord's and he shall have dominion over the nations.'[7] Open the ears of your heart and hear, that 'The God of gods, the Lord, hath spoken; and he hath called the earth, from the rising of the sun even to the going down thereof; out of Sion the loveliness of his beauty.'[8] If you will not understand this, hear the Gospel, where the Lord now speaks with His own mouth and says that, concerning Christ, 'All things must needs be fulfilled, which are written in the Law . . . and in the prophets and in the psalms; and that penance and remission of sins should be preached in his name unto all nations, beginning at Jerusalem.'[9] Where He says in the psalm: 'He hath called the earth, from the rising of the sun even to the going down thereof,' He says in the Gospel: 'unto all nations;' and where the psalm has: 'out of Sion the loveliness of His beauty,' the Gospel has: 'beginning at Jerusalem.'

You imagine that you can escape the intermingling of cockle, before the time of the harvest,[10] because you alone are

---
5 Ps. 21.17-19.
6 John 19.23.
7 Ps. 21.28,29.
8 Ps. 49.1,2.
9 Luke 24.44,47.
10 Matt. 13.24-30.

the cockle. If you were the good seed, you would endure the intermingling of cockle, and you would not cut yourselves off from the harvest of Christ. Of the cockle it is written: 'Because iniquity hath abounded, the charity of many shall grow cold,' but of the good grain it is said: 'He that shall persevere to the end, he shall be saved.'[11] Why do you believe that the cockle has increased and filled the world, but the good seed has diminished and is found only in Africa? You say you are Christians, but, you give the lie to Christ. He said: 'Suffer both to grow until the harvest';[12] He did not say: 'Let the cockle grow, and the good seed diminish.' He said: 'The field is the world;'[13] He did not say: 'The field is Africa.' He said: 'The harvest is the end of the world'; He did not say: 'The harvest is the time of Donatus.' He said: 'The reapers are the angels';[14] He did not say: 'The reapers are the leaders of the Circumcellions.'[15] But, because you make the good seed to be cockle, you show that you yourselves are the cockle, and, what is worse, you have cut yourselves off from the good seed before the time. Of your fathers, in whose accursed separation you persist, some, according to the official records, betrayed the sacred books and the vessels of the Church to the persecutors; others forgave those who committed that crime and continued in communion with them; and both sides came to Carthage in a stormy fight. They condemned without a hearing men charged with betrayal, a crime in which they themselves shared; they ordained bishop against bishop; they set up altar against altar. Afterwards, they sent letters to Emperor Constantine, asking that overseas bishops should judge the case between the

---

11 Matt. 24.12,13.
12 Matt. 13.30.
13 Matt. 13.38.
14 Matt. 13.39.
15 Cf. Letter 23 n. 13.

Africans; when they had the judges they asked for, and these had given a verdict at Rome, they did not yield to it; they accused the bishops to the emperor, of wrong judgment; and, when other bishops had met at Arles, they appealed to the emperor in person; when they had been heard by him and had been found to be in the wrong, they remained fixed in their criminal course of action. Awake to your salvation. Love peace. Return to unity. All these facts we are ready to relate to you, just as they happened, whenever you are willing.

He shares in evil who consents to the deeds of evil-doers, but not he who suffers the cockle to grow in the Lord's field until the harvest, or the chaff to remain until the final winnowing. If you hate evil-doers, you yourselves must turn from the crime of schism; if you feared the contact of evil, you would not have had Optatus[16] living among you for so many years, in such manifest evil conduct. You are now calling him a martyr; consequently, you must call the one for whom he died Christ. Finally, what wrong has the Christian world done you that you have cut yourselves off with such abominable fury? And what did you gain from the Maximianists[17] whom you condemned and drove from their basilicas by public edicts, and then reinstated again in their previous rank? What wrong has the peace of Christ done you, against which you separate yourselves from those whom you defame? Or what good does the peace of Donatus[18] do you, that you reinstate those whom you condemn? Felician of Musti[19] is now with you, but we read that he was formerly condemned in your council, and afterward accused by you in the proconsular court, and was impugned in the public records of the city of Musti.

---

16 Cf. Letter 51 n. 8. Optatus died in prison because of his collusion with Gildo.
17 Cf. Letter 43 n. 51.
18 Cf. Letter 43 n. 6.
19 Cf. Letter 51 n. 3.

If the betrayal of the sacred books is execrable, because God punished with death in war the king who burned the book of Jeremias,[20] how much more execrable is the crime of schism, whose instigators, to whom you compare the Maximianists, were swallowed up alive by the open earth![21] How, then, do you accuse us without proof of the crime of betrayal, and you both condemn and reinstate your own schismatics? If you are just because you have suffered persecution from the emperors, how much more just than you are the Maximianists themselves, whom you persecuted through the judges sent by the Catholic emperors. If you alone have baptism, what was the effect of the baptism of the Maximianists on those whom Felician baptized, who were afterwards reinstated by you, together with Felician whom they had condemned? Otherwise, let your bishops answer these objections to you laymen,[22] if they refuse to discuss them with us, and consider, if you value your salvation, what question it is which they refuse to discuss with us. If the wolves called a council so as not to have to answer to the shepherds, why did the sheep disband the council so as to take refuge in the dens of the wolves?

---

20 Jer. 35.20.30.
21 Num. 16.31.33.
22 In a general council of Africa, held August 25, 403, the Donatist bishops had been ordered to attend a joint meeting with a view to the pacification of the Church, but they had refused with scorn and insult. In this letter, Augustine addresses himself to the laymen, in an attempt to win their support.

77. Augustine gives greeting in the Lord to the beloved lords and justly esteemed brothers, Felix and Hilarinus[1] (404)

I am not surprised that Satan disturbs the minds of the faithful. But, do you resist him, relying strongly on your hope in the promises of God, who cannot deceive, who has not only deigned to promise us eternal rewards if we believe and hope in Him, and remain faithful to His love unto the end, but who has also warned us that temporal scandals will not be wanting, since by such it is fitting that our faith be tried and proved. He said: 'Because iniquity hath abounded, the charity of many shall grow cold'; but He adds at once: 'But he that shall persevere to the end, he shall be saved.'[2] What wonder is it that men should disparage the servants of God and, failing to draw them off from their way of life, should attempt to undermine their reputation, when they daily blaspheme their God and Lord because they find displeasing what He does by a just and secret judgment contrary to their will? Therefore, I exhort your Prudence, beloved lords, deservedly honored brothers, to think over in a most Christian spirit what God has written, telling us beforehand that all these things would happen, and warning us of our duty to be strong against them, and against the scurrilous futilities and rash suspicions of men.

In short, I tell your Charity that I have found the priest Boniface[3] in no wrong-doing, and that I emphatically have

---
1 Citizens of some standing among the Catholics of Hippo.
2 Matt. 24.12,13.
3 A priest of Augustine's diocese, who had accused Spes, a monk in Augustine's monastery, of some wrong-doing. Spes threw the charge back on Boniface. Letter 78 gives the method used by Augustine to decide the case.

not believed and do not believe any such thing of him. How could I order his name to be removed from the list of priests,[4] fearing as I do the vigorous words of the Gospel, where the Lord says: 'With what judgment you judge, you shall be judged'?[5] While the case which has arisen between him and Spes is still subject to divine decision[6] according to their decree which will be read to you, if you wish—who am I to dare to forestall the verdict of God by erasing or suppressing the name of one whom, as bishop, I ought not rashly to suspect of any evil; or how can I as man judge clearly the secret acts of men? Is it not true that even in civil cases, when the right of judgment has been referred to a higher power, as long as circumstances remain unchanged, the verdict, from which no appeal is now allowed, is to be awaited without making any change in the course of the trial, so as not to prejudice the higher judge? Certainly, there is a great difference between the divine power and any human one, even the most exalted. May the mercy of the Lord our God never fail us, beloved lords and honored brothers.

---

4 The diptychs from which the names of the clergy were read out in the churches.
5 Matt. 7.2.
6 Boniface and Spes had been ordered to visit the tomb of St. Felix of Nola, in Italy, so that some miraculous sign might decide who was innocent. This is what Augustine means by 'divine decision.' It is a sort of variation of the mediaeval trial by ordeal.

78. Augustine gives greeting in the Lord to his most beloved brothers, the clergy, the elders and the whole people of the church of Hippo,[1] *whose servant I am, in the love of Christ (404)*

I could wish that you might ponder over the Scripture of God with earnest attention, and in such way that you would not need the help of my words in these recent scandals, and that, rather, He who consoles us should console you, too. It is He who has foretold not only the happiness which He is to bestow on His holy and faithful ones, but also the evils of which this world was to be full, and He has had these written down, so that, as surely as we experience the predicted evils which are to precede the end of the world, so surely shall we await the happiness which is to follow after the end of the world. Therefore, the Apostle says: 'For what things soever were written, were written for our learning; that through patience and the comfort of the Scriptures, we might have hope'[2] in God. But, what was the use of the Lord Jesus Himself saying: 'Then shall the just shine as the sun in the kingdom of their Father,'[3] which is to happen after the end of the world, and even exclaiming: 'Woe to the world because of scandals'[4]—if it was not to keep us from flattering ourselves that we can attain the abodes of everlasting bliss in any other way than by standing firm when we are tried by temporal evils? What was the use of His saying: 'Because iniquity hath abounded the charity of many

---
1 A synod was held at Carthage on June 26, 404. It is supposed that Letters 77 and 78 were written by Augustine while he was attending this council, which would account for his addressing his clergy and people by letter rather than by word of mouth.
2 Rom. 15.4.
3 Matt. 14.43.
4 Matt. 18.7.

shall grow cold,'[5] if it was not that those, of whom he speaks when He adds at once: 'He that shall persevere to the end, he shall be saved,'[6] should not be disturbed, should not be frightened, when they see this charity growing cold with the prevalence of iniquity, should not fall into sadness as at things unanticipated and unexpected? But, seeing those things that were predicted happen before the end, should they not persevere patiently to the end so as to deserve, after the end of time, to reign without care in that life which has no end?

Therefore, dearly beloved, in that scandal connected with the priest Boniface, by which many are troubled, I do not tell you not to grieve—if there are any who do not grieve over such things, the charity of Christ is not in them, and, if there are any who delight in such things, the malice of the Devil abounds in them—not that there has appeared in the above-mentioned priest any evidence worthy of an adverse judgment, but because two members of our household are in such a situation that one of them must undoubtedly be considered lost, and the reputation of the other is blackened with some, shaken with others, even though his own conscience be clear. Grieve over those things, because they are things to be grieved over, but not so that your charity cool toward right living because of your grief. Rather, let it flame up in prayer to the Lord, that, if your priest is innocent, the divine decision may quickly make this evident by its own agency. I am inclined to believe in his innocence, because, when he had experienced the unchaste and impure incitement of the other, he would neither consent to it nor keep silence about it. However, if he has a guilty conscience—which I do not dare to suspect—and was willing to injure the

---

5 Matt. 24.12.
6 Matt. 24.3.

reputation of another when he could not defile his chastity—as that one says, with whom he has the quarrel—let the divine decision not allow him to hide his wickedness. So, what men cannot discover, we must pray may be revealed by divine judgment of one or other of them.

When this case had tortured me for a long time, and I could not see how one of the two was to be convicted, although I put more trust in the priest, I thought at first to leave them both to God, until something should appear in the one whom I suspected, to give me an open and legitimate excuse for expelling him from our dwelling. He had made vehement efforts to be promoted to the priesthood either by me or by letters from me to another bishop, but I could not bring myself to lay the hands of ordination on a man of whom I thought such evil, nor could I introduce him to any brother bishop by my recommendation. It was then he began to make trouble, and to say that, if he could not be promoted to the priesthood, he would not suffer the priest Boniface to be in that state. When I saw that Boniface, under that challenge, out of regard for the weaker brethren and those prone to suspicion, did not wish a scandal to be made out of doubt over his manner of life, and that he was ready to suffer the loss of his honor among men rather than let that quarrel cause a useless disturbance in the Church—and it was one in which he could not display his conscience to ignorant or doubtful men or to those ready to suspect evil —then I decided upon a certain measure. They were both to bind themselves by a strong resolve, to go to a holy place, where the more awe-inspiring intervention of God more easily lays open the uneasy conscience, and through penalty or fear drives it to confession. It is true that God is everywhere, that He is not confined or bounded by any place, because He made everything; and it is fitting for Him to be adored by the true adorers in spirit and truth,⁷ that, hearing them in secret, He may likewise justify and reward them in secret. But, as far as things visibly known to men are concerned, who can search into His purpose, or the reason why these miracles occur in some places but do not occur in others? The holiness of the place where the body of the blessed Felix of Nola is buried is well known to many, and this is the place which I wished them to visit, because, if any divine revelation should be made about either of them, a trustworthy account could more easily be written to us from there. We also know that at Milan, at the shrine of the saints, where the devils make wonderful and terrible confession, a certain thief, who had gone there to strengthen a false oath, was forced to confess his theft, and to restore what he had stolen. But, how about Africa: is it not full of the bodies of holy martyrs? Yet we do not hear of such things happening anywhere. It is that, as the Apostle says, just as all saints do not have the gift of healing, nor do all have the discernment of spirits, so, not in all shrines of the saints does He will that these things happen, and He 'divides to everyone his own according as he will.'⁸

I was unwilling to bring this deep grief of my heart to your attention, because I did not want to trouble you with sharp and useless sorrow, but perhaps God has not willed to leave you in ignorance of it, so that you could apply yourselves to prayer with us, asking Him to deign to make known to us what He knows in this case, but what we cannot know. As for the name of the priest, I have not dared to remove it from the list of his colleagues or to erase it, because I must not seem to do an injury to the Divine Power to whose testing the case has been submitted; and this I should do if

---

7 Cf. John 4.23.
8 Cf. 1 Cor. 12.30,11.

I anticipated His judgment by my pre-judgment. In civil suits, when a doubtful case has been referred to a higher court, the judges would not dare to make any change so long as the appeal is pending. And, in the council of bishops,[9] it was decreed that no cleric, prior to his conviction, is to be suspended from communion with his church, except for failure to appear for the examination of his case. Now, Boniface has submitted to this humiliation of not taking with him on a pilgrimage letters which would give him his clerical rank, and he has done this so that both of them, being equally unknown in that place, should be treated alike. If you now insist on his name not being read out, that in the words of the Apostle we may not give 'occasion to them that desire occasion'[10]— in the case of those who refuse to come to the church—this will not be our doing, but theirs on whose account it is so done. What harm does it do a man that human ignorance does not wish his name to be read from that list, if a guilty conscience does not blot him out of the book of the living?

Therefore, my brothers, you who fear God, remember what the Apostle Peter said: 'Because your adversary the devil, as a roaring lion, goeth about, seeking whom he may devour.'[11] When he cannot devour a man by seducing him into wickedness, he tries to blacken his reputation, to make him lose courage by reason of the insults of men and the detraction of evil tongues, and so to fall into the lion's jaws. But, if he cannot blacken the reputation of an innocent man, he tries, by evil suspicions, to persuade him to judge his brother, and so he is caught in the snares of the Evil One. Can anyone either understand or even enumerate all his tricks and strata-

---

9 Council of Carthage, 397.
10 Cf. 2 Cor. 11.12.
11 1 Peter 5.8.

gems? God speaks thus to us by the Apostle, warning us against these three sins, which concern the present case, and first that you be not led into evil by following bad example, saying: 'Bear not the yoke with unbelievers. For what participation hath justice with injustice? Or what fellowship hath light with darkness?'[12] Likewise, in another place: 'Be not seduced,' he says, 'evil communications corrupt good manners. Be sober, ye just and sin not.'[13] In order that you may not fall into sin through the tongues of detractors, He speaks thus by the Prophet: 'Hearken to me, you that know judgment, my people, who have my law in their heart; fear ye not the reproach of men and be not overcome by their detraction, neither think it any great thing that they despise you. For as a garment they shall be consumed by time, and they shall be eaten as wool by the moth, but my justice remaineth forever.'[14] And, now that you may not perish by suspecting false things, with evil mind, of the servants of God, recall that saying of the Apostle: 'Judge not anything before the time, until the Lord come: who both will bring to light the hidden things of darkness, and will make manifest the counsels of the hearts: and then shall every man have praise from God';[15] and this also which was written: 'Things that are manifest, to us; secret things, to the Lord our God.'[16]

It is evident that those things do not happen in the Church without causing great sadness to the saints and the faithful; may He console us who foretold all these things, and who warned us not to grow cold because of the prevalence of iniquity, but to persevere to the end that we may be saved.

---

12 2 Cor. 6.14.
13 Cf. 1 Cor. 15.33,34.
14 Cf. Isa. 51.7,8.
15 1 Cor. 4.5.
16 Deut. 29.29.

As far as I am concerned, if there is in me the smallest spark of the charity of Christ, 'Who of you is weak, and I am not weak; who is scandalized and I am not on fire?'[17] Do not increase my sufferings, therefore, by falling either into false suspicions or into the sins of others; do not, I beg of you, make me say of you: 'And they have added to the grief of my wounds.'[18] For, those who take pleasure in these sorrows of ours, of whom it was long ago foretold in the person of the body of Christ, 'They that sat in the gate, spoke against me; and they that drank wine made me their song,'[19] are much more readily borne with; indeed, we have learned to pray for them, and to wish them well. But, for what other purpose do they sit there, and what else do they aim at, except, when some bishop or cleric or monk or nun has fallen, that they may believe, assert and contend that all are like that —although it cannot be proved of all? Yet, when some married woman has been found to be an adulteress, they do not cast off their wives or accuse their mothers: but, when it is a case of those who profess a sacred calling, if some false charge has been rumored about or some true one has been published, they take it up, go to work on it, toss it about, so as to have it universally believed. Therefore, of those who take sweetness for their evil tongues from our sorrows, it is easy to compare them to those dogs, if, perchance, we are to take in an adverse sense, those who licked the sores of the beggar who lay before the rich man's gate, and who bore hard and humiliating things until he came to rest in Abraham's bosom.[20]

But, do not torment me further, you who have some hope in God; do not multiply the wounds which they lick, you for whom we are in danger at every hour, having 'combats with-

---
17 2 Cor. 11.29.
18 Ps. 68.27.
19 Ps. 68.13.
20 Luke 16.20-22.

out, fears within,'²¹ 'perils in the city, perils in the wilderness, perils from the Gentiles, perils from false brethren.'²² I know that you suffer, but does anyone suffer more grievously than I? I know that you are troubled, but I fear that he may fall through the tongues of slanderers, and that 'the weak . . . may perish for whom Christ hath died.'²³ Let not our grief increase because of you, because it is not our fault that it has become your grief. For, this is what I had tried to guard against; if it were possible neither to overlook this evil through negligence nor to let it come to your knowledge, whereby the strong would be uselessly saddened and the weak dangerously troubled. May He who has permitted you to be tempted by letting this be known give you strength to bear it and may He teach you according to His law, may He teach you and 'May He give rest from the evil days, till a pit be dug for the wicked.'²⁴

I hear that some of you were further saddened by the case of the lapse of those two deacons who had come over from the sect of Donatus; that some had insulted the flock of Proculeianus,²⁵ boasting about ours, as if nothing of the sort ever happened among the clerics of our flock. Whoever of you did this, I confess to you, you did not do well. See how God has taught us that 'he that glorieth, may glory in the Lord.'²⁶ And do not taunt the heretics, except with not being Catholics, lest you be like them who, having no grounds of defense for their separation, make a show of attacking merely human misdeeds, and falsely make them out to be worse than they are; when they cannot defame and obscure

---

21 2 Cor. 7.5.
22 Cf. 2 Cor. 11.26.
23 Cf. 1 Cor. 8.11.
24 Ps. 93.12,13.
25 Donatist bishop of Hippo; cf. Letter 33.
26 1 Cor. 1.31.

the truth of the Divine Scripture itself, by which the universal Church of Christ is commended, they bring odium upon those by whom it is preached, and about them they invent whatever comes into their mind. 'But you have not so learned Christ, if so be that you have heard him and have been taught in him.'[27] He, indeed, made His own faithful safe against wicked stewards, who do their own evil deeds, but speak His good words, when He said: 'All things therefore whatsoever they shall say to you, observe and do; but according to their works do ye not: for they say and do not.'[28] Pray for me, 'lest perhaps, when I have preached to others, I myself should become a castaway,'[29] and when, notwithstanding, you do glory, let it not be in me, but in the Lord. However much I may be on guard in ruling my household, I am a man, and I live among men, nor do I dare flatter myself that my house is better than the Ark of Noe, where, of eight men, one was found reprobate;[30] or better than the house of Abraham, of which it was said: 'Cast out the bondwoman and her son;'[31] or better than the house of Isaac, of whose twin sons it was said: 'I have loved Jacob, but have hated Esau';[32] or better than the house of Jacob himself, where his son defiled his father's couch;[33] or better than the house of David, whose son lay with his sister;[34] and whose other son revolted against the holy meekness of his father;[35] or better than the dwelling of the Apostle Paul, who would not have

---

27 Eph. 4.20,21.
28 Matt. 23.3.
29 1 Cor. 9.27.
30 Gen. 7.13; 9.27. The reprobate was Cham who was cursed by his father Noe.
31 Gen. 21.10.
32 Mal. 1.2,3.
33 Gen. 49.4.
34 2 Kings 13.14. This son was Ammon.
35 2 Kings 15.12. This son was Absalom.

said what I mentioned above: 'Combats without, fears within,'[36] if he had been living among good people only; nor would he have said, when speaking of the holiness and fidelity of Timothy: 'I have no man, who with sincere affection is solicitous for you; for all seek the things that are their own, not the things that Jesus Christ's';[37] or even better than the dwelling of the Lord Christ Himself, in which eleven good men bore with the traitor and thief Judas; or, finally, better than heaven from which the angels fell.

I confess openly to your Charity before the Lord our God, who has been the witness of my soul from the time when I began to serve Him, that, just as it is hard to find better men than those who live virtuously in monasteries, so I have not found worse than those who have fallen into sin in monasteries, and I think it was written of such in the Apocalpyse: 'He that is just, let him become more just, and he that is filthy let him be filthy still.'[38] And so, although we are saddened by the filth of some, we are consoled by the beauty of many more. Do not, then, because of the dregs by which your eyes are offended, despise the oil-presses, from which the storehouses of the Lord are filled with the harvest of the light-giving olive. May the mercy of the Lord our God preserve you in His peace against all the wiles of the enemy, my dearest brothers.

---

36 2 Cor. 7.5.
37 Phil, 2.20,21.
38 Cf. Apoc. 22.11.

79. [Augustine to a certain Manichaean priest[1]] *(404)*

You have no reason to evade, for it is evident from afar what sort of person you are. The brethren have reported to me what they talked about to you. It is a good thing that you do not fear death, but you ought to fear that death which you are bringing upon yourself by uttering such blasphemies against God. As for your understanding that the visible death which all men know is the separation of soul and body, it is no great thing to understand that. But, when you add of your own that the separation is one of good from evil, if by good you mean the soul and by evil the body, then He is not good who joined them. But, you say that a good God did so join them; in that case, He is either evil or He feared evil. Do you boast that you do not fear man when you fashion for yourself a god who so feared darkness that he joined good and evil? Do not be puffed up in mind, as you wrote, because we only make you out great in order to put an obstacle to your poisons, and to prevent your pestilence from crawling serpent-wise among men. The Apostle who called certain ones dogs did not make them great when he said: 'Beware of dogs,'[2] nor did he make those great whose speech he said spread like a canker.[3] Therefore, I warn you in the name of Christ[4] to solve that question, if you are ready to do so, in which your predecessor Fortunatus[5] failed.

---

1 This letter, without salutation, is addressed to a nameless Manichaean priest, believed to be one Felix, who was worsted in a public debate by Augustine in December, 404. His predecessor is called Fortunatus here, and Felix is named as the successor of Fortunatus in *Retractations* 1.8.
2 Phil. 3.2.
3 2 Tim. 2.17.
4 A lacuna here is suggested in the Vienna Corpus.
5 A Manichaean priest, whom Augustine, while still a priest, had reduced to silence in a public disputation. Cf. *Retractations* 1.16.

He went from here with the resolve never to return unless he could find an answer that he could make against me, after conferring with his own and debating with his brethren. If you are not ready for this, then depart hence; do not 'pervert the ways of the Lord,'[6] or lay your snares, or try to poison weak minds. Otherwise, by the help of the Lord's right hand, you may have to blush as you had not thought to do.

80. Augustine gives greeting in the Lord to his revered and greatly desired brothers, Paulinus and Therasia; holy and deservedly dear to God (405)

When our dearest brother Celsus[1] was asking for answers to carry, I made haste to pay my debt, but I really hurried; for I thought he had still several days to stay with us, but, when he heard suddenly that a ship was to sail, he told me, when it was already night, that his departure was advanced by a day. What could I do? I could not hold him, since he was hastening to you, where he is much better off; nor should I even if I could. So I seized these few thoughts on the wing and had them dictated and sent, with the admission that I owe you a longer letter, to be sent after the early return of our venerable brothers, my colleagues, Theasius and Evodius,[2] from your part of the world, when I shall be satisfied. We hope more and more in the name and by the help of Christ that you will come to us in their hearts and words. A few days

---

6 Acts 13.10.

---

1 Probably a priest belonging to the flock of Paulinus.
2 Two bishops sent as legates to the Emperor Honorius from the Council of Carthage of the previous year, who were now returning from Italy to Africa. They had presumably visited Paulinus at Nola. Evodius, Bishop of Upsala, was one of Augustine's early friends and companions.

before I wrote this, I gave another letter to be delivered to you by our devoted son, Fortunatianus,[3] a priest of the church at Tagaste, who was about to sail for Rome. Now, therefore, according to my wont, I am asking that you do according to yours: that you pray for us, asking the Lord to 'See my abjection and my labor and forgive me all my sins.'[4]

I have a great desire to discuss with you by letter, if you will be so kind, such matters as we could discuss face to face. And here is that little diffculty which I recently proposed to you, setting it forth as if we were personally present to one another, engaged in pleasant conversation. It is true you solved it with Christian understanding and devotion, but too superficially and briefly. Surely, the charm of your speech could have dwelt somewhat longer and more fruitfully upon it, if, when you said that you had decided to live in that place where you were so happy, but in such wise that, if something else were more pleasing to the Lord, you would prefer His will to yours, you had explained more clearly how we are to know the will of God, which is to preferred to our will. Is it found only in the case where we ought to perform something willingly for the very reason that we are forced to it against our will; or is it found also when we do not have to change our plan, in spite of something else happening in which the will of God appears to call on us rather to change it—but not for the reason that ours was wrong, since it was one in which we could rightly have continued if we had not been called by Him to another? In the first case what we do not want happens, but we so change ourselves that we do wish it because He wishes it, recognizing that it

---

[3] A priest of Tagaste who was making a journey to Rome. Any occasion for sending letters was eagerly seized.
[4] Ps. 24.18.

would be wrong to refuse His perfect will and impossible to escape His omnipotence. So, for example, another girded Peter and led him where he would not;[5] nevertheless, he went whither he would not, and willingly submitted to a cruel death. In the second case, it was not wrong for Abraham to nourish and bring up his own son, to the limit of his power and as far as it rested with him, to the end of his life, but, when he was suddenly commanded to kill his son, he changed his plan, which certainly was not wrong up to that time, but which would have been wrong if it had not been changed after the commandment. I am sure you do not differ from this view.

Generally, it is not because of a voice from heaven, nor through a Prophet, nor by the revelation of a dream or of that mental seizure which is called ecstasy that we are forced to recognize a will of God different from our own, but by the accident of circumstances which call us to something other than what we had planned. This might be if we had decided to set out on a journey, and were asked to do something which a true regard for our duty would prevent us from refusing; or if we had resolved to stay at home, and some message was brought to us, because of which, the same regard for duty would require us to go somewhere. It is about this third set of reasons for changing one's plans that I ask you to set out for me more fully and connectedly what you think. We often are upset and find it hard to give up something which really had to be done, not through any unwillingness on our part to change a course of action we had previously decided on. This course need not be anything wrong in itself, but wrong now because something comes up which has to be done first and cannot be omitted; but, if this had not come up, we could stand by our first plan not

---

5 John 21.18,19.

only without blame but even with praise. In a case like this it is difficult not to be deceived, a case called to mind by the voice of the Prophet: 'Who can understand sins?'[6] I would like you to share your thoughts with me on this point, and tell me what you usually do or what you think ought to be done.

81. Jerome gives greeting in Christ to the truly holy lord and blessed prelate, Augustine[1] (405)

When I inquired anxiously of our brother Firmus[2] how you were, I was glad to hear that you are well. But, when in the next place I was—I do not say hoping, but demanding, letters from you—he said he had left Africa without notifying you. So then, I send you back by him this debt of greeting, embracing you with disinterested love, and at the same time I ask you to pardon my diffidence because I could not refuse you the answer you have so long demanded of me. But it is not I that answer you; it is argument answering argument. If I do wrong in answering—please listen patiently —you do much more wrong in challenging me. But, let complaints of this sort be at an end; let there be between us pure brotherly affection, and let us hereafter send each other letters full of charity, not of questions. The holy brothers who serve the Lord with us greet you cordially. I ask you to give my respectful greetings to the saints who bear the light yoke of Christ with you, especially the holy and estimable prelate, Alypius. May Christ, our omnipotent God, keep you safe, and mindful of me, truly holy lord and blessed prelate.

---

6 Ps. 18.13.

1 This letter seems to be a sort of excuse for Letter 75 which had preceded it.
2 Apparently one of Jerome's regular messengers.

If you have read my book of commentaries on Jonas, I imagine you do not consider the question of the gourd-vine[3] a matter of jesting. But, if a friend who has first attacked me with a sword is hit back with a pen, you should make it a matter of fairness and justice to blame the accuser, not the defendant. Let us, if you will, play together in the field of the Scriptures without hurting each other.

82. Augustine gives greeting in the Lord to his holy brother and fellow priest, Jerome, beloved lord, honored in the bowels of Christ (405)

Some time ago, I sent a long letter to your Charity, in answer to that one of yours which you remember that you sent by your holy son, Asterius, now no longer only my brother, but also my colleague.[1] I do not know whether it has deserved to come into your hands, except that you write by our esteemed brother Firmus, that if someone who has first attacked you with a sword is hit back with a pen, I should make it a matter of fairness and justice to blame the accuser, not the defendant.[2] On this very slight evidence I gather that you must have read that letter of mine.[3] In it I expressed my regret at the great dissension that had arisen between you,[4] whose friendship, known wherever fame had published it, had been a subject of brotherly rejoicing. I did this, not by way of reproaching you, my brother—for I should not venture to discern any blame of yours in this matter—

---

3 Cf. Letter 75.

---

1 It appears from this that Asterius, one of Jerome's regular messengers, had become a bishop.
2 Cf. Letter 81.
3 Probably Letter 73.
4 Between Jerome and Rufinus.

but as deploring our human frailty, whose hold on friendships, such as it is, is so unsteady, even when they are cemented by mutual charity. But, what I most wanted to know from your answer—and I would like it said to me very plainly—is whether you granted me the pardon which I asked. A sort of cheerful tone in your letter makes it seem that I have been pardoned—that is, if your letter was sent after you had read mine, something that is not so certain.

You ask, or, rather, with the boldness of charity you command, that we play together in the field of the Scriptures without hurting one another. Indeed, as far as I am concerned, I would rather deal with those matters seriously than in sport. But, if it pleased you to use that word because of your facility in that field, I confess that I ask something greater of your kindly ability, of your learned, exact, experienced, expert and gifted prudence and care, that, in these great and involved questions, by the gift, or rather under the guidance, of the Holy Spirit, you would help me not so much playing in the field as toiling up the mountain of the Scriptures. However, if you thought it proper to use the word 'play' to indicate the good temper which befits dear friends carrying on a discussion, whether the question at issue is simple and easy or complicated and difficult, show me this, I beg of you: how we may manage, if we sometimes speak with too great assurance, not to fall into the suspicion of childish boasting and of trying to win fame for our own name by depreciating great men,[5] when we chance to be stirred by an argument which is not yet adopted by us, through undue caution or slowness in understanding, and we are trying, according to our lights, to see the other side of the case. But, if something sharp is said in the process of refuting an argument, let us, to make it more acceptable,

---

5 A reference to Letter 68.

temper it with milder language, and let us imagine that we wield a sword tipped with honey. Otherwise, in order to avoid the above-mentioned defect or suspicion of defect, we might find ourselves arguing with a more learned friend in such a manner that, whatever he says, we have to agree with it, and we are given no chance of the slightest opposition, not even for the sake of asking a question.

That is the only way we can play in the field without fear of hurt, but I wonder if we are not deluding ourselves. For, I admit to your Charity that it is from those books alone of the Scriptures, which are now called canonical, that I have learned to pay them such honor and respect as to believe most firmly that not one of their authors has erred in writing anything at all. If I do find anything in those books which seems contrary to truth, I decide that either the text is corrupt, or the translator did not follow what was really said, or that I failed to understand it. But, when I read other authors, however eminent they may be in sanctity and learning, I do not necessarily believe a thing is true because they think so, but because they have been able to convince me, either on the authority of the canonical writers or by a probable reason which is not inconsistent with truth. And I think that you, my brother, feel the same way; moreover, I say, I do not believe that you want your books to be read as if they were those of Prophets or Apostles, about whose writings, free of all error, it is unlawful to doubt. Let us not even think such a thing in connection with your humble virtue, and your true opinion of yourself, for, if you were not so endowed, you would certainly not have said: 'How I wish I might deserve to embrace you, and that we might teach or learn something by mutual conversation!'[6]

But if, as I believe, you said that as an expression of your

---
[6] Quoted from Letter 68.

own life and character, and not conventionally or deceitfully, how much more reasonable is it for me to believe that the Apostle Paul thought no other than he wrote, when he said to Barnabas about Peter: 'When I saw that they walked not uprightly unto the truth of the gospel, I said to Peter before them all: If thou, being a Jew, livest after the manner of the gentiles and not as the Jews do: how dost thou compel the gentiles to live as do the Jews?'[7] For, how can I be certain that the Apostles does not deceive me in writing or speaking, if he was deceiving his own sons, of whom he was in labor again until Christ, that is, truth, should be formed in them,[8] when he sent them before him saying: 'But the things which I write to you, behold before God I lie not?'[9] Was he not then writing truly, or was he making use of some sort of official prevarication, when he said that he had seen Peter and Barnabas walking not uprightly unto the truth of the Gospel, and that he had withstood Peter to his face for no other reason than that he was compelling the Gentiles to live like the Jews?[10]

Surely, it is better to believe that the Apostle Paul wrote something untruthful than that the Apostle Peter acted not uprightly. If that is so, then let us say something abhorrent, that it is better to believe that the Gospel lies than that Christ was denied by Peter;[11] and that the Book of Kings lies than that a great Prophet, so eminently chosen by the Lord God, committed adultery by coveting and seducing another man's wife, and was guilty of a revolting murder by killing her husband.[12] On the contrary, I will read the Holy Scripture

---

7 Cf. Gal. 2.14.
8 Gal. 4.19; 1 John 5.6.
9 Gal. 1.20.
10 Gal. 2.11.
11 Matt. 26.69-75.
12 2 Kings 11.2-17.

with complete certainty and confidence in its truth, founded as it is on the highest summit of divine authority; and I would rather learn from it that men were truly approved or corrected or condemned than allow my trust in the Divine Word to be everywhere undermined because I fear to believe that the human conduct of certain excellent and praiseworthy persons is sometimes worthy of blame.

The Manichaeans maintain that many parts of the Divine Scriptures are false, because they cannot twist them to a different meaning, but their detestable error is proved by the perfect clarity of scriptural expressions; and even they do not attribute falsehood to the apostolic writers, but to some supposed corrupters of the texts. But, as they could never prove their case by either more texts or older ones, or even by the authority of an older language from which the Latin books were translated, they come out of this argument defeated and put to shame by a truth so well known to all. Does your holy Prudence not understand what an avenue we open to their malice if we say, not that the apostolic writings were falsified by others, but that the Apostles themselves wrote falsehoods?

It is not to be believed, you say, that Paul blamed Peter for what Paul himself had done. I am not now asking what he did, I am asking what he wrote. The fact that the truth of the Divine Scriptures, so necessary for building up our faith, has been handed down to our memory not on the authority of any chance writers, but of the Apostles themselves, and has been received with the sanction of the highest canonical authority, and that it remains true in every part and not subject to doubt—this fact has the closest bearing on the question which I have raised. If what Peter did was what he ought to have done, then Paul lied when he said that he saw him walking not uprightly unto the truth of the Gospel.

Surely, when anyone does what he ought to do, he acts uprightly, and therefore that man accuses him falsely who says that he has not rightly done what he knew he ought to do. If, however, Paul wrote the truth, then it is true that Peter was not then walking uprightly unto the truth of the Gospel; therefore, he was doing what he ought not to do. And if Paul had done the same thing himself, I prefer to believe that, having been himself corrected, he could not pass over the correction of his fellow Apostle rather than that he put any lying statement in his epistle or in any epistle, much less in the one which he prefaced with the words: 'But the things which I write to you, behold, before God, I lie not.'[13]

For my part, I believe that Peter did act so as to compel the Gentiles to live like the Jews. For, I read that Paul wrote this, and I do not believe he lied. Therefore, Peter was not acting uprightly in this; he was going against the truth of the Gospel, making those who believed in Christ think that they could not be saved without those ancient ceremonial observances. This is what the converts of the circumcision insisted on at Antioch, against whom Paul fought persistently and vigorously. But, this was not Paul's motive for acting when he either circumcised Timothy,[14] or kept his vow at Cenchrae,[15] or followed the advice of James at Jerusalem in providing for the offering of sacrifices according to the Law, in company with men who had made a vow;[16] with the result that he appeared to give credence to the belife that Christian salvation depended on those observances. His purpose was to avoid the appearance of condemning those ceremonies which God had ordered to be performed in earlier times, to which they were appropriate, as fore-

---

[13] Gal. 1.20.
[14] Acts 16.3.
[15] Acts 18.18.
[16] Acts 21.18-26.

shadowings of things to come,[17] while condemnation was to be made of the idolatry of the Gentiles. This is what James said had been reported about him, that he taught the Jews to depart from Moses,[18] and this would certainly be unlawful, to separate those who believe in Christ from a Prophet of Christ, as if they condemned and detested his teaching, when Christ said of him: 'If you did believe Moses, you would believe me also, for he wrote of me.'[19]

I ask you, then, to recall the very words of James: 'Thou seest, brother,' he says, 'how many thousands there are in Judea, who have believed in Christ, and they are all zealots for the law. But they have heard of thee that thou teachest those Jews, who are among the gentiles, to depart from Moses, saying that they ought not to circumcise their children, nor walk according to the custom. What is it therefore? the multitude must needs come together; for they will hear that thou art come. Do therefore this that we say to thee: we have four men, who have a vow on them. Take them and sanctify thyself with them: and bestow on them that they may shave their heads; and all will know that the things which they have heard of thee are false, but that thou thyself followest, keeping the law. But as touching the gentiles that believe, we have given orders, judging that they are to keep nothing of that sort, except that they refrain from that which has been offered to idols, and from blood and from fornication.'[20] It is quite clear, I think, that James gave this advice in order to show the falsity of the views supposed to be Paul's, which certain Jews who had come to believe in Christ, but who were still 'zealous for the law,' had heard about him, namely, that through the teaching of Christ the

---
17 Col. 2.17.
18 Acts 21.21.
19 John 5.46.
20 Cf. Acts 21.20-25.

commandments, written by the direction of God and transmitted by Moses to the fathers, were to be thought sacrilegious and worthy of rejection. These reports were not circulated about Paul by those who understood the spirit in which the Jewish converts felt bound to those observances, namely, because of their being prescribed by a divine authority and for the sake of the prophetic holiness of those ceremonies, but not for the attaining of salvation, which has now been revealed in Christ and is conferred by the sacrament of baptism. Those who spread this rumor about Paul were the ones who wished to make these observances as binding as if without them there could be no salvation in the Gospel for believers. For, they had experienced him as a most vigorous preacher of grace, and as one who taught the exact opposite of their view, that man is not justified by these but by the grace of Jesus Christ, and that all the ordinances of the Law were foreshadowings meant to announce Him. That was why they tried to stir up hatred and persecution against him, making him out to be an enemy of the Law and of the divine commandments, and there was no more fitting way for him to repel the injustice of this false charge than by performing personally the ceremonies which he was supposed to condemn as sacrilegious. In this way he would prove two things: that the Jews were not to be prevented from observing these obligations as if they were wrong and that the Gentiles were not to be forced to observe them as if they were necessary.

Now, if he had truly rejected them, as it had been reported of him, and still undertook to observe them, so as to conceal his real sentiments by a pretended action, James would not have said to him: 'And all will know,' but he would have said: 'all will think "that the things which they have heard of thee false,"' especially since the Apostles had just decreed in Jerusalem itself[21] that no one was to compel the Gentiles to live like the Jews, but they had not decreed that no one was to prevent the Jews from living like Jews, although the Christian teaching did not oblige them to do so. Therefore, if after that decree of the Apostles Peter kept that pretense at Antioch by which he obliged the Gentiles to observe the Mosaic Law, since he was not obliged to it himself—although, because of the commendable words of God which were committed to the Jews,[22] it was not prohibited to him —what wonder if Paul constrained him to express freely what he remembered he had decreed at Jerusalem with the other Apostles?

But, if Peter did this before the council of Jerusalem— which I think more likely—it is not so surprising that Paul wanted him to assert boldly, not to cover up fearfully, what he knew they both thought about it. This may have been because he had conferred with him about the Gospel[23] or because he knew that he had been divinely inspired in this matter in the case of the call to conversion of the centurion Cornelius,[24] or because he had seen him eating with Gentiles at Antioch before the arrival of those whom he feared.[25] We certainly do not deny that Peter had been of that opinion, just as Paul was. Consequently, he was not teaching Peter what was true in that matter, but he was rebuking the pretense by which the Gentiles were compelled to keep the Mosaic Law. He had no other reason for doing this except that all such pretenses were undertaken on the assumption that there was truth in what was said by those who thought

---

21 Acts 15.28.
22 Rom. 3.2.
23 Gal. 2.2.
24 Acts 10.9-16.
25 Gal. 2.12.

that believers could not be saved without circumcision and the other observances, 'Shadows of things to come.'[26]

That is the reason why he circumcised Timothy, that they might not appear to the Jews and especially to Timothy's relations on his mother's side—Gentiles who had come to believe in Christ—to despise circumcision as idolatry is to be despised, since God had commanded the former to be performed, but Satan had suggested the latter. For a different reason he did not circumcise Titus, so as not to give support to those who were claiming that without such circumcision believers could not be saved, and who were boasting, to the detriment of the Gentiles, that Paul thought the same way. He shows this plainly when he himself says: 'But neither Titus, who was with me, being a Greek, was compelled to be circumcised: but because of false brethren unawares brought in, who came in privately to spy our liberty . . . that they might bring us into servitude. To whom we yielded not by subjection, no not for an hour, that the truth of the gospel might continue with you.'[27] Here it is clear that he knew they had grasped his reason for not doing here what he had done to Timothy, because, by acting with such freedom, he showed that these observances were neither to be required as necessary, nor condemned as sacrilegious.

Obviously, we must be careful in this discussion not to speak, as philosophers do, of certain human acts as midway between right and wrong; such as are to be classified neither as good deeds nor as sins; and we are not to be forced to the conclusion that observance of the ceremonies of the Law cannot be an indifferent matter, but is either good or bad. In that case, if we said it was good, we should be obliged to do it ourselves; if we said it was bad, we should have to be-

---
26 Col. 2.17.
27 Gal. 2.3-5.

lieve that, when the Apostles observed it, they were acting for appearance only, and not truthfully. But, I do not so much fear to have the example of philosophers applied to the Apostles, since these do utter some truth in their debates, as I fear that of trial lawyers, who tell lies in defending other men's cases. If it is thought proper to use these latter as an example in that same explanation of the Epistle to the Galatians,[28] in order to give probability to that deceit of Peter and Paul, why should I shrink from bringing up philosophers to you, when they are not untrustworthy because everything they say is false, but because they rely for the most part on untrustworthy sources, and where they are found to speak truth, they are far from the grace of Christ, which is truth itself?

But, why should I not say that those requirements of ancient ceremonies are not good because men are not justified by them; they are figures that foreshadow the grace, by which we are justified; on the other hand, they are not bad, because they were precepts of divine origin, adapted to times and people, although in this estimate I am supported by the prophetic statement in which God said that He had given to that people 'statutes that were not good'?[29] It happens that He did not say that they were bad, but only that they were not good: that is, such that with them men become good; without them, they do not. I would like your kind Sincerity to inform me whether any oriental saint who comes to Rome and fasts on Saturday—except the eve of Easter—is acting deceitfully. If we say that is wrong, we shall condemn the Roman Church and also many places near it and others somewhat further away, where the same custom continues to be observed. If, on the other hand, we think it is wrong

---

28 Jerome, on *Epistle to Galatians* 2.11ff.
29 Ezech. 20.25.

not to fast on Saturday, what boldness is ours to censure so many Eastern Churches, to say nothing of the larger part of the Christian world! Do you agree then that we call it something between the two, which is, notwithstanding, accepted by whoever does it sincerely, respectfully and in suitable surroundings? Still, we do not read in the canonical books that any such thing is binding on Christians. This makes me less willing to call that wrong which I have to admit was enjoined by God, and this I have learned by the very Christian faith which teaches that I am not justified by such things but by the grace of God through our Lord Jesus Christ![30]

I say, therefore, that circumcision and the other ordinances of this sort were divinely revealed to the former people through the Testament which we call Old, as types of future things, which were to be fulfilled by Christ. When this fulfillment had come, those obligations remained for the instruction of Christians, to be read simply for the understanding of the previous prophecy, but not to be performed through necessity, as if men had still to await the coming revelation of the faith which was foreshadowed by these things. However, although they were not to be imposed on the Gentiles, they were not thereby to be removed from the customary life of the Jews, as if they were worthy of scorn and condemnation. Gradually, therefore, and by degrees, through the fervent preaching of the grace of Christ, by which alone believers were to know that they were justified and saved—not by those shadows of things, formerly future, but now present and at hand—through the conversion of those Jews whom the presence of the Lord in the flesh and the times of the Apostles found living thus, all that activity of the shadows was to be ended. This was to be enough

---
30 Rom. 3.24.

praise for it, that it was not to be avoided and despised as idolatry was, but was to have no further development, and was not to be thought necessary, as if salvation either depended on it or could not be had without it. This is what some heretics[31] thought, who wanted to be both Jews and Christians, and could be neither Jews nor Christians. You were so kind as to warn me very earnestly against that opinion, although I have never held it. It was through fear of that opinion that Peter fell, not into consent but into pretense of consent, and that Paul wrote of him in absolute truth that he saw him walking not uprightly unto the truth of the Gospel; and he said truthfully to him that he was forcing the Gentiles to live like the Jews. Paul certainly was not forcing them to do this, because he had a true view of these ancient ordinances, when they had been obligatory; but he pointed out that they were not to be condemned, while he preached forcefully that the faithful were not saved by them, but by the grace of faith which was then revealed, and that no one was to be forced to take them on himself as necessary. I believe that the Apostle Paul acted sincerely in all this, and as I myself neither force nor allow any converted Jew to observe the Mosaic Law as a true obligation, so you, to whom Paul seems to have acted deceitfully, do not force or allow anyone to pretend to such observance.

Perhaps you would like me to say that this is what the question, or rather your opinion, really means: that, after the establishment of the Gospel of Christ, it is right for converted Jews to offer sacrifices, as Paul offered them, to circumcise their sons and keep the sabbath, as Paul acted toward Timothy and all the Jews did, so long as they do these things deceitfully, as a matter of pretense. If that is so, then we shall fall into heresy,—not the Ebionite one or

---
31 Cf. Letter 75 n. 44.

that other which is commonly called Nazarean, or any other old one—but some new one, much more baneful, because it springs from a perverted will, not from a false theory. You may try to save yourself from this conclusion by answering that the Apostles dissembled for a good motive: to prevent the weak-minded from being shocked, because many of the Jews were coming to believe in Christ, and did not yet understand that those observances were to be repudiated; whereas, now, the doctrine of Christ's grace has been built up among so many people, and the reading of the Law and the Prophets is an established custom in all the churches. Nowadays, people understand that these things are read aloud to be understood, not to be practised, and if anyone were to pretend to practise them he would be thought crazy. In that case, I could say that the Apostle Paul and other Christians of upright faith must then have recommended those ancient mysteries by practising them faithfully for a short time, to prevent those observances of prophetic value, kept by the most devout of the fathers, from being despised by their descendants, as if they were diabolic abominations. Now, however, with the coming of faith, foreshadowed as it was by those early mysteries, and revealed after the death and resurrection of the Lord, those former things have lost the life of their binding force. So, then, they are to be treated in such a manner as are the dead bodies of our kindred: they are to be carried out for burial, not as a matter of form, but as a religious duty; they are not immediately to be abandoned or exposed to the attacks of enemies, as to the teeth of dogs. From now on, if any Christian, though he be a converted Jew, should wish to keep these observances in such a way, he will not be a devout funeral attendant or bearer of the body, but an impious violator of a tomb, digging up dead ashes.

I do admit that in that sentence from my letter[32] where I said that Paul had undertaken to observe the ceremonies of the Jews, even after he had become an Apostle of Christ, to teach that they were not harmful to those who wished to keep them, as they had learned them from their parents under the Law, I neglected to add: 'provided it was done at the time when the grace of faith had just been revealed,' for that was the time when they were not harmful. But, with the passing of time, those observances were to be given up by all Christians, because, if they were then retained, there might be no distinction between what God enjoined on his people by Moses and what the unclean spirit of demons set up in the temples of idols. The blame must then be laid on my carelessness in not adding these words rather than on your objection. As a matter of fact, long before I received your letter, I wrote a tract against Faustus, the Manichaean,[33] in which I explained this passage somewhat briefly, but without passing over that point, and if your Benignity will kindly read it, whenever you will, you can be assured by it, as well as by the dear brethren by whom I am sending this letter, that I did dictate that opinion at an earlier date. Believe me on my soul—and speaking before God, I ask this as an obligation of charity—I never held that Jews who become Christians at this time should keep those ancient ordinances with any affection or any attachment, or that it is in any way lawful for them to do so, although I have held my views about Paul since I made my first acquaintance with sacred literature. Similarly, you do not believe that any Jewish convert of today should make a pretence of such observance, although you do believe that the Apostles did so.

Therefore, as you speak and write from the other side,

---

[32] Letter 40.
[33] *Contra Faustum* 1.19.17.
[37] Jer. 31.31.

though with some protest, you announce to the world in
unqualified speech that the ceremonies of the Jews are both
baneful and deadly to Christians, and that whoever keeps
them, whether Jew or Gentile, is doomed to the abyss of
the Devil, so I agree with this utterance of yours at every
point, and I add to it that whoever keeps them not merely
with sincere intention, but even only as a matter of form,
he also is doomed to the abyss of the Devil. What more?
You make a distinction between the dissimulation of the
Apostles and what is proper to do at this time, and I make
a distinction between the true speech of the Apostle Paul,
suitable to all the circumstances of that time, and what is
proper at this time, although his observance of Jewish ceremonies was not at all a pretence, because those ceremonies
were then to be approved, but are now to be repudiated.
So, although we read: 'The law and the prophets were until
John the Baptist,'[34] and that: 'Hereupon therefore, the Jews
sought to kill Christ, because he did not only break the sabbath, but also said that God was his Father, making himself
equal to God,'[35] and that: 'We have received grace for
grace; for the law was given by Moses; but grace and truth
came by Jesus Christ,'[36] and by Jeremias the promise was
made that God would give a new convenant to the house of
Juda, not according to the covenant which He had made with
their fathers[37]—I still do not think that the Lord Himself
was circumcised as a matter of form by His parents, or as
if it was only His age that kept Him from preventing them.
Nor do I think He spoke deceitfully to the leper, who assuredly was made clean by Him, and not by the observance
of the Mosaic Law: 'Go and offer for thee the sacrifice

---

[34] Luke 16.18.
[35] John 5.18.
[36] John 1.16-17.

which Moses commanded for a testimony to them.'[38] And
He did not go up deceitfully to the festival day, since He
went up not openly but secretly, so that He was not trying
to make an impression on men.[39]

But the same Apostle said: 'Behold I, Paul, tell you, that
if you be circumcised, Christ shall profit you nothing.'[40]
Therefore, he deceived Timothy and made Christ profit him
nothing. Or perhaps this was done for form's sake only and
so it did him no harm? But, he himself did not express it
thus, nor say: 'If you be circumcised truly,' any more than
he said: 'for form's sake,' but without exception he said: 'If
you be circumcised, Christ shall profit you nothing.' As you
want this text to support your opinion, and so you would have
the words, 'except as a matter of form,' understood, so I
demand, without shame, that you allow us to understand
that the words, 'if you be circumcised,' were addressed to
those wished to be circumcised, because they thought they
could not be saved otherwise, even in Christ. Whoever, therefore, was circumcised with this state of mind, with this will,
and with that intention, Christ profited him nothing at all,
as he says clearly in another place: 'For if justice be by the
law, then Christ died in vain.'[41] And he asserts what you yourself recalled: 'You are made void of Christ, you who are
justified in the law; you are fallen from grace.'[42] He blames
those who believed that they were justified in the Law, but
not those who with right understanding kept the requirements of the Law in honor of Him who prescribed them,
because they were commanded as a foreshadowing of truth,
and were to last just that long. That is why he said: 'If

---
38 Cf. Mark 1.40-44.
39 John 7.10.
40 Gal. 5.2.
41 Gal. 2.21.
42 Gal. 5.4.

you are led by the spirit, you are not under the law.'[43] From which, as you conclude, it is evident that the one who is under the Law not for form's sake, as you think our predecessors would have it, but in reality, as I understand it, is the one who does not possess the Holy Spirit.

I think it is important to know what it means to be under the Law, in the way which the Apostle condemns. I think he was not referring to circumcision or to those sacrifices which were then offered by the fathers, but are not offered today by Christians, and other things of that sort, but I think he meant this commandment of the Law which says: 'Thou shalt not covet.'[44] We admit that Christians certainly ought to obey this and to preach it as part of the Gospel enlightenment. He says that the Law is holy and the commandment is holy and just and good, and he then adds: 'Was that then which is good, made death unto me? God forbid. But sin, that it may appear sin, by that which is good, wrought death in me; that sin by the commandment might become sinful above measure.'[45] Here he says that sin by the commandment became above measure, and in another place he has this: 'The law entered in that sin might abound. And where sin abounded, grace did more abound';[46] and again, when he spoke above of the dispensation of grace, and says that it gives justification, he asks: 'Why then was the law?' and immediately answers his question: 'It was set because of transgression, until the seed should come to whom the promise was made.'[47] He says, then, that those are under the Law to their own damnation whom the Law makes guilty of not fulfilling the Law, because they do not under-

---
43 Gal. 5.18.
44 Rom. 7.7; 13.9; Exod. 20.17; Deut. 5.21.
45 Rom. 7.13.
46 Rom. 5.20.
47 Cf. Gal. 3.19.

stand the gift of grace and they rely with proud confidence on their own strength to carry out the commandments of God. 'For love is the fulfilling of the law,'[48] but 'the charity of God is poured forth in our hearts,' not by ourselves, but 'by the Holy Ghost Who is given to us.'[49] But, to explain this truth as it ought to be explained, a long treatise or even its own proper volume is needed. So, then, if that commandment of the Law, 'Thou shalt not covet,' keeps a man, subject to it, in a state of guilt, unless his human weakness is helped by the grace of God, and if it rather damns the transgressor than frees the sinner, how much less possible is it for those precepts which were given as types of something to come, such as circumcision and the like, to justify anyone, especially as they were of necessity to be abolished when the revelation of grace had become more widely known! Yet, they were not to be avoided as were the diabolical abominations of the Gentiles, even after the first revelation of grace—which had been foreshadowed by them as figures— but they were to be allowed for a little while, particularly to those who had come from the people to whom they had been given. Afterwards, they were, so to speak, to be buried with honor, and to be given up by all Christians for good and all.

Turning to that expression of yours, 'Not for form's sake, as our elders would have it,' [50] I ask you what that means. It is either what I call the officious lie,[51] so that this formalism makes it a sort of duty to tell an honest lie, or else I do not understand at all what it could be, unless adding the name of 'form's sake' makes a lie not a lie. If this is ridiculous, why not say openly that the officious lie is allowable? Perhaps the

---

48 Rom. 13.10.
49 Rom. 5.5.
50 Cf. Letter 75.
51 Cf. Letter 40 n. 3.

term bothers you, because the word 'duty' is not much used in ecclesiastical books, although our Ambrose was not afraid of it, since he gave the name *On Duties* to certain of his books filled with useful rules of conduct. Or is a person who tells an officious lie to be blamed, but, if he does it for form's sake, is he to be approved? I ask you. It is also an important question whether it is becoming for a good man to lie, or rather for a Christian man, one of the sort to whom it is said: 'Let there be in your mouth Yea, yea, no, no';[52] the sort who hear with faith: 'Thou wilt destroy all that speak a lie,'[53]—as I said, this is another and an important question, but, if anyone thinks this, let him lie when he reads; let him who thinks this choose as he will, when he shall tell his lie, so long as there is unshaken belief in the writers of the Holy Scriptures and especially of the canonical books, and so long as the view is defended that they are entirely free of falsehood. Otherwise, the dispensers of Christ, of whom it is said: 'Here now it is required among dispensers that a man be found faithful,'[54] would seem to have learned faithfully for themselves that it is something great to lie in the imparting of truth. Even the word 'faith' in Latin is said to be called because what is said is done.[55] When what is said is done, there is naturally no place for lying. Unquestionably, the Apostle Paul, a faithful dispenser, shows faith in writing, because he was a dispenser of truth, not of falsehood. Consequently, he wrote truly when he said that he had seen Peter walking not uprightly unto the truth of the Gospel, and that he withstood him to the face, because he was forcing the

---

52 Matt. 5.37; James 5.12.
53 Ps. 5.7.
54 1 Cor. 4.2; the term, 'dispenser', is here used to mean ministers or stewards.
55 This is to take the word *fi-des* as if the first syllable, *fi*, came from *facere* (do), and the second, *des*, from *dicere* (say). Cf. Cicero, *De Off.* 1.7.23.

Gentiles to live like the Jews. But Peter, for his part, received with the mildness of a holy and meek humility the reproof made by Paul, for his good, with the freedom of charity. And so, by not refusing to be corrected, even by his inferiors, for having accidentally left the path of uprightness, he gave a more precious and holy example to posterity than Paul did, who showed how those lower in authority might confidently dare to defend the truth of the Gospel by opposing their elders, with all due regard for fraternal charity. Obviously, it is better in traveling along a road not to turn aside at all than to turn aside ever so little, but it is much more remarkable and more praiseworthy to receive correction willingly than to correct the errant boldly. It seems, therefore, to my limited capacity, that it would have been better to uphold the praise of Paul's just liberty and Peter's holy humility against the false attacks of Porphyry rather than to give him a greater opening for attack, and allow him to charge the Christians, with greater bitterness, either of writing their epistles or of carrying out the ceremonies of their God deceitfully.

You ask me to point out at least one authority whom I follow in this opinion of mine, whereas you listed several by name, who have preceded you in the case which you are building up, and you request that, if I reprove your error in this matter, I allow you to be wrong in the company of such men; but I have to admit that I have not read any of them. But, as there are about six or seven, you yourself weaken the authority of these four: you say that the Laodicean has recently gone out of the Church; Alexander is a former heretic; and I read that Origen and Didymus have been severely criticised in your more recent works, about no trifling questions, although you had once praised Origen extravagantly. I think you will not allow yourself to be wrong in the company of these, but let this be said as if they were not wrong in this opinion. For, who is there who would want to be wrong with anybody at all? There remain, therefore, these three: Eusebius of Emesa, Theodore of Heraclea, and the one whom you mentioned shortly after, John, who recently ruled the Church of Constantinople as bishop.

Moreover if you should inquire or recall what our Ambrose[56] thought about this, or our Cyprian[57] on the same subject, you will find, perhaps, that we, too, have authors to follow in this opinion which we propose. Still, as I said awhile ago, it is only to the canonical Scriptures that I owe such a willing submission that I follow them alone, and believe of them that their authors were not in error anywhere at all in them, nor did they set down anything so as to deceive. Therefore, if I look for a third, so as to set three against three, I imagine I could easily find one if I read a great deal. But truly as a substitute for all of them, or rather as one above them all, the Apostle Paul comes to my mind. I take refuge with him; I appeal to him against all the commentators on his Epistles, who think differently about him; I call on him, asking and inquiring about what he wrote to the Galatians, to the effect that he saw Peter walking not uprightly unto the truth of the Gospel and that he withstood him to the face because he was forcing the Gentiles to dissemble and to live like the Jews; whether he wrote this as the truth or whether he lied by some sort of conventional falsehood. And a little further back in the beginning of his narrative, I hear him crying out to me with a solemn voice: 'But the things which I write to you, behold before God, I lie not.'[58]

---

56 This reference is to St. Ambrose on Paul, *Epistle* to *Galatians* 2.11.14.
57 St. Cyprian, Bishop of Carthage 249-258, a convert from paganism, a prolific and important writer on theological and scriptural subjects. This reference is to his *Letters* 71.3.
58 Gal. 1.20.

Those who think otherwise must pardon me; I would rather believe so great an Apostle taking oath in and for his own Epistles than the most learned person discussing someone else's letters. And I do not fear having it said of me that I defend Paul against the charge that he did not pretend to follow the error, when with apostolic freedom, such as was fitting at the time, he commended those ancient ceremonies by practising them when it was needful. He did this, not with the craftiness of Satan, to deceive men, but by the providence of God, prophetically arranged to foreshadow future things; and he was not truly involved in the error of the Jews, since he not only knew but preached constantly and vigorously against the wrong teaching of those who thought that these burdens should be imposed on the Gentiles as necessary for the salvation of the faithful.

When I said that he became as a Jew to the Jews and as a Gentile to the Gentiles, it was not by a crafty intent to deceive but by a feeling of compassion that he did so, but it seems to me that you did not notice carefully how I said it, or rather, I could not, perhaps, make myself sufficiently clear. I did not mean that he was pretending to feel sympathetic, but, when he acted like the Jews, he was not then acting by pretence; just as he did not act like the Gentiles, a fact which you recalled to me, and thereby helped me, for which I am truly grateful. When I asked you in my letter[59] how he was to be considered to have become a Jew to the Jews, if he only pretended to carry out the observances of the Jews, whereas when he became as a Gentile to the Gentiles, he did not pretend to carry out the sacrifices of the Gentiles, you answered that he became as a Gentile to the Gentiles by receiving the uncircumcised and allowing foods to be eaten without distinction, something which the Jews condemn.

---

59 Letter 40.

Whereupon, I ask whether he did this as a pretence, also, and, if that is utterly ridiculous and untrue, the same holds of those matters in which he conformed to Jewish custom, which he did with prudent freedom, not from slavish necessity, nor, what is worse, by a deceitful pretence, instead of a true conformity.

To the faithful and to those who recognize the truth, according to his testimony, 'Every creature of God is good, and nothing to be rejected that is received with thanksgiving'[60]—unless, perhaps, he is wrong here, too. Therefore, to Paul himself, not only as man, but also as eminently faithful dispenser—not only as learned witness, but also as teacher of truth—every creature of God, especially of food, is good: not as a matter of pretence but in reality. How is it that he became as a Gentile to the Gentiles, not by pretending to submit to their rites and ceremonies, but by thinking and teaching the truth about foods and uncircumcision, and he could not become as a Jew to the Jews except by pretending to conform to their ceremonies? Why did he save the true faith of his ministry for the engrafted wild olive, and spread some kind of a veil of official deceit over the true branches,[61] which are attached to the tree, not outside it? Why, when he became as a Gentile to the Gentiles, did he teach what he thought, and think as he acted; but, when he became as a Jew to the Jews, he shut one thing up in his heart, and uttered another in his words, in his actions, in his writings? I have no use for this sort of wisdom. For he owed to both charity from a pure heart, and a good conscience, and an unfeigned faith,[62] and in this way he 'became all things to all men, that he might gain all,'[63] not by a crafty intent to deceive, but

---

60 1 Tim. 4.4.
61 Rom. 11.17.
62 1 Tim. 1.5.
63 1 Cor. 9.22.

by a feeling of compassion. This he did, not by pretending to commit all the evil deeds of men, but by treating all the evil deeds of all others with the constant remedy of compassion.

By not repudiating those ceremonies of the Old Testament, but by performing them himself, he was not making a pretence, out of kindness—he was not pretending at all—and, while thus commending those observances which had been ordered by the Lord God, as the order of things for a limited time, he distinguished them from the unholy rites of the Gentiles. The time when he became as a Jew to the Jews— not with a crafty intent to deceive, but by a feeling of compassion—was when he tried to free them from that error whereby they either would not believe in Christ or held that they could only be saved and cleansed from sin through their own traditional priesthood and the performance of their own ceremonies. He did this as if he were involved in that error himself, thus manifestly loving his neighbor as himself and doing to others what he wished others to do to him, in case of need. And when the Lord had commanded this, He added: 'For this is the law and the prophets.'[64]

He prescribed this feeling of compassion in the same Epistle to the Galatians, when he said: 'If a man be overtaken in any fault, you, who are spiritual, instruct such a one in the spirit of meekness, considering thyself, lest thou also be tempted.'[65] Notice that he did not say to become like him so as to gain him by going through the motions of committing the same offense, or by pretending to have done so; but to consider in the sin of another what could happen to oneself, and therefore to help the other as compassionately as he would like to be helped by another; and that is what

---

64 Cf. Matt. 22.39-40.
65 Gal. 6.1.

is meant by: 'not by crafty intent to deceive but by a feeling of compassion.' Thus, to the Jew, to the Gentile, to any man of any sort, in error or in any sin committed, Paul became 'all things to all men that he might gain all,'[66] not by pretending to be what he was not, but by showing compassion, because he could have been so, as one who thought himself to be a man.

I beg you to look in upon yourself, for a little while, if you will, upon yourself, I say, in your attitude toward myself, and recall, or, if you have a copy, reread your words in that short letter which you sent me by our brother and my colleague, Cyprian,[67] and note with how true, how brotherly, how affectionate a charity you reproached me for having offended you, and how you added gravely: 'By that conduct friendship is injured and the bonds of intimacy are broken ... but let us not seem to be engaging in a childish contest, or to give grounds of contention to our mutual supporters or detractors.' I feel that these words were uttered by you from your heart and from a kind heart, for my best interest. Finally, you add—and they would be understood even if you did not add them—these words: 'I write this because I wish to love you with pure Christian love, and I would not keep in my heart anything that differs from my words.' O holy man, loved by me with a sincere love as God sees my heart, this very thing which you put into your letters, which I am sure portrays you to me, this very same thing I believe portrayed the Apostle Paul in his letters, not to any one man, but to the Jews and Greeks and to all races, his sons, whom he begot in the Gospel, and of whom he was in labor until he brought them forth,[68] and finally to so many thousands of faithful

---
66 1 Cor. 9.22.
67 Letter 72.
68 Gal. 4.19.

Christians, their successors, for whose sake that Epistle has been handed down to posterity, so that nothing should be kept in his heart which differed from his words.

Surely, you became like me when you thought, not with a crafty intent to deceive, but with a feeling of compassion, that I should not be left in the mistake into which you thought I had fallen, as you would not have wished me to leave you if you had fallen into it. I thank you for your kindness to me, and I ask you at the same time not to be angry with me if I object to something in your works and share my objection with you. I would like the same treatment to be accorded by all to me as I accord it to you, and, if they think there is anything objectionable in my writings, I want them not to bury it in a crafty heart, nor air their criticisms to others, while hiding them from me, for this is the way I think friendship is injured, and the bonds of intimacy are broken. I doubt that those are to be considered Christian friendships in which there is more regard for the popular proverb, 'Flattery creates friends, but truth begets hatred,'[69] than for the scriptural one, 'More trustworthy are the wounds of a friend, than the proffered kisses of an enemy.'[70]

Let us, then, with all the insistence we can put into it, impress this upon our dearest friends, those who are most sincerely interested in our work, and let them know that it is possible between dear friends for something to be objected to in the speech of either, without charity being thereby diminished, without truth begetting hatred. This is something which is owed to friendship, even if what is objected to is true, or whatever it is, so long as it is uttered from a truthful heart, without keeping in the mind what is at variance with the words.

---

69 Terence, *And.* 68.
70 Cf. Prov. 29.6.

Consequently, let our brothers, the members of your household, of whom you bear witness that they are the vessels of Christ, believe that this matter of my letter going through many hands before it could reach you, to whom it was addressed,[71] was not intentional on my part, and it causes me no slight grief. It is too long a story to tell how it happened, and, if I am not mistaken, it would be useless to do so; let it be enough to say—if my explanation is believed—that it was not done with the intention credited to me, and that, in fact, it was entirely without my wish, or arrangement, or consent, or even knowledge that it happened. If they do not believe what I call God to witness, I do not know what more I can do. I should be loath to believe that they made this insinuation to your Holiness with the evil intent to stir up ill will between us—may the mercy of the Lord our God keep that far from us!—but, without any wish to do harm, it is easy to suspect human weakness of a man. This is what I must believe of them, if they are vessels of Christ, that they were made not for dishonor but for honor, and prepared by God in a great house for a good work.[72] If they wish to act thus after this solemn statement of mine—supposing it comes to their knowledge—then you also see how wrongly they act.

When I wrote that I had not sent any book against you to Rome, I meant to distinguish the word 'book' from that letter about which I thought you had heard something entirely different. Besides, I had not sent my letter to Rome, but to you, and I did not think that what I had done in sincere friendship was anything against you, since it was meant for your enlightenment or for our mutual correction. Leaving aside the members of your household, I beg of you personally

---

71 Cf. Letter 72.
72 2 Tim. 2.20-21.

not to think that I was dealing in hypocritical flattery when I mentioned in my letters those talents which the goodness of the Lord has granted you, and, if I have offended you in any way, pardon me. And do not apply to yourself more literally than it was spoken that reference from some poet or other, which I probably used with more ineptness than literary effect, since I added immediately that I did not mean you should regain the eyes of your heart,[73] but that you should turn them back, strong and watchful as they are. If I wrote something, which I should expunge by a later writing, about a single palinode[74] not to be imitated because of the blindness of Stesichorus, which I neither attributed to your heart nor feared for it, I thought it was something to be attained. And I ask you again and again to correct me faithfully whenever you see that I need it. For, although, according to the titles of honor which the usage of the Church has now sanctioned, a bishop ranks higher than a priest, in many things Augustine ranks lower than Jerome. And in any case, correction from an inferior is not to be refused or disdained.

You have convinced me of the value of your translation of the Scriptures which you have wished to make from the Hebrew, with the purpose of bringing to light what has been omitted or corrupted by the Jews. But I wish you would be so kind as to point out what Jews did this; whether it was those who made the translation before the coming of the Lord, and, if so, which ones or which one; or whether it was done by those who came afterwards, who can be supposed to have suppressed or changed certain parts of the Greek texts so as not to be convinced by their proofs for the Christian religion. But, I do not see why the earlier translators would

---

73 Cf. Letter 40.
74 Cf. Letters 40 and 75.

have wanted to do that. Then I ask you to send us your translation of the Septuagint, which I did not know that you had published. And I am also anxious to read that book of yours which you mentioned, on the best method of translating, and I still want to know how a knowledge of languages in a translator is to be balanced against the conjectures of those who expound the Scriptures by annotating them. These must necessarily, even if they are of the one true faith, offer differing opinions, because of the obscurity of many passages, although this difference is not inconsistent with the unity of the same faith, so that one commentator can explain the same passage according to the same faith in one way, and another in another way, since its obscurity allows this.

The reason why I am anxious to have your translation of the Septuagint is to free us, as far as possible, from the great awkwardness of the Latin translators who, such as they are, have dared to make their versions. As for those who think that I am envious of your valuable work, let them at length understand for a little while, if that can be, that I do not wish your translation from the Hebrew to be read in the churches, for fear of upsetting the flock of Christ with a great scandal, by publishing something new, something seemingly contrary to the authority of the Septuagint, which version their ears and hearts are accustomed to hear, and which was accepted even by the Apostles. And if that shrub in Jonas is neither an ivy nor a gourd, but some other sort of thing which springs up, supporting itself with its own trunk, without needing to be supported by any props, I would still rather have 'gourd' read in all the Latin versions, for I think the Seventy put that there because they knew it was like one.

I think I have answered enough—even, perhaps, more than

enough—to your three letters,[75] two of which I received from Cyprian and one from Firmus. Do you answer what you think, for our instruction or that of others. I will take greater care, as far as the Lord helps me, to see that the letters which I write to you reach you before they get into any other hands to be scattered abroad. I admit that I do not want yours to me to have the same fate which you so reasonably complain happened to mine addressed to you. I hope there may reign between us not only the love but even the freedom of friendship, and, if we object to anything in each other's letters, you must not fail to criticise mine as I shall do to yours, but of course it must be with such dispostitions as do not displease the eyes of God in the love of brothers. But, if you think that cannot be between us without a deep injury to love itself, then it must not be. For, that other complete understanding which I wished to have with you is greater, but the lesser is better than none.

---

[75] Letters 72, 75 and 81.

www.ingramcontent.com/pod-product-compliance
Lightning Source LLC
Chambersburg PA
CBHW032023290426
44110CB00012B/638